What Is World Literature?

TRANSLATION | TRANSNATION

SERIES EDITOR **EMILY APTER**

DAVID DAMROSCH

What Is World Literature?

PRINCETON UNIVERSITY PRESS

PRINCETON AND OXFORD

Published by Princeton University Press, 41 William Street, Princeton, New Jersey 08540
In the United Kingdom: Princeton University Press, 3 Market Place, Woodstock, Oxfordshire
OX20 1SY

Library of Congress Cataloging-in-Publication Data
Damrosch, David.
     What is world literature? / David Damrosch.
     p.   cm.
     ISBN 0-691-04985-8 (alk. paper) — ISBN 0-691-04986-6 (pbk. : alk. paper)
     1. Literature—History and criticism.   2. Literature, Comparative.   3. Translating and
interpreting.   4. Canon (Literature).   I. Title.
PN523 .D36 2003
809—dc21

                                                                        2002029272

British Library Cataloging-in-Publication Data is available

This book has been composed in Minion with Gills Sans Display.
Printed on acid-free paper. ⊗
www.pupress.princeton.edu
Printed in the United States of America
10 9 8 7 6 5 4

ISBN-13: 978-0-691-04986-1 (pbk.)

ISBN-10: 0-691-04986-6 (pbk.)

For Michael Holquist

CONTENTS

vii

ACKNOWLEDGMENTS

I have a thousand people to thank concerning this book. Though it is tempting to list each person by name, I can express my gratitude to most of them collectively: over the past decade, my friends and colleagues in the American Comparative Literature Association have provided much food for thought with an extraordinary range of literary explorations in a widening range of venues. As stand-ins for the entire listing, I will mention the association's officers during the years I've been developing the ideas presented here: Jonathan Culler, Eugene Eoyang, Roland Greene, Margaret Higonnet, Elaine Martin, Stuart McDougal, Marjorie Perloff, and Susan Suleiman, together with our principal associates in the ACLA/AAC (Aquatic Activities Caucus), Svetlana Boym, Gail Finney, Herb and Perry Marks, and Maarten van Delden.

I want to thank my students and colleagues in the department of English and Comparative Literature and in Columbia's Center for Comparative Literature and Society, particularly Jonathan Arac, Ann Douglas, Ursula Heise, Jean Howard, Andreas Huyssen, David Kastan, Martin Puchner, Bruce Robbins, Edward Said, Maura Spiegel, and Gayatri Spivak, for conversation, for the bracing example of their writing, and for their creative engagement in giving ideas institutional and curricular form. I want as well to thank those who have given me the opportunity to present some of this material elsewhere: Michael Holquist and Wai Chee Dimock at Yale, Jennifer Wicke at the University of Virginia, Djelal Kadir at Penn State, Svetlana Boym at Harvard, Bruce Mazlish at MIT, Sandra Bermann and Michael Wood at Princeton, E. Ann Kaplan at SUNY Stony Brook, Renate Blumenfeld-Kosinski at Mont Sainte Odile, Theo d'Haen in Leiden, and Eduardo Coutinho in Rio de Janeiro. Preliminary versions of portions of the following chapters appeared in *Civilization, Representations, Symplokē, Pedagogy,* and *British Writers III,* edited by George Stade (Scribner's). Additionally, in my book *Meetings of the Mind*, I summarized a paper by my friend Vic Ad-dams on Mechthild von Magdeburg; Vic's ideas (corrected for his polemi-cal biases) are developed more fully here. Mark Getlein intervened as well with a perfect chapter title. Direct help in the preparation of this volume was admirably provided by the research assistance of Miranda Calderón, Mela-nie Micir, and Dermot Ryan. Lauren Simonetti expertly prepared the index. I am particularly grateful to Emily Apter and Mary Murrell for their support of this project, and to Wai Chee Dimock and Wlad Godzich for very sub-stantive and useful reader's reports.

As if all these debts were not enough, I must also give special thanks to my colleagues on the editorial board of the forthcoming *Longman An-thology of World Literature:* April Alliston, Marshall Brown, Page du Bois, Sabry Hafez, Ursula Heise, Djelal Kadir, David Pike, Sheldon Pollock, Bruce Robbins, Haruo Shirane, Jane Tylus, and Pauline Yu. The broadest possible definition of world literature would simply be: what these people know.

Thirty years ago, in Michael Holquist's section of an experimental undergraduate course entitled "Literature X" (no ordinary course number would do), I first learned how effectively a capacious and creative scholarly mind could bring together a tremendous variety of works—canonical and noncanonical, ancient and modern, from Europe and beyond. In some ultimate sense, this book is Holquist's doing.

In place of the old wants, satisfied by the productions of the country, we find new wants, requiring for their satisfaction the products of distant lands and climates. In place of the old local and national seclusion and self-sufficiency, we have intercourse in every direction, universal interdependence of nations. And as in material, so also in intellectual production. The intellectual creations of individual nations become common property. National one-sidedness and narrow-mindedness become more and more impossible, and from the numerous national and local literatures, there arises a world literature.

—Marx and Engels, *The Communist Manifesto*

(Stoop) if you are abcedminded, to this claybook, what curios of signs (please stoop), in this allaphbed! Can you rede (since We and Thou had it out already) its world?

—James Joyce, *Finnegans Wake*

What Is World Literature?

Goethe Coins a Phrase

"I am more and more convinced," Goethe remarked, "that poetry is the universal possession of mankind, revealing itself everywhere and at all times in hundreds and hundreds of men. . . . I therefore like to look about me in foreign nations, and advise everyone to do the same. National literature is now a rather unmeaning term; the epoch of world literature is at hand, and everyone must strive to hasten its approach." Speaking to his young disciple Johann Peter Eckermann in January 1827, the seventy-seven-year-old Goethe used his newly minted term *Weltliteratur,* which passed into common currency after Eckermann published his *Gespräche mit Goethe in den letzten Jahren seines Lebens* in 1835, three years after the poet's death. The term crystallized both a literary perspective and a new cultural awareness, a sense of an arising global modernity, whose epoch, as Goethe predicted, we now inhabit. Yet the term has also been extraordinarily elusive, from the moment of its formulation onward: What does it really mean to speak of a "world literature"? Which literature, whose world? What relation to the national literatures whose production continued unabated even after Goethe announced their obsolescence? What new relations between Western Europe and the rest of the globe, between antiquity and modernity, between the nascent mass culture and elite productions?

If we look to Goethe for guidance, the perplexities only multiply, fueled by his constantly shifting personality—his unstable mix of modesty and megalomania, cosmopolitanism and jingoism, classicism and Romanticism, wide-ranging curiosity and self-absorbed dogmatism. Eckermann's account is both a portrait of the great man and the record of his inability to grasp his subject; Goethe is a diamond, Eckermann tells us, that casts a different color in every direction. Eckermann, on the other hand, is a diamond in the rough: of humble origins, largely self-taught, an aspiring poet and dramatist, he seeks to model his life and work on Goethe, whom he knows he can never measure up to. Both *Bild* and *Bildungsroman*—objective portrait of Goethe and subjective autobiography of Eckermann himself—the *Conversations with Goethe* is a gallery of scenes of instruction, seduction, influence, and transmission, all of which have much to tell us about the worldliness of literature. Looking at Goethe's *Weltliteratur* within the multiple frames Eckermann provides, we can already find all the major complexities, tensions, and opportunities that we still encounter today as we try to grasp our rapidly expanding world and its exfoliating literatures.

Indeed, for Eckermann Goethe is the living embodiment of world literature, even of world culture as a whole. Late in his account, he records Goethe's remark that "the daemons, to tease and make sport with men, have placed among them single figures so alluring that everyone strives after them, and so great that nobody reaches them"; Goethe names Raphael, Mozart, Shakespeare, and Napoleon as examples. "I thought in silence," Eckermann adds, "that the daemons had intended something of the kind with Goethe—he is a form too alluring not to be striven after, and too great to be reached" (271).

Even to be as close to Goethe as he is, Eckermann has come a long way. Raised in rural poverty, he had managed to find a clerk's job at the local court. "At this time I heard the name *Goethe* for the first time and first acquired a volume of his poetry. I read his poems, and constantly reread them, with a pleasure that no words can describe. . . . it seemed to me that in these poems my own hitherto unknown essence was reflected back to me [*zurückgespiegelt*]. . . . I lived for whole weeks and months in these poems. . . . I thought and spoke of nothing but Goethe" (*Gespräche*, 21).[1] Friends at court arranged a two-year scholarship for Eckermann to study law at Göttingen. His fellowship ending, he could not bear to pursue a legal career. Living penuriously on the last remains of his fellowship, he wrote poems and composed a work of literary criticism, *Contributions to Poetry, with Particular Attention to Goethe,* and sent the manuscript to Goethe, hoping he would recommend it to his publisher. Some weeks passed; hearing nothing, Eckermann decided to risk everything and go see Goethe in person. It took over a week to walk to Weimar. "Along the way, often made wearisome by hot weather, I kept repeating to myself the comforting feeling that I was proceeding under the special protection of benevolent spirits, and that this journey might have important consequences for my later life" (*Gespräche*, 30).

This is an extreme understatement. Eckermann at this point had no

[1] In general I will be quoting from the English translation of Eckermann's book, but that translation is incomplete. Passages I've taken directly from the German will be labeled *Gespräche*.

resources whatever, no prospects; he could only hope that Goethe—one of the most eminent writers in Europe and subject to an incessant stream of visitors, pleas for assistance, requests for references and reviews—would take a special interest in him and help him to some sort of literary career. Cast in the fairy-tale role of donor figure, Goethe does all this and more: he strides into the room, an impressive figure "in a blue frock-coat," Eckermann says, oddly adding, "and with shoes." He sits Eckermann on a sofa and says the magic words: "'I have just come from *you*,' said he; 'I have been reading your writing all morning; it needs no recommendation—it recommends itself'" (*Conversations*, 1). Not only does he arrange immediately for the book's publication; at their next meeting, a few days later, he takes over Eckermann's life. Speaking with "the impetuous and decided manner of a youth" (2), Goethe enlists Eckermann to organize and assess an archive of his early notes and manuscripts, and commands him to move to Jena, where Goethe will be living in the fall.

Goethe's reaction was, in fact, a little less surprising than Eckermann's account suggests. Discussing the book's genesis in an afterword to her definitive edition of the *Gespräche*, Regine Otto notes that when he sent Goethe his manuscript in May, Eckermann had written a cover letter detailing his administrative abilities and indicating his availability for a post as personal secretary, should Goethe have need of someone deeply acquainted with his works and sympathetic to his views (*Gespräche*, 686). As Eckermann reports it, though, Goethe's response is not only spontaneous but magically swift: "I have already written about a lodging for you and other things necessary to make your stay pleasant," Goethe tells him, including letters of introduction to close friends of his in Jena. "'You will enjoy their circle,' said he; 'I have passed many delightful evenings there. Jean Paul, Tieck, the Schlegels, and all the other distinguished men of Germany have visited there, and always with delight; and even now it is the union-point of many learned men, artists, and other persons of note" (*Conversations*, 3). The fairy tale is coming true.

Eckermann's admission to this charmed circle is his introduction to the world of world literature as Goethe practices it: less a set of works than a network. As Fritz Strich has observed, this network had a fundamentally economic character, serving to promote "a traffic in ideas between peoples, a literary market to which the nations bring their intellectual treasures for exchange" (*Goethe and World Literature*, 13). In 1847 Marx and Engels adopted Goethe's term precisely in the context of newly global trade relations: "The bourgeoisie has through its exploitation of the world market given a cosmopolitan character to production and consumption in every country. To the great chagrin of reactionaries it has drawn from under the feet of industry the national ground on which it stood. All old-established national industries have been destroyed or are daily being destroyed" (*Communist Manifesto*, 421). The paragraph that begins with these sentences ends with the lines that form the first epigraph to this book: "National one-sidedness and narrow-mindedness become more and more impossible, and from the numerous national and local literatures there arises a world literature." For Marx and Engels, as for Goethe, world literature is the quintessential literature of modern times.

The dramatic acceleration of globalization since their era, however, has greatly complicated the idea of a world literature. Most immediately, the sheer scope of the term today can breed a kind of scholarly panic. "What can one make of such an idea?" Claudio Guillén has asked. "The sum total of all national literatures? A wild idea, unattainable in practice, worthy not of an actual reader but of a deluded keeper of archives who is also a multimillionaire. The most harebrained editor has never aspired to such a thing" (*The Challenge of Comparative Literature*, 38). Though it has a certain surface plausibility, Guillén's objection is hardly decisive; after all, no one denies that the term "insect" is viable, even though there are so many billions of insects in the world that no one person can ever be bitten by each of them. Still, the sum total of the world's literatures can be sufficiently expressed by the blanket term "literature." The idea of world literature can usefully continue to mean a subset of the plenum of literature. I take world literature to encompass all literary works that circulate beyond their culture of origin, either in translation or in their original language (Virgil was long read in Latin in Europe). In its most expansive sense, world literature could include any work that has ever reached beyond its home base, but Guillén's cautionary focus on actual readers makes good sense: a work only has an *effective* life as world literature whenever, and wherever, it is actively present within a literary system beyond that of its original culture.

A viable concept when delimited in this way, world literature still consists of a huge corpus of works. These works, moreover, stem from widely disparate societies, with very different histories, frames of cultural reference, and poetics. A specialist in classical Chinese poetry can gradually, over years of labor, develop a close familiarity with the vast substratum beneath each brief T'ang Dynasty poem, but most of this context is lost to foreign readers when the poem travels abroad. Lacking specialized knowledge, the foreign reader is likely to impose domestic literary values on the foreign work, and even careful scholarly attempts to read a foreign work in light of a Western critical theory are deeply problematic. As A. Owen Aldridge has said, "it is difficult to point to remarkably successful examples of the pragmatic application of critical systems in a comparative context. The various theories cancel each other out" (*The Reemergence of World Literature*, 33). Or as the Indian scholar D. Prempati has pointedly remarked, "I do not know whether the innumerable Western critical models which, like multinationals, have taken over the Indian critical scene would meaningfully serve any critical purpose at this juncture."[2]

Some scholars have argued that literary works across cultures do exhibit what Northrop Frye thought of as archetypes or what more recently the French comparatist Étiemble has called "invariants." In his lively polemic *Ouverture(s) sur un comparatisme planétaire*, Étiemble argued that common literary patterns must provide the necessary basis for any truly global understanding of literature. Yet such universals quickly shade into vague generalities that hold less and less appeal today, at a time when ideals of melting-pot harmony have faded in favor. Scholars of world literature risk becoming little more than the literary ecotourists described by Susan Lanser, people "who dwell mentally in one or two (usually Western) countries, summer metaphorically in a third, and visit other places for brief interludes" ("Compared to What?" 281).

A central argument of this book will be that, properly understood, world literature is not at all fated to disintegrate into the conflicting multiplicity of separate national traditions; nor, on the other hand, need it be swallowed up in the white noise that Janet Abu-Lughod has called "global babble." My claim is that world literature is not an infinite, ungraspable canon of works but rather a mode of circulation and of reading, a mode that is as applicable to individual works as to bodies of material, available for reading established classics and new discoveries alike. This book is intended to explore this mode of circulation and to clarify the ways in which works of world literature can best be read. It is important from the outset to realize that just as there never has been a single set canon of world literature, so too no single way of reading can be appropriate to all texts, or even to any one text at all times. The variability of a work of world literature is one of its constitutive features—one of its greatest strengths when the work is well presented and read well, and its greatest vulnerability when it is mishandled or misappropriated by its newfound foreign friends.

[2] "Why Comparative Literature in India?" 63. Both Aldridge and Prempati were reacting against efforts, popular in the seventies, to "apply" structuralist and other Western methods directly to foreign works. A cogent critique of this practice can be found in Pauline Yu, "Alienation Effects: Comparative Literature and the Chinese Tradition," though Yu herself holds out hope that more nuanced studies may still be productive.

A work enters into world literature by a double process: first, by being read *as* literature; second, by circulating out into a broader world beyond its linguistic and cultural point of origin. A given work can enter into world literature and then fall out of it again if it shifts beyond a threshold point along either axis, the literary or the worldly. Over the centuries, an unusually shifty work can come in and out of the sphere of world literature several different times; and at any given point, a work may function as world literature for some readers but not others, and for some kinds of reading but not others. The shifts a work may undergo, moreover, do not reflect the unfolding of some internal logic of the work in itself but come about through often complex dynamics of cultural change and contestation. Very few works secure a quick and permanent place in the limited company of perennial World Masterpieces; most works shift around over time, even moving into and out of the category of "the masterpiece," as we will see in the third chapter below.

As it moves into the sphere of world literature, far from inevitably suffering a loss of authenticity or essence, a work can gain in many ways. To follow this process, it is necessary to look closely at the transformations a work undergoes in particular circumstances, which is why this book highlights the issues of circulation and translation and focuses on detailed case studies throughout. To understand the workings of world literature, we need more a phenomenology than an ontology of the work of art: a literary work *manifests* differently abroad than it does at home.

The rich variability of world literature is already fully evident in Goethe's conversations with Eckermann. Goethe had a lively sense of the ways his own books could benefit by translation, even as he himself read voraciously in a surprisingly wide range of foreign literatures. Having found in Eckermann the perfect middleman for his own literary trade, Goethe arranged for his disciple to settle into lodgings near him, first in Jena and then permanently in Weimar. There Eckermann met many of Goethe's visitors from all over Europe and began to take part in the network's activity. He published poems, collaborated on opera libretti, made translations from French, read widely, at Goethe's request, so that he could bring significant new writers to Goethe's attention, and kept a detailed journal recording his conversations with Goethe, with an eye toward eventual publication.

Through these conversations, we gain a nuanced picture of Goethe's manifold encounters with foreign texts. He constantly recommends to Eckermann books he has been reading, in English, French, Italian, and Latin, and he reads translations as readily as originals, even in the case of his own works. "I do not like to read my *Faust* any more in German," he remarks at one point, but in a new French translation he finds his master-work "again fresh, new, and spirited"—even though the translation is mostly in prose (276). Eckermann's initial response to Goethe's poetry, of finding his own essence reflected back to him, thus parallels Goethe's experience of the international circulation of his work, which he regularly describes in terms of "mirroring" (*Spiegelung*). Goethe reads English and French commentaries on German literature with great avidity, finding the foreign perspective sharper and clearer than German criticism can be. As he wrote in an article for his journal *Kunst und Alterthum*, "Left to itself every literature will exhaust its vitality, if it is not refreshed by the interest and con-tributions of a foreign one. What naturalist does not take pleasure in the wonderful things that he sees produced by reflection in a mirror? Now what a mirror in the field of ideas and morals means, everyone has experienced in himself, and once his attention is aroused, he will understand how much of his education he owes to it" ("Some Passages," 8).

Goethe is particularly intrigued when the foreign press reflects his own work back to him, and in his first published use of his new term *Weltliteratur* he sees this process as less a matter of individual than of na-tional pride. Late in January 1827, Goethe wrote an essay on two French re-views of a new play, *Le Tasse: Drame historique en cinq actes,* by the play-wright Alexander Duval, a work closely based on Goethe's own play *Torquato Tasso.* Goethe quotes at length from the two reviews, both of which note Duval's dependence on Goethe's play (what one reviewer calls "felicitous borrowings," we would now call plagiarism). The two reviews give diametrically opposed assessments of the two *Tassos:* one sees Duval as a pale imitation of Goethe, in whose inspiring philosophical discussions "we encounter a full and deep meditation which perhaps the masses have not been able to grasp," whereas the other reviewer sees Duval's play as a marked improvement on Goethe's ("the monotony of its dialogue seems completely unbearable to us").

Quoting evenhandedly from both reviews, Goethe declines to re-spond in his own defense, apart from an ironic aside at foreigners who show their appreciation of German works "by borrowing from us without thanks, and making use of us without acknowledgment." His chief purpose is to stimulate his countrymen to follow the international circulation of works, and he encourages his readers by appealing to their—and his own—na-tional pride: "there is being formed a universal world literature, in which an honorable role is reserved for us Germans. All the nations review our work; they praise, censure, accept, and reject, imitate and misrepresent us, open or close their hearts to us. All this we must accept with equanimity, since this attitude, taken as a whole, is of great value to us."[3] From this point of view, the world beyond is only a larger and better version of the world at home. As he wrote elsewhere, in an essay on a German translation of Carlyle's life of Schiller: "The wide world, extensive as it is, is only an expanded fatherland, and will, if looked at aright, be able to give us no more than what our home soil can endow us with also" ("Some Passages," 10).

To some extent, Goethe's views show the imperial self-projection that Barbara Herrnstein Smith sees in *Contingencies of Value* as a danger lurking within major-power cosmopolitanism: the imperial self's "system of self-securing," she says, is not necessarily "'corrected' by cosmopolitanism. Rather, in enlarging its view 'from China to Peru,' it may become all the more imperialistic, seeing in every horizon of difference new peripheries of its own centrality, new pathologies through which its own normativity may be defined and must be asserted" (54). Goethe, however, lacks the secure cultural standpoint that could allow his imperial view to collapse into a self-confirming narcissism. For all his pride in his own achievements and those of friends like Schiller, Goethe has an uneasy sense that German culture is provincial, lacking a great history, lacking political unity. He can't afford to grant "national literature" too much meaning, since he doesn't even live *in* a proper nation at all.

Despite the strategic sincerity with which he appeals to German national pride in his article on the *Tasso* reviews, Goethe begins that very article by noting that it is France whose stages command "a decisive supremacy" (*eine entschiedene Oberherrschaft*) in the theatrical world. Paris is the cultural crucible in which even German plays must strive for recognition and in which their strengths and weaknesses will most clearly be revealed. It is far from certain, moreover, that the provincial work will manage to meet French and English standards. Lacking a strong literary tradition at home, how can a German writer ever live up to the great models of wealthier traditions? "Shakespeare gives us golden apples in silver dishes," he tells Ecker-

---

[3] The conclusion of Goethe's article is given in Hans-Joachim Schulz, "Johann W. von Goethe: Some Passages Pertaining to the Concept of World Literature," 5. The full article appears in Goethe's *Schriften zur Literatur* 2:171–74, and its composition history is lovingly rehearsed in the extensive apparatus—twice the size of the article itself—given in 5:237–43, where the interested reader can trace the article's evolution from Goethe's first draft through its subsequent emendations in pencil, black ink, red ink, and pencil again. This sumptuous edition, published in 1980 under the auspices of the Akademie der Wissenschaft der DDR, testifies to lasting national pride in Goethe—a pride only heightened by the need of what was then East Germany to assert its cultural identity over against West Germany.

mann, adding ruefully, "We get, indeed, the silver dishes by studying his works; but, unfortunately, we have only potatoes to put into them" (99).

Goethe's stance is thus very different from the triumphalist cosmopolitanism with which a leading French critic, Philarète Euphémon Chasles, introduced a new course, "The Comparison of Foreign Literature," in Paris in January 1835. Opening his lecture with the figures of Cervantes and Shakespeare, poorly understood by their own contemporary countrymen, Chasles announces that his course will study the influence of great minds beyond their own borders—and above all, in France. This focus, he tells his students, simply reflects the fact that "France is the most sensitive of all countries," receptive to the passionate advances of all nations. Contemplating his homeland's charms, Chasles falls into an extended erotic reverie:

> She is a sleepless and restless country that vibrates with all
> impressions and that palpitates and grows enthusiastic for the
> maddest and the noblest ones; a country which loves to seduce
> and be seduced, to receive and communicate sensation, to be
> excited by what charms it, and to propagate the emotion it
> receives. . . . She is the center, but the center of sensitivity; she
> directs civilization, less perhaps by opening up the route to the
> people who border her than by going forward herself with a giddy
> and contagious passion. What Europe is to the rest of the world,
> France is to Europe; everything reverberates toward her,
> everything ends with her. ("Foreign Literature Compared,"
> 21–22)

And so on. Infinitely receptive as Chasles's France is, however, she carefully controls her own borders: she will go out for a mad fling when and where she pleases, but foreigners should not expect to move in with her. A green card is not in the cards, and her rejuvenating forays may open up no new routes at all for the suitors ringing her borders.

The writer from a marginal culture is in a double bind. With little to go on at home, a young writer can only achieve greatness by emulating desirable foreign models—"the need for an intercourse with great predecessors is the sure sign of a higher talent," Goethe says. "Study Molière, study Shakespeare" (150)—yet these models can have a crushing weight. Within their own cultural context, this weight may be bearable: working among great contemporaries like Ben Jonson and Marlowe, Goethe remarks, Shakespeare was like Mont Blanc, only the highest of a range of great Alps. But if Mont Blanc were set down amid the flat fields of the Lüneberg Heath in Lower Saxony, "you would be rendered speechless with astonishment at its immensity" (26). Looking at a set of engravings of scenes from Shakespeare's plays, Goethe cannot repress a shudder:

> "It is even terrifying," said Goethe, "to look through these little pictures. Thus are we first made to feel the infinite wealth and grandeur of Shakespeare. There is no *motif* in human life which he has not exhibited and expressed. And all with what ease and freedom! . . . He is even too rich and too powerful. A productive nature ought not to read more than one of his dramas in a year, if it would not be wrecked entirely. . . . How many excellent Germans have been ruined by him and Calderon!" (99)

If Goethe's provincial anxiety provides one counterbalance to his imperial acquisitiveness, his extraordinary writerly receptivity provides another. He loves foreign works as much for their ineradicable difference from his own practices as for their novel employment of themes and strategies that he finds familiar. These two sides to his response can be seen in his shrewd appraisals of two foreign works, a Serbian poem and a Chinese novel, that he shows Eckermann in the very days he is formulating the term *Weltliteratur*. On 29 January 1827, Eckermann records a conversation that includes discussion of contemporary French poetry, allusions to Horace and to the Persian poet Hafiz, and discussion of Goethe's own just-completed drama *Helena*, a work that begins as a classical tragedy and ends as a modern opera. Turning from the perusal of this hybrid, Goethe picks up a different kind of work. "Here you have something new;—read it," he says:

> He handed to me a translation by Herr Gerhard of a Serbian poem. It was very beautiful, and the translation was so simple and clear that there was no disturbance in the contemplation of the object. It was entitled *The Prison-Key*. I say nothing of the course of the action, except that the conclusion seemed to me abrupt and rather unsatisfactory. (131)

Eckermann is displeased with the poem's abruptness, its violation of neoclassical canons of balance and harmony, but Goethe disagrees: "That," said Goethe, "is the beauty of it; for it thus leaves a sting in the heart. . . . that which is set forth in the poem is really new and beautiful; and the poet acted very wisely in delineating this alone and leaving the rest to the reader" (131).

Two days later, Eckermann comes to see Goethe again, and now Goethe's reading has ranged still farther from Western Europe:

> Dined with Goethe. "Within the last few days, since I saw you," said he, "I have read many things; especially a Chinese novel,

which occupies me still and seems to me very remarkable."

"Chinese novel!" said I; "that must look strange enough."

"Not so much as you might think," said Goethe; "the Chinese think, act, and feel almost exactly like us; and we soon find that we are perfectly like them, except that all they do is more clear, pure, and decorous, than with us.

"With them all is orderly, citizen-like, without great passion or poetic flight; and there is a strong resemblance to my *Hermann and Dorothea*, as well as to the English novels of Richardson." (132)

Goethe—who himself is writing a novella at this time and struggling to find an appropriate ending—sees in the Chinese novel a version of his own ideal, as much social as literary: "It is by this severe moderation in everything that the Chinese Empire has sustained itself for thousands of years, and will endure hereafter." This elevated moderation, moreover, gives him a welcome counter to the dissolute poetry of a leading contemporary French poet, Pierre-Jean de Béranger, whom he is also currently reading (brothels and bars are Béranger's settings of choice): "I find a highly remarkable contrast to this Chinese novel in the *Chansons de Béranger*, which have, almost every one, some immoral licentious subject for their foundation, and which would be extremely odious to me if managed by a genius inferior to Béranger."

Even as he takes heart from the kinship he senses with imperial Chinese prose writers, Goethe acutely perceives a range of distinctive features of Chinese literary practice. Legends, he remarks, are constantly alluded to, forming a running commentary on the action; nature is not realistically presented but is symbolic of human character ("There is much talk about the moon, but it does not alter the landscape, its light is conceived to be as bright as day itself"). Even furniture serves to illustrate character: "For instance, 'I heard the lovely girls laughing, and when I got sight of them they were sitting on cane chairs.' There you have, at once, the prettiest situation; for cane chairs are necessarily associated with the greatest lightness and elegance" (132).

These observations show a fascinating mix of elements. Goethe is partly responding to cultural difference (the weight given to exemplary legends), partly projecting his own values outward (he takes the cane chairs to signify what *he* would have used them to mean), and partly finding in the foreign text a middle quality, a distinctive novelty that is like-but-unlike practice at home (the intimate connection of character and landscape had been a staple of intensely subjective Romantic poetry, but Goethe sees the connection in the Chinese novel as showing a more restrained and ordered universe of correspondences). Any full response to a foreign text is likely to operate along all three of these dimensions: a sharp *difference* we enjoy for its sheer novelty; a gratifying *similarity* that we find in the text or project onto it; and a middle range of what is *like-but-unlike*—the sort of relation most likely to make a productive change in our own perceptions and practices.

Eckermann seems resistant to finding so much of interest in so foreign a text. He interposes a skeptical question, apparently hoping that at least he won't have to read *too many* Chinese novels: "'But then,' I said, 'is this Chinese novel perhaps one of their most superior ones?'" It is in reply to this reservation that Goethe shares with him the concept of *Weltliteratur*:

> "By no means," said Goethe; "the Chinese have thousands of them, and had when our forefathers were still living in the woods.
> "I am more and more convinced," he continued, "that poetry is the universal possession of mankind. . . . the epoch of world literature is at hand, and everyone must strive to hasten its approach." (132)

Goethe is no multiculturalist, however: Western Europe remains the privileged modern world of reference for him, and Greece and Rome provide the crucial antiquity to which he always returns. No sooner does he tell Eckermann to strive to hasten the epoch of world literature than he adds a limiting, or delimiting, condition:

> "But, while we thus value what is foreign, we must not bind ourselves to some particular thing, and regard it as a model. We must not give this value to the Chinese, or the Serbian, or Calderon, or the *Nibelungen;* but, if we really want a pattern, we must always return to the ancient Greeks, in whose works the beauty of mankind is constantly represented. All the rest we must look at only historically; appropriating to ourselves what is good, so far as it goes." (132)

Thinking always as a practicing writer, Goethe responds most of all to what he can appropriate in anything he reads, and he shares with many of his contemporaries a sense of classical antiquity as the ultimate treasury to plunder for themes, formal models, and even language. Indeed, he actually prefers a Latin translation of one of his own works to the original: "there it seems to me nobler, and as if it had returned to its original form" (67).

In the variability of Goethe's valuations of the foreign, we see a crucial feature of the system of world literature: on examination, it resolves always into a *variety* of worlds. These different worlds vary by region, audience, and cultural prestige. Moreover, the impact of a given world can change for us over time, and it can be strongly affected from the start by the age at which we first encounter it. Goethe's devotion to classical antiquity can be so heartfelt and unambiguous in large part because it developed once he had reached a substantial maturity as a writer. This is a lesson he often forgets when telling young admirers to "study the old Greeks, and only the Greeks": he himself actually benefited, he now feels, by growing up amid the relatively weak culture of the Germany of his youth, which allowed him more freedom to strike out on his own, only discovering Greek literature once he was sure of himself as a writer. "Had I earlier known how many excellent things have been in existence for hundreds and thousands of years, I should not have written a line" (104).

The provincial writer is thus at once cut off but also free from the bonds of an inherited tradition, and in principle can engage all the more fully, and by mature choice, with a broader literary world: Joyce and Walcott are far more cosmopolitan writers than Proust or Woolf. Whether of provincial or metropolitan origin, in fact, a given writer or reader is likely both to inherit and to seek out a variety of networks of transmission and reception, engaging differently with works from each world. These worlds will be variously delineated by different observers, and even by the same person in different moods. While in January of 1827 Goethe is praising the artistic refinement of Serbian poetry to a dubious Eckermann, a year later we find him dismissing Serbian poetry out of hand, lumping it together with medieval Germanic poetry as emblems of barbaric crudity: "'From these old-German gloomy times,' said Goethe, 'we can obtain as little as from the Serbian songs and similar barbaric popular poetry. We can read it and be interested for a while, but merely to cast it aside and to let it lie behind us'" (213).

This is not, or not primarily, Eurocentrism; here Goethe is discussing a modern French poet's unsatisfactory attempt to place a tale in Germany during the days of the Minnesingers. An elegant Chinese novel can find a more secure place within Goethe's gallery of world masterpieces than the *Nibelungenlied*. His Eurocentrism is highly permeable, in part because of a competing value: his elitism. It is popular poetry, of whatever origin, that has only limited appeal for Goethe, and the world literature he prefers is the production of a guiding elite whose international brotherhood compensates for their small numbers and neglect by the masses. As he wrote on Carlyle's life of Schiller:

> What pleases the crowd spreads itself over a limitless field, and, as we already see, meets with approval in all countries and regions.

The serious and intellectual meets with less success, but . . . there are everywhere in the world such men, to whom the truth and the progress of humanity are of interest and concern. . . . the serious-minded must therefore form a quiet, almost secret, company, since it would be futile to set themselves against the current of the day; rather must they manfully strive to maintain their position till the flood has passed. ("Some Passages," 10)

Goethe is uncomfortably aware that there is a form of world literature flooding over "all countries and regions" that does not include his work or similarly elite productions, and that even threatens to submerge him altogether. Goethe was far from alone in this concern: already in 1800, Wordsworth had used similar flood imagery in his preface to *Lyrical Ballads,* warning darkly that serious English poetry was being drowned in a rising tide of "frantic novels, sickly and stupid German Tragedies"—surely not Goethe's—"and deluges of idle and extravagant stories in verse" (Preface, 449). The worlds of world literature are often worlds in collision.

Goethe's conversations with Eckermann signal a major shift in the range of what could be taken seriously as world literature. In this book, I will have relatively little interest in attempting any firm definition of literature as such, since this is a question that really only has meaning within a given literary system. Any global perspective on literature must acknowledge the tremendous variability in what has counted as literature from one place to another and from one era to another; in this sense, literature can best be defined pragmatically as whatever texts a given community of readers *takes* as literature. Even within the Euro-American tradition, there has always been considerable variety in what counts as literature, including that foundationally canonical work the Bible. In 1862, troubled by his difficulties in translating the Scriptures into Zulu, Bishop John William Colenso was moved to write *The Pentateuch and Book of Joshua Critically Examined,* in which he shocked many readers by treating the Flood story as a literary legend rather than as the unmediated word of God, a dispute that inspired enormous public interest a few years later in the recovery of *The Epic of Gilgamesh,* as I will be discussing in my first chapter.

The Bible's status has not been questioned only in earlier eras: as recently as 1982, Northrop Frye gave his book *The Great Code* the subtitle *The Bible and Literature,* arguing in his preface that to work on "the Bible *as* literature" is to make a category error. Less canonical works, of course, figured prominently in the culture wars of the eighties and early nineties: in 1991 Dinesh D'Souza attacked *I, Rigoberta Menchú* as unworthy of inclusion alongside European masterworks, while in *Against Literature* (1993) John Beverley championed Burgos and Menchú's book precisely for its exploding of traditional definitions of the literary.

This sort of variability involves constantly competing ideas of literature, and our contemporary definitional debate can be seen as an episode in the shifting relations among three general conceptions. World literature has often been seen in one or more of three ways: as an established body of *classics,* as an evolving canon of *masterpieces,* or as multiple *windows on the world.* The "classic" is a work of transcendent, even foundational value, often identified particularly with Greek and Roman literature (still taught today in departments of Classics) and often closely associated with imperial values, as Frank Kermode has shown in his book *The Classic.* The "masterpiece," on the other hand, can be an ancient or a modern work and need not have had any foundational cultural force. Goethe clearly considers his own best works, and those of his friends, to be modern masterpieces. The "masterpiece," indeed, came into prominence in the nineteenth century as literary studies began to deemphasize the dominant Greco-Roman classics, elevating the modern masterpiece to a level of near equality with the long-established classics. In this literary analog of a liberal democracy, the (often middle-class) masterworks could engage in a "great conversation" with their aristocratic forebears, a conversation in which their culture and class of origin mattered less than the great ideas they expressed anew. Finally, Goethe's disquisitions on Chinese novels and Serbian poems show a nascent interest in works that would serve as windows into foreign worlds, whether or not these works could be construed as masterpieces and regardless of whether these differing worlds had any visible links to each other at all.

These three conceptions are not mutually exclusive, though sometimes people of decided taste champion one or another and even attempt to portray their favored mode as the one form of literature worth serious attention. Goethe, however, holds all three conceptions together, as have many readers since. There is really no good reason why we shouldn't allow all three categories their ongoing value, particularly as a single work may effectively be classified under two or even all three headings. Virgil's *Aeneid* is the very type of a timeless classic, but it is also a masterpiece of its genre, registering one stage of development in the long series of works from *Gilgamesh* and the *Iliad* up to Joyce's *Ulysses* and Walcott's *Omeros.* Equally, the *Aeneid* is a window on the world of imperial Rome; though it is set before Rome's founding and treats legendary materials, in its underworld scenes and epic similes it opens out with unconcealed directness toward Virgil's contemporary world.

In the nineteenth century, devotees of the classics were distressed that modern European masterpieces were displacing Anacreon, Statius, and even Virgil. In recent decades, lovers of the European masterpieces have felt a comparable alarm in turn, as literary studies in an increasingly multicultural North America have opened the canon to more and more works in the third category: hence D'Souza's outrage—and Beverley's satisfaction—at the widespread adoption of *I, Rigoberta Menchú* in many world literature and "Western Civ" courses. In an influential 1993 report to the American Comparative Literature Association on the state of the discipline, a committee chaired by Charles Bernheimer urged that comparatists should be actively engaged in reconceiving the canon, paying particular attention to "various contestatory, marginal, or subaltern perspectives" (*Comparative Literature in the Age of Multiculturalism*, 44). Introducing the report and a set of responses to it, Bernheimer emphasized the contemporary relevance of comparative study: "In the age of multiculturalism," he concluded, "the comparatist's anxiety has finally found a field adequate to the questions that generated it" (16).

The Bernheimer report was intended as a call to expand rather than abandon the older canon, and in the last decade there has been a growing consensus that all three categories of world literature are still viable. Equally important, but perhaps less widely recognized, is the fact that world literature is multitemporal as well as multicultural. Too often, shifts in focus from classics to masterpieces to windows on the world have underwritten a concomitant shift from earlier to later periods. John Guillory has remarked that the traditional European canon has been a white male affair in large part because, until fairly recently, few women and minority writers had access to literacy, much less publication. He goes on to say that

> obviously in order to "open" this canon, one would have to *modernize* it, to displace the preponderance of works from earlier to later. And there are of course many good reasons to do so. The pressure to modernize the curriculum has succeeded again and again despite the inertial conservatism of the educational institution, and it is this presure which is largely responsible for many historically significant *exclusions:* The fact that we read Plato but not Xenophon, Virgil but not Statius, has nothing to do with the social identities of Xenophon or Statius . . . but the

necessity of choosing between them has everything to do with the modernization of the curriculum, with the imperative of *making room* for such later writers as Locke or Rousseau. (*Cultural Capital*, 32)

Though this modernizing tendency has been widespread, it need not and should not entail the sheer overwhelming of the past by the present. All too often, students of imperialism, colonialism, nationalism, and globalization do indeed define their topics in such a way as to restrict their investigations to just the last five hundred years of human history, or the last hundred years, or even the last few years. If we do so, however, we reproduce one of the least appealing characteristics of modern American—and global commercial—culture: the insistent *presentism* that erases the past as a serious factor, leaving at best a few nostalgic postmodern references, the historical equivalent of the "local color" tipped in to distinguish the lobby of the Jakarta Hilton from that of its Cancún counterpart.

Not only does this presentism deprive us of the ability to learn from a much wider range of empires, colonies, polities, and migrations; it also leaves out of account the dramatic ways in which the canons of the earlier periods themselves are being reshaped through new attention to all sorts of long-neglected but utterly fascinating texts. The following chapters will treat materials written as far back as four thousand years ago and as recently as the late 1990s, and will include discussions of the current reshaping of our understanding of Hellenistic Egypt, thirteenth-century Europe, and seventeenth-century Mexico. One of the most exciting features of contemporary literary studies is the fact that all periods as well as all places are up for fresh examination and open to new configurations.

This is not to deny that the contemporary world offers an extraordinarily vibrant and varied literary landscape, and several of the following chapters will focus on work written across the span of the twentieth century. Yet the tremendous and ongoing expansion of the field of contemporary world literature raises serious questions as well. It is not only cultural conservatives like Dinesh D'Souza or William Bennett who have expressed qualms about the opening of so many windows onto such disparate parts of the world: many scholars to their left are deeply ambivalent about this whole process. Are these brave new texts a testimony to a wealth of cultural diversity, or are they being sucked up in the Disneyfication of the globe? The problem here is partly one of reception. Masao Miyoshi (in *Off Center*) and Lawrence Venuti (in *The Scandals of Translation*) have shown how the postwar reception of texts from Japan or from Italy often had more to do with

American interests and needs than with genuine openness to other cultures. Even today, foreign works will rarely be translated at all in the United States, much less widely distributed, unless they reflect American concerns and fit comfortably with American images of the foreign culture in question.

The problem of reception is compounded today by questions of production as well. In recent decades a growing proportion of works has been produced primarily for foreign consumption—a process that will be the focus of the final third of this book. This is a fundamentally new literary development: for the first time in history, authors of highly successful works can hope to have them translated into twenty or thirty languages within a few years of publication, and foreign countries may even provide the primary readership for writers who have small audiences at home or who are censored by their governments. In earlier centuries, writers like Dante rarely thought of themselves as writing anything resembling this kind of "world literature"; though they might hope to be read abroad, their patrons and most immediate audience were at home. Dante, indeed, wrote his *Commedia* in the vernacular precisely in order to be read by the widest possible audience in Italy, instead of using Latin to reach a large European public.

Writing for publication abroad can be a heroic act of resistance against censorship and an affirmation of global values against local parochialism; yet it can also be only a further stage in the leveling process of a spreading global consumerism. According to Tim Brennan:

> Several younger writers have entered a genre of third-world
> metropolitan fiction whose conventions have given their novels
> the unfortunate feel of ready-mades. Less about an inauthenticity
> of vision than the context of reception, such novels—typically
> grouped together in the display cases of library foyers—unjustly
> come off as a kind of writing by numbers. . . . Placed in the
> company of other hybrid subjects, they take their part in a
> collective lesson for American readers of a global pluralism.
> (*At Home in the World*, 203)

This is almost the opposite of the long-recognized problems of cultural distance and difficulty: these new globally directed works may be all too *easy* to understand. Brennan places the blame chiefly on distributors and readers, but others have criticized the writers themselves. According to Tariq Ali: "From New York to Beijing, via Moscow and Vladivostok, you can eat the same junk food, watch the same junk on television, and, increasingly, read the same junk novels. . . . Instead of 'socialist realism' we have 'market realism'" ("Literature and Market Realism," 140–44). Non-Western works from earlier periods have often been excluded from world literature courses on the grounds that they are too difficult to understand and absorb in the time available. Now the converse fear is often expressed: that contemporary world literature isn't worth the effort it doesn't require.

Brennan and Ali tactfully avoid mentioning any new-global-economy writers by name, but others have been less discreet. The prominent Sinologist Steven Owen provoked a severe reaction when he advanced a comparable critique of contemporary Chinese poetry, in a 1990 review essay significantly titled "What Is World Poetry?" Owen's occasion was the publication of *The August Sleepwalker,* the collected poetry of the prominent dissident poet Bei Dao. Writing for nonspecialist readers in the *New Republic,* Owen argued that third-world poets are increasingly running afoul of the literary hegemony of the major Western powers, with the result that they begin to write a "world poetry" that is little more than a watered-down Western modernism:

> Poets who write in the "wrong language" (even exceedingly populous languages like Chinese) not only must imagine themselves being translated in order to reach an audience of a satisfying magnitude, they must also engage in the peculiar act of imagining a world poetry and placing themselves within it. And, although it is supposedly free of all local history, this "world poetry" turns out, unsurprisingly, to be a version of Anglo-American modernism or French modernism, depending on which wave of colonial culture first washed over the intellectuals of the country in question. This situation is the quintessence of cultural hegemony, when an essentially local tradition (Anglo-European) is widely taken for granted as universal. (28)

In Owen's view, this surrender to Euro-American modernism—often introduced into China in the form of mediocre translations several decades ago—entails the erasure of local literary and cultural history, leaving the writer with no vital tradition to work from. This new world poetry floats free of context, merely decorated with a little local ethnic color. Though such poems lack real literary power, Owen says, "it may be that the international readers of poetry do not come in search of poetry at all, but rather in search of windows upon other cultural phenomena. They may be looking for some exotic religious tradition or political struggle. These Western fashions in exotica and causes are ephemeral things. Who now reads Tagore? He is a bargain that fills the shelves of poetry sections in used book stores" (29). Having established this broad, depressing framework, Owen proceeds to discuss

Bei Dao's poetry as a secondhand American modernism, given momentary currency thanks to its author's close involvement in dissident activities leading up to the massacre in Tiananmen Square. Owen sees Bei Dao's lyrics as sporadically vivid but ultimately empty: "most of these poems translate themselves. They could just as easily be translated from a Slovak or an Estonian or a Philippine poet. . . . The poetry of *The August Sleepwalker* is a poetry written to travel well" (31).

Owen's position has been widely criticized, most notably by Rey Chow, who opened her 1993 book *Writing Diaspora* with a wholesale attack on his essay. Calling Owen's views orientalist and even "racist" (2 n. 2), Chow argued that the problem is not with the poetry but with the Western critic's loss of authority:

> Basic to Owen's disdain for the new "world poetry" is a sense of loss and, consequently, an anxiety over his own intellectual position. . . . This is the anxiety that the Chinese past which he has undertaken to penetrate is evaporating and that the Sinologist himself is the abandoned subject. . . . Concluding his essay sourly with the statement, "Welcome to the late twentieth century," Owen's real complaint is that *he* is the victim of a monstrous world order in front of which a sulking impotence like his is the only claim to truth. (3–4)

The problem for a nonspecialist reader—apart from the danger of the critical prose bursting into flames in your hands—is that Chow is so deeply committed to her position that she doesn't see any need to combat Owen's views by discussing a single line of Bei Dao's poetry. Owen's article does give some brief quotations, but he spends little time on them. Further, having taken the position that Bei Dao's poems "translate themselves," he says little about the work of the poems' actual translator, Bonnie McDougall. Readers unable to consult Bei Dao in the original may wonder how we can possibly assess these radically differing views.

We can make some headway by looking directly at *The August Sleepwalker,* and if we do so, we can find verses that show Bei Dao's own acute awareness of the difficulties his poetry faces abroad. Thus his poem "Language" begins by saying that

> many languages
> fly around the world
> producing sparks when they collide

sometimes of hate
sometimes of love

(121)

Appropriately enough, I first encountered this poem in Jayana Clerk and
Ruth Siegel's 1995 anthology *Modern Literature of the Non-Western World,*
whose back-cover copy (no doubt written by the HarperCollins marketing
department rather than by the editors) positions the collection as just the
sort of literary jet-setting that Owen condemns: "Travel to 61 countries and
experience a vast selection of poetry, fiction, drama, and memoirs," the cover
urges us; "make stops in Asia, Southeast Asia, the Middle East, Africa, Latin
America, and the Caribbean. . . . Your passport? *Modern Literature of the
Non-Western World.*" Bei Dao's own poem, however, ends by deconstructing this very process of circulation:

> many languages
> fly around the world
> the production of languages
> can neither increase nor decrease
> mankind's silent suffering

Bei Dao seems less confident of his work's value abroad than Chow herself is; at the same time, he may have a more thoughtful, ironic stance toward home tradition and foreign audiences alike than Owen allows. To
pursue this question in detail, it would be necessary to look at a range of
issues: the ways in which Chinese poets in the generation before Bei Dao
translated American and French poets as a form of self-expression as they
sought new resources to revitalize the ancient classical repertoire; the ways
in which midcentury American and Chinese poets alike were influenced
by translations of earlier Spanish-language poets like Rubén Darío and
Federico García Lorca; the ways in which the surface simplicity of Bei
Dao's prosody may be subverting Maoist calls to abandon the complexities of aristocratic poetry and return to the purity of the old *Shih Ching
(Book of Songs),* that ancient folk classic marked, as Eugene Eoyang has
said, by simple diction and "intensely commonplace sentiments, with a
universality which the song does not try to hide" ("The Many 'Worlds' in
World Literature," 249).

Such investigations could take us deep into specialist territory, but
it is important to realize that we don't face a strict either/or choice between
total immersion and an airy vapidity. A full appreciation of world literature

requires us to see it as at once "locally inflected and translocally mobile," as Vilashini Cooppan has said ("World Literature and Global Theory," 33). Our reading of Bei Dao, or of Dante, will benefit from a leavening of local knowledge, an amount that may vary from work to work and from reader to reader but that will remain less than is needed for a full contextual understanding of a work within its home tradition. As such, world literature can be aligned with the nuanced, localized cosmopolitanism championed by Bruce Robbins: "No one actually is or ever can be a cosmopolitan in the sense of belonging nowhere. . . . The interest of the term *cosmopolitanism* is located, then, not in its full theoretical extension, where it becomes a paranoid fantasy of ubiquity and omniscience, but rather (paradoxically) in its local applications" ("Comparative Cosmopolitanisms," 260). Far from being a rootless cosmopolitan, Bei Dao is doubly or multiply linked to events and audiences at home and abroad; indeed, as an exile since the early nineties, he has occupied an increasingly multiple relation to the very terms "home" and "abroad."

To read Bei Dao's poems in English we should be alive to relevant aspects of the context of their production, but we don't finally need the Chinese context in all its particularity. When all is said and done, Bei Dao in English *isn't* Bei Dao in Chinese, and Steven Owen is really describing the life of any work of world literature when he asks, "Is this Chinese literature, or literature that began in the Chinese language?" ("What Is World Poetry?" 31). Owen means to express the poet's limitations by this formulation, but the criticism only partly holds, even if Bei Dao's poetry is in fact superficial in the original. Not only is this something that those of us who don't read Chinese cannot judge; it is actually irrelevant to the poem's existence abroad. *All* works cease to be the exclusive products of their original culture once they are translated; all become works that only "began" in their original language.

The crucial issue for the foreign reader is how well the poems work in the new language; such cultural information as may be practical to acquire and relevant to apply must still make sense in the translation if it is to be useful at all. Here we can gain in understanding by looking at different translations of Bei Dao's work. Thanks to his global popularity, he has already been translated by a number of people, and even individual poems can be found variously translated. Here, for example, are two versions of the opening stanza of his most famous poem, "The Answer," which became a rallying cry for the Tiananmen protestors:

Debasement is the password of the base.
Nobility the epitaph of the noble.

See how the gilded sky is covered
With the drifting twisted shadows of the dead.

(McDougall tr.)

The scoundrel carries his baseness around like an ID card.
The honest man bears his honor like an epitaph.
Look—the gilded sky is swimming
with undulant reflections of the dead.

(Finkel tr.)[4]

McDougall's translation clearly tries to convey an underlying word play in the original, but the result is stilted and unpoetic English; Finkel's translation is freer but also more readable, and without the constraint of making the end of the opening lines echo the beginning, he is able to set up a more effective contrast of identity card to epitaph. Further, his version plays with modernist shifts of verbal register: the stanza opens with prosaic, even clunky, language to describe the bureaucratic "scoundrel," and then moves to the poetic eloquence of the "undulant reflections of the dead."

As the poem continues, Finkel also brings out uses of modernist motifs that aren't visible in McDougall's version. Where McDougall has "I don't believe in thunder's echoes," Finkel has "I don't believe what the thunder says," ironically recalling the heading in Eliot's "Waste Land" when the speaker turns to the East for timeless wisdom to refresh his dried-up Western roots. In Bei Dao's concluding stanza, a group of stars that McDougall renders as "pictographs" becomes in Finkel "that ancient ideogram," using Ezra Pound's term of choice for Chinese characters. These echoes assort well with the debt to American modernism that Owen and others have identified in Bei Dao's work. Rather than connecting the poem to modernism in this way, McDougall continues to do her best to suggest Chinese theories of correspondence and history, as in her version of the concluding stanza:

A new conjunction and glimmering stars
Adorn the unobstructed sky now:
They are the pictographs from five thousand years.
They are the watchful eyes of future generations.

Compare Finkel:

The earth revolves. A glittering constellation
pricks the vast defenseless sky.

[4] McDougall's version is from her translation of *The August Sleepwalker*, 33; Donald Finkel's is from *The Splintered Mirror*, 9–10.

Can you see it there? that ancient ideogram—
the eye of the future, gazing back.

Compared to McDougall's cautious and literalistic renderings, Finkel's version is at once more eloquent and more creative in holding Chinese and modernist contexts together in view. The prosaic prosody and lurking sentimentality that Owen dislikes in Bei Dao's poetry are much more evident features of McDougall's translations than of Finkel's, which actually gain in poetic effect by emphasizing the modernist connections that Owen regrets and McDougall plays down.

This brief look at Bei Dao can suggest what I will be exploring in detail in the chapters to follow: works of world literature take on a new life as they move into the world at large, and to understand this new life we need to look closely at the ways the work becomes reframed in its translations and in its new cultural contexts. Translation is always involved in what Fernando Ortiz described in 1940 as *transculturación*,[5] and if we do want to see the work of world literature as a window on different parts of the world, we have to take into account the way its images have been multiply refracted in the process of transculturation. World literature can be described, to borrow a phrase from Vinay Dharwadker, as "a montage of overlapping maps in motion" (*Cosmopolitan Geographies,* 3), and this movement involves shifting relations both of literary history and of cultural power. Works rarely cross borders on a basis of full equality; if the classics and masterpieces long dominant in world literature have typically enjoyed high prestige and authoritative weight in their new homes, the power relations are often reversed when noncanonical works come into North America today. Tim Brennan and others have criticized the manipulations by which the political edge has often been taken from works imported into the American context, but it is not enough to have our politics in the right place. All works are subject to manipulation and even deformation in their foreign reception, but established classics usually gain a degree of protection by their cultural prestige: editors and publishers will be less likely, for example, to silently truncate a classic text or reorganize it outright, a fate that is commonly experienced by noncanonical works even at the hands of highly sympathetic translators. As will be seen below in examples from Mechthild von Magdeburg to Rigoberta Menchú, works by non-Western authors or by provincial or subordinate

[5] Cited by Gustavo Pérez-Firmat, who describes the space of *transculturación* as "a liminal zone or 'impassioned margin' where diverse cultures converge without merging" (*The Cuban Condition,* 25).

Western writers are always particularly liable to be assimilated to the immediate interests and agendas of those who edit, translate, and interpret them. This book is written in the belief that we can do better justice to our texts, whether perennial classics or contemporary works, if we really attend to what we are doing when we import them and introduce them into new contexts.

In emphasizing the shaping force of local contexts, I mean to distinguish world literature from a notional "global literature" that might be read solely in airline terminals, unaffected by any specific context whatever. The world's literature is not yet sold by a Borders Books Without Borders. The airport bookstore is stocked by buyers who operate first and foremost within a national context and its distribution system, and the bookstore's customers, mostly traveling to or from home, continue to read in ways profoundly shaped by home-country norms. For all the power of the Internet, even Amazon.com has been setting up distinct subsidiaries abroad rather than relying on its American-based website to achieve a global reach.

Modern literature can be studied in global terms within the "polysystems" framework developed by translation theorists like Itamar Even-Zohar, or the sociopolitical "world systems" approach based in the writings of Immanuel Wallerstein. A notable example of such work is Franco Moretti's ambitious mapping of the spread of the novel, beginning with his *Atlas of the European Novel, 1800–1900.* As he has carried his work beyond Europe, Moretti has found that the global system of literary production and reception is highly variable locally, and he has described the difficulty of dealing directly with the masses of disparate material that a global approach should encompass. Moretti has gone so far as to recommend that we abjure close reading altogether, analyzing broad patterns rather than individual works. "Literary history," he says, "will become 'second hand': a patchwork of other people's research, *without a single direct textual reading.* Still ambitious, and actually even more so than before (world literature!); but the ambition is now directly proportional *to the distance from the text* ("Conjectures on World Literature," 57). Though his emphasis is political rather than archetypal, Moretti in this sense recalls Northrop Frye's method in *Anatomy of Criticism,* where Frye gave rapid surveys of patterns and motifs in a wide range of works. In his article, Moretti draws a sharp distinction between two metaphoric approaches to change: trees and waves. Individual works can be studied by specialists as offshoots of a family tree, an exfoliating national system; global comparatism, on the other hand, should concentrate on wave patterns of transformations sweeping around the world.

Are students of world literature really going to have to leave the analysis of actual works to specialists in national literatures, as Moretti proposes? Those of us unable to tear ourselves so resolutely away from the pleasures of the text are likely to disagree. A world systems approach to literature has many of the virtues earlier found in structuralist approaches, but it also shares some of the problems experienced by those who attempted to apply the insights of structural linguistics directly to complex literary works. Deep structures could be elucidated, but literary effects are often achieved by highly individual means, and generative grammars of narrative had difficulty providing much insight into works more elaborate than folktales or detective stories. As with texts, so with cultures at large: individual cultures only partly lend themselves to analysis of common global patterns. As Wallerstein himself has said, "the history of the world has been the very opposite of a trend towards cultural homogenization; it has rather been a trend towards cultural differentiation, or cultural elaboration, or cultural complexity" ("The National and the Universal: Can There Be Such a Thing as World Culture?", 96). As a result, systemic approaches need to be counterbalanced with close attention to particular languages, specific texts: we need to see both the forest and the trees.

This is a problem that Moretti acknowledges. Going beyond a simple form-and-content account of the spread of the novel (the Western form imitatively adapted to convey local content), Moretti argues for the importance of a third term, narrative voice—a primary feature of indigenous tradition that critically affects the interplay of content and form. As he says, however, we can't study narrative voice at a linguistic remove in the way that we can trace patterns of book sales or broad movements of motifs ("Conjectures," 66). But how to mediate between broad, but often reductive, overviews and intensive, but often atomistic, close readings?

One solution is to recognize that we don't face an either/or choice between global systematicity and infinite textual multiplicity, for world literature itself is constituted very differently in different cultures. Much can be learned from a close attention to the workings of a given cultural system, at a scale of analysis that also allows for extended discussion of specific works. A culture's norms and needs profoundly shape the selection of works that enter into it as world literature, influencing the ways they are translated, marketed, and read. In India, for example, world literature takes on a very particular valence in the dual contexts of the multiplicity of India's disparate languages and the ongoing presence of English in post-Raj India. English can be seen in comparative terms as three distinct entities in India: as the language of the British literature that featured so prominently in colonial Indian education; as the worldwide phenomenon of contemporary global

English; and as Indo-English, with its ambiguous status somewhere between a foreign and a native language.

Amiya Dev has pointed out that India's twenty-two principal literary languages themselves form a plenum comparable to that of European literature, and the different Indian literatures are always strongly colored by the other languages in use around them. As a result, Dev says, no Indian literature is ever itself alone: "Bengali will be Bengali +, Panjabi Panjabi +, and Tamil Tamil +. In a multilingual situation there cannot be a true appreciation of a single literature in absolute isolation" (*The Idea of Comparative Literature in India*, 14). "The very structure of Indian literature is comparative," as Sisir Kumar Das has said; "its framework is comparative and its texts and contexts Indian" (quoted in Chandra Mohan, "Comparative Indian Literature," 97).

By contrast, world literature in Brazil has long been shaped by a very different set of forces: by complex relations between people of indigenous, European, or mixed descent; by inter-American relations within Latin America and vis-à-vis North America; and by lasting cultural ties to Portugal, to Spain, and to France. In works like Oswald de Andrade's *Manifesto Antropofágico*, "international modernism" helped form a specifically Brazilian cultural identity, as Beatriz Resende has recently emphasized ("A Formação de Identidades Plurais no Brasil Moderno"). Relatedly, whereas European scholars have often seen world literature as radiating outward from metropolitan centers toward relatively passive provincial recipients, a number of contemporary Brazilian scholars are moving beyond the paradigm of "Paris, cultural capital of Latin America" to emphasize a two-way process, one that is grounded as much in Brazil's dynamic heterogeneity as in French cultural authority.[6]

For any given observer, even a genuinely global perspective remains a perspective *from somewhere*, and global patterns of the circulation of world literature take shape in their local manifestations. With this in mind, in the following chapters I will be concentrating particularly (though not exclusively) on world literature as it has been construed over the past century in a specific cultural space, that of the formerly provincial and now

---

[6] This is the subject of an illuminating article by Tania Carvalhal, "Culturas e Contextos" (2001). In her balanced presentation of a two-way exchange, Carvalhal avoids the implicit triumphalism seen in a work like Pascale Casanova's *La République mondiale des lettres* (1999), which might better be titled *La République parisienne des lettres*. An unsatisfactory account of world literature in general, Casanova's book is actually a good account of the operation of world literature within the modern French context.

metropolitan United States. This focus gives time for detailed treatment of exemplary works, allowing for an interplay of general issues and actual cases. Further, while avoiding the hubris of supposing that we *are* the world, an account of world literature in this setting may bring out patterns that can be suggestive for accounts of world literature elsewhere.

A final look at Johann Peter Eckermann at home and abroad can suggest some of the issues involved when a provincial author reaches a metropolitan audience. Both in his encounters with Goethe and then in the subsequent reception of his *Conversations* in England and in America, Eckermann gives us a vivid illustration of the problematic power relations between elite and popular worlds. Whereas Goethe can praise Chinese novelists for already enjoying a highly refined level of culture "when our forefathers were still living in the woods," Eckermann's own family, as his introduction informs us, had only gotten a few hundred yards away from the woods, to which he regularly returned to gather kindling. He begins his book with a twenty-page story of his own life up to his arrival in Weimar, entitled "Introduction: The Author Gives an Account Concerning his Person and Origins and the Beginning of his Relation to Goethe." This is a story whose elements can all be found in Vladimir Propp's *Morphology of the Folktale.* Eckermann is born in 1792 in a village in northern Germany, youngest child of a second marriage. His family is very poor—"the chief source of our small family's nourishment was a cow" (*Gespräche,* 11)—and young Johann spends his childhood gathering straw from the fields and firewood from the forest, working the family's vegetable plot, and walking with his father from village to village, wooden boxes on their backs, selling ribbons, thread, and cloth. Fascinated one night by the picture of a horse on his father's tobacco pouch, Johann devotes the evening to copying it, and his parents are charmed by the result. All night, he can scarcely sleep, looking forward to seeing his drawing again the next morning.

He obtains paper and charcoal, and draws incessantly. A well-to-do villager takes an interest, offering to send him to Hamburg to learn painting. His parents refuse, pointing out that it is difficult and even dangerous work, especially as the houses in Hamburg—house painting is the only painting trade they know of—are so tall. Discouraged, Johann stays at home, but his drawings do inspire some neighbors to pay his fees at the village school. At sixteen, he gets a job as secretary to the local judge. He serves briefly in the army as Napoleon's forces are driven out of Germany; stationed in Flanders, he sees actual paintings for the first time. ("Now that I saw what it was to be a painter, I could have wept that it had been forbidden me to follow such a path" *Gespräche,* 16). The war ends, and he returns home, to find his father deceased, his older sister and her family now sharing his mother's cottage; he walks for days through snow-covered fields to reach Hamburg, finds lodging with a friend from his village, and attempts to become an artist.

Checked in this ambition by poverty and ill health, he finds a clerk's job at the local royal court, and begins to read and to try his hand at poetry. He is twenty-four. He studies privately, painfully aware that he lacks the education enjoyed by the great writers whose biographies he constantly reads. Still, his poems meet with approval, and he ventures printing a small volume of them. He sends a copy to Goethe, who writes him a kindly note. They have no further contact until he concludes his fellowship at Göttingen, writes his manuscript on poetry, and hazards his letter and visit.

Eckermann succeeds in leaving his childhood surroundings behind, but his provincial roots are hard to sever entirely. Once he is installed in Goethe's circle, the social differences continually reappear in his account, often displaced into a difference of gender. Throughout the *Conversations,* Eckermann plays the shy, admiring maiden to Goethe's heroic authority. At their very first conversation on Goethe's sofa, Eckermann says: "We sat a long while together, in a tranquil affectionate mood. I forgot to speak for looking at him—I could not look enough. His face is powerful and brown—full of wrinkles, and each wrinkle full of expression! [*und jede Falte voller Ausdruck!*] . . . With him I was indescribably happy" (2).

As can be seen, Eckermann's maidenly reserve entails a silence in the face of Goethe's vast powers of expression, which extend even to his wrinkles. A year later, Eckermann is still speaking in the tones of young love, stimulated ever anew by Goethe's poetry as mediated by the poet's voice and by his entire body: "He brought some manuscript poems, which he read aloud to me. Not only did the original force and freshness of the poems excite me to a high degree; but also, by his manner of reading them, he showed himself to me in a phase hitherto unknown but highly important. What variety and force in his voice! What life and expression in the noble countenance, so full of wrinkles! And what eyes!" (45). Five years into their association, Eckermann is still making a point of arriving early when invited to dinner, so as to have his hero to himself: "I found him, as I wished, still alone, expecting the company. He wore his black coat and star, with which I so much like to see him" (219). They now have a discussion in which Goethe confides that he will never be popular with the multitude; he writes only for like-minded individuals. The other guests arrive and dinner begins, but Eckermann is lost in thought:

I could pay no attention to the conversation that was going on; Goethe's words entirely occupied my mind.

Meanwhile, all around me were jesting and talking, and partaking of the good fare. I spoke now and then a word, but without exactly knowing what I said. A lady put a question to me; to which, it seems, I did not render a very appropriate answer: they all laughed at me.

"Leave Eckermann alone," said Goethe. "He is always absent, except when he is at the theater."

Biscuits and some very fine grapes were brought for dessert. The latter had been sent from a distance, and Goethe would not say whence they came. He divided them, and handed me a very ripe branch across the table.

I highly enjoyed the grapes from Goethe's hand, and was now quite near him in both body and soul. (220–21)

This is as near as Eckermann will ever get, savoring the grapes sent to Goethe by an unnamed admirer; he never succeeds in appropriating his hero's literary power as a poet. Goethe himself hardly helps matters by instructing him, at the start of their acquaintance, to abandon a projected long poem on the seasons: "I especially warn you against great inventions of your own . . . for that purpose youth [Eckermann is *thirty*!] is seldom ripe" (7). Yet if Goethe, nearing the end of his life, feels his audience to be a declining few, Eckermann can make a book out of their conversations and in this way bring his image before a wider audience. This act of piety is at the same time his most successful act of appropriation, as he shows in the opening words of a preface that precedes his autobiographical introduction in the original German edition: "This collection of conversations and discussions with Goethe stems above all from the natural drive that dwells within me to appropriate to myself, through writing, whatever lived experience seems worthy or notable" (*Gespräche*, 7). Though the diamantine Goethe presents very different facets to different people, Eckermann says, "this is *my* Goethe" (8; Eckermann's emphasis).

Eckermann takes up the process of mirroring or *Spiegelung* that Goethe associates with the network of world literature and applies it to his portrait of Goethe himself: "This word ["*my*"] applies not only to the way he presented himself to me, but more especially to the way I was able to grasp him and represent him in turn. In such cases a mirroring occurs, and it very rarely happens that in passing through another individual no specific characteristics will be lost and nothing foreign will be mixed in" (8). Eckermann thus mixes some of his own foreign substance into the portrait, and in the process the silent, maidenly hearer gets the last word.

Interestingly, in a further installment of the *Conversations* published twelve years after the original, Eckermann ends his account by aligning himself with the Virgin Mary. His final entry centers on discussion of the Bible. He has just bought a copy but is annoyed to find that it lacks the Apocrypha. Goethe comments that the Church erred in closing the canon of scripture, as God's creative work still continues, notably in the activity of great spirits like Mozart, Raphael, and Shakespeare, "who can draw their lesser contemporaries higher" (*Gespräche*, 667). Following these words—the last words of Goethe's that Eckermann records—a one-line paragraph appears: "Goethe fell silent. I, however, preserved his great and good words in my heart" (667). This phrasing echoes Luke 2:51, in which the young Jesus preaches in the temple; though his hearers don't understand him, "his mother kept all these words in her heart."

The biblical ending to Eckermann's sequel mirrors the classical ending to his original account. Eckermann has always experienced Goethe's house as a sort of museum of classical art. The first thing he notices on his first visit are "the casts from antique statues, placed upon the stairs" (1), and Goethe himself is the cherished exhibit at the heart of the house: "This evening, I went for the first time to a large tea-party at Goethe's. I arrived first, and enjoyed the view of the brilliantly lighted apartments, which, through open doors, led one into the other. In one of the farthest, I found Goethe, dressed in black, and wearing his star—which became him so well. We were for a while alone" (8). Now, at the end of the book, the Goethe whom Eckermann wishes to monumentalize turns into a funerary monument. After recounting a last conversation on Greek tragedy and the role of the artist, Eckermann passes over any mention of Goethe's final illness or death. There is simply a gap, and then a haunting, and haunted, closing paragraph:

> The morning after Goethe's death, a deep desire seized me to look once again upon his earthly garment. His faithful servant, Frederick, opened for me the chamber in which he was laid out. Stretched upon his back, he reposed as if asleep; profound peace and security reigned in the features of his sublimely noble countenance. The mighty brow seemed yet to harbour thoughts. I wished for a lock of his hair; but reverence prevented me from cutting it off. The body lay naked, only wrapped in a white sheet; large pieces of ice had been placed near it, to keep it fresh as long

as possible. Frederick drew aside the sheet, and I was astonished at the divine magnificence of the limbs. The breast was powerful, broad, and arched; the arms and thighs were full, and softly muscular; the feet were elegant, and of the most perfect shape; nowhere, on the whole body, was there a trace either of fat or of leanness and decay. A perfect man lay in great beauty before me; and the rapture the sight caused made me forget for a moment that the immortal spirit had left such an abode. I laid my hand on his heart—there was a deep silence—and I turned away to give free vent to my suppressed tears. (344–45)

The deep silence of the scene only heightens its stark visual power. Eckermann has achieved a strange synthesis in prose of the pictures he once hoped to paint and the dramatic poetry he continued to compose.

None of Eckermann's efforts at writing in "high" genres made any impact at all, but in the more popular form of the journal he achieved a decisive entry into world literature. His book was translated into "all the European languages," as the *Encyclopaedia Britannica* informs us, and even into "all the languages of civilization," as Havelock Ellis put it in 1930 in an introduction to the *Conversations* (a phrase that, though grandiose, at least allows for the Japanese translation). He became through his book the widely traveled cosmopolite he could never be in life, even emerging in Spanish translation as the dashing Juan Pedro Eckermann.

    The book's rapid foreign success stands in sharp contrast to its early reception at home. Though it was put out by a prominent publisher, Brockhaus, it sold poorly and attracted only a handful of reviews. Goethe's work was indeed falling into neglect in Germany, and his lofty, conservative perspective had little appeal for the German literati of the turbulent years leading up to 1848. Eckermann had considerable difficulty finding a publisher for his sequel, which did even more poorly than the original version. The *Gespräche* only began to gain a substantial audience in Germany twenty years later, when Brockhaus took over the sequel and reissued it along with the original version. Eckermann's book thus provides an interesting example of a work that only achieves an effective presence in its country of origin after it has already entered world literature; in a movement that would hardly have surprised Goethe, the book's reception abroad set the stage for its subsequent revival at home.

    The *Conversations* did particularly well in English translation; both the first version and the sequel were rapidly translated and soon found many admirers. An abridged translation—made, interestingly, by the American feminist Margaret Fuller—appeared as early as 1838, and only two years after Eckermann published his 1848 sequel an English translator, John Oxenford, expanded Fuller's translation, adding substantial entries from the sequel. In translation, the book not only gained new readers but also achieved new coherence, for Oxenford redid the entire series of conversations to produce an integrated sequence, whereas Eckermann himself had had to issue his new material as an independent volume, having broken with his original publisher after the first edition failed to attract the wide acclaim he was sure it should have received.

The *Conversations* gained in this way in translation. Yet Eckermann himself lost, for the book entitled *Gespräche mit Goethe* became *Conversations with Eckermann:* Oxenford gave Goethe, not Eckermann, as the book's actual author. Eckermann's authority over his text diminished along with his authorship: from Oxenford on, translators and editors have felt free to rework his entries and even his prose, according full respect only to the text's quotations from Goethe—even though the quotations themselves are usually Eckermann's reconstructions, often years after the event, and are shaped, like the framing narrative itself, by Eckermann's interpretation of Goethe and his work. As Eckermann put it in a letter to a friend, his book was not "merely the mechanical production of a good memory. . . . even though I made nothing up and *everything is completely true,* it has nonetheless been *selected"* (*Gespräche,* 680). Or as he bitterly remarked in another letter, "were I such a nonentity as many believe, how could Goethe's worth and nobility have so fully preserved themselves in passing through my spirit?" (*Gespräche,* 694).

All too often, Eckermann's translators actually seem to have felt that he wasn't insignificant *enough.* In his 1850 version, Oxenford systematically reduced Eckermann's presence throughout the book. He drastically abridged Eckermann's autobiographical introduction, and in the body of the text he silently omitted phrases that seemed too emotive or self-conscious ("with him I was indescribably happy"; "I rejoiced greatly at these words"). Further, he dropped whole entries, usually ones in which Eckermann has as large a role as Goethe, such as the final entry from the sequel, with its discussion of the Bible and Eckermann's implicit comparison of himself to Mary.

Havelock Ellis deplored the nineteenth-century diminishment of Eckermann's life and authorship. In his preface to the 1930 edition of Oxenford's translation in the Everyman Library, Ellis praised a recent biography of Eckermann as long overdue and asserted that "Eckermann will not be forgotten again. . . . he has moulded the portrait by which we all best know the greatest modern figure in the world of the spirit" (xviii). Yet in this very edition, Havelock's praise for Eckermann is followed by a stern note from one J. K. Moorhead, the Everyman edition's editor, who has actually gone farther than Oxenford himself in reining Eckermann in: "Nearly one-eighth of the original book," Moorhead tell us, "has been got rid of by chastening [!] Eckermann's extreme verbosity and what he himself might have consented to call his subjectiveness" (xxi).

The situation is even worse in a recent reissue of Oxenford's translation, in a quality paperback edition from the North Point Press (1984). Not only is the book yet again titled *Conversations with Eckermann*, with Goethe given as the book's author, but Goethe himself is taken out of history. Whereas the *Conversations* begins with Goethe aged seventy-four and ends with his death at eighty-three, the North Point edition's cover shows Goethe at about forty years of age. The North Point edition goes even further in a frontispiece, which gives a Roman-style bust of Goethe as a young man (figure 1). Goethe has seen his dearest wish fulfilled: he has indeed become nobler, more Latin—and also decades younger—in translation.

Crossing the English Channel, Goethe revives like Dracula from his bier and becomes the author of the book that records his own death. Eckermann's life, meanwhile, dissolves along with his authorship: whereas earlier editions tended to abridge Eckermann's preface and autobiographical introduction, the North Point reprint drops them entirely. This makes the book's beginning a little mysterious ("Weimar, June 10, 1823. I arrived here a few days ago, but did not see Goethe till today"), but the deletions preserve Goethe's authorship from any challenge from the person who is now construed merely as his amanuensis. "JOHANN WOLFGANG VON GOETHE," the cover tells us, "was an intellectual giant. . . . Of all his works, *Conversations with Eckermann* perhaps best demonstrates the range of his interests and the depth of his command of them." Eckermann, meanwhile, is simply "a young friend," as a brief "Note on the Text" explains, who transcribed and published Goethe's remarks. Having given new life to his cosmopolitan hero, the provincial author fades into the obscurity cast by the lengthening shadow of the portrait he himself has painted.

I will be centrally concerned, in the following chapters, with tracing what is lost and what is gained in translation, looking at the intertwined shifts of language, era, region, religion, social status, and literary context that a work can incur as it moves from its point of origin out into a new cultural sphere. Today we are making more and more translations from and among an un-

Figure 1. Roman Goethe

precedented range of literary worlds; done well, these multiple translations can give us a unique purchase on the scope of the world's cultures, past and present. All too often, though, things slip in the process, and we can gain a work of world literature but lose the author's soul. Our sophisticated critical methods and refined cultural sensitivity have not yet sufficed to keep us from falling into errors and abuses that were common a hundred and even a thousand years ago. We ought to do better, but this will require a better sense of what it is we do when we circulate works through the shifting spheres of world literature. What follows is an essay in definition, a celebration of new opportunities, and a gallery of cautionary tales.

Circulation

PART ONE

Circulation

Gilgamesh's Quest

In the summer of 1839 two young Englishmen, Edward Mitford and Austen Henry Layard, left London on a journey to Ceylon, where both had family connections and where jobs were waiting for them. Severely susceptible to seasickness, Mitford preferred to travel overland rather than make a long voyage by sea. The land route would also allow Mitford to indulge his favorite hobby, which he pursued with a typically Victorian intensity: bird-watching. Mitford planned for a leisurely journey, birding his way across the Ottoman Empire and on through India. His wishes dovetailed with Layard's own private goal: to find some compelling excuse along the way that would keep him from ever reaching Ceylon at all. Restless, impetuous, impatient of routine and scornful of authority, Layard was dependent on the financial support of a loving aunt and uncle, whose fondest wish was that he would pursue a quiet career in his uncle's law offices in London. As it gradually became clear to all concerned that this plan just wouldn't fly, the family pressed Layard to take the colonial route to respectability: young Austen Henry could see the world while absorbing the training and discipline of work as a magistrate in Ceylon. Layard hoped that if he and Mitford wandered around the Middle East long enough en route, he might hit upon something more dramatic to do with his life.

These are the motives that led to the discovery of the lost city of Nineveh, whose ruins would yield the cuneiform tablets bearing the text of *The Epic of Gilgamesh*. The scholarly adventurers who recovered and deciphered the epic found themselves dealing in new ways with the ambiguities of history and culture, as the poem forced them to reassess ancient sacred history at a time when modern imperial conflict was developing. Oscillating between antiquity and modernity, traveling between Western Europe and the Ottoman Empire, Layard and his fellow archaeologists confronted a newly deepened antiquity beneath a shifting political landscape. Even as Goethe had been formulating his ideas on world literature just a few years before, the pioneering French Egyptologist Jean-François Champollion was solving the mysteries of Egyptian hieroglyphics, crucially aided by the Rosetta stone, found in 1799 during Napoleon's brief occupation of Egypt. Over the course of the nineteenth century, the dual recoveries of ancient Egyptian and Mesopotamian cultures provided one of the greatest of all modern expansions in the domain of world literature: for the first time in many centuries, a wealth of literature from the second and even third millennia B.C.E. could once again be read, the oldest texts to have survived anywhere in the world, and indeed the first literatures ever written. Discovered and deciphered at the high tide of European imperial expansion, these works opened up vistas far older—and farther east and south—than the biblical and classical writings long taken to be the originary documents of "Western" culture.

Widely agreed to be the greatest literary discovery from the entire region, the *Epic of Gilgamesh* gives a vivid illustration of the struggles entailed in trying to make sense of a genuinely foreign work. Looking closely at the story of its reappearance, it turns out that the people involved in the recovery and interpretation of Mesopotamian culture were a surprisingly varied group, and they approached and assessed their astonishing finds from a variety of perspectives and with very different motives. If their first efforts inevitably involved a high degree of assimilation toward the already known (most especially the Bible and its history), they were often remarkably alive to the uncanny strangeness of the epic and the other artifacts they were uncovering. At times brilliantly perceptive, at times absurdly obtuse, these early scholars set the stage for the more accurate understandings of the epic that were to follow in the next century. If we then look ahead to the epic's subsequent reception, we will find something of the converse as well: *Gilgamesh*'s more recent editors and translators have not always been very successful at understanding and conveying the epic's cultural difference—or its deep connections to later Western culture. Layard and his successors still have much to teach us today.

One of the greatest civilizations of the ancient world, by the start of the nineteenth century the Assyro-Babylonian culture of Mesopotamia had been deeply buried by millennia of warfare, resettlement, and drifting sand: not a single structure remained above ground; not a single sculpture was preserved in any museum; and two thousand years of imperial history were known only from passing references in the Bible and a few classical authors.

The cuneiform tablets occasionally turned up by farmers' plows were completely incomprehensible; some scholars even doubted that they contained writing at all. As late as 1842, the novelist and historian J. Baillie Fraser could only regret the paucity of sources:

> Mesopotamia and Assyria, if not actually the cradle of mankind, were, at all events, the theatre on which the descendants of Noah performed their first conspicuous part. . . . Events so various and important must invest the countries where they occurred with a deep interest; and that portion of them, in particular, which has reference to the early postdiluvian ages, cannot fail to excite the curiosity of those who delight in marking the moral progress of mankind. But all hope of tracing clearly the events of their early history is checked by the scantiness of means. (*Mesopotamia*, 18)

Layard himself did not start out with any intention of exploring the enigmatic mounds in Mesopotamia that were rumored to be the ruins of Nineveh, Babylon, and Ur; he and Mitford spent months touring Turkey, Syria, and Palestine, traveling with no fixed agenda or goal. Eventually Layard decided to visit the more distant and obscure sites farther east. The young discipline of archaeology had largely been focusing on the more dramatic monumental remains of Egypt, Greece, and Rome, but Layard's imagination was fired by the very desolation of the Mesopotamian mounds. The traveler beyond the Euphrates, he later wrote, seeks in vain "the graceful column rising above the thick foliage of the myrtle" or the gentle slope of an amphitheater overlooking the sparkling Aegean:

> He has left the land where nature is still lovely, where, in his mind's eye, he can rebuild the temple or the theater, half doubting whether they would have made a more grateful impression upon the senses than the ruin before him. He is now at a loss to give any form to the ruin before him . . . the more he conjectures, the more vague the results appear. The scene around is worthy of the ruin he is contemplating; desolation meets desolation; a feeling of awe succeeds to wonder; for there is nothing to relieve the mind, to lead to hope, or to tell of what has gone by. These huge mounds of Assyria made a deeper impression upon me, gave rise to more serious thought and more earnest reflection, than the temples of Balbec or the theatres of Ionia. (*Nineveh and Its Remains*, 1:29)

When Mitford finally went on to Ceylon Layard stayed behind, working for Sir Stratford Canning, British ambassador in Constantinople, as a political analyst and intelligence agent. He became fascinated with the local cultures and with the larger imperial struggles underway between the Turks, Russia, and England. He learned Arabic, Persian, and Turkish, and began meeting secretly with reformists opposed to the Turkish government then in power.

Layard could not resist striking out on his own as well. In intervals between assignments from Sir Stratford Canning, he would disappear into distant, conflict-filled regions for months at a time, emerging to send his aunt glowing letters describing narrow escapes from death, romantic encounters with dark-eyed maidens, and visits to mysterious and long-forgotten ruins. He made an extended stay in the remote mountain court of Mohamed Taki Khan, chief of the Bakhtiari tribes in the western Persian mountains. Appointing himself an unofficial ambassador for the Bakhtiari, he tried unsuccessfully to stave off the khan's destruction at the hands of the Persians. Part tourist and part freedom fighter, Layard was living a Byronic existence. Ill with malaria at one point, he was even bled in Constantinople by the very doctor who had killed Byron in Greece fifteen years earlier (Waterfield, *Layard of Nineveh*, 30).

In *Orientalism*, Edward Said has demonstrated the important role of European travelers and their writings in the elaboration of the orientalist discourse that undergirded subsequent European imperial adventures. Such writing affected the shape of the nascent concept of world literature as well—often quite directly, when European travelers to the East returned home with linguistic and cultural knowledge that enabled them to create pioneering translations and editions of non-European works. Edward Lane and Sir Richard Burton, who figure prominently in Said's account, both produced influential translations of the *Arabian Nights*. Both were deeply involved in elaborating the programmatic contrasts of "East" versus "West" that Said deconstructs with such devastating effect in his book, and their translations helped solidify the hold of imperial orientalism on the imagination of the British public. Austen Henry Layard, however, had only a tangential relation to orientalist perspectives. He was not notably motivated by any simple contrast of cultures and in fact was exceptionally alive to the cultural multiplicity within "East" and "West" alike. Across his career and across the Mediterranean world, Layard was repeatedly galvanized into action by a rather different conflict: the struggle between tyranny and liberty. He sided actively with Italian revolutionaries against the Austro-Hungarian empire, with Montenegrin separatists against the Ottoman empire, with Polish patriots and with Turkish reformers against the Russians, and with his Bakhtiari friends against the expansionist Persian government.

Layard's fascination with the cultures he was encountering eventually led to his break with his traveling companion, who really did want to assume his colonial duties in Ceylon. Mitford, indeed, was very much a British orientalist in Said's sense, a traveler for whom the Levant was a prelude to greater things: "to pass through the Near Orient was therefore to pass en route to a major colony. Already, then, the room available for imaginative play was limited by the realities of administration, territorial legality, and executive power" (*Orientalism*, 169). Mitford's own regrettably plodding memoir, *A Land March from England to Ceylon Forty Years* Ago (1884), is a catalogue of ossified orientalist tropes. Unlike his far more conventional friend, however, Layard developed complex engagements with the cultures he encountered, and these gradually led him quite literally to look beneath the surface of the lands he was traversing.

No poet himself, Layard was always alive to the poetic novelty of the modern cultures he was encountering, and to the poetic antiquity of the monumental ruins he sought out in his travels. During his time in Constantinople, his friend Paul Botta, French vice-consul in Mosul, made a spectacular discovery at Khorsabad, ten miles from Mosul: he unearthed the palace of Sargon II, the first ancient structure ever found in Mesopotamia in modern times. In this period a British army officer, Major (later Sir) Henry Rawlinson, made several trips to a monumental relief carved high in a cliff at Bihistun in Persia. There, perched atop a ladder set on a two-foot-wide ledge two hundred feet above the ground, he painstakingly copied a long trilingual inscription of Darius the Great, written in Old Persian, Elamite, and Akkadian cuneiform. By the mid-1840s Rawlinson had succeeded in deciphering the alphabetic Old Persian text; by comparing it with the Akkadian text, he was starting to decipher kings' names and a few other words from the Babylonian version. The necessary pieces for the recovery of the ancient civilization were beginning to emerge.

Layard's diplomatic career was going nowhere at this point. Though Sir Stratford Canning greatly valued his intelligence and industry, Layard's impetuosity and independence made him enemies in the career civil service, and Canning was unable to secure him a permanent post. Fortunately for Layard, Canning shared his interest in Rawlinson's and Botta's discoveries, and in the fall of 1845 Canning put up five hundred pounds to finance an exploratory dig in the mounds outside Mosul. Layard decided to try the unexplored mound at the village of Nimroud, twenty miles south of the city. Arriving there early in November, Layard set up camp. He was too excited to sleep: "Hopes, long cherished, were now to be realised, or were to end in disappointment. Visions of palaces underground, of gigantic monsters, of sculptured figures, and endless inscriptions, floated before me. After forming plan after plan for removing the earth, and extricating these treasures, I fancied myself wandering in a maze of chambers from which I could find no outlet" (*Nineveh*, 1:25). Underground palaces tenanted by gigantic monsters: in his dream, Layard was merging Botta's discoveries with his own early reading of *The Thousand and One Nights*. Layard credited that book, in fact, as an important influence on his career. As he wrote late in life: "My admiration for the *Arabian Nights* has never left me. . . . They have had no little influence upon my life and career; for to them I attribute that love of travel and adventure which took me to the East, and led me to the discovery of the ruins of Nineveh" (*Autobiography*, 1:26–27). It is ironically appropriate that one of the most orientalist of texts—Galland's *Mille et une nuits*, a translational mirage—inspired Layard to achieve his great advance in the recovery of the region's real history.

In keeping with the magical quality of this source text, Layard's dream came true the very next day. He set his crew to work in the morning, and within hours they had begun to uncover palace walls lined with spectacular bas-reliefs of kings and warriors. Layard pursued his digging, both at Nimroud and then at Kuyunjik, across the Tigris from Mosul, which proved to be the site of Nineveh itself. In his first excavations, he uncovered the monumental winged, human-headed bulls that became centerpieces of the British Museum's Mesopotamian collection, and with which Layard was ever after identified in the public mind. As these objects emerged, they produced considerable excitement and uncertainty among the local residents, as illustrated in Layard's sketch of the first emergence of one of the winged bull's heads (figure 2).[1] The diggers at first thought that what they were uncovering was no statue at all but the giant body of Nimrod himself, mighty hunter of antiquity. The local Arab sheikh, Abd-ur-rahman, came to inspect the find:

> It was some time before the Sheikh could be prevailed upon to
> descend into the pit, and convince himself that the image he saw

---

[1] In his excellent history of Assyriology, *The Conquest of Assyria*, Mogens Trolle Larsen has commented shrewdly on this illustration: "The image of Arab superstition may be compared with the pictures from *Illustrated London News* which show the coolly observant gaze of the visitors to the British Museum [as they view Layard's finds] . . . clearly, the Europeans are related to the ancient past, not the Arabs" (91). Or we might also say: clearly the Arabs are *immersed* in this past, whereas the British can stand back from it and possess it as an object of knowledge.

Figure 2. "Discovery of the Gigantic Head"

was of stone. "This is not the work of men's hands," exclaimed he, "but of those infidel giants of whom the Prophet, peace be with him! has said, that they were higher than the tallest date tree; this is one of the idols which Noah, peace be with him! cursed before the flood." (*Nineveh*, 1:73)

Assessing this newly uncovered wonder in light of the Koran, the sheikh is reacting very much as the European public was soon to do: the discoveries aroused intense interest not as relics of Assyro-Babylonian culture but as testimonies to the sacred history they already knew. On further reflection, the sheikh becomes more and more puzzled as to why the English would pay to have such items dug up and sent back to England. It never occurs to him that the sculptures could have a purely aesthetic value, both because idols are so repugnant to his beliefs and because his experience of Englishmen has given him a very different sense of their aptitudes and interests. Some time later, he asks Layard:

> In the name of the Most High, tell me, O Bey, what you are going to do with these stones. So many thousands of purses spent upon such things! Can it be, as you say, that your people learn wisdom from them; or is it, as his reverence the Cadi declares, that they are to go to the palace of your Queen, who, with the rest of the unbelievers, worships these idols? As for wisdom, these figures will not teach you to make any better knives, or scissors, or chintzes; and it is in the making of those things that the English show their wisdom. But God is great! God is great! (2:71)

The British government was not, in fact, particularly interested in recovering ancient artifacts with no commercial value, and Layard and Canning spent the next several years trying with little success to get government grants for further excavation. The British Museum did come up with a small grant, one that Layard felt was absurdly insufficient; he continued his work, under protest, using his own slender resources to supplement the museum's funds. He began to consider writing up his discoveries in a popular form so as to rouse public interest directly. Encouraging this idea, his friend Sir Charles Alison shrewdly urged him to play up the biblical angle: "Write a whopper with lots of plates; fish up old legends and anecdotes, and if you can by any means humbug people into the belief that you have established any points in the Bible, you are a made man" (quoted in Waterfield, 171).

Home in England for several months in 1848, Layard did just this, rapidly writing a vivid account of his explorations. He made sure not only to play up the biblical angle but to tie his work into the British fascination with tales of travel to imperial outposts, a theme well indicated by his book's full title: *Nineveh and Its Remains: With an Account of a Visit to the Chaldaean Christians of Kurdistan, and the Yezedis, or Devil-Worshippers; and an Inquiry into the Manners and Arts of the Ancient Assyrians.* The book became a best-seller upon its appearance in 1849, and support for Assyriological work increased to a modest but steady trickle. The book also revived Layard's lagging diplomatic career: he became sought after as an authority on Middle Eastern cultures and politics and in 1852 was offered his first significant government post, as under secretary of the Foreign Office. He subse-

THE MEMBER FOR NINEVEH DIGS OUT THE BRITISH BULL.

Figure 3. Layard as parliamentary reformer

quently became a member of Parliament and ambassador to Spain, and the popular press continued to identify him as the discoverer of the Assyrian bulls, curiously transformed by *Punch* into John Bull, embodiment of Britishness itself (figure 3). Twenty years later, as ambassador to Turkey, Layard was accused by conservatives of taking an overly pro-Turkish stance, and now *Punch* gave the bull Layard's own face, making him crash through the diplomatic china shop (figure 4).

With Layard having gone into the government, in 1853 the British Museum turned to Layard's friend and principal assistant, Hormuzd Rassam, to mount a new expedition to Nineveh, most of which lay still beneath the ground. Rassam was a young Nestorian Christian from Mosul, where his older brother was employed by the British diplomatic service as their local representative. Originally hired at age seventeen as Layard's paymaster for his first digs, Rassam had become a close friend of Layard's and came back with him to England. Returning to Mosul in 1853 as head of the museum's new expedition, Rassam dug for several months in Layard's sites, with scanty results. He decided to try an area near the north edge of the mound at Kuyunjik, where Layard had made some initial explorations without finding anything significant. Digging under cover of night with a few men—a

PUNCH'S ESSENCE OF PARLIAMENT.

Figure 4. Layard as a bull in a china shop

rival French team had a neglected claim to the area—Rassam hit the jack-pot: the palace of Ashurbanipal, King of the World and King of Assyria in the mid–seventh century B.C.E. Rassam found many beautiful works of art in the palace, but his most important find was literary. As his workmen dug through the palace's chambers, they came upon one of the largest troves of texts ever found in a site from the ancient world: some twenty-five thousand tablets from Ashurbanipal's extensive library, including a wealth of histori-cal, religious, and poetic material.

　　Culturally weighted struggles of memory and oblivion attended the recovery as well as the destruction of Assyria's monuments and written records. Rassam's decisive role in this discovery was often minimized or de-nied outright—most likely, as Layard later wrote to a friend, "because he is a 'nigger' and because Rawlinson, as is his habit, appropriated to himself the credit of Rassam's discoveries" (Waterfield, 478). Late in life Rassam wrote his own memoirs to try to restore his credit for his finds, in a work whose title pointedly details the extent of his explorations.[2] As evidence of former recognition of his role, he quotes an 1856 article from the *Illustrated London News,* which properly credits him with the discovery of the palace. Even this article, though, slides into portraying Rassam simply as Layard's faithful retainer, saying that Layard must have been pleased to find "an Oriental—generally indifferent to all works of art—so thoroughly interested in the undertaking and impregnated with English energy to carry his individual labors to a successful conclusion" (40). The article goes on to praise Rassam for performing so well even though he was "a foreigner in an Englishman's position" (41). Rassam makes no comment on the strangeness of the paper's characterizing him as "a foreigner" excavating the mounds outside his own birthplace.

There is poetic justice in the fact that the Gilgamesh epic, perhaps the first true work of world literature, should have been recovered through the combined efforts of Austen Henry Layard and Hormuzd Rassam, who were themselves microcosms of cultural circulation and exchange. Descended from French Huguenot stock, Layard spent much of his childhood in Italy and France, where his classmates tormented him as a Protestant; sent to school in England, he was taunted by his classmates as "an organ-grinder" (*Autobiography,* 1:38). In his later travels, as he became fluent in Middle Eastern languages Layard took pleasure in melting into the crowd, casting off his European appearance at will; at various points, Europeans took him for an Arab, Arabs took him for a Turk, and Turks took him for a Kurd.

Hormuzd Rassam, conversely, rapidly became a proper English gentleman. After their initial excavations together, Layard brought him back to England and arranged for him to enroll at Oxford, where he spent two years before the British Museum hired him away from his studies to continue the excavations outside Mosul. Rassam went on to have a long career in the British diplomatic service and made his permanent home in London, where he joined learned societies. Increasingly uncomfortable wearing "native" dress even when in the Middle East (figure 5, top), he presented himself in the frontispiece to his memoir as a true Victorian gentleman (figure

[2] *Asshur and the Land of Nimrod: Being an Account of the Discoveries Made in the Ancient Ruins of Nineveh, Asshur, Sepharvaim, Calah, Babylon, Borsippa, Cuthah, and Van, including a Narrative of Different Journeys in Mesopotamia, Assyria, Asia Minor, and Koordistan* (1897).

Figure 5. Hormuzd Rassam in
native dress and in later life

5, bottom). By then, comfortably settled in retirement in Brighton, Rassam was certainly more at home in England than he would have been at Mosul. Like his fellow immigrant Joseph Conrad, he developed a prose style replete with more Britishisms than most English authors would use, and in an 1883 essay he even portrayed English as descended from his own first language, "Aramaic, or what is commonly known as Chaldee." Listing several similar-sounding words in both languages, he ended by observing that "the most quaint resemblance that I have seen between the English and Semitic languages is in the common phrase 'tally-ho'; because *tally* in Chaldean means fox. When a fox-hunter, therefore, calls out 'tally-ho,' it means, in Chaldean, the 'fox-ho.' . . . If this resemblance occurs only as a coincidence, it is certainly a very curious accident" (*Babylonian Cities*, 18). Between Layard's ethnic outfits and Rassam's fox hunts, *Gilgamesh* was reentering a world of increasing cultural flux.

Though Rassam had dug up the Gilgamesh epic amid his mass of tablets, in 1853 no one could yet read them or even tell what they were. Rassam shipped them all back to the British Museum, where they were carefully stored in wool-lined racks. Sir Henry Rawlinson (now director of the museum's Division of Near Eastern Antiquities) and several assistants set about piecing shattered tablets together and trying to decipher them. By the mid-1860s, British and Continental scholars had achieved a basic working knowledge of the script and of the Akkadian language of most of the tablets. By good fortune, at this time a young bank note engraver, George Smith, fell under the spell of Rassam's trove of ancient tablets. Unable to afford a university education, Smith had become fascinated by newspaper accounts of the new finds, and he began spending all his spare time at the British Museum. He taught himself Akkadian and started studying the tablets for references to people and events mentioned in the Bible. Impressed by his dedication, Rawlinson hired him to help with the painstaking task of cleaning and organizing the masses of fragmentary tablets. Smith proved to have an exceptional combination of talents: precocious linguistic ability, an acute visual memory, and extraordinary patience and manual dexterity (his engraving work stood him in good stead). These skills brought him signal success in piecing tablets together, and he was able to decipher them with exceptional intuitive and analytical skill.

Smith soon made valuable discoveries among the tablets, especially in establishing the historical setting of events in the Bible. This was an area of intense interest in Europe in the later nineteenth century. On internal evidence, German biblical scholars (and occasionally even Englishmen, like

Bishop Colenso) had come to argue with increasing persuasiveness that the Pentateuch could not have been written by Moses, as traditionally believed, but was instead a composite work, written over time in several distinct stages and from partly conflicting perspectives. With the literal accuracy of the Bible's primordial history undercut first by the findings of modern geology and then by the theory of evolutionary biology, people were left wondering what, if anything, they could trust in the biblical narrative. No extrabiblical written records had survived from ancient Israel itself, and a major interest in the Assyro-Babylonian texts now being recovered from Mesopotamia lay in the hope that they could provide independent confirmation of the biblical accounts.

Poring over the British Museum's collection in the fall of 1872, Smith came upon a fragmentary tablet that seemed to tell the story of a worldwide flood, with details closely resembling the Noah story. This was what proved to be the eleventh tablet of *The Epic of Gilgamesh,* the section in which Gilgamesh travels to visit his ancestor Utnapishtim, who recounts the story of the Flood. Most of the tablet was obscured by a thick limestone deposit that Smith couldn't remove, so he needed the help of the museum's chief restorer, George Ready. Ready was a former tobacconist who had begun collecting medieval seals as a hobby and had developed sophisticated methods to clean them—methods he treated as proprietary secrets, revealing them only to his sons later in life. He had been hired by the museum as repairer of coins and seals and had become the key figure in the restoration of the more badly encrusted cuneiform tablets.

Ready, however, was out of town on private business when Smith came upon the Flood tablet. E. A. Wallis Budge, later a leading Egyptologist, was then a student associate at the museum; as he recalled the situation in his book *The Rise and Progress of Assyriology,* "Smith was constitutionally a highly nervous, sensitive man; and his irritation at Ready's absence knew no bounds" (152–53). Finally Ready returned and after several days of meticulous work he brought Smith the tablet, now beautifully legible:

> Smith took the tablet and began to read over the lines which Ready had brought to light; and when he saw that they contained the portion of the legend he had hoped to find there, he said, "I am the first man to read that after more than two thousand years of oblivion." Setting the tablet on the table, he jumped up and rushed about the room in a great state of excitement, and, to the astonishment of those present, began to undress himself! (153)

Word of his find spread rapidly, and Prime Minister Gladstone was in the audience when Smith presented his preliminary translation of the Flood story in a lecture to the recently founded Biblical Archaeology Society on December 3, 1872. "This must be the only occasion," Andrew George has dryly noted, "on which a British Prime Minister in office has attended a lecture on Babylonian literature" (*The Epic of Gilgamesh*, xxiii). During the discussion following Smith's presentation, Gladstone rose to offer extensive remarks, with two major themes. He praised the new discoveries in Meso-potamia, not so much for their relevance to the Bible as for giving "a solid-ity to much of the old Greek traditions which they never before possessed," bringing new understanding to the reading of Homer, "the friend of my youth, the friend of my middle age, the friend of my old age, from whom I hope never to part as long as I have any faculty of breath left in my body"— sentiments, the *Times* reported, greeted with cheers from the audience. Sec-ondly, Gladstone said that while he appreciated the earnestness with which several speakers that evening had called for the government to mount an ex-pedition to continue the excavations, "it has been the distinction and the pride of this country to do very many things by individual effort that in other countries would only be effected by what Sir Robert Peel used to call 'the vulgar expedient of applying to the Consolidated Fund'"—the national Treasury.[3] This sentiment does not appear to have been greeted with cheers from the archaeological audience.

With Gladstone having artfully stifled the call for public financing by the unanswerable charge of "vulgarity," it was left for a more forthrightly vulgar source to provide further funding. The broken tablet Smith had found at the museum was substantial but tantalizing: it lacked the begin-ning of the story. Within hours of his lecture, the London *Daily Telegraph* offered Smith a thousand guineas to mount an expedition back to Nineveh in search of the balance of the tablet. (A nice touch, setting the grant in guineas rather than in pounds sterling: originally a gold coin worth twenty-one shillings, the guinea had ceased to be used in the 1830s, but the term survived to price luxury goods, often including books.) The newspapers of the day had a penchant for dramatic search-and-rescue operations. In set-ting up this expedition, the *Daily Telegraph* may have wanted to outdo the *New York Herald*, which earlier that year had trumpeted the success of their commission to the journalist-explorer Henry Morton Stanley, whom they had sent to Africa to find the missing Doctor Livingstone. The parallel was not lost on Smith's American publishers. In the back of Scribner's edition of Smith's *Assyrian Discoveries* (1875), the publisher lists various titles of re-

[3] As reported in the *Times* (London), 4 December 1872, 7.

lated interest, including *Modern Doubt and Christian Belief* and *The Super-human Origin of the Bible*—and Stanley's recent best-seller, *How I Found Livingstone.*

Like Stanley's expedition, Smith's search would be a long shot at best: the palace at Nineveh had been burned when it was sacked, almost twenty-five hundred years earlier, and the library's contents had fallen through the floor into the palace's basement. Even if the remainder of the tablet hadn't been pulverized in the process, Smith would be trying to find a fragment of baked clay a few inches square amid a mass of thousands of similar fragments, all mixed among tons of rubble and damaged over the centuries by water seeping into the area. Well aware that the search would be long and unlikely to yield the desired lines, Smith jumped at the chance to bring home a new trove of tablets, as he knew that Layard and Rassam had lacked the time and resources for a full excavation of the site. After an arduous seven-week journey, Smith reached the ruins of Nineveh in May of 1873. With a local workforce that came to number six hundred laborers, he began to uncover the corner of the palace that had contained the royal library. Tablets started to emerge amid the rubble and, astonishingly, after just a week he found the beginning of the Flood story.

A few days later, Smith telegraphed news of his discoveries home to the aptly named *Daily Telegraph*, and the news was reported by papers around the world. There was something particularly compelling about the transmission of Smith's report via the ultramodern technology of the telegraph. The world's first telecommunications system, commercial telegraphy had been pioneered by Morse in the 1840s and only started to become a global network in the 1860s; the first successful transatlantic telegraph line was laid in 1866, just seven years before the *Daily Telegraph* sent Smith to Mesopotamia. A few days after the first report of Smith's arrival at the site, the *New York Times* ran an unsigned article reflecting on this overlay of ancient and modern modes of communication:

> It is hardly possible to conceive of two more opposite literary productions than the modern newspaper and the crumbling and mysterious records found among the ruins of antiquity. A telegraph dispatch and a cuneiform inscription are both composed of letters, and are alike *media* for the transmission of intelligence; and yet how immeasurably different are the ideas of life, time, and space which the mention of the two suggests. The one is gray with the dust and mist of the past, the other fresh and

throbbing with the life of the present. One is fading out of all practical suggestiveness, the other deals with nothing else.

How to relate these two opposed media? The writer of the article proposes an inversion of poetry and prose, an inversion performed by time itself:

> The one [i.e., the cuneiform tablet], which was essentially prosaic, is made poetic by time; the other, which is essentially poetic, is made prosaic by newness and utility. There is something startling in associating the two together, in thrusting them into sudden and unexpected juxtaposition; and this is what has just been done by a London journal, which has sent Mr. GEORGE SMITH, the well-known archaeologist, to puzzle out the antique inscriptions of Assyria.[4]

The ancient texts are creating new and startling literary juxtapositions as they begin to circulate into the modern world.

Smith himself described his find two years later in sober, scholarly terms—no running about, no undressing—in his book *Assyrian Discoveries:*

> The bottom of the pit was now full of massive fragments of stone from the basement wall of the palace jammed in between heaps of small fragments of stone, cement, bricks, and clay, all in utter confusion. On removing some of these stones with a crowbar, and digging in the rubbish behind them, there appeared half of a curious tablet copied from a Babylonian original, giving warnings to kings and judges of the evils which would follow the neglect of justice in the country. On continuing the trench some distance further, the other half of this tablet was discovered, it having evidently been broken before it came among the rubbish.
>
> On the 14th of May my friend, Mr. Charles Kerr, whom I had left at Aleppo, visited me at Mosul, and as I rode into the khan where I was staying, I met him. After mutual congratulations I sat down to examine the store of fragments of cuneiform inscription from the day's digging, taking out and brushing off the earth from the fragments to read their contents. On cleaning one of them I found to my surprise and gratification that it contained the greater portion of seventeen lines of inscription belonging to

[4] "Journalism and Archaeology," *New York Times,* 14 May 1873, 6.

the first column of the Chaldean account of the Deluge, and fitting into the only place where there was a serious blank in the story. When I had first published the account of this tablet I had conjectured that there were about fifteen lines wanting in this part of the story, and now with this portion I was enabled to make it nearly complete. (97)

An understated enough way to describe one of the most dramatic finds in the history of archaeology; yet the passage is resonant in its juxtapositions, both textual and social. The missing fragment of the Deluge story comes to light directly after the recovery of an Assyrian copy of an emblematic Babylonian warning of the evils of misrule. This copy would have been made at the direction of the Assyrian king Ashurbanipal, who set about assembling his great library after he had suppressed a major rebellion by Babylon in 648 B.C.E. and plundered its riches; scribes around his empire were instructed to send him copies of any texts that would be useful to him in governing his large and restive lands. In an all too vivid illustration of the text's cautionary theme, the copy in turn had apparently been broken asunder by the resurgent Babylonians themselves in 612, when they allied with their erstwhile enemies the Medes, overran Nineveh, and sacked Ashurbanipal's palace. As his workmen burrow into the library's ruins, Smith restores the warning tablet from "utter confusion" to wholeness and, almost as though a magic key has been fit into a lock, the long-sought treasure now comes to light.

The Flood story's discovery, moreover, is made in a social context. Though Smith did no digging himself, he uses impersonal constructions ("On removing some of these stones . . . there appeared") which effectively remove his native assistants from view. Their place is taken by Smith's visiting friend Charles Kerr—the first Englishman Smith mentions seeing in weeks—and the great discovery is directly preceded by their "mutual congratulations" upon Kerr's arrival. Snatched from the wreckage of Near Eastern history, the climactic tablet of *The Epic of Gilgamesh* finds a new and very English audience ready to take it up and take it home.

Actually, neither the *Daily Telegraph* nor George Smith himself had much interest in the epic as such. Smith viewed the poem chiefly as corroboration for the Bible; he published his first translation in 1874 under the title *The Chaldean Account of the Deluge,* a title that forthrightly treats the epic as a parallel to the biblical Flood account, even though the story of Utnapishtim takes up less than a tenth of the text and only secondarily involves the epic's true hero. Admittedly, in 1874 Smith was only just beginning to make sense of the tablets he had begun to piece together; but a similar emphasis pre-dominated two years later, when he gave a quite full translation. This appeared in a volume in which Smith gave a synoptic account of the range of known cuneiform literature, concentrating especially on the creation epic *Enuma Elish* and on *Gilgamesh*. No longer able to associate this varied material to the Flood story alone, Smith simply widened his focus to include more of Genesis. The volume is titled *The Chaldean Account of Genesis*, and in his translations and discussions alike he programmatically assimilates his texts to the stories in Genesis 1–11, even to the point of reading a quasi-biblical story of the Fall of Man into a few obscure lines in *Enuma Elish* that can now be seen to refer simply to temple duties. This framing was just what was wanted: the book became a major best-seller, hotly debated pro and con by those who saw the Mesopotamian stories either as confirming the Bible's historical truthfulness or as revealing its fictionality.[5]

Smith's work is a telling example of a profoundly assimilative reception, and indeed in his drive to associate the epic to historical events Smith takes it almost entirely out of the realm of literature as such. Regarding the tablets as "principally of interest for their containing the Chaldean account of the Deluge" (*Chaldean Account of Genesis*, 167), he even seems to regret that the story has been "disfigured by the poetical adornments deemed necessary to give interest to the narrative" (208). He devotes more attention to his speculative reconstruction of the epic's historical core than to Gilgamesh's friendship with Enkidu, his rejection of Ishtar's duplicitous love, or his quest for immortality—the literary themes by which the epic would enter more fully into world literature in the twentieth century.

In assimilating the cuneiform texts so closely to the Bible, Smith was carrying through intellectually what he and Rassam had already done physically: *saving* them, as Smith saw it, from their own self-destructive culture. The full dimensions of this saving activity can be seen in his longest and most ambitious work, *Assyrian Discoveries: An Account of Explorations and Discoveries on the Site of Nineveh, during 1873 and 1874*. Realizing that the excitement surrounding his discoveries provided a golden opportunity

[5] The ambiguity of the material is already discussed in one of the *New York Times's* first reports of Smith's translation of "Noah's log of the deluge." The article correctly predicts that "this discovery is evidently destined to excite a lively controversy. For the present the orthodox people are in great delight, and are very much prepossessed by the corroboration which [the tablet] affords to Biblical history. It is possible, however, as has been pointed out, that the Chaldean inscription, if genuine, may be regarded as a confirmation of the statement that there are various traditions of the deluge apart from the Biblical one, which are perhaps legendary like the rest" (22 December 1872, 1).

to advance the cause of research in his field, Smith followed Layard's lead and created a hybrid book, part scholarship and part adventure story. His opening chapters dramatize the travails of travel as he makes his way by boat across the Mediterranean and then by mule across the mountains and deserts of Syria and what is now Iraq, coping with floods, bandit-ridden mountain passes, and corrupt officials at every turn. In the process, Smith becomes a kind of raider of the lost ark (Noah's, in his case), an archaeologist-adventurer whose exploits are intended to engage not only his readers' interest but their financial support as well. This agenda is brought forward in his concluding chapter, as can be seen from the summary headings in the table of contents. "Difficulty of work.—Short time.—Good results," the headings begin encouragingly, going on to "New light on the Bible.—Origin of Babylonian civilization. Turanian race.—Semitic conquest.—Flood legends.—Mythology.—Connection with Grecian mythology" before announcing the book's concluding theme, "Importance of future excavations."[6]

As he travels through remote villages on his way to the ruins of Nineveh, Smith is struck by a sense of continuity with the past: he sees clay-brick houses whose style he recognizes from ancient reliefs and encounters a threshing machine "similar to those which are found in prehistoric deposits. The use of such an instrument shows the small amount of change produced by thousands of years in the East" (*Assyrian Discoveries,* 37). In a humorous vein, he even presents a meal as an all-too-perfect example of a persisting antiquity: "The single course consisted of a tough fowl that might have remembered the Assyrian empire" (27). In the unchanging East, the Gilgamesh epic itself may live on in folktale form: hearing a local tale of a monster in a cave, "I could not help remarking the striking similarity of this story to one of the Izdubar legends." ("Izdubar" is Smith's preliminary rendering of the name that proved to be vocalized as "Gilgamesh.") He concludes that "I believe this is a modern version of this ancient story, and that the legend has been handed down in this country since the days of Izdubar" (52).

The continuities he senses all around him, however, hardly inspire Smith to seek enlightenment from present-day dwellers of the region as he

[6] The fund-raising peroration has become a staple of Mesopotamian scholarship for general audiences. Thus Andrew George laments that "such is the lack of professional Assyriologists everywhere that we have yet to study properly many thousands of tablets that have long been in museum collections." He adds that "the eventual recovery of this literature is assured by the durability of the writing medium. It is only a matter of time—providing, of course, that the society in which we live continues to place value on such things and to support the scholars who study them" (*The Epic of Gilgamesh,* xxx).

tries to decipher his ancient tablets. A generation later, Milman Parry would revolutionize Homeric scholarship by studying the oral epic techniques still in use among Yugoslavian bards; such an approach would never cross Smith's mind, as the living culture of the Levant repelled him in fundamental ways. Brilliantly endowed and self-trained as a student of ancient texts, Smith was poorly equipped as an observer of a modern foreign culture. Unlike the restless—and socially advantaged—Layard, Smith had never left England before he made his trips to the ruins of Nineveh and Babylon; indeed, he had probably rarely set foot outside London before he embarked for the Middle East. In Smyrna, his introduction to Turkish territory, he is baffled by foreign customs, jostled by crowds, upset by untidiness and dirt, and thrown for a loop even by the sight of shish kebab: "Here and there were Eastern refreshment houses, where natives were cooking dirty-looking messes; one of these dishes appeared to me particularly repulsive, it consisted of small portions of meat and intestines of kids strung on skewers like cat's meat" (23).

Even passing through Europe en route to Smyrna, Smith is none too pleased by cultural differences that challenge his political and religious loyalties. He speaks mockingly of a Frenchman he meets while crossing the English Channel, who "amused me very much by his endeavours to whitewash the late French government, and to persuade me to read some recent passages in history through his spectacles" (16). Still more objectionable are religious differences. Stopping over in Sicily, the loyal Protestant Smith is confronted with the sight of the sacrament of confession being openly practiced in a Catholic church: "The point that seemed most painful to English eyes was the confessional, which was carried out during the service and in the church" (19).

For a scholar whose lifework involves cleaning ancient tablets in order to devote searching scrutiny to minute wedge-shaped patterns, clear sight and the right spectacles are critical tools and dirt is the great enemy. Yet dirt is everywhere in the Middle East, apparently an outright cultural value, as Smith sees it. His "Asiatic" shipmates en route to Smyrna are "exceedingly devout and equally filthy" (24); a bathhouse "is in a state of indescribable filthiness" (96); when he stays in the town of Nimroud, though his host is "a man of influence among the Arabs here" and his wife is "a woman of some intelligence for an Arab," their children live "like so many pigs, any washing or attention being quite out of the question" (81).

A low point in Smith's travels comes at a Syrian village whose sole lodging house "consisted simply of rough wooden rooms and benches, with a strong suspicion of vermin" (26). After a miserable dinner and dreading an uncomfortable night to come, Smith and two fellow travelers are forewarned by comments in the inn's guest book:

> Yakub, the proprietor, brought to us a book, in which his various visitors had written their experience of this place. Yakub, who could not read, thought that these entries were all praise, and begged us to add some notice of our satisfaction to the collection. We took the book and looked it through; it was full of the richest and most appropriate remarks about the "hotel": one discoursed about the age of the fowls, another about the vermin; others gave cautions to the travellers who might come after; one advised his successors not to fall through the holes in the floor, as they would be astonished at the appearance of the apartment below, another wrote that the place was comfortable, and the holes in the floor "very convenient." After inserting some remarks in this book, Mr. Forbes left, and Mr. Kerr and myself commenced a battle with the fleas; ultimately our weariness got the better of us, and we fell asleep. (27–28)

If the culture is baffling, the political situation Smith encounters in the waning phase of the Ottoman Empire is altogether horrifying. A succession of corrupt Turkish governors had been maintaining their hold over the region by dividing and oppressing their constituent populations. Venality and outright violence were widespread, with little to choose between local bandits and government troops. At one point, Smith is taking refreshment with a local Turkish officer, when a man is brought in who has been set upon by one of the officer's Circassian irregular troops; "there were six long sword-cuts on his back, which presented a sickening spectacle, resembling a piece of hacked meat" (111). Smith meets Turks, Kurds, Chetchens, and Arabs, and rarely finds the groups on good terms with one another. Sharply critical of the Turkish government for its duplicity toward foreigners and its own citizens alike, Smith nonetheless seems to regard the region's violence as a feature of the landscape, another point of continuity with ancient times: "The hand of the wandering Arab is to-day, as ever, against every man's hand, and their hand against his," he remarks (109), now reading modern culture through biblical spectacles: he is paraphrasing the Bible's depiction of Ishmael, Abraham's rejected son, supposed father of the Arab peoples (Genesis 16:12).

The overlay of ancient and modern violence is particularly vivid when Smith visits ruins at Hammum Ali, a village just south of his principal site of Nineveh:

War was at the time raging among the Arab tribes on the west of the Tigris. The great tribe of the Aneiza, which occupies the desert between Aleppo and the Tigris, had been moving as usual for plunder. . . . A few days before my visit to Hammum Ali, they had a brush in that neighborhood with a division of the Shammer Arabs, and had plundered them of all their flocks and herds. The various wandering tribes on the west of the Tigris were now flying across the river to escape the Aneiza, and we met on the way to Hammum Ali numbers of the fugitives carrying all their goods and driving their cattle before them. . . . Early in the morning I rose, and having procured some breakfast went to visit the mounds. There are several artificial elevations here, giving indications of the existence at one time of a considerable city. (95)

This incident directly precedes his account of the discovery of the Flood story, two pages later.

Calmly observing what he takes to be immemorial violence, Smith reserves his outrage for the refusal of the Turkish government to protect the antiquities in the lands under its rule. "The Turkish officials," he bitterly remarks, "while always ready to oppose researches and prevent the discovery or removal of monuments, never hinder the natives from destroying antiquities" (427). Modern warfare is actually less destructive to his sites than everyday life, as for centuries the local villagers have been mining the old mounds to extract stones and bricks for their own building projects. At the ruins of Babylon: "The natives have established a regular trade in these bricks for building purposes. A number of men are always engaged digging out the bricks from the ruins. . . . Every day when at Hillah I used to see this work going on as it had gone on for centuries, Babylon thus slowly disappearing, without an effort being made to ascertain the dimensions and buildings of the city, or recover what remains of its monuments" (62). Smith returns to this theme at the end of his book, just before he begins his concluding account of the urgency of further excavations: at Nineveh, "the later inhabitants have in a great measure gradually destroyed the great works which their predecessors had raised" (436).

Smith's hostility toward the Turkish officials is matched only by their growing suspicion of him. Indifferent toward the ancient history of the lands they are occupying in Mesopotamia, and even less interested in verifying the historical accuracy of the Bible, the officials Smith deals with simply cannot believe that he is really hunting for the kind of shattered clay tablets he shows them. On his way home, at the head of a caravan of mules laden with boxes full of his precious tablets, Smith is stopped in Aleppo by customs officials who try to impound his collection. Even when Smith produces his firman proving his right to the antiquities, the officials insist that he unpack them all for inspection. "The Turkish officers laughed at the appearance of the old fragments of inscriptions, and called them rubbish, making fun at the idea of taking care of such things" (115). Everything seems resolved, and they give Smith a letter authorizing the goods to be cleared at the port of Alexandretta—"but although the things were worthless in their eyes, they could not resist the temptation to play me false, and I found later, on presenting my letter, that it was an order to seize my boxes. . . . the Turkish officials having made me the bearer of a letter directed against myself" (115, 117).

"Such was the conduct of the Turkish officials," Smith remarks with wounded dignity, "to the agent of a nation which had been foremost in upholding Turkey" (117). He has to sail without his treasures; they are only released following the intervention of the British ambassador in Constantinople and eventually reach England safe and sound. Consumed with indignation as he recalls this episode, Smith fails to note the poetic justice whereby his companions' earlier trick on the illiterate innkeeper is now mirrored by the customs officials' reliance on his own inability to read Turkish. The world's greatest living authority on cuneiform writing is caught in a web of warring scripts that he can't decipher.

Relations only worsened when Smith returned the following year. To Smith's deep regret, the *Daily Telegraph* had recalled him as soon as he announced his quick find of the Flood tablet fragment, perfidiously insinuating to their readers that Smith himself had chosen to end his mission.[7] After due deliberation, the British Museum finally provided funds for a proper expedition. Smith secured a new firman from Constantinople authorizing a second period of digging and returned the next winter. Now, convinced that he must have spirited away some really valuable objects on his first trip, the local officials delay his work with a succession of bureaucratic hurdles. A new pasha has been installed in Baghdad, and unlike his predecessor he takes a keen and suspicious interest in Smith's work—a suspicion only increased, to Smith's surprise, by familiarity with European culture: "I was told that Rajid Pacha understood French and was acquainted

---

[7] As it happens, the fragment Smith so rapidly found was not from *Gilgamesh* at all; it was the opening of the Flood story in the *Atrahasis Epic,* the source for the *Gilgamesh* version. Had he realized this, Smith might have been able to argue that his assignment had not been completed, though he actually had gotten what he was sent to find, the opening of the story.

with something of European civilization, but instead of learning from the West I was informed that his policy at Baghdad was hostile to all foreigners" (136). The pasha is further emboldened by reports that Smith was not in fact an agent of the British government at all but "only a newspaper correspondent and he might do as he liked with me" (138).

Following Rajid's lead, the local officials in Mosul now insist that Smith give them half of everything he finds—standard archaeological practice today, but premium terms in Smith's time. Smith replies that his authorization from Constantinople says nothing of such a division, and in any event he's looking for tablets, which he knows have no value to the Turks. Moreover, dividing up half the fragments before they are even studied will undercut the whole purpose of his follow-up expedition. He offers instead to take the officials into his trenches to show them what he is really getting and proposes to point out to them any large artifacts he may happen to come upon, so that they can excavate them once he has completed his work. "At this reasoning the Turks laughed; they said they did not understand antiquities, and if I pointed anything out I should point out worthless things to them and they must have half the things I collected to make sure they had good ones." The meeting ends with both sides dissatisfied, "and from that time I was subject to perpetual annoyance" (138).

Though Smith's book is chiefly designed to gain support for archaeological work, in his preface he suggests the larger political stakes involved, linking his difficulties with those encountered by Christian missionaries in the region:

> I have been working in the territory of the Turkish empire, and it is with regret that I have had to mention the unsatisfactory conduct of many of its agents. I have not made the most of this; I have omitted many incidents of bad conduct, and have stated those I have mentioned as moderately and slightly as possible; but I could not have passed the subject over entirely without falsifying my narrative. I have not the smallest doubt that in the government of Asia the Turks are not alive to their own interests, and particularly in the oppressive laws and persecution of the Christians. The American missions in Asiatic Turkey are doing a noble work in the country, but they can only be useful in proportion to the amount of official support they receive from England and America. (vii–viii)

He rather pointedly offers thanks to "M. Péretié, the French consul at Mosul, who was of great assistance to me in my dealings with the Turkish officials, and took as much interest in my affairs as if I had been a fellow-subject with himself," and then closes his preface with the observation that "it is extremely unfortunate that in the wide extent of country between Aleppo and Baghdad there is not a single British representative" (viii).

Smith's treatment of *Gilgamesh* was informed by his political concerns. When he was not assimilating "the Chaldean account of the Deluge" to the Bible, he read it in terms of nineteenth-century European ideals of national autonomy and national identity. As he began to reconstruct the body of the epic leading up to the flood narrative, Smith sought a unifying theme in Gilgamesh's adventures. He discovered this theme by triangulating between Gilgamesh's story, the Bible, and Greek epic. Smith was sure that Gilgamesh was in reality the same person as Nimrod, identified in Genesis 10 as Noah's great-grandson and described as a mighty hunter and founder of the major cities of Mesopotamia, including Babylon, Nineveh, and Erech— the biblical version of Uruk, Gilgamesh's actual city. Moving from biblical history to literary expression via ancient Greece, Smith determined that the Gilgamesh epic was "a national poem to the Babylonians, similar in some respects to those of Homer among the Greeks. Izdubar [Gilgamesh] himself was often afterwards esteemed a deity, and at Nineveh I found part of a tablet with a prayer addressed to him" (204).

So far, so good—but what was this national epic really about? Smith located the heart of the epic in Gilgamesh and Enkidu's journey to the Cedar Forest in tablet 5, where they defeat a demon called Humbaba. In his expanded analysis of the poem in *The Chaldean Account of Genesis*, Smith saw Humbaba not as a chthonic monster but as an Elamite king who had invaded the region and oppressed its people. "It appears that Izdubar did not assume the crown until after he had slain the tyrant Humbaba, and this leads to the conclusion that it was Humbaba, or at least the race to which he belonged, that conquered and tyrannized over Erech and probably over the whole of Babylonia. . . . the death of the oppressor being the signal for the proclamation of Babylonian freedom and the reign of Izdubar" (185, 216).

Smith was completely wrong in this reading. Gilgamesh is the ruler of his city from the very outset, and his defeat of Humbaba has no effect on his political status: he ends the epic as he began, not a "national" hero but the ruler of his own local city-state. Humbaba is no Elamite tyrant but a solitary giant, living alone in his Cedar Forest and oppressing no one, least of all Gilgamesh's subjects in distant Uruk. But fundamentally mistaken though it is, Smith's interpretation is actually a brilliant piece of detective work, building plausibly on external evidence to help him make sense of the fragmentary text before him. His writings are full of discoveries that have stood the test of time, often involving impressive intuitive leaps: he was the first scholar, for instance, to realize that Tiamat, the primordial sea monster whom Marduk defeats in *Enuma Elish,* is cognate with the Bible's *tehom,* the watery chaos over which God's spirit broods in Genesis 1:2. Smith's analyses set the stage for the contemporary understanding of Genesis 1–11 as a polemical, monotheistic rewriting of the older Babylonian epics.

His accomplishment is all the more impressive as he was building his interpretations on his best guesses as to the meanings of words which he was sometimes the first person ever to have deciphered, from what were often mere fragments of the original lines of verse. In *The Chaldean Account of Genesis,* Smith begins his chapter "Destruction of the Tyrant Humbaba" by frankly acknowledging that "I have had considerable difficulty in writing this chapter; in fact I have arranged the matter now three times, and such is the wretched broken condition of the fragments that I am even now uncertain if I have the correct order" (207). The chapter has some fairly connected passages, but many others that look like this:

> 7. Humbaba . . .
> 8. he did not come . . .
> 9. he did not . . .
>
> (Seven lines lost.)
>
> 17. heavy . . .
> 18. Heabani opened his mouth . . .
> 19. . . . Humbaba in . . .
> 20. . . . one by one and . . .
>
> (Many other broken lines.)
>
> (215–16)

Smith's reconstruction was a real tour de force, certainly more successful than any other scholar of his generation could have achieved; yet the text's very obscurity aided him in assimilating the work simultaneously to biblical history and to modern national concerns, constructing Gilgamesh as the king who had given the Babylonians "that unity without which they were powerless as a nation" (294).

In the century and a quarter since Smith made his dramatic discoveries, we have learned a great deal about the development of the Gilgamesh epic and about the culture within which it grew. What would it now mean to read the epic as a work of world literature in light of this culture-specific knowledge? The result can be a much better modulated relation between the temporal poles of ancient distance and modern presence that scholars and translators have grappled with from George Smith's time to ours. When it is not artificially overrestored to good-as-new condition, the text itself varies from shattered fragments to perfectly preserved passages sometimes over a hundred lines long, so that we constantly shift between readability and uncertainty. Even in well-preserved passages we often find lines that simply make no sense to us today, immediately followed by lines that could have been written by a modern poet. Recovering the ancient context helps us to understand much that would otherwise remain incomprehensible—and it also helps us gain some distance on what we would otherwise too easily take to be just what a modern poet would have meant, in the way that Goethe took the cane chairs in the Chinese novel to mean what he would have used them to mean.

New continuities and new discontinuities alike emerge when the standard form of the epic comes into view against a three-dimensional literary and historical background. The Akkadian epic's core motifs are almost all to be found in an older loose cycle of Sumerian poems about a hero named Bilgames and his servant Enkidu: Bilgames and Enkidu slay the monster Huwawa in the Cedar Forest, to the annoyance of some of the gods but to Bilgames's own glory. Enkidu descends to the Netherworld (to retrieve a ball and mallet dropped by Bilgames); his ghost emerges to give a chilling account of the realm of Ereshkigal, not enthroned as she is in other texts but lying prostrate on the ground, mourning her dead son Ninazu, her clothing ripped away in grief, tearing her hair with her fingernails as though she were raking a bed of leeks. Bilgames travels to the distant home of Ziusudra, immortal survivor of the Deluge, and brings home lost knowledge of proper service to the gods.[8]

The old Sumerian poems—four thousand years old in their present form and based on earlier oral traditions—take us back to customs very far removed from our own. In "The Death of Bilgames," Bilgames's entire household is buried alive with him, and the burial is described in formal, repetitive verse that only underscores the distant horror of the event:

> His beloved wife, his beloved child,
> his beloved senior wife and junior wife,
> his beloved minstrel, steward and . . . ,
> his beloved barber, [his beloved] . . . ,

---

[8] The relevant Sumerian Bilgames stories are included as a supplement to Andrew George's translation of *Gilgamesh* (141–208).

[his beloved] attendants and servants,
[his] beloved goods . . . ,
were laid down in their places,
  like a palace-review in the midst of Uruk.
Bilgames, the son of the goddess Ninsun,
set out their audience-gifts for Ereshkigal,
set out their presents for Namtar,
set out their surprises for Dimpikug,
set out their gifts for Bitti,
set out their gifts for Ningishzida and Dumuzi,
for Enki and Ninki, Enmul and Ninmul,
for Endukuga and Nindukuga
. . . .
He lay himself down on . . . overlaid with . . .
Bilgames, the son of the goddess Ninsun,
. . . .
. . . They took . . . inside (the tomb), they [sealed] its doorway.
They opened the Euphrates,
its waters swept over,
his [*resting place*] the waters removed (from view).

(George, 206–7)

Few episodes in Mesopotamian literature are more dramatically distant from our modern outlook than this scene. Today such an event would be available to our imagination only as the pitiful insanity of a Jonestown massacre or, at the opposite extreme, in the make-believe world of farce: "It's such a *stuffy* death!" exclaims Gilbert and Sullivan's Yum-Yum, told that she is to be buried alive with her husband Nanki-Poo (*The Mikado,* 378). Yet the Sumerian poet is not making up this scenario at all; a royal mass interment is attested from third-millennium Ur, thirty miles downstream from Uruk. Clearly the poem's frame of reference is radically different from any that we would use today: far from recoiling from the desperate self-destruction of a madman and his cult followers, the poet recounts with calm formality the noble end of a great hero.

The poetry that describes these utterly foreign events was ancient even in Homer's day, and yet all the same in this very episode we find lines that suddenly leap out with a freshness and a vivid realism to which we can immediately respond. To hide his tomb from robbers, Bilgames orders his townspeople to divert the Euphrates from its course and to dig his tomb in the river's bed:

they breached the Euphrates, they emptied it of water,
its pebbles gazed on the Sun God in wonder.
Then in the bed of the Euphrates the earth cracked dry.

(205–6)

A modern poet could be pleased to have thought of the charming personi-
fication of the astonished pebbles, and this image is followed in the next line
by the novelistic realism of the riverbed's cracking as it rapidly dries under
the sun's unaccustomed heat. Here a modern reader may feel entirely at
home, and yet only a few lines later the beloved senior wife, junior wife,
child, and servants are all being buried alive.

A similar mixture of continuity and discontinuity persists as we
come to examine the formation of the Akkadian epic proper. The Old and
Middle Babylonian poets who created it took the Sumerian material and
linked it together to form their far-reaching account, and their shaping activity often makes perfect novelistic sense, yet at other times diverges dramatically from what a modern writer would do. Understandably enough,
the epic's creators developed the relationship of Gilgamesh and Enkidu
(variously described in the Sumerian poems) and played it up for increased
drama: Enkidu is now a wild man, seduced into city life by the harlot
Shamhat, in scenes that set up the epic's theme of the gains and losses of civ-
ilized life. The formerly separate adventures of the slaying of Huwawa and
the fight against the Bull of Heaven are now integrated, and the gods' wrath
over these events becomes the motivation for Enkidu's early death, which in
turn now motivates Gilgamesh's fear of death and his quest for immortality. Whereas Bilgames simply went to visit the Flood hero Ziusudra in order
to recover ritual knowledge from him, now Gilgamesh goes in search of immortality and hears the entire story of the Flood—a global catastrophe that
mirrors his personal concern with death and rebirth. Taken together, these
structural changes create a unified story and fashion Gilgamesh's adventures
into the frame for a searching portrayal of human civilization over against
the two realms of nature and the divine.[9]

These developments are so readily legible to us today that we may
well fall into reading the epic as though it were a novel—a very early novel.
Here, however, we run up against the fact that the epic's ancient authors had
little or no interest in the novelistic depiction of character. Modern commentators have often depicted the epic as a virtual bildungsroman, "a story

---

[9] The fullest account of the history of the epic's text is Jeffrey Tigay, *The Evolution of
the Gilgamesh Epic.*

of learning to face reality, a story of 'growing up,'" in Thorkild Jacobsen's phrase ("The Gilgamesh Epic," 231). Developing this theme, Andrew George sees Gilgamesh as an immature youth who does everything wrong in the body of the epic, until he finally achieves a sober maturity at the poem's end. Thus Gilgamesh is wrong to venture forth to attack Humbaba: "Full of youthful bravado he turns down sage counsel and makes the perilous journey to the Cedar Forest. There he and Enkidu kill the ogre Humbaba, in the full knowledge that the god Enlil, the greatest power on earth, had given Humbaba the job of guarding the cedar. There, too, Gilgamesh does not hold back from desecrating the sacred groves of the gods" (xlvii–xlviii).

The evidence for such character-based interpretations is limited at best. It is true that the elders of Uruk urge Gilgamesh not to go looking for Humbaba, but the scene is so sparely described that we really have no way to tell whether the elders are displaying sagacity or timidity. Heroes, from antiquity through the distant future of science fiction, have often been known for boldly going where no one has gone before, but on the other hand it might well be that the epic reflects a traditional, gerontocratic society in which such youthful adventurousness would be considered foolhardy. The dialogue with the elders simply doesn't give us good grounds to decide, and the narrator relates the discussion without comment.

Opinions on Gilgamesh's adventure are voiced elsewhere by the gods, but the problem here is that George's interpretation is more consistent than the text itself. *Some* of the gods object to the killing of Humbaba, yet Gilgamesh's mother, the divine Ninsun, prays to the sun god Shamash to support Gilgamesh in his journey, "until he slays ferocious Humbaba / and annihilates from the land the Evil Thing you abhor" (24). In this passage, Humbaba is a Grendel-style predator, hated even by the gods. The poet is building on his Sumerian source, a poem called "The Lord to the Living One's Mountain," in which the sun god Utu (the Sumerian name for Shamash) explicitly encourages Bilgames to go after Huwawa and lights the way for him: "Thus he put the Cedar Smiter in happy mood, / he put the lord Bilgames in happy mood" (152). At the end of the Sumerian poem, the captive Huwawa pleads with Bilgames, and then with Utu, to spare his life, but Utu doesn't intervene and Enkidu kills him, after arguing that Huwawa is too treacherous to be released. They take his head back to Enlil, apparently not expecting him to be upset. He is furious, however, saying that Bilgames and Enkidu should have befriended Huwawa, and he takes away the prizes they have brought home and distributes them to others. Even so, it is unclear whether Bilgames has been rash or Enlil is being naive; Enkidu's arguments in favor of killing Huwawa reflect very real problems of treachery and truce breaking. The poem closes not by condemning the slaying or praising Enlil but by giving "Honor to the mighty Bilgames, / praise to the goddess Nissaba," goddess of writing (161).

In creating the connected epic, the later poets retained the Sumerian sun god's support for Gilgamesh's adventure even while playing up Enlil's anger so as to provide a motivation for the slaying of Enkidu. As it now stands, the epic is openly inconsistent, but the Babylonian poets had a greater tolerance for inconsistency than would a modern novelist: like the early redactors of the Hebrew Bible, they often use conflicting traditions without feeling any special need to reconcile them. This is no problem for them, as their interests lie elsewhere; they don't share the concern with individual character which leads modern commentators to want to know whether Gilgamesh is being rash or brave, hubristic or noble, in his attack on Humbaba. In this instance, as in a variety of others in the epic, attending to the text's history can help us to sort out the degree of difference that persists between our values and those of the ancient writers.

Nowhere is this difference more pronounced than in the ancient poets' treatment of the gods and their relations with mortals. Observing Gilgamesh's highly independent and at times openly hostile attitude toward the divinities he encounters, modern commentators have often seen the poem as "a document of ancient humanism" (W. L. Moran), fundamentally concerned with human life on its own terms, with the gods relegated to the background of the story. Alternatively, N. K. Sandars reads the poem as showing "a profoundly pessimistic attitude to human life and the world," displaying an inveterate hostility between mortals and the gods, "these frightening and unpredictable beings" (*The Epic of Gilgamesh,* 22–23). In Sandars's view, the Babylonians suffered from the multiplicity of their gods, unable to establish a secure bond as the Israelites did with their single, loving God. This is the moral she draws from the climactic account of the Flood, as compared with the biblical version:

> Instead of the rainbow pledge, there is only Ishtar fingering her
> necklace and exclaiming that she will not "forget these days."
> But this is the word of the most notoriously faithless of all the
> gods. So, too, the immortality and semi-divine status which
> Utnapishtim, Atra-hasis and Ziusudra win for themselves and
> their families is very different from the solemn covenant of the
> Bible, between God and a still entirely human Noah, through
> whom all mankind is given respite from anxiety. Part of the cause

of the malaise present in the Mesopotamian psychology was this insecurity under which the people lived out their lives: the lack of a covenant. (42)

A century earlier, George Smith had read the epic against a double background of biblical history and modern nationalism; it is not much of an improvement to see Sandars mixing biblical theology with modern psychology to read the epic as an exploration of the neurosis, as she sees it, of polytheism.

Certainly the epic is grounded in a profound psychological insight into the human fear of death; certainly, too, the poem focuses—like the Homeric epics—on human relations and concerns, with the gods playing an important but secondary role. The issue is to try to understand the poem's psychology, and its "humanism," without collapsing these terms into our modern understanding. Here again it is helpful to look at the epic's Sumerian prehistory, for the theme of mortality is already prominent in poems that give a far stronger role to the gods. In the Sumerian story of Bilgames's attack on Huwawa, Bilgames is motivated precisely by a wish to win fame in order to compensate for the brevity of life: "O Enkidu," he cries at the start of the poem, "since no man can escape life's end, / I will enter the mountain and set up my name" (George, 151). Enkidu urges Bilgames to consult with the sun god Utu, whose mountain it is, and Utu questions the point of the journey. Bilgames replies with a haunting cri de coeur:

> O Utu, let me speak a word to you, give ear to what I say!
> Let me tell you something, may you give thought to it!
> In my city a man dies, and the heart is stricken,
> a man perishes, and the heart feels pain.
> I raised my head on the rampart,
> my gaze fell on a corpse drifting down the river,
>   afloat on the water:
> I too shall become like that, just so shall I be!
>
> (151)

Utu responds tenderly—none of Sandars's Mesopotamian harshness here: "Utu accepted his tears as he would a gift, / like a man of compassion he showed him pity" (151–52). He is moved enough to give Bilgames seven warriors to accompany him, and he lights the path for his journey. In the Sumerian poems, the gods are far from indifferent to the sorrows of mortality; instead, they support Bilgames in his quest for earthly fame. In the poem that tells of Bilgames's death, the gods console him for his mortal lot by raising him to prominence as a judge in the underworld. "Be not in despair, be not heart-stricken," the cosmic ruler Enlil tells him, "for now [you will number] among the Anunna gods" (204).

If the Gilgamesh epic can be seen as a document of a genuinely *ancient* humanism, this humanism extends beyond humanity to include the gods as well. Already in the Sumerian cycle Utu's generous response is that of "a *man* of compassion," and throughout the Gilgamesh poems the gods' generosity, their fickleness, even their hatred are expressed in very human terms. The Babylonian gods differ profoundly from mortals in that they live forever—though even this attribute is qualified: they don't die of natural causes, but they can, in fact, be slain. But in many respects they remain closer to humankind than is the God of Israel: though powerful, they are not omnipotent; though far-seeing, they are far from omniscient; though dangerous, they can be played off against one another, and Gilgamesh can rely on his patron god, Shamash, to protect him even when he insults Ishtar, goddess of love, by refusing to become her lover.

Far from setting Gilgamesh in opposition to the gods, the epic stresses that he is actually *two-thirds* divine himself: his immortal mother, Ninsun, has evidently had twice the genetic influence of his mortal father, Lugalbanda. In this sense Gilgamesh is still a degree closer to the gods than his later epic confrere Achilles, who also has a divine mother, Thetis, but who is marked as mortal from the start of his story. Achilles stands correspondingly farther down the earthly social scale as well, the greatest of warriors but not a king like Agamemnon, whereas Gilgamesh is the undisputed ruler of the greatest city of his day.

Gilgamesh remained a prominent figure even outside the boundaries of his epic: he was worshiped as an underworld judge during the second millennium, and the poets of the Akkadian epic presumably expected their audience to be aware of this. Yet the epic stops short of Gilgamesh's death and ultimate reward, leaving him bereft of the plant of rejuvenation and mourning the loss of immortality:

> Then Gilgamesh sat down and wept,
> down his cheeks the tears were coursing.
> . . . [*he spoke*] to Ur-shanabi the boatman:
> "[For whom,] Ur-shanabi, toiled my arms so hard,
> for whom ran dry the blood of my heart?
>
> (99)

The gods no longer step in to give Gilgamesh special status in the afterlife; the poem ends with him taking what comfort he can in surveying the great walls he has built around his city. The epic reached its full form around 1200 B.C.E. through a final revision and expansion by a Babylonian priest named Sîn-liqe-unninni, who gave new emphasis to the Flood story and also added the poem's prologue. In its final form, the epic confines the gods' special dispensation to the distant past. According to Utnapishtim's account, once Enlil finally repented of having brought about the Flood, he took Utnapishtim and his wife by hand, and declared:

> In the past Utnapishtim was a mortal man,
> but now he and his wife shall become like us gods!
> Utnapishtim shall dwell far away, where the rivers flow forth!
> So far away they took me, and settled me where the rivers flow
> forth.

(95)

Far from encouraging Gilgamesh to hope for a similar fate, Utnapishtim closes his narrative by underscoring the difference:

> But you now, who will convene for you the gods' assembly,
> so that you can find the life you search for?

(95)

The epic doesn't cast the difference between his fate and Gilgamesh's in terms of their respective characters, as though Gilgamesh has some tragic flaw that prevents him from achieving his goal. Indeed, Gilgamesh remarks on their essential similarity when he first sees Utnapishtim:

> Said Gilgamesh to him, to Utnapishtim the Distant:
> "I look at you, Utnapishtim:
> your form is no different, you are just like me,
> you are not any different, you are just like me."

(88)

The difference is not one of character but of era: the day is past when the gods would convene in assembly to change a man's destiny on earth. In many ways, the standard version of the epic is a self-consciously modern work—if we understand "modern" within the ancient context. Sîn-liqe-unninni reshaped the epic in full awareness that he was inheriting an ancient tradition that stretched back to times very different from his own, and he made the exploration of antiquity an explicit theme of his version. When Gilgamesh visits Utnapishtim, history visits the world of myth, to learn from it and at the same time to measure the distance of modern times from the days of Utnapishtim the Distant.

It is a pity that George Smith devoted so little attention to the poem's literary themes. Caught up in his historical speculations, he missed the poem's genuine parallels to his own life. He actually had a good deal in common with Gilgamesh himself—not because Smith was a modern superhero, but because Gilgamesh was an ancient archaeologist. More precisely, Sîn-liqe-unninni *represents* Gilgamesh as exemplifying the care for old monuments that a monarch of the poet's era was supposed to display. Royal inscriptions of the period regularly extol the king's efforts to preserve and restore his ancestors' public works; in one relief Ashurbanipal, in whose library the epic was preserved, is actually represented as personally carrying a basket of material to rebuild the temple of Esagila in Babylon (figure 6).[10] In the prologue that Sîn-liqe-unninni added to his version of the epic, he emphasizes the theme of the loss and recovery of the past. There we are told that Gilgamesh "restored the cult-centres destroyed by the Deluge, / and set in place for the people the rites of the cosmos" (2), and his search for Utnapishtim is presented as a quest for ancient knowledge as much as for personal gain. Traveling like Smith by mule and by boat, Gilgamesh undertakes an arduous journey and retrieves the story of the Flood, writing up his findings upon his return home. Like Smith's *Assyrian Discoveries,* Gilgamesh's narrative at once transmits the Flood story and details his own adventures in acquiring it:

> He saw what was secret, discovered what was hidden,
> he brought back a tale from before the Deluge.
> He came a far road, was weary, found peace,
> and set all his labours on a tablet of stone.

> (1)

At the epic's end, denied the literal immortality he loses when the proto-biblical serpent steals the root of rejuvenation that Utnapishtim has given him, Gilgamesh takes comfort in surveying his city's walls, a task that Smith hoped to undertake at Babylon. In the poem's closing lines, Gilgamesh invites his audience to join him in this activity:

[10] Sîn-liqe-unninni is not the only ancient Near Eastern writer to have emphasized such interests in a hero: a whole cycle of late-Egyptian stories was written about a prince named Setne Khamwas, famous for having studied old inscriptions and restored decaying monuments. Two of these stories can be found in Miriam Lichtheim, *Ancient Egyptian Literature,* 3:125–51.

Figure 6. Ashurbanipal as a restorer of temples

O Ur-shanabi, climb Uruk's wall and walk back and forth!
  Survey its foundations, examine the brickwork!
Were its bricks not fired in an oven?
  Did the Seven Sages not lay its foundation?
A square mile is city, a square mile date-grove,
  a square mile is clay-pit, half a square mile the temple of Ishtar:
  three square miles and a half is Uruk's expanse.

(99)

Like Gilgamesh, Smith achieved fame through his travels and discoveries, which gave him entrée into diplomatic circles whose members would otherwise only have handled the bank notes he was expected to spend his life engraving. His writings gave him a measure of literary immortality as well—like that of Gilgamesh, Layard, and Rassam, an immortality always contingent upon the preservation of a written account.

If Smith resembles Gilgamesh as a restorer of monuments and a retriever of ancient tales, he also can be compared to Gilgamesh's uncultured, adventurous friend Enkidu, struck down young by a jealous Ishtar. For Smith's adventures killed him as well. On his second journey he even had, like Enkidu, a vision of untimely death. Passing through the Syrian port of Alexandretta in November of 1873, he visited the British consul, who had assisted him on his first journey and whose wife had given him lunch "and packed up some useful things for the road" (*Assyrian Discoveries,* 25). They renewed their friendship on this second visit: "Mr. and Madame Franck received me very kindly," Smith says, "and my arrangements were soon made for going up the country. On the same day I bid farewell to the consul and Madame Franck, little thinking that for one of us it was the last time. Soon afterwards, while Mr. Franck had gone to England on business, Madame Franck was taken suddenly ill and died" (120).

When Smith returned to England from this expedition, he set about planning a third and more extensive excavation. Having completed his *Assyrian Discoveries* and *The Chaldean Account of Genesis,* in the spring of 1876 he set out once again. In Constantinople he met a Scandinavian Assyriologist named Eneberg, and they decided to journey together. E.A.W. Budge comments sadly that "the truth is that no two men who were called upon by Fate to travel in Mesopotamia, considering what travel was in those days, were ever more unfitted for their work. Both were enthusiastic, excitable, and optimistic; and both were sadly chafed in mind by their difficulty in obtaining food and good sleeping accommodation" (117). Eneberg was smitten with cholera as they traveled from Aleppo down toward Baghdad, and died. Smith himself eventually reached Mosul after long delays caused by tribal warfare, by which time it was July, and no workmen could be persuaded to dig in the intense heat. Deeply frustrated, Smith decided to return to Aleppo, impatiently traveling across the desert during the day, at a time of year when local residents would only travel by night. Exhausted and dehydrated, he was prostrated by dysenteric fever at Ikisji, a small village forty miles from Aleppo. Carried by litter into Aleppo, he died there four days later, at the age of thirty-six, not quite four years after he had become the first person to read Utnapishtim's account of the Flood after two thousand years of oblivion.

2

The Pope's Blowgun

I, Lord Xicotencatl, am the one who says, "Pass away, and not in vain!" ...
So let them follow onward. Go carefully! And yonder we're assembled....
Friends, willow men, behold the pope,
who's representing God, who speaks for him.
The pope is on God's mat and seat and speaks for him.
Who is this reclining on a golden chair? Look! It's the pope.
He has his turquoise blowgun and he's shooting in the world.
It seems it's true, he has his cross and golden staff,
and these are shining in the world.
I grieve in Rome and see his flesh, and he's San Pedro, San Pablo!
It seems that from the four directions they've been captured:
you've made them enter the golden refuge, and it's shining.
It seems the pope's home lies painted in golden butterflies. It's beaming.

—*Cantares Mexicanos,* Song 68

The court poets of the Aztec empire created an exquisite body of poetry in the fifteenth and early sixteenth centuries, celebrating friendship, flowers, quetzal plumes, and the violent beauties of warfare. After the fall of Tenochtitlán in 1521 the surviving poets preserved their poetic traditions, singing old songs and making new ones to take account of their radically changed circumstances. We might know nothing of these songs today, as the conquistadores burned almost all of the old painted books they found, taking them as products of idolatry, and the living tradition of art poetry began to die out as the century went on. Fortunately, however, a few Spanish friars saw the importance of understanding the culture of the natives they wished to convert, and several important collections of traditional information were made from the 1550s through the 1580s, written in Nahuatl by native informants using the Roman alphabet.

Among these compendia were two important collections of poetry: a manuscript with sixty poems known as the *Romances de los Señores de la Nueva España* (Ballads of the Lords of New Spain), and the collection of ninety-one poems known as the *Cantares Mexicanos*. Together these manuscripts preserved the largest body of native poetry ever collected in the New World during the lifetimes of those who had experienced the first shock of European contact and conquest. Like the *Romances*, the *Cantares Mexicanos* circulated only in manuscript for a time and then fell out of sight altogether. Its obscurity at least saved it from outright destruction: later ecclesiastics came to regard such texts as a kind of moral obscenity, unworthy of preservation on any account. The greatest single compendium of information on traditional Aztec culture, the *Historia General de las Cosas de Nueva España* (1547–69), by the pioneering ethnographer Bernardino de Sahagún, was never published; two manuscript copies survived in European libraries, and it is known today as the Florentine Codex. Sahagún's *Psalmodia Christiana*, a collection of psalms that he composed in Nahuatl for church use, did actually get printed during his lifetime and was used in some parishes during the ensuing century; but then it was denounced by a bishop in eighteenth-century Mexico, and the existing copies were systematically destroyed. Only five complete copies are known today, all in libraries in the United States; a "badly mutilated" copy survives as well, in Madrid (*Psalmodia*, xiii).

By the middle of the nineteenth century, however, the native cultures began to be studied by scholars who were fascinated rather than dismayed by the religious and political content of the sources. Yet the scholars who created "Mesoamerica" as a field of study had their own agendas, comparable to George Smith's drive to use Mesopotamian records to reconstruct an early cultural history. Like "Mesopotamia," indeed, the concept of "Mesoamerica" can be seen as a nineteenth-century creation, and in many ways the early scholars who established these area studies set the tone and the terms for later inquiry. In studying both the ancient Near East and the native cultures of Mesoamerica, nineteenth-century scholars tended to favor earlier periods over later ones, and texts from later periods were either neglected or used primarily as evidence for the persistence of older customs and beliefs. In consequence, though the *Cantares Mexicanos* and the *Romances* were recorded half a century after the Conquest, scholarly attention focused almost exclusively on what could be identified as pre-Conquest poems and motifs. Christian elements in the poems were regularly set aside as later accretions onto an original core, and poems that clearly reflected events and attitudes more than a few years after the Conquest itself were rarely discussed at all.

Freed from their Colonial context, when the poems came to the attention of literary scholars and general readers, they were typically read as expressing a delicate and life-affirming aestheticism. The poems were selectively quoted and studied to bring out these themes, an approach well exemplified by articles like Andrew Wiget's "Aztec Lyrics: Poetry in a World of Continually Perishing Flowers" (1980). Books on Aztec art and culture regularly include samples of the poetry, but the pope does not shoot his turquoise blowgun in any of the selections that I've seen, nor is the reader presented with poems in praise of the Virgin Mary. The poems quoted are those that can be read as at once ancient and timeless:

> We lift our songs, our flowers,
> these songs of the Only Spirit.
> Then friends embrace,
> the companions in each other's arms.
> So it has been said by Tochihuitzin,
> So it has been said by Coyolchiuqui:
> We come here only to sleep,
> we come here only to dream;
> it is not true, it is not true
> that we come to live on earth.[1]

In pressing backward through their sources to the pre-Conquest era, the Mesoamericanists were engaged in a deeply interesting and even noble undertaking: the historical reconstruction of societies that had been severely disrupted by the Conquest and its aftermath of plagues, repression, and abuse. At the same time, the field's nineteenth-century founders were working within a broad historical model inherited from the Enlightenment, in which a culture could be conceived, Leviathan-like, as a sort of human being writ large. Like an individual person, a culture was born, grew into

---

[1] *Cantares Mexicanos,* poem 18, stanza 39. (Future citations from the *Cantares* will also be by poem and stanza, as the stanzas are written in paragraph form.) For a good example of a selection of the poems for a general public, see Eduardo Matos Moctezuma, *The Aztecs,* 164–72, which begins with a poem describing the fall of Tenochtitlán and then gives ten "very intensely lyrical poems, all of which discuss the brevity of life and the uncertainty of life after death" (165), followed by four poems on warfare. None of the selections contains any Christian elements or any direct reference to any post-Conquest events, and even the opening poem on the fall of Tenochtitlán serves to illustrate the eternal theme of ephemerality rather than to introduce any poems about life *after* the Conquest.

maturity, then gradually decayed into senility, a pattern codified for Greek art by Johann Joachim Winckelmann in the mid-eighteenth century. Working on this assumption, for instance, nineteenth-century Egyptologists divided Egyptian history into three principal periods: the Old Kingdom, the Middle Kingdom, and the New Kingdom (separated by two "Intermediate Periods" of political unrest and short-lived governments). These periods were purely the Egyptologists' invention, a way of organizing modern knowledge and of identifying certain broad patterns of cultural development, but they have continued in use to this day. Few scholars today would actually subscribe—consciously, at least—to Winckelmann's enthusiastic overlaying of human biology onto thousands of years of cultural history, and yet until very recent times Egyptology retained a Winckelmannian bias toward earlier, "purer" periods of cultural youth and maturity and tended to avoid later periods of hybridity (or "decay").

True, the New Kingdom was always an important focus of study, not least because this was the period of Hebrew involvement with Ramses the Great and his successors—but the "New" Kingdom itself was taken as ending in around 1090 B.C.E. Egyptian culture persisted, however, for well over a thousand years beyond this terminus, in what Egyptologists labeled "the Late Period," a catch-all term for a variety of eras of greater or lesser dependency on external powers. It was generally agreed that the culture of the Late Period was of comparatively little interest, and it was much less studied than that of the earlier periods. Language study would begin with Middle Egyptian and then go back to Old Egyptian and forward to Late Egyptian, but as recently as the 1970s most people stopped there: "demotic" Egyptian, both the language and its literature, were decidedly beyond the pale. This emphasis predominated as well in anthologies for nonspecialized audiences, such as Siegfried Schott's *Altägyptisches Liebeslieder* (1950) and W. K. Simpson's *Ancient Egyptian Literature* (1972), both of which stopped at the very threshold of the Late Period.

A similar periodization, also weighted toward earlier periods, was devised for Mesoamerica and is still in use today. Here too, three overall periods were created (each divided into early and late subperiods): the Formative Period, the Classic Period, and the Post-Classic Period. As these terms imply, the height of Mesoamerican culture was taken to be the Classic Period—an era that was defined as ending in around 900 C.E. with the decline of the Maya. The entire history of the Aztecs, and even of their Toltec predecessors, occurred in what was labeled the Post-Classic, a period that itself ended in the ashes of the Conquest of 1519–21, to be followed by the Colonial Period. Like the Late Period in Egypt, the Colonial Period in

Mesoamerica was largely seen as only the aftermath of the three key earlier periods, and even the centuries of Aztec rule as a kind of imitative echo of the morally and artistically superior Classic. As Mary Miller and Karl Taube have noted, the Aztecs became the derivative, militaristic Romans to the Mayas' noble Greeks (*Gods and Symbols of Ancient Mexico,* 11).

This weighting of periods held sway well into the 1970s, among Mesoamericanists as among Egyptologists. Writing in the *Encyclopaedia Britannica* in 1976, William Sanders noted that things were finally beginning to change:

> It has been asserted . . . that the Classic period was one of relatively peaceful contact between polities, of the absence of large imperialistic states and empires (and of the militaristic élan and organization that accompanies such states). The Classic has been further characterized by the absence of true cities, by theocratic rather than secular government, and by an overall superiority of arts and crafts. . . . In contrast, the Post-Classic was characterized as a period of intense warfare and highly organized military organization, of empires and cities, of secular government, and of overall artistic decline. (Coe and Sanders, "History of Meso-American Civilization," 947)

Sanders was describing the (then still common) bifurcation between the peaceful, rural Maya and the bloodthirsty, city-dwelling Aztecs. Classic native culture, as exemplified by otherworldly Mayan astrologers and nurturing, corn-growing earth mothers, was made to represent everything that modern European culture wasn't, and so the Aztec imperialists could only be decadents, their steroidal warrior-priests using human sacrifice as an instrument of conquest, their corruption extending even to their art. Sanders went on to note that "recent research, however, has cast considerable doubt on these conclusions." The Maya were found to have had large cities, to have practiced extensive human sacrifice, and to have engaged in frequent warfare, while a new appreciation developed for the positive role of religion in Aztec society and for the specific beauties of their art. Sanders concluded that "the separation between Post-Classic and Classic is therefore little more than a convenient way of splitting up the long chronicle of Meso-American cultural development into manageable units for discussion and analysis."

As alive as Sanders was to the artificiality of these distinctions, a rather different view was expressed in the same article by his co-author Michael Coe, who wrote the section on Mayan culture immediately preceding Sanders's contribution on Post-Classic history. Discussing the Maya of the Classic Period, Coe argued that "most of what is known about ancient Maya religion is inferred from the descriptions that the Spanish friars have left of Maya life and thought on the eve of the conquest. All modern scholars have stressed the deep religious conservatism and resistance to change of the Maya, and it is highly likely that the 16th-century picture was not appreciably different from that prevailing in the Late Classic, in spite of centuries of Mexican contact" (946). There is no question that Colonial-era texts are invaluable aids to the reconstruction of pre-Conquest culture, but it is still a remarkable claim that several hundred years of contact with the Toltecs and Aztecs had not "appreciably" altered the features of Mayan religion, despite the far-reaching similarities visible in sixteenth-century sources between Mayan and Aztec practices and beliefs. If even six centuries of contact with Aztec culture could be bracketed in this way, then six decades of interaction with the encroaching Spanish culture could all the more readily be erased from the sources, which could then be read as faithful transcripts of ancient beliefs.

Compelling results have indeed been achieved by scholars who have sought to tease out the shape of pre-Conquest culture from post-Conquest sources. Miguel Léon-Portilla, for example, used the collections of Aztec poetry as evidence for his eloquent evocation of pre-Conquest philosophies of life in his book *Aztec Thought and Culture* (1963). More recently, Inga Clendinnen has made brilliant use of Sahagún's *General History* in her magnificent cultural reconstruction *Aztecs: An Interpretation* (1991). Yet until very recently, Colonial-era literary texts were rarely used to examine the actual culture within which they were recorded. When they were not neglected altogether, early colonial texts suffered a sort of temporal bifurcation along ethnic lines: while indigenous elements in the sources were typically read backward toward the pre-Conquest period, European elements in the sources were read *forward* as early stages in the region's march toward independence. Works like Sahagún's *Psalmodia Christiana*—psalms written in Nahuatl by Sahagún himself in direct engagement with his Aztec parishioners—were on few scholars' radar screens. The *Psalmodia*, in fact, was never republished after it was banned in the early eighteenth century, and as late as 1990 it had never been translated into Spanish or any other language.

This entire picture has changed dramatically over the past two decades. A powerful combination of social and intellectual changes has disrupted the older patterns of selective attention and widespread neglect that had persisted ever since Winckelmann's time. New patterns of immigration, rapid changes in college and university populations, and the general rise of ethnic consciousness have given a new impetus to studies of hybridity, creolization, and métissage, in the United States as elsewhere. These changes have greatly strengthened the internal dynamic natural to scholarly inquiry, particularly in times like the present, when many people are producing scholarship in many areas: as central texts and problems come to be frequently explored and well understood, there is a natural intellectual drive toward the margins—new texts, new issues, new areas and periods of study. These social and intellectual forces have combined to reinforce one another, with the result that late periods and their products are now interesting, and are interesting precisely for the hybridity that once made them look decadent or derivative. Materials that even specialists never used to read are now being made available to a broader public.

In the case of Egyptology, a notable departure from the perennial focus on earlier periods occurred with Miriam Lichtheim's ambitious three-volume anthology *Ancient Egyptian Literature* (1975–80). In an earlier time such an anthology would have been arranged to follow the favored division of Old, Middle, and New Kingdoms. Lichtheim, however, combined the Old and Middle Kingdoms in her first volume, assigned the second volume to the New Kingdom, and devoted the entire third volume to the Late Period, arguing in her introduction to the final volume that this rich and complex period should no longer be "summarily treated as a phase of decline" (3). Still a new perspective in 1980, Lichtheim's attention to late materials has become common today. Ancient-history sections of university bookstores now regularly feature titles like *Religion in Roman Egypt* side by side with studies of the earlier periods that once had the shelves to themselves.

This shift has enormous consequences for the shape of world literature today: a wealth of neglected older material is now appearing, often for the first time in centuries, in high-quality translations intended to be readable by specialists and nonspecialists alike. Taking this new material seriously, however, will require major changes in the way we read works of world literature. Otherwise, we are unlikely to avoid mapping the old essentialisms onto this new material; worse yet, we may merely replace a Europe-based ideal of universalism with an equally insistent and self-confirming particularism. To avoid or at least to mitigate these dangers, our new ways of reading will require new understandings of cultural identity and cross-cultural interactions, and will reflect back on those understandings, modifying them in turn.

In the last chapter, I focused on the travails of appropriation and misappropriation that *Gilgamesh* has undergone from the nineteenth century to the present. In this chapter, I want to emphasize the contrary: the immense gains that come from having so much new material in view. I want to look in particular at three hybrid documents from colonial Mexico, all of which have received their first full English translation only since 1980. All three are collections of poetry (or what we may now call poetry), and in all three cases the meaning of the poems is inseparable from the drama of the colonial situation itself. As I hope to show, the social context must be understood in order to make sense of the poems and appreciate their power and beauty. Moreover, attention to the poems' aesthetic effects can tell us much, in turn, about the social context, complicating and enriching our understanding of events that we may otherwise understand only in terms of simplistic oppositions between Spaniard and native, malevolent conqueror and helpless victim.

In 1529 the Franciscan friar Bernardino de Sahagún came to New Spain, as it was then called, and began to serve in a series of posts in and around Mexico City, the new colonial capital that was rising on the ruins of the Aztecs' double capital city of Tenochtitlán-Tlatelolco. Unlike many of the new arrivals from Spain, the Franciscans saw force as an undesirable and finally ineffective means to conversion of the masses of natives now in their charge. Language became a key focus of their efforts. Latin was always the language of choice for church use; as early as 1536 the Royal College of Santa Cruz was established in Tlatelolco, where native seminarians were taught Latin as well as Spanish and even became adept at composing Latin verse. They taught the friars Nahuatl in turn, enabling them to communicate directly with their parishioners, rather than having to rely on interpreters. The Franciscans came to see that Indians who were required to give up all their old customs outright tended to avoid church at every opportunity, and several friars began experimenting with adapting the natives' traditional songs and dances to Christian uses, so that they could be performed on feast days outside church and at home, even while Latin canticles would be sung in church.

No friar in sixteenth-century Mexico became more intimately familiar with native culture than Sahagún. He attained true fluency in Nahuatl and began assembling a great archive of documents, including both native codices and interviews with native informants, conducted by Sahagún himself or by native seminarians in his employ. The *General History* was the most extensive result of these activities. As interested as he was in native culture, Sahagún had no doubt that the religious beliefs and rituals he was recording were the work of the Devil; he needed to understand the Enemy's machinations in order to combat them. He understood too that the combat would be cultural as well as theological: he would not succeed if his parishioners merely gave lip service to Christian doctrine and then went on with most of their old customs as before.

The better Sahagún got to know his parishioners, the more concerned he became that they were neither forsaking their old songs nor warming to the Latin canticles they were being given. Hence he decided to take a decisive step: to compose an entire year's cycle of psalms directly in Nahuatl, using all the resources of traditional Nahuatl poetry. As he says in his preface to the *Psalmodia*:

> Since the time they were baptized efforts have been made to force them to abandon those old canticles of praise to their false gods and to sing only in praise of God and His saints. . . . And for this purpose in many places they have been given canticles about God and His saints, so that they may abandon the other old canticles, and they have accepted and sung them, and still sing them in some places. But in other places—in most places—they persist in going back to singing their old canticles in their houses or their palaces (a circumstance that arouses a good deal of suspicion as to the sincerity of their Christian Faith); for in the old canticles mostly idolatrous things are sung in a style so obscure that none can understand them well except they themselves. (7)

The natives' insistence on singing the old canticles "in other places—in most places" calls into question not only the sincerity of their faith but also the security of their obedience to Spanish rule: "they use other canticles to persuade the population to do what they want, or about war or other matters that are not good; for they have canticles composed for these purposes that they refuse to abandon." To this end, Sahagún says, he has composed his book of psalms, "so that they will completely abandon the old canticles, a penalty being imposed applicable to any who go back to singing the old canticles" (7).

Sahagún immersed himself in the study of existing native lyrics, and the result was an extraordinary poetic amalgamation of Bible stories, saints' lives, and dogma, all versified using the resources of traditional Aztec poetry, which had been lovingly elaborated by generations of court poets in the principal cities of the Valley of Mexico. As Arthur Anderson says in the introduction to his translation: "In that these psalms vary in style from good, solid prose to sometimes striking poetry, they may be said to be of uneven quality. They cannot, however, be said to be of poor quality" (xxxiii); they serve a range of purposes, from material for sermons to lyrical effusions suited to major holidays. Not all of these poems are likely ever to register as true literature, world or otherwise, and yet Sahagún's most poetic psalms achieve a weird and haunting beauty, well captured in Anderson's sensitive translations. Their beauty is inseparable from the strangeness of the cultural mixture that Sahagún is undertaking, in which Nahuatl images, filtered through a Spanish sensibility, suffuse the Holy Land.

Particularly notable are psalms that deal directly with moments of transition between worlds. On Pentecost, a shower of Mexican flowers descends upon earth as the apostles miraculously begin to speak in all languages at once:

> The apostles honored God in languages of all people of the world.
> And God's beloved Saint Peter clarified the many features of
>   God's Word before the people of Jerusalem, by commandment
>   of the Holy Spirit.
> Ah, let golden rattles jingle. Let jade-popcorn flowers rain down;
>   let quetzal-trefoil sprinkle down; let them be planted.
> Our beloved father is Saint Peter; he was a mighty preacher,
>   mighty knower of God's Word.

(165)

Sahagún freely mixes Latin terms into his Nahuatl, as with *tonantzi sancta Iglesia* ("our holy Mother Church," 164). He often gives Spanish versions of biblical names—God is Dios, not Deus, and Saint Peter is "sant Pedro"— yet he also gives native inflections to biblical terms: thus the apostles are rendered as *Apostolosme*, using the plural form for Nahuatl nouns.

Sahagún's mergings, in fact, go well beyond what would be needed simply to adapt foreign terms: he clearly fell in love with the combinatory resources of Nahuatl, an "agglutinative" language in which words are often run together into complex chains. It appears that a mark of a traditional poet's skill had been the ability to create new and striking combinations. In one war poem in the *Cantares*, for example, the poet invents a nonexistent flower, the *itzimiquilxochitl,* or "knife-death-flower," in a complex play on the terms *miquiztli* (death) and *quilitl* (plant) that inverts as well the term for ritual battle, *xochimiquitzli,* or "flower war." In his own poems, Sahagún makes liberal use of existing compounds (in the Pentecost psalm quoted above, "jade-popcorn flowers" is a single term, *chalchiuhizquisuchitl*), and he uses similar principles to create neologisms of his own: Saint Peter is a "mighty knower of God's word," *teutlatolmatini,* a term that Sahagún has invented by combining *teotl,* "god," with *tlatotl,* "word," and *matini,* "knowing." Sahagún's poetic experiments reach a climax at the close of the volume, in a series of psalms celebrating the birth of Jesus, who has earlier been rather strikingly described in a hymn to Mary as "your jewel, the quetzal feather of your womb" (22).[2] The series ends with several psalms to be sung on the final day of a three-day Christmas celebration, and now Sahagún pulls out all the stops, in a hallucinatory scene that he carefully grounds scripturally through Latin glosses in the margin next to his verses. The first psalm begins in a heaven filled with Mexican birds, and interestingly it is the birds' ecstatic singing that inspires the angels in turn:

> In heaven all kinds of precious troupials, trogons, rosy spoonbills
>   came to make so memorable a din of precious rattle-bell-like
>   sounds that angels also chanted. (*Multitudo coelistis, alleluia.*)

Baroque poets of the day like Góngora loved intricate patterns of verbal play, but no Spanish contemporary of Sahagún's could have gotten away with coining a neologism like the one that Sahagún uses in his next verse: *unquetzalchalchiuhtlapitzalicaoatiaque,* which could be literally translated "they-feathered-jade-flute-have-come-warbling." (Anderson unpacks this as "the angels have come warbling as with the finest of jade flutes.") This bravura verbal construct appropriately has a multiple subject as well, for the birds actually begin to shade over into the angels themselves:

> The various birds, the precious birds, the birds of springtime, the
>   angels have come warbling as with the finest of jade flutes,
>   have come to make a memorable sound of rattle-bells. Alleluia.
>   (*Laudantiū deum, alleluia.*)
> Goodly were the flowery troupial, chachalaca, emerald toucanet,
>   momotus birds. With goodly songs the angels chanted: May
>   God, God in Heaven, be praised. Alleluia, alleluia. (*Dicentiū
>   gloria ī excelsis deo, alleluia.*)
> All the various precious little birds in Heaven flew like quetzal
>   birds. They said in song: May there be peace on earth. Alleluia.
>   (*Et in terra pax.*)

(373)

Tropical though this heaven may be, the earthly setting is not in doubt, as the second psalm twice points out: "It all occurred in Bethlehem" (*omuchiuh in umpa Bethlem*). Yet in the third psalm the overlay of regions only becomes

---

[2] Sahagún is here drawing on his ethnographic knowledge: conception was traditionally described metaphorically as the gods' sending of a quetzal feather into the womb.

more pronounced: "Castilian flowers, frangipani are outspreading like the early light of dawn. Alleluia, alleluia" (373). The landscape of Palestine is covered in fragrant American *cacalosuchitl* (not yet renamed for the sixteenth-century Italian count Frangipani who derived a perfume from its blossoms), and its scent mingles with that of the doubly transplanted *Castillan suchitl*, "Spanish flowers"—a generic name that no flower in Spain itself would ever carry but which imported flowers were collectively called in Nahuatl.

One of the most remarkable attempts to bridge the Spanish and Aztec worlds, Sahagún's *Psalmodia Christiana* held no interest at all for scholars exclusively invested in the study of pre-Conquest culture. Yet it gives striking testimony to the ongoing vitality of Aztec culture and its poetic traditions; even as he worked to suppress those traditions, Sahagún was moved to take them up and give them a strange, and strangely beautiful, new application. In order to carry out his project, he had to learn the old techniques from within, and his book carried them over to uses in churches around Mexico, displacing the imported Latin hymns.

More than that: it is likely that this very project is what motivated Sahagún to have the *Cantares* assembled in the first place: not needed for his *General History,* the poems seem to have served Sahagún as his data base for his own poetic endeavor. The *Romances* in turn were compiled on similar principles by a member of Sahagún's circle.[3] Had Sahagún not wished to overwrite the native traditions by beating the court poets at their own game, the native songs would probably never have been recorded, just when the poets and their tradition were about to disappear forever. As Sahagún says in the closing words of his preface, his book was intended "to bring about the purpose here sought, that our Lord be praised by His believers with Catholic, Christian praises, and that the praises of idols and idolatry be buried as they deserve" (8). A profound poetic irony: the very ingenuity with which Sahagún sought to suppress the old poetry led to its preservation for us today.

Turning now to the *Cantares Mexicanos* themselves, we can better appreciate the boldness with which the surviving court poets recast their materials in the wake of the Conquest. Keeping in mind that the poems as we have them were written down thirty to sixty years after the Conquest itself, they

---

[3] In his introduction to the *Cantares Mexicanos,* John Bierhorst gives samples of phrases used in the *Psalmodia* that are found in the *Cantares* and in no other source (86). On the related compilation of the *Romances,* see Bierhorst (85) and Garibay, *Poesía Náhuatl,* 1:x–xi.

represent a profound meditation on what had occurred, rather than an eye-witness account from 1520, as they are often taken to be. They reflect an on-going negotiation with present realities in which the power of poetry is a crucial force for maintaining cultural identity and courage in the face of devastating change. How did the surviving court poets employ their old image repertoire now that they were no longer the voice of the most powerful empire ever seen in the New World? How did they adapt their work as they participated—unwillingly no doubt, but actively nonetheless—in the creation of a new society, built on elements that had never been brought together before?

I will take as an area for examination what may be the single most striking change in the poetry: the displacement of the old gods by the new. Traditionally, the court poets had worked under the watchful guidance of the Aztec priests, and their compositions were performed on public occasions, ordinarily as part of religious celebrations and rituals. In the codices of the *Cantares* and the *Romances,* however, actual names of Aztec divinities almost never appear. What we do find are a variety of epithets that Sahagún and other chroniclers list as names for the gods, such as Ipalnemoani, "Giver of Life," a traditional appellation of Tezcatlipoca, patron of rulers and warriors. It is generally impossible to say whether a poem addressed to Ipalnemoani represents a veiled appeal to Tezcatlipoca, or whether the term now refers to the Christian God—as seems more certainly to be the case with Icelteotl, "Sole God," a term occasionally used for major deities before the Conquest but now very explicitly associated with the biblical God in post-Conquest poetry.

Very often, the names of God (*Dios,* or *Tios,* or *Tiox*) and other Christian figures appear in the manuscripts, and here too it is hard to say how often these names reflect the poet's own beliefs, or a deliberate ruse on the poet's part to escape censorship, or a pious emendation by the native informants who collected the songs for Sahagún. The two poetic codices appear to take somewhat different formal approaches to the problem of emendation. In the *Romances,* the scribe often gives a marginal gloss to a traditional epithet. For example, next to the line *Acan huel ichan Moyocoyatzin,* "In no place is found the home of The One Who Creates Himself"—an epithet of Tezcatlipoca—the scribe notes in the margin, *yehuan ya dios glosa,* "this is to be read as 'God.'" (Something of the complexity of the cultural situation may be seen from this trilingual gloss, written as it is in a mixture of Nahuatl, Spanish, and Latin.) At other times, a marginal emendation appears where a divine name has simply been omitted, or else replaced with the generic term *teotl,* "god." By contrast, the *Cantares* manuscript often pairs terms within the line itself, so that we encounter lines such as this: "titeotl yehuan Dios an tinechmiquitlani," which can be translated either as an apostrophe—"O Spirit, O God, you want me dead"—or as an emendation: "O Spirit [i.e., God], you want me dead" (poem 18, stanza 21).

As ambiguous as these namings often are, it is still more difficult to say what sort of cultural shift has taken place when Christian names *are* used by the poet. There are some poems in which we may feel that the old gods have simply disappeared, but there are others in which it seems more as though the old pantheon is now being enlarged by the arrival of figures like Tiox, *spilitu xanto* (Espíritu Santo), and Santa Malia. The poems make no mention of Ometeotl, the "Dual God" or "God of Duality," simultaneously male and female, who had created all the other gods; but now, in some poems, Tiox and Santa Malia seem to rule together as king and queen of heaven, at times in quite un-Catholic settings:

> I scatter a multitude of flowers. Ho! I've come to offer songs.
> There's flower-drunkenness. And I'm a leering ribald. . . .
> You've come to give him pleasure, and it would seem that he is
> Tiox, that he is the Giver of Life, that she is Santa Malia, that
> she is our mother. The flowers are stirring, ah!"

(80.5, 9)

The Christian deities now become the patrons of song: "Santa María the ever virgin comes loosening, comes unfolding, song marvels, flower paintings. Hear them! In Butterfly House, House of Pictures, God's home, in Roseate House she sings, she arrives, she, Santa María" (32.5–6). "To the white willows, where white rushes grow, to Mexico, you, Blue Egret Bird, come flying, you, O spirit, O Espíritu Santo! . . . You're here singing in Mexico" (35.3–4). In another poem, Espíritu Santo takes on a form suspiciously like that of a disguised Quetzalcoatl, the traditional patron of Aztec culture: "You come created, O Quetzal-bird"—*quetzaltototl*, a term notably close to *Quetzalcoatl*—"O spilitu xanto. You arrive! You come bringing your quechols, these angels [*ageloti*], these flower garlands, that loosen their songs and give you pleasure, O Giver of Life!" (71.5). It is no wonder that his parishioners' persistence in singing their old songs aroused Sahagún's suspicion as to the sincerity of their Christian faith, though the problem may have been that they were all too enthusiastically adapting their new faith to their underlying modes of thought and expression.

Poetry had often celebrated warfare in the pre-Conquest era, with the victorious ruler-warrior at times explicitly becoming a poet or artist of battle. The linkage of poetry and warfare continues in the late poems, and the same Tiox and Jesucristo who are the new patrons of song are also the new patrons of war, in poems that signal and perhaps incite a direct resistance to the Spaniards:

> Gold is shining in your sapodilla house of trogons. Your home
>   abounds in jade water whorls, O prince, O Jesucristo. You're
>   singing in Anahuac. . . .
> You're hidden away at Seven Caves, where the mesquite grows.
>   The eagle cries, the jaguar whines; you, in the midst of the
>   field—a roseate quechol—fly onward, in the Place Unknown.

(33.3–8)

Here the military reference is covert, encoded in the terms "mesquite," "eagle," and "jaguar," all traditional terms for warriors; the cry of the eagle, further, is a battle cry. Jesucristo is "hidden away at Seven Caves, where the mesquite grows," as though he is training warriors in the Aztecs' ancestral northern homeland in preparation for a return in force. In other poems, these references are more overt: "This jaguar earth is shaking, and the screaming skies begin to rip. Spilitu Xanto, Giver of Life, descends. Chalked shields are strewn away with love. And they that come to stand on earth are spines of His from Flower-Tassel Land" (71.1).

God himself, it seems, is encouraging the Mexicans to fight against the Spaniards who brought him:

> Montezuma, you creature of heaven, you sing in Mexico, in
>   Tenochtitlan.
> Here where eagle multitudes were ruined, your bracelet house
>   stands shining—there in the home of Tiox our father.
>   . . . . .
> Onward, friends! We'll dare to go where fame, where glory's
>   gotten, where nobility is gotten, where flower death is won.
> Your name and honor live, O princes. Prince Tlacahuepan!
>   Ixtlilcuechahuac! You've gone and won war death.

(76.1–6)

The old ideas are still here—but nothing is the same. In fact, the "old" ideas and images themselves are transformed. Not only is warfare a different proposition for a defeated people than for seemingly unconquerable armies, but the relations of beauty, the divine, and mortal life are all altered. In the lines just quoted, the bracelet house (a warriors' house) still stands shining, an enduring human artifact—but it is now Tiox's house, and it survives amid the ruins of the warriors who themselves used to inhabit it.

The flower death of heroic individuals used to take place against the backdrop of the ever-expanding empire, with its unshakable center, Tenochtitlán; now, the heroic death of the warrior achieves no certain result for the culture. The ephemerality of human culture, newly observed on an unprecedented scale, extends to the gods as well. Even as Tiox is enlisted in the struggle, his foreignness and his unpredictability remain apparent to the poets, and they seek to comprehend this fickleness. One poem begins with two ringing verses celebrating warriors in battle, but then comes up short:

> I grieve, I weep. What good is this? The shield flowers are carried away, they're sent aloft. Ah, where can I find what my heart desires?
> Incomparable war death! Incomparable flower death! The Giver of Life has blessed it.
> I seek the good songs whence they come—and I am poor. Let me not sing.

(31.5–7)

The poet then confronts the possibility that the same Giver of Life who has blessed both warfare and poetry may not, after all, reward either:

> Perhaps these glorious jades and bracelets are your hearts and loved ones, O father, O Dios, Giver of Life. So many do I utter near you and in your presence—I, Totoquihuaztli. How could you run weary? How could you run slack?
> Easily, in a moment might you slacken, O father, O Dios.

(31.13–14)

The poem ends with the knowledge that the poet can become intoxicated only with dreams of war, with his songs, while instead of celebrating great feats in battle and splendid flower deaths, the people must be content that anyone is still left alive:

> They make my heart drunk: they flower, they intoxicate me here on earth: I am drunk with war flowers.
> He shows mercy to everyone. Thus people are alive on earth. Heaven comes here! And I am drunk with war flowers.

(31.15–16)

If songs cannot continue to reflect the enduring glory of the empire and the ageless fame of its victorious warriors, they still retain power, fortifying the singer through a newly deepened awareness of the possibilities for beauty in an existence far more ephemeral than anyone had imagined. "Only sad flowers, sad songs, lie here in Mexico, in Tlatelolco. Beyond is the Place Where Recognition Is Achieved. O Giver of Life, it's good to know that you will favor us, and we underlings will die" (13.1–2). In this poem, a raining mist comes down not from the beneficent Tlaloc, god of rain, but from the tears of the vanquished:

> Tears are pouring, teardrops are raining there in Tlatelolco. The
>   Mexican women have gone into the lagoon. It's truly thus. So
>   all are going. And where to, comrades?
> True it is. They forsake the city of Mexico. The smoke is rising,
>   the haze is spreading. This is your doing, O Giver of Life.
> Mexicans, remember that he who sends down on us his agony, his
>   fear, is none but Dios, alas, there in Coyonazco.

(13.5–7)

The poem closes by affirming the power of song even in such devastating circumstances. The poet recalls the captivity of the Mexican leaders Motelchiuh and Tlacotzin, whom the Spaniards tortured with fire in hopes of learning the location of hidden gold:

> Weep and be guilty, friends. You've forsaken the Mexican nation,
>   alas. The water is bitter, and the food is bitter as well. This is
>   the doing of the Giver of Life in Tlatelolco.
> Yet peacefully were Motelchiuh and Tlacotzin taken away. They
>   fortified themselves with song in Acachinanco when they went
>   to be delivered to the fire in Coyohuacan.

(13.9–10)

Strength and beauty can shine out even in defeat. The poet's song can persist too, perhaps no longer as the splendid embodiment of the ever-renewing flowers of empire, but rather as a newly ephemeral artifact. In the fullest expression of this theme, the long sixty-eighth song in the *Cantares* describes Cortés's arrival in Tenochtitlán, the fall of the city, and a real or imagined visit to Rome, where the natives meet the pope:

> The pope [*i papa*] is on Tiox's mat and seat and speaks for him.
> Who is this reclining on a golden chair? Look! It's the pope.
> He has his turquoise blowgun and he's shooting in the world.

(68.65).

Cortés has apparently sent the Aztecs along with a shipment of gold for the pope: "He's said: What do I need? Gold! Everybody bow down! Call out to Tiox in excelsis!" (68.100).

If the Europeans want all the gold, the Aztecs are left trying to preserve their water. The song is entitled "Atequilizcuicatl," "Water-Pouring Song," and in this poem "water" comes to stand for Mexico itself. One name for Tenochtitlán, reflecting its construction on islands in the Lake of Mexico, was Atliyaitic, "The Water's Midst." Water and fire were the great gifts of the two gods worshiped on the Templo Mayor in Tenochtitlán, the fertile Tlaloc and the war god Huitzilopochtli. Now, in this poem, Tiox has taken control of both of these forces. Concerning fire: "Tiox and Only Spirit, you and you alone lay down the mirror and the flame that stands here in the world" (68.36), with the power over mirror and flame implicitly taken over from the god Tezcatlipoca, whose name means "Smoking Mirror." God's envoy Cortés enters the city with smoking guns: "Now woe! He gives off smoke! This is how he enters, this conquistador, this Captain" (68.9).

Those who control the fire control the water as well. The Mexicans are forced to pour out their water for the invaders, and here water becomes a metaphor for the entire culture:

> We who've come to Water's Midst to marvel are Tlaxcalans:
>   Mexican princes are pouring out their waters! Lord
>   Motehcuzoma's hauling vats of water. And the city passes on,
>   ensconced in water-whorl flowers. Thus Mexico is handed
>   over. Oh! The waters are His, and He drinks them, it's true.
> Iye! The lady María comes shouting. María comes saying, "O
>   Mexicans, your water jars go here! Let all the lords come
>   carrying." And Acolhuacan's Quetzalacxoycatl arrives. And
>   Cuauhpopoca. Oh! the waters are His, and He drinks them,
>   it's true.

(68.10–11)

As often in poems that link poems and flowers together, the poet has found an appropriate flower to symbolize his theme, as the city passes away "ensconced in water-whorl flowers." Perhaps there is also a play between "water-whorl flowers," *amalacoxochitl*, and "paper flowers," *amacaxochitl*, used in 60.55 to mean "poems"; the root, *amatl*, means "paper, book, song-book." The poet has also chosen his nobles deliberately, in order to contrast their humble duties as water carriers with the glorious possibilities suggested by their names. Cuauhpopoca, "Smoking Eagle," is a warrior's name par excellence, while Quetzalacxoycatl, "Plumed Needle," refers to the *acxoycatl*, an instrument used in ritual bloodletting and mock combats.

The poet sees only one refuge from the harsh labor being imposed on his people: to break the carved and painted jars that have been pressed into the lowly service of hauling water, even as the people are being broken by the Spaniards: "O Giver of Life, these urgently required ones have been broken, these, our water jars, and we are Mexicans. A cry goes up. They're picking them off at Eagle Gate, where recognition is achieved. Oh! the waters are His, and He drinks them, it's true" (68.12–13).

As his people die, the poet sees his poem itself as a water jar, carrying his culture. And so his poem is to be broken along with the people:

> O nephews, hail! And hear a work assignment: we've come to do
> our water pouring. Now who will go and fetch the jadestone
> jars that we must carry? And yonder we're assembled, at Shore
> of the Bells, at the Place of Green Waters.
> Oh none among us shall work for tribute. We're to pass away. Our
> guardian Don Diego Tehuetzquiti is to lead us.
> . . . . .
> I weep, I sorrow, and I sing: I've broken these, my turquoise gems,
> my pearls, these water jars.
> And let it be thus that I return them. Chirping for these flowers,
> let me head for home. At Flower Waters let me weep,
> composing them: I've broken these, my turquoise gems, my
> pearls, these water jars.

(68.25–33)

Poems like the "Water-Pouring Song" were obviously new compositions made in the aftermath of the Conquest, perhaps close in time to the actual events, or perhaps decades later as the poets synthesized their experiences and meditated on their meaning. Yet older poems too continued to be sung, and these poems took on new meanings in the Colonial era. Indeed, most of the poems in the *Cantares* and the *Romances* fall into an ambiguous grey area: they may be seen as coming from either the pre-Conquest era or from the Colonial period, or, in a very real sense, from both. Within their own lifetimes, the Aztec poets were compelled to sing their poems in light of the overturning of the world in which they were first composed, and the surviving poems are filled both with a sense of dramatic loss and with a sense of underlying continuity. It is, indeed, this mixture of loss and of continuity that enables and even requires us to read many of the poems against both pre- and post-Conquest history together.

In many cases, poems change their valences dramatically across the great divide of 1519–21. The theme of ephemerality in the poems, for example, has often been read in modern times as expressing a detached, existential—even existential*ist*—philosophy. It is increasingly clear, however, that the poems were always closely tied to urgent religious and political concerns, and by this very engagement their meaning altered radically with the Conquest. The same images and verses that aided and even heightened the brutality of the imperial regime were turned to a new purpose some years later: to strengthen the resolve of a conquered people to resist their total destruction.

Understanding this sort of shift helps us to read these poems more fully, and it has larger implications as well. The Aztec poems illustrate in exemplary fashion some of the ways in which any text alters and renews its meaning as it circulates across time and across cultures. In their double historical grounding, these poems provide a real-life instance of the shifting of meaning over time explored fictively in Borges's story "Pierre Menard, Author of the *Quixote*": "Not for nothing have three hundred years elapsed, freighted with the most complex events. . . . the Cervantes text and the Menard text are verbally identical, but the second is almost infinitely richer" (93–94). In the case of Aztec poetry, though, the crucial passage of time was three years rather than three hundred, and in consequence the Aztec poets of the sixteenth century were among the first to be forced to confront this problem directly. The ways in which they did so bear comparison with Renaissance poets' struggles with their cultural heritage on the other side of the Atlantic, though the vanishing past in Mexico was not that of a remote antiquity but of the poets' own youth.

The theme may also be seen in poems that make no reference to the Conquest and that have no Christian elements at all, poems that may well be pre-Conquest compositions. To give one example, the forty-ninth poem in the *Romances* codex[4] modulates the theme of the brevity of human life through a series of ironic changes. It begins with a standard evocation of the joys of fellowship:

> Make your beginning, you who sing.
> May you beat again your flowered drum,
> may you give joy to my lords, the eagles, the jaguars.
> Briefly we are here together.

This last line is then given a surprising twist in the next stanza:

[4] Text and Spanish translation in Garibay, *Poesía Náhuatl*, 1:76–77.

> The one heart's desire of the Giver of Life
> is jewels, is quetzal plumes: to tear them apart.
> This is his desire: to scatter apart the eagles, the jaguars.
> Briefly we are here together.

The brevity of existence has moved from a neutral fact of life to the direct consequence of a divine will to destruction. As the poem continues, the poet reverses the traditional image of the song as the bearer of immortality for mortal heroes:

> And these our songs, these our flowers,
> they are our shrouds. So be happy:
> woven into them is the eagle, the jaguar;
> we will go with them, there where it is all the same.

Like the broken water jar in the "Water-Pouring Song," poetry now shares in the destruction it is elsewhere represented as surviving. This poem has no elements that mark it explicitly either as a pre-Conquest or a post-Conquest composition; depending on which setting one sees it in, its message reads rather differently. In both contexts, though, the poem offers its audience a severe consolation, as in its closing lines, in which the problem of the brevity of life becomes its own ironic solution, the very source of strength:

> So let us now rejoice within our hearts,
> all who are on earth;
> only briefly do we know one another,
> only here are we together.
> So do not be saddened, my lords:
> no one, no one is left behind on earth.

The challenge these poems offer us is to read them in multiple senses, a multiplicity commonly taken on by texts over time, but in this case inscribed within the poems themselves, shaped as they have been by the poets' own multiple perspective on their past triumphs and their present struggles. As they sang the old songs and composed new ones, perhaps some of the poets of the 1550s and 1560s recalled the archaic "Legend of the Suns," the central mythic description of the world's five ages, in which the Aztecs accounted themselves as living in the fifth age: 4-Movement, the age of earthquakes. Perhaps, too, they thought that this final age of the world shared something of the violent second age as well:

> It was called the Jaguar Sun.
> Then it happened that the sky was crushed,

the Sun did not follow its course.
When the Sun arrived at midday,
immediately it was night;
and when it became dark,
jaguars ate the people.
In this Sun giants lived.
The old ones said the giants greeted each other thus:
"Do not fall down," for whoever falls,
he falls forever.[5]

The elaborate traditions of Nahuatl art poetry gradually died out, along with the court poets who had been trained in the pre-Conquest *cuicacalli*, "houses of song." The common people, however, had never shared much of the wealth the nobility had gathered to themselves, and the Conquest had a less drastic effect on their everyday culture than on the culture of the ruling class. This is not to say that the entire population didn't suffer severely, particularly as disease and mistreatment led to a shocking loss of life: by the middle of the seventeenth century, the native population of New Spain was probably less than a tenth of what it had been on the eve of the Conquest. Yet the still substantial surviving native population of some two million people adapted to new living conditions that in some respects resembled older oppressions. Cortés, after all, could never have taken Tenochtitlán with his few hundred Spanish troops alone: he succeeded because his arrival became the catalyst for a general uprising of many of the Aztecs' enemies and allies alike. From the time of Cortés's first arrival on the mainland they began to come to him, complaining bitterly of their mistreatment by their Aztec overlords, who stole their gold, levied crushing taxes, and pressed them into forced labor. In a cruel irony, the new world order that Cortés brought them was all too familiar.

The wasteful brutality of the Spanish *encomienda* system, in which native workers were effectively enslaved to work under conditions of high mortality on farms and in mines, bore a grim family resemblance to the Aztecs' policy of taking many of their sacrificial victims from nearby populations. This had not been a traditional feature of Mesoamerican life but began after a king named Itzcoatl ascended the throne in 1428. His chief

[5] *Anales de Cuauhtitlan*, fol. 2; quoted in Miguel Léon-Portilla, *Pre-Columbian Literatures*, 36. In an article on "The Nahua Myth of the Suns," Wayne Elzey has argued that the fifth age was in fact regarded as embodying the characteristics of the earlier ages. For an illuminating discussion of the political uses of these and other myths, see Davíd Carrasco, *Quetzalcoatl and the Irony of Empire*.

strategist and ideologue, Tlacaelel, promoted a new and shocking level of human sacrifice, turning small-scale rituals into a large-scale theater of terror as the Aztecs expanded their new empire and tried to cement their hold over the entire region. One sixteenth-century account records Tlacaelel's explanation of why he insisted on sacrificing so many local victims, despite the obvious dangers of political unrest. The war god Huitzilopochtli, he reportedly said, would not accept sacrifices from distant regions: "Those places are too remote, and, furthermore, our god does not like the flesh of those barbarous people. They are like hard, yellowish, tasteless tortillas in his mouth." Sacrificial victims from nearby cities, on the other hand, "will come to our god like warm tortillas, soft, tasty, straight from the fire."[6]

The sufferings of the common people under Spanish rule, then, were not exactly unprecedented in their experience, and throughout the sixteenth and seventeenth centuries, Aztec farmers and laborers preserved many of their traditional means for dealing with adversity. Though they might now sing Sahagún's Nahuatl psalms in church, they turned for help with many daily problems to their traditional supports: the community's healer-diviners, the *nahualli,* and each individual's personal spirit double, the *tonal,* typically embodied in an animal, whom every child received at birth as a private guiding spirit. Indeed, powerful diviners could even change themselves into their animal forms at will, and they developed rituals, aided by elaborate incantations, to bring about these transformations, to cure illness, and to affect people's fortunes in love and in situations of need or conflict.

We know a good deal about these beliefs and practices thanks to a treatise completed in 1629 by Hernando Ruiz de Alarcón, a parish priest in the town of Atenango in the rural state of Guerrero, south of Mexico City. His archbishop had appointed him to serve as the ecclesiastical judge for his region, and so he had the responsibility to investigate and punish deviations from orthodoxy. Devoted to his parishioners but profoundly hostile to pagan practices, like Sahagún before him Ruiz de Alarcón realized the importance of gaining a full understanding of the practices he was charged with suppressing. To this end, he wrote a long, bilingual treatise that he entitled *Tratado de las Supersticiones y Costumbres Gentílicas que hoy Viven entre los Indios Naturales desta Nueva España* (Treatise on the Superstitions

---

[6] Diego Durán, *The Aztecs: History of the Indies of New Spain,* 231–32. Durán's work is one of the major accounts of pre-Conquest history, based on extensive interviews with native informants. Particularly where speeches are involved, it is of course hard to say how accurate Durán is, but at the very least it is significant that Durán's informants in the 1570s *thought* of Tlacaelel's policy as having been formulated in these cold-blooded terms.

and Pagan Customs That Survive Today among the Native Indians of this New Spain). He wanted his fellow clerics to be able to recognize and understand the spells and prayers that diviners and common people would chant as they performed their rituals, and so he included many of these incantations directly in his text, in Nahuatl together with a loose Spanish translation. Altogether his treatise is the fullest surviving record of seventeenth-century popular rituals and of the mesmerizing poetic incantations that accompanied them.

Ruiz de Alarcón's treatise found even less of an audience than Sahagún's works. Though he wrote up a fair copy and presented it to his archbishop, it was never printed for parish use as he had hoped. The manuscript was preserved at a rural estate until, two and a half centuries later, it was bought by Francisco del Paso y Troncoso, one of the scholars who began to take an interest in old native materials during the later nineteenth century. Paso y Troncoso published the treatise in 1892, but few people paid attention to a work so far removed from the drama of the Conquest and from the high culture of the Aztec nobility. It was reprinted only once, in 1953, sixty years after its first publication. In the early 1970s Alfredo López Austin made a fresh and more accurate translation of the Nahuatl incantations, but he left out most of Ruiz de Alarcón's own commentary, which occupies more than half the volume. Finally, in the early eighties, the treatise received its first full translation into any language, and indeed two different translations appeared almost simultaneously. I will focus on the first of these, published in 1982 by Michael Coe and Gordon Whittaker under the title *Aztec Sorcerers in Seventeenth-Century Mexico: The Treatise on Superstitions by Hernando Ruiz de Alarcón*. Though this is a scholarly translation that retains the Nahuatl originals along with the commentaries, Coe and Whittaker were at pains to make their edition accessible to general readers.[7] Not only did they give the treatise an extensive introduction, locating the work in its time and place for the benefit of nonspecialists, but they sought to attract readers by inventing a dramatic title for the book (*Aztec Sorcerers . . .*) and even by commissioning a series of evocative drawings to illustrate the treatise and Ruiz de Alarcón's own life (see figure 7 for an example).

The Nahuatl texts in this treatise are very different from the elevated poetry of the Aztec nobility: they are far simpler in form and in diction, with incantatory repetitions that give them a vivid power of their own.

---

[7] The other translation, by J. Richard Andrews and Ross Hassig, appeared in 1984 under the more accurate title *Treatise on the Heathen Superstitions and Customs That Today Live among the Indians Native to This New Spain, 1629.* This version is a fuller critical edition, addressed more directly to a scholarly audience.

Figure 7. "Imaginary Portrait of Hernando Ruiz de Alarcón in his parish house at Atenango"

Whether they should be considered poetry at all could be debated, but they certainly carry a real poetic force, and in their translation Coe and Whittaker have opted to give them a poetic form as well, breaking what are long paragraph-style stanzas in the manuscript into short lines that bring out the phrasings of the original. As they say in their preface, "we have considered the spells as poetry, but it is not poetry as the Western world understands it" (40). Following the ethnopoetician Dennis Tedlock, they argue that "in practically all American Indian poetry and poetic expression, versification is semantic, and rhyme and meter are generally unknown" (40). This, then, is a poetry based on repetition, parallelism, and variations of phrases and ideas rather than on rhyme or even set meters. Whereas other translators of Nahuatl chant have often left out some of the repetitions for fear of putting readers off, Coe and Whittaker say that "we hope that we have done justice to the power of the original Nahuatl by not excluding them" (41).

Here is one of the incantations, "a spell for attracting and creating affection," with Ruiz de Alarcón's preceding (and interrupting) commentary:

> The superstition of attracting the affection of another's will is of the kind referred to before, and is used by those in love to see if it will be of benefit to them, and so it begins here in its proper place. This superstition is based on words alone, to which they attribute the power of making whomever one fancies yield to one's will. They say, then, the words of the spell:

tezcatepec	On the mountain of mirrors,
nenamicoyā	In the place of encounters,
niçihuanotza	I call to women,
niçihuacuica	I sing to women.
nonnentlamati	I am unhappy there,
nihualnentlamati	I am unhappy here.
ye nocōhuica	Already I am carrying off
in nohueltiuh in xochiquetzal	My elder sister Flower Plume;
ce coatl ica	With 1 Serpent
cuitlalpitihuitz	She comes girded
tzonilpitiuitz	She comes braided.
ye yalhua	Yesterday,
ye huiptla	The day before,
ica nichoca	I wept over it,
ica ninentlamati	I was unhappy about it.
ca mach nelli teotl	For indeed she is truly a goddess,
ca mach nelli mahuiztic	For indeed she is truly marvelous.
cuix quin moztla	Is it tomorrow?
cuix quin huiptla	Is it the day after?
niman aman	Right now!
nomatca nehuatl	I myself,
nitelpochtli	I am the Youth
ni yaotl	I am the Adversary,
nonitonac	I have shone forth,
nonitlathuic	I have dawned.
cuix çan cana onihualla	Have I come forth just anywhere?
cuix çan cana onihualquiz	Have I set forth just anywhere?

ompa onihualla	Over there I have come forth.
ompa onihualquiz	Over there I have set forth.

The rest of the words, even though somewhat disguised, are such that they are not put here for reasons of modesty and chaste ears. Finally they conclude, saying:

ca mach nelli teotl	For indeed she is truly a goddess,
ca mach nelli mahuiztic	For indeed she is truly marvelous.
cuix quin moztla	Is it tomorrow,
cuix quin huiptla	Is it the day after
niquitaz	That I shall see her?
nyman aman	Right now!
nomatca nehuatl	I myself,
nitelpochtli	I am the Youth
niyaotl	I am the Adversary.
cuix nelli niyaotl	Am I truly the Adversary?
ahmo nelli niyaotl	I am not truly the Adversary,
çan nicihuayaotl	Just the Adversary of Women.

(189–90)

This incantation is much more immediately accessible than the earlier court poetry: the phrasing is simple, and the verbal play is limited but often charming, as in the final reversal in which the speaker undercuts his own boasting and announces himself more modestly as only a lady-killer (*cihuayaotl*). At the same time, the poem presents real obscurities, chiefly because the speakers in these spells rarely name the divinities they invoke, either out of respect for the gods or from caution before the priest who is recording their chant. As a result, this incantation's opening phrase, *tezcatepec*, gives a kind of Borgesian effect: what exactly would a "mountain of mirrors" be? I suspect that this is not meant as a visual image at all but is a veiled reference to the warrior god Tezcatlipoca ("Smoking Mirror"): the speaker is on a mountain sacred to this god, whom he invokes along with Tezcatlipoca's consort Xochiquetzal ("Flower Plume"), goddess of love. At the end of the incantation, in fact, the speaker identifies himself as "the Adversary," a traditional epithet of Tezcatlipoca. In then denying that he is literally the great god himself, the speaker closes by acknowledging his humanity and his need for the god's aid.[8]

---

[8] Translating *tezcatepec* simply as a place name ("Mirror Mountain") in their edition of the treatise, Andrews and Hassig express surprise that this incantation reads more like a

Disturbed as Ruiz de Alarcón was by the persistence of old beliefs, he was even more outraged by the syncretism well under way in his community a hundred years after the Conquest. In his treatise he describes these mixed practices as deceptive ruses whereby the natives attempt to continue their old ways under the guise of Christian worship. The sacred cross itself becomes a hiding place for the old gods: "They also used to place the idols in the pedestals of crosses, especially those in deserted places, for two ends: the first, because no one would suspect the mixture *quae conventio lucis ad tenebris.* The second, because they venerate and worship the idols under that cover, repeatedly placing before them lit candles, incense, bouquets, and other things of that kind" (91). Ruiz de Alarcón has no idea that anyone could really be making such a combination for its own sake, and his Latin quotation paraphrases a scriptural passage in which Saint Paul rejects any accommodation of Christianity with pagan practices: "What fellowship has light with darkness? And what covenant has Christ with Belial?" (1 Corinthians 6:14–15). Any such mixing can only be a deliberate deception, and Ruiz de Alarcón notes with satisfaction that God himself has exposed some of these ruses: "I have also found out that in many other parts things of this nature have been discovered by Our Lord God making them known, as happened in the mountains of Meztitlan, of the Augustinian friars, where he sent lightning from heaven onto the pedestal of a cross so many times that the friars had it destroyed in their presence. They found an idol within it; since its removal, lightning has not struck again in more than twelve years" (91).

It is far from certain, though, that mere deception is at work here, especially as the natives are setting their idols in deserted regions and on mountains—the traditional locales for offering worship and sacrifices to the gods. Rather than simply trying to carry on their old rites in disguise under the watchful eyes of the priests in town, these natives seem instead to have begun combining old and new elements together in a deliberate mixing. This tendency was recognized by some observers at the time. In a "Brief Relation of the Gods and Rites of Heathenism," a contemporary of Ruiz de Alarcón's named Don Pedro Ponce warns that Satan is inspiring the people

---

European poem than a native production: "It hardly seems like an incantation at all; no powerful ally is summoned to help the speaker attain his goal, nor on the other hand is the beloved one appealed to. In fact, no one is addressed and the speaker seems to be talking to himself, so there is a lyriclike expression of feeling and a stating of desires that reminds one of a Renaissance love complaint" (281). Recognizing Tezcatlipoca's veiled presence solves this puzzle and restores the incantation to its local context, giving an answer for Andrews and Hassig's speculation that it must really be spoken to an "unspecified addressee" of supernatural powers.

to deal with Christ simply by adding him to their existing pantheon: "Among all these gods they put Christ, Our Lord and Redeemer, for they received Him as the last God, and in certain paintings about how sacrifices are to be made to their Gods, one finds the cross, nails, and scourge tied to the column and crucified [Christ] and the priests saying mass. And at this time their dogmatizers make their sacrifices according to their ancient custom" (211). Ruiz de Alarcón seems oblivious to this process, and yet, shortly after he reports God's blasting of the mountain cross, he goes on to describe a highly syncretistic dream-vision experienced by a native diviner under the influence of a hallucinogenic drink made from the seeds of the *ololiuhqui* (morning glory):

> In the settlement of Iguala . . . I arrested an Indian woman named Mariana, a sorceress, charlatan, and curer of the kind they call *ticitl*. This Mariana declared that she had learned the sorceries and tricks which she knew and practiced from another Indian woman, Mariana's sister, and the said sister had learned them from no one, but that they had been revealed to her; because when the said sister consulted the ololiuhqui about the cure of an old ulcer, and she had become intoxicated with the force of the drink, she summoned the patient and blew on the ulcer over some hot coals, by which she cured the ulcer; and following the blowing, there immediately appeared to her a boy whom she judged to be an angel. He consoled her, saying, "Do not be troubled, for behold! God is granting you a favor and a boon, for you live poor and in great misery. Through this favor you will have chili and salt (that is to say, sustenance). You will cure sores, and rashes and pox, just by licking them. If you do not respond to this, you will die." After this, the said boy gave her a cross, and was there the whole night crucifying her on it and hammering nails in her hands. While the said Indian woman was on the cross, the boy taught her the ways which he knew for curing, which were seven or more exorcisms and incantations. (94–95)

This remarkable vision reworks the gospel accounts of Christ's death and resurrection, enabling Mariana's sister to see herself both as the biblical Mary, comforted by the angel, and as Christ himself on the cross, not expiating sin but receiving sacred knowledge. For his part, Ruiz de Alarcón has no doubt at all that the woman did receive secret knowledge through this vision. He is sure, though, that it was sent by the Devil himself: "With these fancies, fictions, and diabolical performances which the Devil puts into their imagination, they consider themselves almost divine beings. . . . For in this also the Devil attempts more semblances, or to put it better, casts shadows on the brilliant enlightenment of the Evangelist" (95).

Reading Ruiz de Alarcón's commentary, it becomes increasingly apparent that the syncretism was going both ways. Though he remains secure in his orthodoxy as regards church doctrine, he and many of his fellow priests had accepted some of the natives' key beliefs. Not only does Ruiz de Alarcón credit many miraculous events (albeit as the work of the Devil rather than Tezcatlipoca), but he even reports several instances in which diviners successfully changed themselves into their animal doubles. His very first chapter is titled "Of the basis of idolatries. Of the adoration and worship of different things, especially fire. Of *nahual* sorcerers and how such can exist" (63–67). In this chapter he gives several instances of reports by Indians and even by fellow clergy ("witnesses who are faultless") describing mysterious transformations and exchanges between sorcerers and their animal doubles. To take one example:

> Father Andrés Ximénez of the Dominican Order told me that when two fathers of his faith were in a cell towards nightfall, a bat—much larger than usual—came in through a window. The two monks followed the bat, throwing their hats and other things at it, until it escaped them and departed. The next day, an old Indian woman came to the porter's lodge of the monastery; summoning one of the two monks, she asked why he had mistreated her so, and had he wanted to kill her. The monk in turn asked her if she was crazy, for where and how could that be. She replied by asking if it were true that on the previous night he and the other monk had mistreated and many times struck a bat that had entered a cell by a window. On the monk saying, "Can this be so?", the Indian woman said, "For the bat was I, and I am still very tired." Hearing this in wonder, the monk wished to summon his companion to meet the Indian woman, and, to detain her, he asked her to wait, that he would go inside to get some alms. He went in, and returning with his companion, he discovered neither the Indian woman, nor where she had gone. (64)

Ruiz de Alarcón adds that "I have known many other cases of this sort. . . . although curious and outside what is known of the nations and peoples accustomed to having a pact with the Devil" (64–65). The missionaries found their own conceptions changing even as they worked to change those of their parishioners.

Born at the outer edge of the European world, Ruiz de Alarcón moved off the map altogether when he took holy orders, serving in obscurity in the mountains of Guerrero, some hundred and fifty miles southwest of Mexico City. This was a move in the opposite direction from the path taken by his older brother Juan. Juan earned a degree in law at the University of Mexico in 1600, from which his brother would graduate six years later. Small, dark, hunchbacked, ambitious, and irascible, Juan could not manage to establish himself in Mexico. Eventually he settled in Spain, where he began to write plays. In an interesting reversal of fact, in his great play *La Verdad Sospechosa,* "The Truth Suspected," the protagonist is a compulsive liar who *pretends* to be a wealthy colonist just arrived back in Madrid from the New World. To this day, Juan Ruiz de Alarcón is regarded as one of the greatest playwrights of Spain's "Golden Age." By contrast, Hernando turned his back on worldly ambition and on the world of European culture he knew. Living in his rural town of Atenango, locked in a triangular struggle with the Devil over his parishioners' fidelity, he fell into writing his long treatise, a work much more ambitious and unsettling than his bishop had expected—or wanted—to receive. Unpublished for centuries and never intended as literature at all, the *Tratado sobre las Supersticiones y Costumbres Gentílicas* has preserved for us an unequaled treasury of the native poetry of its era, wrapped within Ruiz de Alarcón's account of his own tragicomic efforts to master the shifting cultural currents around him. By turns sympathetic and hostile, insightful and baffled, disturbed by the power of chants whose content repelled him, he struggled with truths more suspicious than any encountered by his brother's heroes and heroines on stage.

All the texts examined in this chapter give the lie to the traditional consensus that native Mexican culture ended almost overnight upon the arrival of the Spanish. William Sanders closes his *Britannica* article on "The History of Meso-American Civilization" with a typically sweeping expression of this view: "The Post-Classic civilizations of Meso-America came to an abrupt end with the coming of the Spanish in the early sixteenth century. (For the history of the Spanish Conquest, see LATIN AMERICA AND THE CARIBBEAN, COLONIAL)" (954). The article on colonial Latin America says nothing about the ongoing life of native cultures: its focus is on the Spanish colonists and the political and economic arrangements they created, and the natives appear only in their relations with Spanish culture. The implication in both articles is that the native cultures as a whole disappeared in 1521, a view uncomfortably close to the wishful thinking of the conquistadores themselves. Writing his memoirs late in life, Cortés's soldier Bernal Díaz del Castillo remarked with a kind of melancholy wonder that of all the marvels he and his comrades saw as they marched into the Valley of Mexico, "Ahora todo está por el suelo, perdido, que no hay cosa": "Today everything is torn down, lost, so there is nothing left" (*Historia verdadera,* 159). Díaz was wrong: native culture lived on, and it has become newly visible in the haunting poems that are now being recovered from forgotten manuscripts of those ambiguous times.

3

From the Old World to the Whole World

If the scope of world literature now extends from Akkadian epics to Aztec incantations, the question of what is world literature could almost be put in opposite terms: What *isn't* world literature? A category from which nothing can be excluded is essentially useless. Until recently, world literature has often been defined in North America all too specifically as Western European literature. This definition at least had virtues of coherence and relative manageability, particularly when works written in the less commonly spoken European languages, such as Dutch and Yiddish, were ignored and the remaining canon was largely restricted to a core of masterpieces within the favored few national traditions. As the comparatist Horst Rüdiger asserted in 1971, world literature should not be "a UN General Assembly, in which the voices of the great powers count no more than those of the political provinces. It is the *liber aureus* of aesthetically successful and historically effective works in all languages" (*Zur Theorie der vergleichenden Literaturwissenschaft,* 4). Rüdiger was reacting against incipient efforts to broaden the scope of the field. A decade earlier, for instance, Werner Friederich, founder of the *Yearbook of Comparative and General Literature,* had roundly criticized the use of so broad a term as "world literature" for so narrow a geographical range of material:

> Apart from the fact that such a presumptuous term makes for
> shallowness and partisanship which should not be tolerated in a
> good university, it is simply bad public relations to use this term
> and to offend more than half of humanity. . . . Sometimes, in
> flippant moments, I think we should call our programs NATO
> Literatures—yet even that would be extravagant, for we do not

usually deal with more than one fourth of the 15 NATO-Nations. ("On the Integrity of Our Planning," 14–15)

In the decades since then, Friederich's position has more and more won out against Rüdiger's, and today there are many advantages to widening our field of vision beyond the great books of the great powers. Yet in so doing, we have to find new ways of assessing and working with texts that now range from the earliest Sumerian poetry to the most recent fictional experiments of the Tibetan postmodernists (there is now such a category) Jamyang Norbu and Zhaxi Dawa. The problem becomes acute if we also want to continue to give substantial attention to the older canons of classics and masterpieces. How can we have it all? World literature may in some sense exist as an ideal order, a hypothetical mental construct, but in practice it is experienced as what is available to read, in classrooms and on bookstore shelves, on course syllabi and in anthologies for students and general readers, and questions of scale and of coherence come to the fore in such practical contexts.

It isn't clear just what framework can contain Kalidasa's poetry, the epic of Son-Jara, and Dante's *Commedia*. Even if we confine attention to a single genre like lyric poetry, what cultural context needs to be provided— and what cultural context *can* feasibly be provided—for nonspecialists to have meaningful encounters with Petrarchan sonnets, Japanese *renga,* and Mozarabic *kharjas*? Finally, if we do somehow devise ways to compare such disparate works, we will inevitably be reading them mostly in translation, thereby forswearing an intimate encounter with the original works in their original language. Why settle for reading at a cultural and linguistic remove when we can spend our limited time on works from our own language and immediate tradition?

We encounter these issues already with regard to Western literature, even before we think of venturing more widely around the globe. A true purist may regard material in translation as unavailable for serious study: we should only focus on works that we can read in our native tongue, or at most in the few languages that we may happen to know intimately. This was the stance of no less a figure than Roland Barthes. He had no interest in engaging literature in translation, and though his theoretical framework was resolutely international, he confined his literary discussions almost entirely to French works. In his self-portrait, *Roland Barthes by Roland Barthes,* he describes himself as having "little enjoyment of, or talent for, foreign languages. . . . little taste for foreign literature, constant pessimism with regard to translation, confusion when confronted by questions of translators, since so often they appear to be ignorant of precisely what I regard as the very meaning of a word: the connotation" (115). Fortunately for Barthes's large international audience, his translators have repeatedly succeeded in surmounting his confusion and their own ignorance; the poetic prose of *Roland Barthes par Roland Barthes* itself has been luminously translated by the noted poet and translator Richard Howard. Even so, whether in the original languages or in translation, no one reader can even begin to encompass the literatures of the major Western European and American traditions. How are we to make choices? How can we make our inevitably selective choices cohere?

What a consciousness of sin is to the saint, an awareness of ignorance is to the scholar. The most ambitious readers have been acutely aware of how little they have managed to read. In his magisterial study *Mimesis: The Representation of Reality in Western Literature,* Erich Auerbach ranged from Homer and the Bible up to Proust and Virginia Woolf, treating texts in classical and medieval Latin, old and modern French, Italian, German, Spanish, and English: yet he began his book with an epigraph (from Andrew Marvell) expressing regret for everything he had left out: "Had we but world enough and time . . . ." The time is long past when a scholar could aspire to know "everything," like Erasmus, or even to know everything *worth* knowing, like the Victorian classicist Benjamin Jowett. A couplet that circulated when Jowett was master of Balliol College, Oxford, declared that

> Mr. Jowett is master of this college;
> What Jowett don't know, ain't knowledge.

No such claim would be made of any scholar today. At the very most, a particularly voracious reader may come close to mastering the full range of a single national literature. Harold Bloom is famous for being able to quote from memory virtually any significant poem ever written in English; in the case of C. S. Lewis, who had a similar gift, it became a sort of parlor game for visitors to try and stump him by challenging him with the most outrageously obscure old works they could think of. In one such incident, a visiting Rhodes Scholar pulled down from Lewis's shelves *The Siege of Thebes,* a sixteen-thousand-line epic by the fifteenth-century poet John Lydgate, and read a passage at random. "'Stop!' shouted Lewis, as he raised his eyes toward the ceiling and continued the passage from memory. . . . The American closed the book slowly and sat down" (Griffin, *Clive Staples Lewis,* 360). Lacking such total recall, most literary scholars today specialize in some manageable slice of literature, working within definite boundaries of language and of period.

It is harder still to move beyond the traditional Euro-American sphere. In the seventies, literary theory seemed to many comparatists to provide the necessary basis for work across cultures, and it was mostly people hostile to Continental theory who objected to its application outside the West. Now, though, it is often the most theoretically engaged scholars who question the global uses of Euro-American theory. As Jonathan Culler has said, "The intertextual nature of meaning . . . makes literary study essentially, fundamentally comparative, but it also produces a situation in which comparability depends upon a cultural system, a general field that underwrites comparisons. . . . The more sophisticated one's understanding of discourse, the harder it is to compare Western and non-Western texts" ("Comparability," 268). Worse yet, non-Western traditions may be almost impossible for Westerners to assess without falling into neocolonial patterns of projection and outright appropriation. Now we are likely to find ourselves dealing with dramatic disparities of power and the vexed legacies of colonialism. Either the foreign tradition is reduced to an exotic version of our own, or else an opening out to the wider world may degenerate into a search for new markets, a mining of literary raw materials to be brought back for theoretical processing through the academic factories of Europe and the United States. The unequal linkages thus established may enrich Western culture but depress the variety and originality of the local literary cultures elsewhere.

A number of critics have argued that the United States in particular has been maintaining a dramatically uneven balance of literary trade. Lawrence Venuti, for instance, has pointed out that translations often reinforce American stereotypes of foreign cultures, and that a very uneven pattern of the production of translations currently does much more to spread American culture abroad than to bring the world home to America. In 1987, he notes, Brazilian publishers brought out over fifteen hundred translations of English-language books, while only *fourteen* translations of Brazilian literature were issued in England or the United States. British and American publishers rely on sales of foreign rights for an increasing share of their profits, yet foreign publishers are not reaping a comparable benefit in return. As Venuti says, "Quite simply, a lot of money is made from translating English, but little is invested into translating into it" (*The Scandals of Translation*, 160–61).

Increasingly, globalization figures not only in scholarly discussions but in literary works themselves. The cultural politics of globalization was already the subject of a remarkable novel published a quarter of a century ago, *Giambatista Viko; ou, Le Viol du discours africain* (1975), by the Zairean/

Congolese writer Mbwil a M. Ngal. Ngal's own life has spanned the globe: having completed college in what was then Zaire, he earned a doctorate in Fribourg, Switzerland, with a thesis on Aimé Césaire; he then taught at various universities in Africa and Europe (including the Sorbonne) and later in Canada. The hero of his novel is not the eighteenth-century Italian philosopher of similar name but rather an African intellectual. Viko has been struggling for two years with writer's block as he attempts to write the great African novel, a work that will infuse the imported European form of the novel with the riches of traditional African orality. Professor at an unnamed West African university, Viko belongs to an Institute of African Studies that is riven between rootless cosmopolitans who worship Europe and upholders of "africanolâtrie" who reject European culture out of hand (31). Viko is eager to finish his novel so that he can be invited to join the Club of Rome, but instead of actually writing his book, he spends his time on the phone with friends and sycophants, scheming against his Africanist colleagues, debating the merits of Marxist literary theory, and looking for ways to pad his résumé.

Having his work appear in the right languages is an important part of his plans. As he tells his faithful sidekick and confidant Niaiseux, "No intellectual today can do without a knowledge of several international languages. Knowing English—not to mention French, that goes without saying—and Spanish, Russian, that's good. Japanese, better yet. Chinese is ten times better—key to the future, which belongs to Asia, especially China. The Occidentals are terribly afraid of the yellow peril. . . . Translations! That would be a way to lengthen the list of my publications" (45). Not that Viko knows Japanese or Chinese himself; but he plans to ask his visiting colleagues Sing-chiang Chu and Hitachi Huyafusiayama to translate some of his articles. He hopes to get them published with the translators' names suppressed, so as to give the impression that he has done his own translations. Marxist that he is, Viko has a passing qualm about the ethics of exploiting his colleagues' labor in this way, but his friend Niaiseux reassures him that "deontologically speaking, it isn't intellectual dishonesty at all" but simple collegiality (45).

Viko knows that he must produce a major work if he is to achieve his goal of becoming "le Napoléon des lettres africaines" (39), but he knows it is no simple matter to join African orality with European literacy. For all his vanity and self-promotion, Viko is a shrewd observer of the scene around him; he sees "africanolâtrie," for example, as a particularly subtle form of Westernization. For his part, he cannot decide how to proceed with his writing: "As far as I'm concerned, my choice is clear. More precisely, I don't have one at all. A humanist culture—Greco-Roman—seasoned with the erudition that everyone grants me! Where would you have me find a place for it? I believe neither in métissage nor in the integration of cultures. Juxtaposition? Perhaps! Who could marry Cartesian logic to Bantu logic?" (32). Viko recalls the *New Science* of his namesake, Giambattista Vico, whose ambitious cultural history asserted that all writing began in the poetic cries of primitive people. Contemplating his own project, Viko waxes eloquent:

> It would take a *Scienza nuova* to rediscover the spiritual forces
> that our technological universe has lost and which have been
> preserved by the oral societies dismissively called primitive. . . .
> An acoustic space, or more precisely an audio-visual one. That
> of the storyteller! What undefined riches! What freedom in the
> story's unfolding! None of the novel's rigidity! Novelistic space—
> veritable circle of hell! I dream of a novel on the model of the
> tale. (13)

As he develops his ideas in conversation with his friends, Viko reaches the point of readiness to write his great book, using a revolutionary style: "A style that will cross-breed many contradictory tendencies: the incantatory, the learned, the moving, the oracular. . . . abrupt opacities here, profound transparencies there. . . . Punctuation? Don't even mention it!" (45–46).

But then disaster strikes. The Afrocentrists gain the upper hand at the institute, and they go public with a whole series of accusations against him: of having articles ghostwritten by assistants; of "writing" poems that are nothing but plagiarisms of Catullus; of sexual indiscretions with a visiting Italian structuralist; of excluding Africans from the institute; and above all, of betraying Africa by plotting to prostitute the mysteries of oral culture for Western exploitation (the *viol*, or rape, of African discourse referred to in the novel's subtitle). Aroused to action, a consortium of tribal leaders kidnaps Viko and Niaiseux and brings them to trial. Dressed in a goat skin, silver bracelets on his arms and a crown of pearls and parrot feathers on his head, an imposing native elder announces the charges against them, speaking through an intermediary:

> Dogs and sons of dogs! My dignity, my honor forbid me to
> address you directly. Your crime is immeasurable. You will pay
> for it with the last drop of your blood. . . . The fundamental
> reason that keeps me from addressing you directly is that our
> universes—speech and writing—have nothing in common. You
> have impiously set an abyss between yourselves and us. You have

chosen the universe of the book—the space of inscription—
abandoning that which nourished your childhood, fed your
dreams, and furnished your subconscious. . . . The gravity of your
impiety resides in your attempt to desacralize orality. You have
wanted to reappropriate the freedom, the space, the time of the
storyteller; to introduce them into novelistic discourse. An
atheist's attempt, destitute of faith! (89)

Part of the comedy of this scene, of course, lies in the strongly Westernized
quality of the elder's own discourse, which begins in Enlightenment ca-
dences that Rousseau's noble savages might have used and then slides into
terms borrowed from cutting-edge French philosophy. To be sure, these
terms may or may not have been used by the goatskin-clad elder himself; his
views are conveyed by his translator, "an elegantly dressed young gentleman"
(88) who accompanies him. We actually have no direct access to the elder's
own speech; it reaches us, in Ngal's novel, thoroughly imbued with the very
discourse it rejects.

Ngal's account is unsparing of the elders' reflexive conservatism
and their repressive use of violence. They treat Niaiseux with brutal indifference, having him beaten so severely that several of his teeth fall on the
floor; noticing this, the elders order Niaiseux to pick them up. A trial ensues,
in which a series of elders harangue Viko, condemning him unheard. In a
concession to modernity, the elders do allow speeches to be made by some
of their own sons, up-and-coming young technocrats who try to please both
sides at once but who constantly bicker among themselves; they are far less
interested in Viko than in displaying how much they've learned at their respective Western universities. In the end, the elders relent to the extent of
not imposing a death sentence. Instead, they condemn Viko and Niaiseux to
spend their lives wandering through Africa's villages, reconnecting themselves to orality and to their lost spiritual values. These wanderings form the
subject of a sequel, entitled *L'Errance* (1979).

An extraordinary dissection of problems of communication and
identity in a globalizing world, *Giambatista Viko* can be seen as a path-
breaking work both of and *about* world literature in a world of unequal
power relations, where vanity, self-defensiveness, and a will to power pervade every group. As such, Ngal's novel gave no comfort to any side in the
decolonization debates of the seventies and eighties, and it has been almost
entirely neglected by scholars as well as general readers: the *MLA International Bibliography* lists a grand total of three published articles on Ngal in

the twenty-five years since it was published.[1] Though this bibliography is admittedly light on African sources, *Giambatista Viko* has been published in Paris since 1984, when it was reissued by Hatier, which has offices as well in Switzerland, Belgium, Canada, and half a dozen francophone African and Caribbean countries. Yet the book seems to have attracted very little attention outside the Democratic Republic of Congo, if even there.

So far as I know, *Giambatista Viko* has never been translated, and even the three articles cited in the MLA bibliography are all written in French. And yet none of these articles appeared in France itself: two were published in Canada, one in South Africa. Viko thinks of himself as virtually French ("I dream of the day when I will find myself once again in Paris. Everything in me yearns, like Lucien de Rubempré, for Paris" [51]), but his story hasn't found much of a footing there. A brilliant fictive example of "where French theory has gone and is going as it defines itself beyond the hexagon. . . . in postcolonial and postnational critiques of identity," to recall Emily Apter's theme in *Continental Drift* (x), Ngal's novel has yet to achieve any resonance within the hexagon itself. All too appropriately, Hatier's Paris offices have served largely as a transit point for an import-export trade in *le viol du discours africain*.

The tale of Viko's tale is a sobering reminder that foreign works have difficulty entering a new arena if they don't conform to the receiving country's image of what the foreign culture should be, and the difficulties become all the greater if a work doesn't seem useful in meeting local needs abroad. These needs can be purely individual, as people take up works, find them compelling or not, quickly forget them, or continue to think about them and to recommend them to friends. Such individual encounters, however, are profoundly mediated by what is made available to read at any given time: what is translated, published, reviewed, stocked in stores, or assigned in courses. No doubt just because our own literary tradition is comparatively brief, Americans have often given particular prominence to world literature as an important component in education and self-improvement; publishers, schools, and libraries have striven to meet this need, shaping and reinforcing a canon of world literature in the process.

[1] I myself only heard of this novel through a brief reference in a valuable article by Wlad Godzich, "Emergent Literature and the Field of Comparative Literature." Godzich's theme is the blindness of comparative studies to the literatures of many smaller countries, which challenge the dimensions of a field hitherto organized around the literature of a few great powers.

In tracing the contemporary shift from a focus on the Old World to a broader picture of the whole world, it is important to understand the range of purposes the earlier Europe-based canon served. Our present constructions of world literature don't so much represent a dramatic break with the past as a set of expansive variations on century-old themes. A good place to begin to see how the issues were framed on the eve of the twentieth century is with the front portico to the opulent and exuberantly democratic Library of Congress, completed in 1897. When the building was being planned, the Librarian of Congress, Ainsworth Rand Spofford, selected nine figures to be portrayed in busts above the library's main entrance. Benjamin Franklin, in the center, is flanked on the left by Demosthenes, Emerson, Irving, and Goethe, and on the right by Macaulay, Hawthorne, Scott, and an indomitable Dante, somewhat incongruously surmounted by a naked *putto* (figure 8). A living pantheon of founders of Western culture, or an elephant's graveyard of dead white males?

On a second look, what is most remarkable about this grouping is its modernity: in a sharp departure from the still common classical emphasis, Spofford included only a single ancient figure, Demosthenes, among his nine male Muses. Indeed, six of the nine were people active in the nineteenth century itself. The eighteenth century was represented only by Franklin and the young Goethe, and all previous history only by Dante and Demosthenes. Many scholars of Spofford's day would have seen Spofford's list as an affront to past culture, with modern American lightweights (as they would have conceived them) like Irving and Hawthorne edging out European masters like Homer and Milton.

Spofford's choices, however, were strategic: he wished his library to connect America and Europe, past and present, literature and politics, through an obviously incomplete but infinitely expandable grouping, selected to blend classical authority and popular appeal. No "book and school of the ages" (as Harold Bloom has subtitled his book *The Western Canon*), the Library of Congress tableau was arranged with a modern American audience in mind. According to a book on the library's iconography, Spofford also had a less public principle of organization: faced with many more candidates than the portal could accommodate, he simply chose *his favorite authors* for his tableau (Cole, *On These Walls*, 22). From the start, constructions of world literature have always been motivated by a mixture of public concern and private pleasure.

By the turn of the century, publishers began to put together sets of great books, but different collections took very different approaches, reflecting the editors' profoundly different attitudes both toward the past ma-

Figure 8. Dante and friend

terial and toward the present audience. Here I will look at a pair of ambitious multivolume anthologies that were prepared in the first decade of the century: *The Best of the World's Classics*, in ten volumes, published in 1909 by Funk and Wagnalls under the editorship of Senator Henry Cabot Lodge; and the still more ambitious fifty-volume series *The Harvard Classics*, published just a year later by P. F. Collier and Son, under the general editorship of Harvard's president, Charles W. Eliot. In many ways, these anthologies are similar in intent: both are designed for a general-interest market and appear to have been projects developed by their publishers, who then sought out a prominent figure to serve as the (fairly nominal) overall editor; the actual work in each case was done by subordinates. Both anthologies reflect the shift of attention away from classical studies toward modern culture and the rapid expansion in higher education then under way. All sorts of new works were now being taught on campus, and the publishers clearly saw an opportunity to market them to a wider public as well, people who had heard of these changes but had not had the opportunity to experience them: the romance of higher education was taking hold in America, yet few people could afford to go to college. As Eliot put it, Colliers invited him "to make such a selection as any intellectually ambitious American family might use to advantage, even if their early opportunities of education had been scanty" (*The Harvard Classics*, 50:1). Henry Cabot Lodge anticipates a similar audience, and he affirms that his series will offer his readers both intellectual and moral benefits:

> To that larger public whose lives are not spent among books and
> libraries, and for whose delectation such a collection as this is
> primarily intended, these volumes rightly read at odd times, in
> idle moments, in out-of-the-way places, on the ship or the train,
> offer much. They will bring the reader in contact with many of
> the greatest intellects of all time. . . . There is no man who will not
> be the better, for the moment at least, by reading what Cicero says
> about old age, Seneca about death, and Socrates about love, to go
> no further for examples than to
>
> > "The glory that was Greece,
> > And the grandeur that was Rome."
>
> (1:xiv–xv)

Both Eliot and Lodge intend their anthologies to assist in the formation of a new and better American citizen—more refined, thoughtful, self-aware and self-controlled, better able to participate intelligently in public debate—and yet their anthologies show a fundamental difference in the ways they wish to orient their readers toward the world. This difference, indeed, was already signaled by the publishers' respective choices for their general editors (a university president versus a senator), and this difference well illustrates John Guillory's point that *who* reads, and why, matters as much as what specific texts are read as canonical (*Cultural Capital*, 18).[2]

Writing from his university setting, Eliot takes a cosmopolitan, Arnoldian view, arguing that the purpose of world literature is to broaden the reader's horizons through the encounter with cultural difference: "The sentiments and opinions these authors express are frequently not acceptable to present-day readers, who have to be often saying to themselves: 'This is not true, or not correct, or not in accordance with our beliefs.' It is, however, precisely this encounter with the mental states of other generations which enlarges the outlook and sympathies of the cultivated man, and persuades him of the upward tendency of the human race" (50:5). Generous though it is, this formulation leaves unquestioned the superiority of present perspectives, but Eliot went a step further in a preface to the second edition of the series, in 1917, arguing for an irreducible and desirable global diversity: "From these volumes, the thorough reader may learn valuable lessons in comparative literature. He can see how various the contributions of the different languages and epochs have been; and he will inevitably come to the conclusion that striking national differences in this respect ought in the interest of mankind to be perpetuated and developed, and not obliterated, averaged, or harrowed down" (50:14). Eliot is already posing a central question of today's debates over globalization: can expanding communication and interconnection open up a world of rich diversity, or will the result be a spreading *loss* of minority cultures and their languages, a "harrowing down" that would leave only a commercialized global monoculture?

Henry Cabot Lodge's perspective was dramatically different. One of the leading members of the United States Senate at the time he wrote his

---

[2] This is not to say that *all* that matters is how works are read. Guillory's book is in part an entry in the running debate between content-oriented people like Paul Lauter, who argue for an inclusive canon, and theorists who have emphasized instead the importance of sophisticated and critical reading of established works. Granting Guillory's point that a broadened canon doesn't automatically "represent" excluded minorities in a meaningful way, I nonetheless agree with Lauter that our readings, as well as our views of the world, can be greatly enriched if we broaden our base of material. (See Lauter, "Canon Theory and Emergent Practice.") Guillory's own discussion could have benefited from a wider literary frame: though he notes that the Western canon is partly defined against what lies beyond, it is remarkable that in almost four hundred closely argued pages on "the problem of literary canon formation" (Guillory's subtitle) he never has occasion to mention a single non-Western author or work by name.

preface, he was deeply concerned that the United States not overextend it-self on the world stage. Though he supported American involvement in the First World War, he bitterly opposed Woodrow Wilson's proposal for the League of Nations. Lodge organized and led the opposition that doomed American acceptance of the League and in turn destroyed Wilson's presi-dency. The attitudes that would underlie Lodge's actions in 1919 are already evident in his introduction to *The Best of the World's Classics* in 1909. Though the bulk of its contents are classical and Continental, Lodge places great weight in his introduction on the value of the anthology's English-language readings:

> The most important part of the collection is that which gives selections from those writers whose native tongue is English. No translation even of prose can ever quite reproduce its original, and as a rule can not hope to equal it. . . . it may safely be said that the soul of a language and the beauties of style which it is capable of exhibiting can only be found and studied in the productions of writers who not only think in the language in which they write, but to whom that speech is native, the inalienable birthright and heritage of their race or country. (1:xvi–xvii)

Lodge's jingoism allows him to move seamlessly from discussing the limita-tions of translation to denouncing the pretensions of immigrants ever to be full participants in their adopted culture. Where Eliot's collection is meant to inspire a cosmopolitan and even relativistic regard for the variety of the world's cultures, Lodge is promoting a nativist public discourse, for which an elevated English style will serve as emblem and reinforcement of a uni-tary racial and cultural heritage. "No one," he says in conclusion, "can read the masterpieces of English prose and not have both lesson and responsi-bility brought home . . . and thus make them more mindful of the ineffable value to them and their children of the great language which is at once their birthright and their inheritance" (1:xxviii–xxix).

Lodge's forthright statement of his views is worth keeping in mind, as it is far from certain that we have yet cast off the comforting teleology that can organize the world's literature into a progression up through history to a satisfying conclusion on our own doorstep. Indeed, Charles Eliot's con-trasting cosmopolitanism itself admitted a nativist emphasis of its own. Lodge's series at least begins at a remove from America, with volumes on Greece and Rome. The first volume of Eliot's *Harvard Classics*, by contrast, was devoted to the writings of American "Founding Fathers": Benjamin

Franklin, John Woolman, and William Penn. Volume 2 then doubles back to Greco-Roman philosophy (Plato, Epictetus, and Marcus Aurelius), before coming forward to Milton, Bacon, and Browne (volumes 3 and 4), coming home again with Emerson (volume 5) and then going back to Britain for Robert Burns (volume 6). Burns and Milton are given such early prominence, Eliot tells us, precisely for their value to a student of democracy:

> The poems of John Milton and Robert Burns are given in full; because the works of these two very unlike poets contain social, religious, and governmental teachings of vital concern for modern democracies. Milton was the great poet of civil and religious liberty, and Burns was the great poet of democracy. The two together cover the fundamental principles of free government, education, and democratic social structure, and will serve as guides to much good reading on those subjects provided in the collection. (50:7)

As world literature was defined at the start of the twentieth century, then, cosmopolitanism itself showed elements of a higher form of nativism. Oriented as it was toward the proper training of a broad American public, literature had to be read selectively to provide an Arnoldian high seriousness. In celebrating Burns as "the great poet of democracy," Eliot clearly had little use for the full range of Burns's actual poetry, such as his famous poem "Comin' Thro' the Rye," replete (in its uncensored version) with stanzas like the following:

> Gin a body meet a body,
> Comin' thro' the grain,
> Gin a body fuck a body,
> Cunt's a body's ain.

Such poems display a lusty sexuality which was perhaps only too democratic in effect but which would hardly have provided the tone that Eliot wished to set. Burns's poem ends, in fact, by mocking the moralists who would censor his verses:

> Mony a body meets a body,
> They dare na weel avow;
> Mony a body fucks a body,
> Ye wadna think it true.[3]

---

[3] *The Merry Muses of Caledonia*, 144. Needless to say, this side of Burns's work is not represented in the *Harvard Classics'* "complete" Burns volume.

If the study of world literature in Charles Eliot's time still carried with it a strong element of Victorian earnestness, things began to change by the middle decades of the century. Popular as well as elevated literary works began to come directly into play, and the map of the world itself was beginning to shift, with America's place on the map open for reconsideration. A good index of the shape of world literature in midcentury America can be found in a widely used reference work, Frank Magill's *Masterpieces of World Literature in Digest Form* (also known as *Masterplots*). Written by a team of experts under Magill's direction, this work was first published in 1949, giving summaries and brief analyses of 510 major works (the editors had intended to summarize 500 key works but couldn't quite decide on the final cut). Well aware that there were more works worth including, in 1955 they produced a "Second Series" with a further 500 titles; a third volume gave 500 more summaries in 1960; and a final volume, with another 500 works, appeared in 1969.

From the outset, the collection defined "the world" unhesitatingly as the Western world: "The array of literature represented in this book," Magill wrote in his preface, "is drawn from the vast reservoir of literary achievements which has been accumulating since the legendary beginnings of Western civilization. All the great literature is not here; perhaps all that is here is not great. But these stories are representative of the places and the times from which they sprang and they have helped to tint the fabric which makes up the composite imprint of our culture" (v). Of the 1,010 works discussed in the first two volumes, only 3 are non-Western: *The Thousand and One Nights, The Tale of Genji,* and the *Shakuntala* of Kalidasa (beloved of Goethe, and introduced as "the Shakespeare of India" [2:931]). In 1960, the year Friederich made his plea to broaden the term "world literature" or abandon it altogether, the third volume finally made a modest attempt to include "a few titles from the vast reservoir of Oriental literature, an area of world culture long neglected by Western readers" (3:v), and a further handful of non-Western works were added in the fourth volume. In the end, the four volumes of the series included a total of 1,008 authors; 23 in all are non-Western, or 2.7 percent of the total.

This minimal proportion shows no improvement over that of prewar works like John Macy's 1925 survey *The Story of the World's Literature.* Over five hundred pages long, Macy's book confines non-Western materials to a single fifteen-page chapter actually called "The Mysterious East." Macy does at least express regret that he doesn't have more time to unfold these mysteries: he allows that "there is no doubt much in the Chinese mind which is sympathetic with us, and probably we are making a profound mistake not to get better acquainted with it" (38). Yet when it comes right down to it, "the disproportion is to some extent justified by the magnitude of the literatures which are blood of our blood and bone of our bone" (24–25). Macy here turns to the biblical creation story to evoke an essentialist idea of culture: an American Adam needs an ethnically appropriate Eve. But timeless essences aren't Macy's only defense against the mysterious East, for modernity imposes its own demands: "The West has been thinking so fast," Macy tells us, "that we have not time for the timeless East" (25).

Magill's collection of summaries was likewise intended for readers who needed to think fast. More precisely, his book was meant for a combination of *former* and *would-be* general readers. The extensive plot summaries would help you if you wanted to recall the plot or the characters in a book you'd read some time ago; they would also be useful if you'd heard of a book and wanted to learn more about it so as to decide whether to read it. (Nowhere does Magill allow that his book might also be used by a third group: *nonreaders,* who could use the summaries to get through a quiz on material they were supposed to have read for a class.) Whereas both Charles Eliot and Henry Cabot Lodge had focused exclusively on established major authors, Magill freely mixed classics together with popular work: Arthur Conan Doyle and Pearl Buck appear as early as volume 1, along with Homer and Shakespeare—taking up places that might otherwise have been used for Ovid's *Metamorphoses* or Goethe's *Wilhelm Meister,* both of which eventually appeared, but not until volume 3.

If Magill's preface sounds a little defensive in allowing that "perhaps all that is here is not great," he may be reacting to the gentle mockery provided in an introduction to his very own volume, written by Clifton Fadiman. In soliciting this introduction from Fadiman, guiding spirit of the Book of the Month Club's editorial committee, Magill presumably anticipated a warm testimonial from a kindred spirit. This isn't quite what he got. Fadiman does approve of the project overall and stresses its crossover appeal to a wide range of users: "It should make its way at once to the shelf of the writer, publisher, editor, teacher, lecturer, after-dinner speaker, literary agent, bookseller, librarian, radio and television director or editor or producer, motion picture ditto, and of many students and general readers" (1:ix). So far, so good; but Fadiman then spends the bulk of his introduction belittling Magill's choices of popular authors:

> One finds, as is natural, titles the grounds for whose inclusion
> appear incomprehensible. . . . thus Rex Beach lies down with
> Aristophanes and Dickens with Lloyd Douglas. Grandiose

trumpery (*Ben Hur, Quo Vadis*) is here, and so is *The Magic Mountain*. . . . The editors have not tried to limit their titles to the "best," whatever that may be. The aim is not to elevate taste, nor even to instruct . . . but simply to furnish the interested reader with a useful reference tool. (1:x)

Fadiman isn't being fair here. It is, admittedly, a little disorienting to find *The Sound and the Fury* followed directly by Rex Beach's 1906 Yukon tale *The Spoilers*—"a lusty book about a raw new land filled with adventures and gamblers of all kinds. Blood and thunder leap forth from every page" (1:919). Yet Magill and his contributors are constantly instructing their readers in what to look for, showing them how to appreciate works that are unfamiliar to them, to broaden their world beyond that of current best-sellers and the standard classics taught in school. Here is their pitch for a little-read nineteenth-century French novelist, Edmond About: "Practically unknown in this country, About's novel deserves to be more widely read, for it is ingenious, clever, and witty. Edmond About, who was well-known and honored in his own country, is the equal of many French writers whom we consider great" (2:534).

This argument is interesting: it tries to extend the bounds of what "we consider great" by recourse to About's standing in his own culture in his own era, suggesting that world literature should take account of the values of the originary culture as well as the values of the receiving culture.[4] Even though he stops short of really describing About's novel *as* a "great book"— "ingenious, clever, and witty" are rather modest superlatives, after all—the writer of this entry has apparently been moved to include About because he was both "well-known" *and* "honored" by his countrymen: both a commercial success and a respected figure, his novel appropriate to read among the ranks of elite books, even if not a towering masterpiece itself.

This crossover evangelism in turn informs the collection's advocacy on behalf of the difficult, elite works it presents side by side with *A Study in Scarlet* and *Young Captain Hornblower*. Faulkner's novel, for example, is introduced as though it were a worthy companion to Rex Beach's Yukon pot-

---

[4] A subsequent entry notes the converse, that a work may have greater appeal abroad than at home: "*The Little Clay Pot* is more like Western drama than any other Sanskrit play, in structure, characterization, and tone. This similarity to Occidental drama may account for the fact that its Indian critics have been less enthusiastic than those of the Western world" (3:586)— an even-handed formulation that encourages the American reader to expect the play to be approachable, while admitting that this very approachability arises from qualities that make it uncharacteristic of Sanskrit drama in general.

boiler: "Beneath its involved and difficult techniques, *The Sound and the Fury* is a compelling study of an old Southern family gone to seed. The members of the Compson family are victims of lust, incest, suicide" (1:916). Yet once it has hooked the reader with its dramatic lead-in, the Faulkner entry gives a lucid exposition that devotes as much attention to the novel's difficult techniques as to its melodramatic plot, and it closes by encouraging the reader to persevere to the novel's end, for "only in the last two parts does the story fall into a clear pattern. Then the pieces of the puzzle begin to fit into place and the reader finds that he is experiencing stark tragedy and horrible reality" (1:917).

Encompassing both popular and elite literature from the start, Magill's collection shows in its later series the steady expansion of the category of "literature" as the century progressed. While the first two volumes focus almost exclusively on novels, drama, and narrative poetry, the Third Series in 1960 acknowledges "the broadening of categories" then under way (3:v). The first two volumes had included a few memoirs and autobiographies, such as Dana's *Two Years Before the Mast* and *The Travels of Marco Polo*, but volume 3 offers a considerably wider range of literary nonfiction: Caesar's *Commentaries*, Abelard's *Historia Calamitatum*, Darwin's *Origin of Species*. The fourth volume went farther still in 1969, including anthropological and psychological writers—Boas, Freud—and even literary criticism (I. A. Richards).

Magill's collection gives a good picture of the shape of world literature in postwar America: a largely Euro-American world, opened a little to some "major" non-Western cultures by the sixties, and increasingly encompassing a range of literary works that would not have been classified as literature a few decades earlier. Intended for a general readership, this account of world literature included popular as well as elite work, even as it presented a populist vision of the accessibility of elite masterpieces.

As modest as were Magill's non-Western ventures in the fifties and sixties, his 2.7 percent went beyond what was typically found in college "World Lit" courses. With academic literary study sharply divided by language and by region, most world literature courses through the 1980s continued to have an exclusively European or Euro-American focus. Consider *The Norton Anthology of World Masterpieces,* probably the most widely used anthology in world literature courses around the country from its appearance in 1956 to the present. As recently as the fifth edition of 1985, the Norton's "World" meant Western Europe and the United States. Finally, the sixth edition of 1992 added a handful of non-Western authors in a newly expanded concluding section called "Contemporary Explorations."

In contrast to Magill's collection, the *Norton Anthology* focused from the start on masterworks. The field of world literature was represented by only seventy-three authors (rather than Magill's 1,008), and almost all of these writers came from the traditional literary "great powers": Greece, Italy, France, Germany, England, and the United States. Norton's canon, unlike Magill's, was also exclusively male: though the anthology found room for various men of less than major world reputation (such as Aleksander Blok and the little-known Portuguese writer Raul Brandão), not a single woman author was to be found within the book's 2,400 pages. Again in the second edition of 1965, with more authors and over 3,300 pages, no women writers at all appear. Finally, the third edition of 1976 succeeded in finding room for two pages of Sappho.

Norton's masterpiece orientation—or occidentation—gave pride of place to traditionally major figures within the great-power canon: in the 1976 edition, for example, one-third of the anthology's 102 authors took up three-quarters of the anthology. The selections, moreover, were almost entirely literature in the strict sense of poetry, plays, and fiction, plus some examples of literary essays and autobiography (Montaigne; Augustine's and Rousseau's *Confessions*). A similar focus and balance were found in the other most often assigned anthology, Wilkie and Hurt's *Literature of the Western World*—whose title at least had the good grace to admit its bias openly.

The picture has changed dramatically since the early nineties. World literature anthologies now typically show a far wider geographical and literary range, usually with extensive selections from non-Western literatures, and some have jettisoned the "masterpiece" approach in favor of briefer selections from a wider range of writers. Thus *The HarperCollins World Reader* (1994) included no fewer than 475 writers and attempted to give something approaching proportionate representation to all the world's major literary traditions, and even some serious attention to many less extensive traditions as well. This resulted in greatly shortened selections from Western figures like Homer and Dante, making room for the inclusion of work not only from China, Japan, and India but also from Vietnam, Singapore, and Micronesia, among many other areas. Literature itself has become an increasingly fluid category: the HarperCollins text includes Confucius, Boethius, and the journal of Christopher Columbus, and it has extensive and very interesting sections on African oral epic and on Native American orature, works that are not even literature in the root sense of a written text.

At the same time that the HarperCollins anthology was in preparation, the Norton anthology awoke from its European slumber and came out in an "Expanded Edition" in 1995, adding two thousand pages of non-

Western material to its four thousand Western pages. While the Norton retained its core of "masterpieces"—including the entire texts of the *Odyssey,* the *Inferno, Candide,* and the first part of *Faust*—it added many works that don't fit the older masterpiece model at all. The section on the twentieth century, for instance, newly edited by Sarah Lawall, begins with a Navajo "Night Chant," followed by selections from Sigmund Freud (another example of the opening up of "literature" beyond its traditional boundaries) before moving on to canonical authors like Yeats, Mann, and Woolf. One edition later, the book's title changed to accommodate its new literary range; with Sarah Lawall as its new general editor, it dropped "Masterpieces" to become *The Norton Anthology of World Literature* (second edition, 2002). Whereas Maynard Mack had been squarely located within English studies and closely associated with the Yale New Criticism, Lawall is a comparatist who works on European literature and theory, with an active interest in the world beyond the West. Even before the Expanded Edition appeared, she had been involved in rethinking the curricular shape of world literature, and in a wide-ranging introduction to an edited volume, *Reading World Literature* (1994), she was openly critical of existing arrangements:

> the variety and complexity of theories devised to account for the presence (or absence) of "world" in the text have had little impact on the most visible example of the study of world literature: its solidly established presence in the academic curriculum. . . . Efforts to rethink the study of world literature will continue, nevertheless, as long as there is a discrepancy between the lively expectations generated by the term "world" and the pinched reality elicited by conventional approaches. (45)

Long satisfied to concentrate on a well-known canon of European masterpieces, Norton was ready to try new approaches. During the same period, even Wilkie and Hurt's explicitly Western two-volume anthology expanded its "West" to include a number of Arabic selections (the Koran, *The 1001 Nights*), and in 1999 their publisher, Prentice-Hall, introduced a "companion volume" edited by Willis and Tony Barnstone, called *Literatures of Asia, Africa, and Latin America.*[5]

All these new developments testify to the excitement surrounding the widening of the literary field, as the focus of world literature enlarges

[5] On the back cover, apparently wishing to reassure us that this collection of regions can be read as a coherent whole, the publisher describes the anthology as presenting "an enormous province of literature."

from the Old World toward the whole world, and from literature strictly defined as poetry, drama, and fiction to the literary in general. Yet all of these anthologies reveal the perplexities involved in our rapidly shifting situation. What, really, does belong in such a collection, and how should all these new materials be ordered and presented? The anthologies just mentioned have taken very different approaches to the problem, and while each offers a wealth of new material, none of them has found a really effective presentation for all these riches. The Barnstones' *Literatures of Asia, Africa, and Latin America* works rather awkwardly as a supplement to Wilkie and Hurt's *Literature of the Western World,* edited as it is by different people, with a different organizational structure, and with the Western volumes not revised to take account of their new "companion." *The HarperCollins World Reader* proceeds essentially by exploding the "old world," making room for a vivid gallery of snapshots of the "whole world," yet the result is fragmentary, inconsistent, a disorienting series of abrupt leaps from one brief selection to another: it is hard to get much from two and a half pages of Augustine or five pages of Cervantes.

By contrast, in its pre-twentieth-century sections the "expanded" Norton of 1995 layered its non-Western material onto a largely unchanged European core, in ways that often seem tokenistic and incoherent. Thus, the expanded edition introduced the ambitiously titled section "Native America and Europe in the New World" to follow their traditional five-hundred-page section on the European Renaissance—but (in 2002 as in 1995) this New World section is only thirty-two pages long, consisting of a few Aztec poems and selections from the Mayan *Popol Vuh;* neither the Spanish explorers nor native responses to the Europeans are represented. Similarly, a new section, "Urdu Poetry in North India," has been inserted in between the long sections devoted to European Romanticism and European realism and symbolism—but it consists of a slender ten pages' worth of ghazals by a single poet, Ghalib. Oddly out of place amid almost seven hundred pages of European literature, the North Indian section is in one sense quite clearly put *in* its place by the seventy-to-one ratio between the space allotted here to Europe and the space allotted to the Indian subcontinent.

Departing from the often highly skewed regional divisions of the earlier sections, the twentieth-century section gives up regional divisions altogether and goes global, with a much fuller proportion of non-Western to Western works. Its basic organizing principle, though, is simply chronological, by author's date of birth. In the 1995 edition, this arrangement placed six pages of Inuit Songs in between Kafka and D. H. Lawrence—giving a new meaning, perhaps, to the term "Eskimo Pie" but offering little foothold for reader or teacher. The new edition of 2002 has reshuffled the deck somewhat, giving the Inuit some company by moving up a few pages of Zuni ritual poetry that had appeared later in the section. The Zuni now come in between Kafka and the Inuit, who are now followed by Tanizaki (Lawrence having been dropped) and then T. S. Eliot. The old march of Western masterpieces is gone, but it's not at all clear what forms of organization are going to take its place.

If the house of world literature became a little unstable as its walls fell away, a new set of problems is emerging now that the floor has begun to drop out as well. Western literature traditionally relied on a well-defined double origin in Athens and Jerusalem. Homer and Plato, the Yahwist and Isaiah could reasonably be taken as starting points when next to nothing was known of the cultures that preceded them. The explosion of knowledge concerning the ancient Near East during the past century and a half, however, has given us a very different landscape, and anthologies are beginning to reflect this. The Norton *World Masterpieces,* for instance, had traditionally begun the section "Masterpieces of the Ancient World" with a bit of Bible before getting down to business in Greece and Rome, but the expanded edition introduced a new opening section called "The Invention of Writing and the Earliest Literatures." This section begins with *The Epic of Gilgamesh* and a judicious selection of ancient Egyptian poetry before going on to readings from Genesis, Job, the Psalms, and the Prophets. This section now reaches a millennium and a half farther back in time than previously, as well as farther east and south than ever before.

A laudable expansion; yet the editors don't quite know what to do with all this new antiquity. As they confess in their introduction to *The Epic of Gilgamesh*:

> A great lost work like *Gilgamesh* poses particular problems of understanding beyond those posed by the discovery of a lost masterpiece by a known author or of a known time. The meaning of a work of literature is partly contextual—it is established by the culture that produced that work. Yet the whole context of *Gilgamesh* was lost along with the text. The names of the gods and humans who people the epic, the cities and lands in which they lived, and the whole of their history vanished for thousands of years from common memory. . . . That strangeness has diminished each year as more tablets have been discovered and translated and as our understanding of the languages and cultures of the ancient Middle East has increased, but what we know is

still relatively slight compared with what we know of the cultures that succeeded them. Today the names of Ulysses and Achilles and the gods and goddesses of Mount Olympus are familiar even to many who have not read Homer. The names of Gilgamesh, Enkidu, Utnapishtim, Enlil, and Eanna are virtually unknown outside the poem itself. (1:10)

The end of this paragraph forgets what the middle knows: we now have a wealth of information about the culture that produced the epic, and many recovered texts concern great gods like Enlil and Ishtar.[6] The general reader may know little of them, but then again the average college freshman, the anthology's most common reader, has little prior knowledge of Hera, say, or even Achilles: the anthology's extensive introductions and notes are designed to supply the cultural context in a way that general readers can absorb. Further, it is simply not true that the ancient Near East is an entirely separate world, unconnected to classical culture and the Olympian gods: the major Near Eastern gods all have cousins on Olympus. Moreover, though the oldest stories of Gilgamesh antedate Homer, Sîn-liqe-unninni created the standard form of *Gilgamesh* in around 1200 B.C.E., at just the time when Homeric oral epic was beginning to develop among the Greek-speaking communities of Asia Minor and the Peloponnesus. *Gilgamesh* then circulated around the Near East—including the Hittite Empire in Asia Minor, a crucial link to the Greek world—and the story was retold in Greek in the fourth century B.C.E. by the Babylonian historian Berossus. The epic continued to circulate in the original as well; a copy has been found that was made in around 130 B.C.E. by a temple trainee named Bel-ahhe-usur.

The Norton editors sever this temporal continuity throughout their introduction. They begin by incorrectly dating the epic to "ca. 2500—1500 B.C.," a range that takes us from the era when the early Sumerian poems of Bilgames were composed (long before the epic itself was) and leaves off in the Old Babylonian period, some three centuries before Sîn-liqe-unninni created the standard form of the epic. Describing *Gilgamesh* as "a poem of unparalleled antiquity," they claim that "then, at a time when the civilizations of the Hebrews, Greeks, and Romans had only just developed beyond

---

[6] This introduction is reprinted unchanged in the 2002 edition. It is a little puzzling that the Norton editors cite Eanna as an example of a vanished name, as this is not a major figure whose Greek equivalent would be known to readers of Homer today: it is simply the name of a temple in Uruk. We no more need a prior knowledge of this name than we would need to come to Homer knowing the name of Agamemnon's horse. Possibly the editors were conflating Ea, god of the ocean, and Inanna, Sumerian goddess of love?

their infancy, *Gilgamesh* vanished from memory" (1:10). Having themselves performed this vanishing act on the epic, the editors are freed from any necessity to set *Gilgamesh* into an active relation with its own cultural traditions or with the classical texts that follow in "Ancient Greece and the Formation of the Western Mind." Instead, they head for the high ground of universal truth. On this plane the poem's antiquity can remain unexamined because it turns into a magical protomodernity: "The story of Gilgamesh and his companion, Enkidu, speaks to contemporary readers with astonishing immediacy. . . . It is both humbling and thrilling to hear so familiar a voice from so vast a distance" (1:10,12). At once amazingly ancient and astonishingly immediate, this *Gilgamesh* is notably unconnected to anything in between.

From Henry Cabot Lodge and Charles Eliot to the HarperCollins and Norton anthologies, world literature has oscillated between extremes of assimilation and discontinuity: either the earlier and distant works reflect a consciousness *just like ours,* or they are unutterably alien, curiosities whose foreignness finally tells us nothing and can only reinforce our sense of separate identity. But why should we have to choose between a self-centered construction of the world and a radically decentered one? Instead, we need more of an elliptical approach, to use the image of the geometric figure that is generated from two foci at once. We never truly cease to be ourselves as we read, and our present concerns and modes of reading will always provide one focus of our understanding, but the literature of other times and eras presents us with another focus as well, and we read in the field of force generated between these two foci.

The past itself may never change, but our vision of it does: the ellipse can shift significantly as its modern focus moves. Consider the changing fortunes of Dante, Goethe, and Shakespeare, the trio whom Joyce considered to be his prime rivals for European eminence, and whom he accordingly amalgamated into "that primed favorite continental poet, Daunty, Gouty and Shopkeeper" (*Finnegans Wake,* 539). Shakespeare looked less canonical in his own day than his classicist contemporary Ben Jonson, and his plays were little read for more than a century after his death. Dante, so daunting to Joyce and central in most twentieth-century accounts of the Western tradition, had been virtually ignored for centuries until he was finally rediscovered in the Romantic era. Goethe's fortunes ebbed and flowed in his own time and may be ebbing again now; as Harold Bloom remarks, "Of all the strongest Western writers, Goethe now seems the least available to our sensibility. . . . Goethe is no longer our ancestor, as he was Emerson's and Carlyle's" (*The Western Canon,* 190). If Bloom is right, then Goethe may be receding to an increasingly nominal place in the pantheon.

Within a given writer's oeuvre as well, great variability can be seen over time. To take the example of Goethe, his *Faust* remains a staple of many world literature courses and would no doubt still qualify for membership as a "core" masterpiece of Western or even world literature. But what of his play *Egmont*? It doesn't appear in a single current American anthology of world literature and is rarely read outside Germany except by people with a specialist's interest in German literature or in the history of drama. Yet as recently as 1955, Magill included it in his second series as one of the 1,010 key works of Western literature—giving it precedence over *Wilhelm Meister* and *Elective Affinities,* which are probably a good deal better known today but which he added only in his third volume of 1960.

Shifts of this sort constantly occur, and an entire author can rapidly come into or drop out of an active presence in the general canon of world literature. In 1949 Magill included no fewer than three of Smollett's novels among the 510 titles of his first series; today, far from being a major figure of world literature, Smollett has hardly any active life even in the more specific canon of "English literature." As you read these words, can you readily name three of his novels, to say nothing of having actually read them? Smollett is now rarely read by anyone but specialists in eighteenth-century literature. Even within eighteenth-century studies, only two of Magill's Smollett choices, *Humphrey Clinker* and *Roderick Random,* still receive real attention; the third, *Peregrine Pickle,* has all but disappeared. The *MLA Bibliography* lists a modest total of twenty-four books and articles from the 1990s that focus on *Humphrey Clinker;* six more are on *Roderick Random;* only a single article from the entire decade is devoted to *Peregrine Pickle.* Both in the field and beyond, Smollett is less visible today than a number of Restoration and eighteenth-century writers, like Aphra Behn and William Godwin, who were scarcely thought of a generation ago. Cataloguing incomprehensible choices in Magill's first series, Clifton Fadiman remarked that "No one— well, hardly anyone—reads poor Godwin nowadays" (*Masterpieces,* 1:x); today he would have to substitute poor Smollett for lucky Godwin, who is very much back in fashion.

Given the variability in the fortunes even of Goethe and Dante, we lose more than we gain if we confine our attention to "the masterworks of the ages," or more precisely to what we perceive as the masterworks of the ages *at this moment.* Even in these dark days before the Roderick Random Revival of 2020 (a great year for hindsight), Smollett lives on within the personal canons of world literature of those happy few who continue to read him, and perhaps also of those who fondly remember having once read him.[7] Major canonical masterpieces are worthy of sustained attention both for aesthetic and for cultural reasons, but they persist so strongly, after all, not because they float forever in some eternal realm but because they adapt so effectively to the changing needs of different times and places, and the transformation now occurring in the shape of world literature is having a major impact on the ways we read even the greatest of great books.

This is not to say that works must always and only be read as documents of a specific time and place. Great works of literature do have a transcendent quality that enables them to reach across time and space and speak directly to us today. As Wai Chee Dimock says, discussing Osip Mandelstam's creative appropriations of Dante in the 1930s, at a time of great personal need and political pressure:

> Not stuck in one national context—and saying predictable things in that context—a literary text becomes a new semantic template, a new form of the legible, each time it crosses a national border. Global transit extends, triangulates, and transforms its meaning. This fact alone challenges the power of the territorial as a determining force in literature. The space-time coordinates of any text are not only fluid when they first come into being, poorly captured by the map of geopolitics, they are also subsequently and unforeseeably revisable, induced by their temporal and spatial displacements to play new tricks with the static borders of the nation. ("Literature for the Planet," 177)

The issue is to stay alive to the works' real difference from us without trapping them within their original context or subordinating them entirely to our own immediate moment and needs. An emphasis on universality can be a powerful aid in protecting the work from either of those extremes, so long as this universality isn't created by a process of stripping away much of what is really distinctive about the work.

At the same time, we should be aware that universality itself is not an eternal and unchanging concept. Rather, it has often been a culturally situated, strategic emphasis, as was notably the case at midcentury. Recoiling from the disasters of the two world wars, many comparatists looked to litera-

---

[7] Variation here too: though I read *Roderick Random* with great pleasure thirty years ago, I can hardly remember a thing about it, and so it retains only a very nominal place in world literature for me, whereas *The Expedition of Humphrey Clinker* impressed me deeply with its riotous play of rival epistles and continues to resonate for me today. *Peregrine Pickle*, it must be said, was something of a chore to get through even when I was under Smollett's spell.

ture as a basis to transcend the national divisions that had torn Europe apart. Like their political counterparts, they sought to create a United Nations of literature, in which local differences would be harmonized under the banner of universal principles of aesthetic order and cross-cultural tradition. This emphasis is well illustrated by a 1959 essay by the leading comparatist René Wellek entitled "The Crisis of Comparative Literature." He begins with the observation that "The world (or rather our world) has been in a state of permanent crisis since, at least, the year 1914" (282). Comparative literature has a role to play in resolving this crisis, as it "has the immense merit of combating the false isolation of national literary histories" (282–83). At the same time, Wellek insists, comparative literature must become far more than what it had often been, a study of the "foreign trade" of national literatures, a study that too often served to underscore the greatness of the comparatist's home culture, praised either for radiating its influence beyond its borders or conversely for its receptivity to the best of foreign thought. Wellek condemned this sort of comparison as entailing "a cultural power politics" in which "everything serves only the strength of one's nation" (283).

For Wellek, the antidote for such covert nationalism will be a search for more general literary patterns that transcend national boundaries altogether, and such patterns are to be found in the aesthetic coordinates of the works themselves. Reflecting his early associations as a Prague formalist, Wellek urges his audience to conceive the work of art as "a stratified structure of signs and meanings which is totally distinct from the mental processes of the author at the time of composition." He goes on to argue for "what has rightly been called an 'ontological gap' between the psychology of the author and a work of art, between life and society on the one hand and the aesthetic object" (293). Yet Wellek isn't advocating formalism for formalism's sake. He has his own cultural-political agenda in mind: by excavating the work's stratified structures of signs and meanings, the comparatist should finally arrive at the bedrock of universal brotherhood, and now the artwork's "ontological gap" shades over into America's saving distance from European conflict:

> Here, in America, looking from the other shore at Europe as a whole we may easily achieve a certain detachment, though we may have to pay the price of uprootedness and spiritual exile. . . . Once we grasp the nature of art and poetry, its victory over human mortality and destiny, its creation of a new world of the imagination, national vanities will disappear. Man, universal man, man everywhere and at all time, in all his variety, emerges and

literary scholarship ceases to be an antiquarian pastime, a
calculus of national credits and debts and even a mapping of
networks of relationships. Literary scholarship becomes an act of
the imagination, like art itself, and thus a preserver and creator of
the highest values of mankind. (295)

These heartfelt words reflect a double uprootedness: of the work from its
point of origin and of the reader from present-day society. As an émigré,
Wellek perhaps had little need to relate his European heritage to his new
American home, but later American scholars have not always been so ready
to accept so direct a loss. Further, as the gender specificity of Wellek's phrasing may suggest, not all readers of the sixties and seventies were able to find
themselves fully reflected in the figure of "man, universal man, man everywhere and at any time." If such a formulation seems less adequate today than
it did in the early postwar era, this may be because of social and intellectual
changes that make universalism less of an all-encompassing concept. Universalism may be best described at present as an important aspect of a work's
effects, rather than as its eternal essence.

It may also be the case that some works have a more marked universal dimension than others. The Book of Job, hardly an orthodox work
and one whose characters are not even Israelites, was always less localized in
its biblical context than the Book of Genesis. Genesis, in turn, contains versions of many widespread Near Eastern tales and is less purely located within
Israelite culture than, say, the books of Deuteronomy or Jeremiah. A perennially universalized work is The Thousand and One Nights, which writers
from the eighteenth century to John Barth and Salman Rushdie in the twentieth have taken as a fountainhead of "the sea of stories." Though many stories are explicitly set in the Baghdad of Haroun al-Rashid, this Baghdad is
clearly a largely imaginary realm. Certain of the tales do track specific historical characters, and the late sequence on "Ja'afar and the Fall of the Bar-
makids" closely follows the historical account of al-Tabari, but the usually
selective translations published in Europe have almost always excluded such
localized stories, preferring to emphasize "universal" tales like those of Sind-
bad and Aladdin.

In so doing, the European editions are only furthering the process
of delocalization already evident in much of the collection itself. Though the
book is written in Arabic and is even sometimes called The Arabian Nights,
the frame tale's characters are Persian—at least in name, though hardly in
many cultural specifics—and the ensuing collection incorporates tales from
Persia and India as well as the Arab world, usually more or less detached

from any historical or cultural point of origin. Having developed over the course of centuries across a range of cultures, *The Thousand and One Nights* can quite appropriately be read as a collection of universally appealing tales and a metafictional meditation on storytelling itself. It becomes all the more easy to read the book in this way given the fact that it was not traditionally considered part of Arabic literature at all, but rather was thought of as a sub-literary work, popular in form and suspiciously heterodox in content (hence the recent move in Egypt to ban it). This is a dramatic case of a work that first enters the field of literature only after it has traveled beyond its region of origin; only in the twentieth century, partly influenced by the book's Western reception, have Arab writers like Naguib Mahfouz and Assia Dje-bar begun to make active use of it as a basis for their own writing.

Universalizing modes of presentation have often been more prob-lematic than in this instance, involving the erasure of basic elements of the original work and a bland response in which the "universal" is only a cover for an unconscious process of assimilation to one's own prior values. Since 1960 *The Epic of Gilgamesh* has most often been read in English in the Pen-guin Classic translation by N. K. Sandars. Sandars decided to bring the epic to a nonspecialist audience by emphasizing its universal features. In her in-troduction, she says that the ancient poems about Gilgamesh "have a right to a place in the world's literature . . . mainly because of the quality and char-acter of the story that they tell. It is a mixture of pure adventure, of moral-ity, and of tragedy." Gilgamesh "is at once the most sympathetic to us, and most typical of individual man in his search for life and understanding" (7).

This universalizing perspective underwrites a variety of strategies by which Sandars removes the work from its context in order to bring it close to the reader. To begin with, she renders the poem as prose, in what the book's own cover describes as "a straightforward English version." In a sort of novelization of the epic, the poem's haunting repetitions are reduced, re-placed with more linear dialogue and action. At the same time, Sandars elides the text's complex history, silently splicing together passages from dif-ferent versions and filling in fragmentary passages at will. A typical passage from the standard version, in Andrew George's careful new rendering, has many gaps, together with brackets for probable reconstructions and italics for less certain guesses:

> Standing there, Enkidu heard [what she said,]
>   and thinking it over, he sat [down *weeping*.]
> His eyes brimmed with [tears,]
>   his arms fell limp, [his] strength [*ebbed away*.]

> They took hold of each other and . . . ,
>> they [*linked*] their hands like . . .
> Gilgamesh . . .
>> To Enkidu he spoke a word, [saying:]
> "Why, my friend, [did your eye] brim [with tears,]
>> Your arms fall limp, [your strength *ebb away*?]"

(17–18)

In Sandars's rendering, this passage is cleared right up: "The eyes of Enkidu were full of tears and his heart was sick. He sighed bitterly and Gilgamesh met his eye and said, 'My friend, why do you sigh so bitterly?'" (70). Little wonder that the Norton anthology, which uses Sandars's translation, finds it "thrilling to hear so familiar a voice from so vast a distance."

Sandars's version is certainly readable, yet it loses both the scene's poetic movement and also the text's strangely appropriate fragmentation, the physical embodiment of the poem's own great theme of the transience of human life and the fragility of material culture.[8] In her introduction Sandars argues that a more accurate reflection of the text perhaps "gives the student and specialist what he needs, but presents the ordinary reader with a page which may look rather like an unfinished crossword puzzle" (50). Sandars cheerfully fills in the blanks for us, but this is a puzzle that she herself was not equipped to solve: though trained as an archaeologist, she worked chiefly on prehistoric Europe and knew none of the relevant Near Eastern languages. Penguin apparently felt that the epic's meaning was sufficiently "universal" that the text could be translated at a second remove by paraphrasing the existing scholarly translations, presenting a novelized content while suppressing poetic and textual form alike.[9]

Works of world literature are best read with an awareness of the work's original cultural context, but they typically wear this context rather lightly. Read as a work of Italian literature, Dante's *Commedia* is naturally seen in close

---

[8] In an apt illustration of this theme, Andrew George reproduces an engraving of the shattered tablet containing the lines "no one at all sees Death . . . then all of a sudden nothing is there" (87).

[9] In 1999 Penguin brought out Andrew George's new verse translation as an alternative to Sandars, which interestingly remains in print as well. Though George too makes concessions to readability, filling in gaps in the standard version by use of other versions, he always notes these additions openly. As he says: "While there is a temptation for a modern editor to ignore the gaps, to gloss them over or to join up disconnected fragments of text, I believe that no adult reader is well served by such a procedure" (xxviii).

connection to a host of medieval poets, theologians, and political thinkers, most of whose works are likely to be entirely unknown outside Italy except to specialists. As Wai Chee Dimock says, Dante's poem changes shape as it crosses borders: it is a fundamentally *different* work abroad, and even in Italy it was a very different work for Italo Calvino and Primo Levi in the twentieth century than it was for Boccaccio in the fourteenth. Yet the *Commedia*'s effects will always be shaped by the reader's powerful sense of it as a poem from a very different time and place from our own. In *The Western Canon*, Harold Bloom has a point in criticizing scholars who overwhelm their objects of study with their own erudition, effectively recreating past authors in their own image: thus he mocks contemporary Dante specialists, alive to every nuance of Augustinian theology, who present us with "a doctrinal Dante, so abstrusely learned and so amazingly pious that he can be fully apprehended only by his American professors" (75). Yet Bloom seriously overstates the problem: surely it can enrich our reading of Dante to know what in Hell the poet was referring to, and modern scholars have done much to recover long-forgotten identities and doctrinal disputes that Dante did indeed expect his readers to recognize. A lively awareness of a work's original context is an important safeguard against its outright assimilation to the reader's own immediate moment. Bloom's chapter on Dante argues forcefully against any orthodox reading of Dante's work; he sees Dante's fierce inventiveness (as Auerbach had earlier seen his earthly humanism) as breaking the theological mold in which he was working. Yet Bloom's reading is an exercise in willed incomprehension, a systematic refusal to allow Dante any creative engagement with his culture, forcing onto this deeply religious medieval poet a model of secular poetic strife lifted unchanged from Bloom's early studies in British Romanticism.

Just how much context is needed will vary, depending on the work itself and on the purposes for which it is being read. A work will sometimes be explicit enough for its cultural assumptions to be fairly clear just from the text itself, but even in those cases one real value of the work will be its connection to a time or place different from our own. This connection is rarely, if ever, direct: the Gilgamesh of the epic is no longer the historical king of Uruk, any more than the pope on his mat, in the Aztec poem, is an accurate portrait of Leo X. Yet all works come out of a world and speak to that world as well as to us, and we gain by attending to both sides of the conversation. Even when we read in private and for our personal pleasure, our reading is in part a kind of social engagement. Bloom insistently condemns new historicists and feminists for emphasizing the links between literature and society, but he doesn't do this just to free the works from scholarly entrapment within their society of origin. Like René Wellek before him, he also wants to hold off the work—and even the reader—from any contact with our *own* society. "Aesthetic authority," he claims, expresses "energies that are essentially solitary rather than social" (35). The canon itself is "the image of the individual thinking" (34), and Bloom's individual is thinking very private thoughts, chiefly of death. Hence Hamlet "is death's ambassador to us," and this relationship "is altogether solitary, despite all of tradition's obscene attempts to socialize it" (30).

A strangely one-sided reading of Hamlet: ambassador from the empty kingdom of Death, but not also to and from the crowded courts of Elsinore, England, and Wittenberg? Society melts away in the vast echo chamber of Bloom's mind, replaced by the warring voices of the few great Titans of the literary universe. The fewer the better: a scholarly Goneril, Bloom continually narrows his authors' already narrow circle. *The Western Canon* treats twenty-six writers, but what need twenty-six? "Most simply, the Canon is Plato and Shakespeare" (34). What need even two? "At once no one and everyone, nothing and everything, Shakespeare is the Western Canon" (71).

Yet even Bloom finally relents. Having spent almost five hundred pages extolling the greatness of the few greatest writers at the heart of his version of the Western canon, he closes with an appendix listing several *thousand* works by more than eight hundred and fifty writers whom he considers to be the key figures in the Western canon as a whole. For all his diatribes against the resentful feminists, his listing includes many women (such as Alice Munro, Edna O'Brien, Jeanette Winterson) who would never have been on a Yale reading list thirty years ago and would not be there now but for feminist scholarship. True, the standard remains higher for the women, all of whom are people of considerable talent, while Bloom's list includes a number of quite minor male authors, such as the early-twentieth-century poet Robert Bridges. I would venture that Bridges is known to readers today, if at all, only through Wyndham Lewis and Ezra Pound's sarcastic reference in their Vorticist Manifesto to the flabby British sky that "can manufacture no snow, but can only drop the sea on us in a drizzle like a poem by Mr. Robert Bridges."

Bloom has previously informed us that we really don't have time to spare for lesser figures:

> Yet we must choose: As there is only so much time, do we reread Elizabeth Bishop or Adrienne Rich? Do I again go in search of lost time with Marcel Proust, or am I to attempt yet another rereading

of Alice Walker's stirring denunciations of all males, black and white? . . . If we were literally immortal, or even if our span were doubled to seven score of years, say, we could give up all argument about canons. But we have an interval only, and then our place knows us no more, and stuffing that interval with bad writing, in the name of whatever social justice, does not seem to me to be the responsibility of the literary critic. (29–30)

Apparently Bloom sees some excellence in Bridges' poetry that most readers have missed—a real possibility, given Bloom's idiosyncratic acuity—and yet even Bloom would hardly class Bridges in the first or even the second rank of canonical figures. The question of quality is answered by the fact that Bridges appears on Bloom's list at all: even if we grant a privileged status to the really major figures, we are still likely to want to expand our literary range. We may often prefer to traverse a varied landscape rather than merely jump from one peak to the next. As it happens, I recently taught Bridges for the first time in a class called "Modernism and Its Enemies." I didn't find any forgotten masterpieces among Bridges's collected poems, but they were very useful to show the literary landscape from which, and against which, Pound and Lewis were emerging.

If we are interested in literature as a great conversation, whether we conceive of this conversation as fundamentally social *or* as essentially aesthetic in nature, following this conversation naturally leads us to an expanding study of the great figures' interlocutors. As they are writing, most writers believe or at least hope that they will prove to be among the great voices of their age, and they find themselves in dialogue not only with the few friends whom they admit to their own ranks but also with a much larger number of also-rans and outright impostors, many of whom are unaccountably being taken quite seriously by a misguided public. When Lewis and Pound wrote the Vorticist Manifesto in 1914, they were the unknowns; their target Robert Bridges, forgotten today, had just been named Poet Laureate, a post he held until his death in 1930. His success may now look suspiciously like a triumph of connections over talent, but to Lewis and Pound he was the foremost representative of the dominant literary values they were seeking to shatter (their manifesto is the opening salvo in their short-lived magazine *Blast*). So it is important to read Bridges in order to hear the full conversation—or altercation—that Lewis and Pound were having with the literary establishment, and in the process we can encounter little-known poems of real value. Bridges may never recover a major place in British literature, still less in world literature generally, yet his poems do offer quiet pleasures uniquely their own, and they are pleasures we may turn to at those moments when we want something different from the querulous brilliance of Pound's Pisan Cantos or the melancholy sonorities of "The Waste Land."

Harold Bloom fails to find Alice Walker worthy to stand next to Robert Bridges, but if this is his conclusion after reading *The Color Purple* twice, as he says he has done, there is certainly no reason he should force himself to undertake yet another reading, any more than someone who admires *The Color Purple* should be compelled to drop it in favor of Bridges's charming hymns to the Gulf Stream (bearer of the drizzle that so incensed Lewis and Pound). All the same, even Bloom's expanded canon is far more capacious than his rhetoric would have led us to expect. Not only are many women now on Bloom's list, but he even includes a range of twentieth-century figures from outside the traditional Euro-American sphere, including Derek Walcott, Mahmud Darwish, Gabriel Okara, and even the Marxist philosopher and cricket enthusiast C.L.R. James. With the probable exception of Walcott, none of these figures would be on many Americans' radar screens now but for the rise of postcolonial criticism, another of Bloom's prime targets in "the School of Resentment."   •

The world is looking much wider today than it did twenty-five years ago. Difficulties of circulation, translation, and assessment remain, and these will be explored through the case studies in the following chapters. Yet the opening up of the canon gives us all sorts of new opportunities for a genuine engagement with the world around us, together with a greatly broadened range of aesthetic possibility. As sharply as he satirizes the mutual incomprehension of the tribal gerontocrats and the self-promoting and even self-hating Giambatista Viko, Mbwil Ngal doesn't invite his readers to share the judges' insistence on maintaining "two universes, each with its own history lost in the depths of the ages. Opposed trajectories. Two types of humanity" (90). The very Viko who wonders how he can recover a lost tribal orality spends his time talking, endlessly, on the telephone, sometimes with a receiver at each ear, communicating with two friends at once (41). At the close of his trial, "the youngest counselor present" issues a passionate plea, not in defense of Viko's own condescending and neocolonialist efforts, but in favor of a genuinely new science of writing, a science of true intercultural understanding:

> Let me make myself clear. Far be it from me to approve what this young man has done. But I would like to point out that . . . what one of our comrades has just called "an assault on our security" is nothing more than "an assault on our specificity," on our

withdrawal within ourselves. But let us not forget that a "specificity" prepares its own asphyxiation to the degree that it receives no oxygen from outside. Cultures survive only by opening up to other cultures that can liberate them from their tendency to collective narcissism. (112)

Ngal himself both gained and lost by the heightening of nationalistic specificity in the postcolonial period. He first went to Europe at a time when a high degree of assimilation was expected of any immigrant, and he published his first books not as Mbwil Ngal but as *Georges* Ngal. He regained his name with the publication of *Giambatista Viko*, yet to date his novel has been read mostly by a few specialists in African literature. Translation of his novel is long overdue, and we will have a world literature worthy of the name when a novel like Ngal's can be seen at once in multiple frames: as a work of African, and French, and world, literature.

PART TWO

Translation

4

Love in the Necropolis

In the second year of the reign of Ramses V, in the third month of the inundation season, a scribe in Thebes made a collection of literary texts: a long, comic story of intrigue among the gods; some hymns; an encomium to the king. "The Contendings of Horus and Seth," as we now call the story, took up most of the front side (the recto) of the scribe's papyrus roll; with a little space left at the end, he decided to include some short love poems, before turning over to the verso to write the encomium and the hymns. The lyrics appear under the heading "The Sweet Sayings Found in a Scroll Composed by the Scribe of the Necropolis, Nakht-Sobek." In W. K. Simpson's vivid translation, the shortest of these lyrics goes as follows:

> Why need you hold converse with your heart?
> To embrace her is all my desire.
> As Amun lives, I come to you,
> my loincloth on my shoulder.

(*The Literature of Ancient Egypt*, 324)

One of the oldest lyrics to have survived anywhere in the world, this poem addresses us with a powerful immediacy. In its brevity and its simplicity, it stands as a kind of minimum of literary expression, and I will use it as a testing ground to explore the irreducible problems that translation always faces, however simple the text in question, however uncomplicated the history of its transmission and reception. In this respect too, this poem presents as simple a case as we could readily find. Whereas many works of world literature come to us already shaped by complex dynamics of transmission, often involving vexed relations between the originating culture and our own, this text has almost no history at all intervening between us and the moment of its inscription in 1160 B.C.E. Produced for private enjoyment, the papyrus passed into other hands; inspired by the poems on the recto, another writer added a more extensive collection of love poems on the verso, under the heading "The Songs of Extreme Happiness." Soon, though, the papyrus fell out of the sphere of literary usage. The demand for papyrus far outstripped supply in the Ramesside period, and within a few years the blank pages remaining at the end of the verso were being used, and reused, for business memoranda: recording now the sale of a bull, now the gift of a box to a general of the War Office. Buried in some cache of administrative records, the papyrus vanished for three thousand years. Discovered by one of the peasants who conducted their own private, for-profit excavations in the Theban necropolis in competition with government-sanctioned university digs, this papyrus was acquired in the late 1920s by A. Chester Beatty, a wealthy American mining engineer who had settled in England and was devoting himself to collecting all sorts of neglected artifacts: Chinese snuff boxes and rhinoceros-horn cups, medieval woodblock prints, and ancient religious manuscripts from around the world. He happened upon "Papyrus Chester Beatty," as it became known, while wintering in Cairo for his health. Beatty underwrote its publication by Oxford University Press in 1931, in a beautiful folio edition, complete with transcriptions, dozens of photographic plates, and a detailed analysis by a leading Egyptologist of the day, A. H. Gardiner (later Sir Alan, himself a man of extensive means), under the title *The Library of A. Chester Beatty: Description of a Hieratic Papyrus with a Mythological Story, Love-Songs, and Other Miscellaneous Texts, by Alan H. Gardiner, F.B.A.*

The poems thus come to us unencumbered by any transmission history whatever from the twelfth century B.C.E. to the early twentieth century C.E., when the lyrics in this papyrus were quickly seen, as Gardiner says in his introduction, to be "of inestimable value, not merely for archaeology, but still more for the world-history of poetry and of lyric expression" (27). And yet, as Gardiner and subsequent translators have tried to give the poems their rightful place in world literature, they have had to struggle with surprisingly intractable problems, even in the case of the simple quatrain quoted above—problems of decipherment, of grammar, of vocabulary, and of cultural framing. Attending to these problems can show us much about the choices that have to be made as a work is brought from its original time and place into our own world.

Gardiner's initial publication itself oscillates between two quite different frames of reference for the poems: historical and transcendent. With extensive philological notes, his edition presents the papyrus as a document of Ramesside history and culture ("Where else have we similar records of the conveyance of foreign news by a system of relays?" [29]), and he waxes eloquent over the orthography: "An astonishing and, so far as I know, unparalleled ligature found in the Encomium, but not on the *recto,* is that for ꟿ (*verso* B 23.26)" (5). Yet at the same time this lavish edition is an aesthetic object in its own right: an oversize folio with three-inch margins, amply illustrated, and with elegant transcriptions employing the delicate hieroglyphic font that Gardiner's father had commissioned for him several years earlier. ("It is to my Father that I owe all my leisure and opportunities for research," Gardiner gratefully noted in the preface to his great *Egyptian Grammar* of 1926, "and it is he who now, more than thirty years later, has defrayed the cost of my new hieroglyphic font.")

At once a paleographer and an aesthete, Gardiner judiciously assesses the scribe's calligraphic style: "The hand is neither very regular nor yet very tidy, but it possesses plenty of character and is not without a certain beauty of its own." He praises "the spirited ꟿ, and ꟿ with the foremost arm ending in a daring flourish," and urbanely mentions "the misshapen ꟿ" as one of the scribe's characteristic usages (5). He prefers, however, to emphasize the physical at the level of form rather than of content. Discussing the anatomy of the beloved's body in one poem ("Long of neck and radiant of nipple . . . / Drooping of buttocks, firm-girt in her midst"), he comments that "here already we mark how purely physical was the gentle passion as felt by these ancient Orientals" (28). Turning quickly from this ancient, oriental physicality, he stresses that "apart from this, the emotions expressed differ in no wise from those of lovers of all ages and climes." The poems achieve their inestimable value for world poetry by their universality—a universality that proves to tally closely with their *similarity* to modern European verse: one poem closes "with some verses which are Heine pure and simple" (he now quotes Heine, in German, [28]); another expresses "a thought not unlike one found upon the lips of Romeo" (whom he also quotes [29]).

It is not an easy matter, though, to translate the poems safely into the Euro-universal world where Gardiner wishes to see them enshrined, even though the papyrus itself has made it to twentieth-century England almost intact, apart from the tearing off of one or more initial pages "by the rapacious and destructive hands of the fellaheen" (1). The balance of the papyrus is in good condition, and yet Gardiner still faces severe challenges in getting from the physical marks on the page to the universality of an achieved work of art. "The text is evidently corrupt," the first two poems "are so obscure as to be almost untranslatable," while "Stanza the fifth is Stygian darkness" (29). Even the quatrain I am examining here, free of any lacunae or even of any unknown words, contains riddles of orthography and grammar that make it difficult to decide even so basic an issue as who is supposed to be speaking in the poem: A man? A woman? A man and his friend? The man's friend only? The friend and the woman? All of these options have been tried by Gardiner and his successors, with no consensus yet in sight.

Gardiner himself took the speaker to be a woman, translating the poem as follows:

> When thou speakest with thy heart,
> Prithee after her, that I may embrace her;
> By Amūn, it is I who come to thee,
> My tunic upon my arm.

(37)

He glosses the poem as signifying that "the maiden tells her lover that pursuit is superfluous, she is a willing quarry" (37 n. 3). Gardiner, however, produced this lucid rendering at the cost of suppressing the grammatical structure of the first two lines. The opening phrase, *ir.n djed-k,* is a simple interrogative and would normally be translated "Why do you speak?" rather than "When you speak." The second line, moreover, is an infinitive phrase rather than a command: "To embrace her is all my desire," rather than "Prithee after her." Just how these lines work together is unclear: Egyptian writing was unpunctuated, and the four lines could represent one, two, or three sentences. Further, as hieroglyphs record consonants and semivowels but not vowels proper, it can often be difficult to say just which form of a verb is being used and which are dependent rather than independent clauses. Sorting these questions out as best they can, the two most scholarly translators of more recent years, W. K. Simpson of Yale and Miriam Lichtheim of the University of California, have both opted for a tripartite rendering, consisting of a question, a reply or exhortation, and an announcement of action. In Lichtheim's version, this becomes:

> Why do you argue with your heart?
> Go after her, embrace her!
> As Amun lives, I come to you,
> My cloak over my arm.

(*Ancient Egyptian Literature,* 2:188)

Like all translations—like all reading—Lichtheim's version is informed by context. Her translation recalls other Egyptian poems in which a hesitating young lover is offered advice by a third party. Papyrus Chester Beatty itself contains several such poems. In one cycle of three poems, the speaker might be either the man's friend or a go-between sent by the woman herself:

> Please come quick to the lady love
> like a king's agent
> whose master is impatient
> for his letters
> and desires to hear them.
> . . . .
> Before you have kissed your hand four times,
> you shall have reached her hideaway
> as you chase the lady love.
> For it is the Golden Goddess
> who has set her aside for you, friend.

> (Simpson, 321–23)

The set of seven poems that includes our verse begins with two poems that are both spoken by a friend, in this instance a none-too-scrupulous male confidant of the lover himself:

> Supply her with song and dance,
> wine and ale are her desire,
> confuse her wits,
> and gain her this night.
> She'll tell you:
> put me in your arms;
> when day breaks
> let's start again.

> (Simpson, 323)

Lichtheim extends this context to our quatrain, construing it as a miniature dialogue in which the friend chides the lover for his hesitation and urges him on; the lover then fortifies himself with a vow to Amun and goes in to the woman.

So far, so good: Lichtheim has solved the grammatical problem of the first line. Yet she has retained Gardiner's insertion of an imperative mode into the second line, actually breaking the line into two separate commands ("Go after her, embrace her!") though there is only one verb in the original. Further, the wider context tends to argue against a rapid change of speakers in midverse: no surviving Egyptian poem makes such a change. Lichtheim may have created a dialogue where none existed to begin with.

Admittedly, a negative argument from context can only be made very tentatively, given the small number of poems to have survived from ancient Egypt: only four dozen poems have come down to us more or less intact, and it would only take a further discovery to extend the range of known possibility in any number of ways. If one particular set of three poems had never been found, for example, we would have observed that every extant Egyptian poem is spoken by a man, a woman, or both, and we might naturally assume this to have always been the case. A papyrus now preserved in Turin, however, has a cycle of three poems whose speakers are *trees,* which testify to the charms of the lovers who meet beneath their branches (Simpson, 312–15).

Tentative though it is, such contextual evidence as we have at least favors the idea of a single speaker, or rather, a single singer, as these poems were composed as song lyrics. Particularly if we remove the implausible imperatives introduced by Gardiner and Lichtheim, our quatrain can readily be translated as involving a single speaker. This is the view taken by Simpson in the translation with which I began, and he makes his view of the speaker's gender clear by his choice of garment:

> Why need you hold converse with your heart?
> To embrace her is all my desire.
> As Amun lives, I come to you,
> my loincloth on my shoulder.

(324)

Simpson's rendering draws on a wider context—including other love poems but also other texts—in which a person debates an issue with his heart or spirit before coming to a decision. The most extended Egyptian use of this theme is found in a haunting twelfth-dynasty text known as "The Dispute between a Man and His *Ba*" (Lichtheim, 1:163–69; Simpson, 201–9). "To whom shall I speak today?" the speaker asks. "Faces are blank, / Everyone turns his face from his brothers." He despairs of life, but his own spirit replies to him ("Are you not a man? Are you not alive?"), urging him not to commit suicide; internal debate here carries the weight given to Job's argument with his three friends in the Book of Job. A typical instance of internal dialogue in love poetry occurs in Papyrus Harris 500, from Memphis:

> I say to my heart within me in prayer:
> if far away from me is my lover tonight,
> then I am like someone already in the grave.
> Are you not indeed well-being and life?

Joy has come to me through your well-being,
my heart seeks you out.

(Simpson, 304)

Simpson's version of our quatrain is attractive, works grammatically, and fits plausibly within the context of surviving Egyptian poetry. On the other hand, it is perfectly possible to build upon Gardiner's original assumption that the speaker is the beloved woman rather than the man, if we correct his verbs but follow his lead in taking the second line as the woman's paraphrase of what she thinks her lover is saying as he hesitates in coming to her. Several other extant poems have a speaker reporting another's speech, as in the following example, which is probably the world's oldest surviving aubade, a poem in which the lovers complain at the rising of the sun. Here the woman reports two different speeches in a single verse:

The voice of the dove is calling,
it says: "It's day! Where are you?"
O bird, stop scolding me!
I found my lover on his bed,
my heart was overjoyed.
Each said, "I shall not leave you,
my hand is in your hand;
you and I shall wander
in all the places fair."
He makes me the foremost of women,
he does not aggrieve my heart.

(Lichtheim, 2:190–91)

The woman in our quatrain could similarly be quoting another's speech, in her case mocking her lover's internal debates as she takes direct action and approaches him. This reading allows us to give, as Gardiner already did, full force to the emphatic phrasing "*it is I who* come to you," for which the original employs the independent pronoun *inek,* a stronger statement than a simple "I come" would be. Such a reading would assort well with other poems in which a woman speaker impulsively rushes to her beloved without pausing to finish dressing:

My heart remembers well your love.
One half of my temple was combed,
I came rushing to see you,
and I forgot my hair.

(Simpson, 305)

An example from Papyrus Chester Beatty itself, featuring another conversation with one's heart:

> My heart flutters hastily
> when I think of my love of you;
> it lets me not act sensibly,
> it leaps from its place.
> It lets me not put on a dress,
> nor wrap my scarf around me;
> I put no paint upon my eyes,
> I'm not even anointed.
> "Don't wait, go there," says it to me,
> as often as I think of him.
> My heart, don't act so stupidly,
> why do you play the fool?

(Lichtheim, 2:183–84)

With such a context in mind, we can render our quatrain entirely within the woman's voice, using reported speech to avoid violating any grammatical norms:

> Why do you dispute with your heart—
> "To embrace her is all my desire"?
> As Amun lives, it is I who come to you,
> my clothing on my arm.

Very well. It appears that two quite different options work grammatically and make sense within the context of the surviving corpus of Egyptian poetry: the poem records either a man's internal debate and resolution or a woman's decisive action. Is there any way to decide between these renderings?

In principle, the question of gender should be readily answered by the original text itself, since the pronouns "I" and "my" are written with the hieroglyph of a seated man or a seated woman, depending on the gender in question. Looking at the text, this proves to be the case, as can be seen in Gardiner's hieroglyphic transcription:[1]

---

[1] The papyrus is actually written in cursive "hieratic," an abbreviated, rapidly written script that employs many simplifications of characters. Intensive study of a given scribe's style is needed to make out many readings in hieratic texts, and Egyptologists usually rely on hieroglyphic transcriptions made by the person who publishes the text. Gardiner's fascination with our scribe's orthography is based on many hours of studying his style.

ir-m   djed-ki   r   m-ha't   ib-k
why   do you speak words in front of your heart

m-sa'   st   n-i   kniw   st
satiety it is to me embracing her

wa'h   Imn   inek   iw n-k
endures Amun it is I   who come to you

iw   ta-y   mss   hr   ka'ht-i
there is my   tunic on my shoulder/arm

The problem here is that the signs are inconsistent: "It is I who come to you" in the third line is written with a seated woman as the "I," but then in the next line, "my" tunic has a *man* as its determinative. The photographic plate of the original indicates that Gardiner has correctly transcribed these signs. So how should we resolve this inconsistency?

One way or another, the scribe has made a slip of the brush. Egyptian scribes were notoriously casual in their uses of pronouns, and furthermore in hieratic script the seated man and the seated woman are often much less distinct than they appear in their full-dress hieroglyphic form. This scribe, as it happens, draws them almost identically: in each case the figure is shown as a single oval shape with a curving stroke at the bottom to indicate the leg and foot. A seated woman differs, in his orthography, only by having an added stroke at the top to indicate her headdress. This stroke is clearly present in the "I" of line three, but just as clearly absent in the "my" of "my tunic." In the case of the final "my" of "my shoulder," there is an ambiguous stroke that may well be the headdress but might also simply be part of the next sign over.

Ordinarily, the speaker's clothing would resolve this matter, as most Egyptian garments were worn only by one sex or the other. Unfortunately, it so happens that the *mss*, a kind of tunic, is the one garment that was commonly worn by *both* sexes.[2] This variability hasn't stopped the poem's trans-

---

[2] A detailed discussion of the *mss* is found in J. J. Janssen, *Commodity Prices from the Ramessid Period*, 259–62. Appropriately for our quatrain, Janssen notes that it was "worn mostly in the evenings as a protection against the cold." This would suggest that rather than leaving home naked, the speaker has entered his/her beloved's house at night, undressing while entering the bedroom. Several poems show the speaker making a surprise visit to the beloved's home.

lators from making a more specific choice of garment, always one that reinforces their interpretation of the speaker's gender. Thus Simpson makes the *mss* a man's loincloth, while another translator, Barbara Fowler, makes the speaker a woman and the garment a dress:

> While you argued with your heart—
> "Take her in your embrace"—
> by Amon, I came to you,
>   My dress still disarranged.

(*Love Lyrics of Ancient Egypt*, 71)

Our mistake, however, may lie in assuming that we need to make a definite choice. The scribe's casual alternation of genders may reflect an openness in the poem's original usage. The Egyptian lyrics we have appear to have been composed as songs, and the singer's gender is often left unspecified. Perhaps we need to think of this poem less in a context of Heine and Shakespeare and more in a context of Willie Nelson and Linda Ronstadt. The understood gender would then change simply according to who is singing the song at a given time. The best translation could be one that leaves the option open, freeing us to envision the scene whichever way our inclinations lead us at a given time.

A harder problem is actually posed by the term *mss* itself, as we have no equivalent garment. Janssen says that a comparable item is still in use in some Arab countries and proposes that "the modern word *ghalabiyah* is the best translation" (*Commodity Prices*, 260), yet this solution works only for speakers of Arabic and would produce an oddly ethnographic effect if used in an English translation. "Tunic" has an all too Roman sound to it, while a more neutral term like "garment" lacks the vivid specificity of a particular item of clothing. Lichtheim's "my cloak over my arm" fails even to suggest a state of undress, giving more the impression of a visit to the dry cleaner. From this point of view, Simpson's "loincloth," though strictly speaking inaccurate ("loincloth" is *da'iw*, not *mss*), is an effective choice, giving the line a strong erotic charge while also preserving a sense of cultural distance.

There are limits to the extent to which a translation can or even should attempt to convey the full cultural specificity of the original, though one strand of translation theory has always dreamed of a mystical mirroring process that would somehow bring the original work, entire, into the translation. This utopian view was eloquently expressed by Walter Benjamin in "The Task of the Translator":

> A real translation is transparent; it does not cover the original,
> does not block its light, but allows the pure language, as though

reinforced by its own medium, to shine upon the original all the more fully. This may be achieved, above all, by a literal rendering of the syntax which proves words rather than sentences to be the primary element of the translator. For if the sentence is the wall before the language of the original, literalness is the arcade. (79)

Benjamin himself was wise enough not to attempt to actually produce such a union of original and translation, though he ends his essay by invoking interlinear Bible translations as a radical alternative to always-incomplete adaptive translations. Others, however, have attempted literalistic translations that convey qualities of the original text so faithfully that they are hardly readable at all. At the extreme, this approach leads to Nabokov's awkwardly phrased and monumentally annotated translation of Pushkin's *Eugene Onegin*, which resolutely attempts to reproduce Russian grammatical effects and to convey all the nuances that each word would have in the original. As he wrote while working on his project, "I want translations with copious footnotes, footnotes reaching up like skyscrapers to the top of this or that page so as to leave only the gleam of one textual line between commentary and eternity" ("Problems of Translation," 83).

In Nabokov's *Onegin*, the actual poem takes up only one-seventh of the edition's fourteen hundred pages. It was published in a beautiful two-volume edition in Princeton's Bollingen Series, but even Princeton hesitated to impose the full weight of Nabokov's erudition on the reader; the poem appears in a slender first volume, while Nabokov's notes (actually the best part of his edition) are relegated to the massive volume 2. Yet Nabokov himself could translate works very differently when he was thinking in terms of world literature rather than in terms of re-creating the vanished Russia of his past: in his wonderfully inventive 1923 Russian translation of *Alice in Wonderland*, he eschewed footnotes and gave himself over to the delights of creating Russian equivalents for Carroll's seemingly untranslatable chains of puns. Thus, when the Mock Turtle describes his studies in "reeling and writhing," Nabokov has him study *chesat' i pitat'* (combing and feeding) instead of *chitat' i pisat'* (reading and writing).[3] The Mock Turtle himself becomes "Chepupakha," an elegant combination of *chepukha* (nonsense) and *cherepakha* (tortoise). In such puns Nabokov made no effort to have his translation convey the flavor of life—or of soup—in Victorian England, but sought instead to see Carroll's uncanny wonderland through a Russian lens.

Already foreshadowing the fractured universes of novels like *Pale Fire* and *Ada*, Nabokov's translation hovers between Russian and English

[3] Lewis Carroll, *Аня въ странѣ чудесъ*, 85.

worlds. Later in this scene, for instance, he slyly inserts a reference to the text's original language: when the Mock Turtle regrets not having taken "Laughing and Grief" with the classics instructor, Nabokov borrows a pun from the Venerable Bede, and has him sigh over never having studied *Angel'skii yazik*, "the Angels' language," instead of "the English language," *Angliiskii yazik* (86). A striking transposition: living in exile in Berlin at the time he made this translation from his future literary language back into his lost native tongue, Nabokov has the Mock Turtle unwittingly reflect an exile's anxiety, regretting that he cannot understand the angelic analog of the language from which he has himself been translated. Neither a mere linguistic compromise nor an arbitrary transposition, this moment in the text can stand as an emblem for the way in which sensitive readers bring a work variously to life through personal associations: English and Russian *are* for Nabokov the true languages of laughing and grief.

The Egyptian poem can be presented as a document of Ramesside culture, complete with pyramids of footnotes, as in Gardiner's original edition, and yet for the nonspecialist reader the supplying of the full wealth of relevant information would entail a loss of primary experience. By this I don't at all mean that a translation should wrench the poem outright into our own world and our own terms; rather, I mean that the original context should not be made to overpower us, interfering with our engagement with the fictive world the poem creates for us to enter. To appreciate the Egyptian poem, it is important to know that the speaker is undressing, but it doesn't greatly matter just what garment the speaker is stripping off. The general reader will supply a rather vague but perfectly sufficient image of a garment: something off-white, made of cotton or linen, its actual shape and stitching unspecified. It would add little to our appreciation of the poem to have a pocket insert in our volume with a fabric sample. Indeed, loading us up with much information of this sort would make it hard to experience the poem as literature, turning it instead into an object of study: just what we want if we're writing a book on Ramesside Commodity Prices, but not what we need to enjoy the poem as such.

Our understanding of the poem can, of course, be further enriched by more contextual knowledge, and anyone who falls in love with a body of work from another time or place will wish to learn more about the works' context. Some literary works, indeed, may be so closely dependent on detailed, culture-specific knowledge that they can only be meaningful to members of the originating culture or to specialists in that culture; these are works that remain within the sphere of a national literature and never achieve an effective life in world literature. Yet many works, like our present quatrain, already begin to work their magic before all their references are understood and all their cultural assumptions are elucidated. Like the quatrain as a whole, its individual elements float in between Nahkt-Sobek's world and our own: however *mss* may be translated, most modern readers will be unable to visualize the ancient garment in all its authentic particularity. Yet as long as the translation doesn't impose a wholesale modernization, we won't assimilate the *mss* directly to our contemporary experience; we will remain aware that we're reading an ancient poem. Whatever we think a *mss* is, we won't envision it as a Gortex windbreaker, though this might be the modern equivalent of the original item. All the same, we can never hold the poem entirely away from our own experience, nor should we. As we read, we triangulate not only between ancient and modern worlds but also between general and personal meanings: however *mss* is translated, different readers will visualize it very differently, and this variability helps the poem to resonate with memories from the reader's own life.

As with Goethe's reading of the Serbian and Chinese works, the Egyptian poem operates for us today on three registers: of likeness, of unlikeness, and of a shifting like-but-unlike relation to our own world. As accessible as the poem is, though, some translators have been unable to resist making it more immediate still, even to the point of expunging its most culturally specific element, the reference to Amun ("As Amun lives, I come to you"). In a particularly unfortunate rendering, John L. Foster gives the conclusion as: "For god's sake, sweet man, it's me coming at you, / My tunic loose at the shoulder!" (*Love Lyrics of Ancient Egypt*, 9). Foster has perhaps taken his cue from the very free re-translations that Ezra Pound and Noel Stock made from an Italian translation by Pound's Egyptologist son-in-law, Boris de Rachewiltz. Stock (the translator of this poem) not only erases the appeal to Amun, but even turns the blessing into a curse: "Damn it all, man, / Go to her, and try to look as if you mean business!" (*Love Poems of Ancient Egypt*, 29).

Foster at least retains a version of the ambiguous garment, which Stock transforms into some sort of personal grooming tip, yet Foster's "for god's sake" is little better than Stock's urging the lover on with faint damnation. Foster's weak, lower-case monotheism provides no equivalent for Amun, whose presence in the poem is important in more than one way. First, as the patron god of Thebes, Amun grounds the poem in a particular time and place—an ancient time, we must recall, in which someone would invoke one god among many, themselves often bitter rivals with one another, as in "The Contendings of Horus and Seth" in this very papyrus. Egyptian writers can be playful in their references to the gods, but they are rarely casual: "your embraces alone give life to my heart," the speaker says to her lover in one poem: "may Amun give me what I have found / for all eternity" (Simpson, 304).

Amun's presence in our quatrain gives depth to the opening line's query, "Why need you hold converse with your heart?" In the Book of the Dead the heart is weighed against the feather of truth; the pure heart will rise upward, while the guilty heart, weighed down with evil, will sink on the scale, and the soul will be doomed to torment. Often in the love poems, lovers are separated because there is some social or moral barrier to their love (rank; a rival; family disapproval of unmarried or adulterous passion). The poem asserts that desire takes primacy over ethical debate, and then underscores the rightness of this choice by invoking the enduring power of Amun—who, moreover, as sun god, can warm the lovers with his beneficent rays and encourage their undressing.

Taken together, the love poems cast a slanting sidelight onto the official temple and funerary practices that were being conducted around Nakht-Sobek in the necropolis of Thebes. One collection of love poems, preserved in Papyrus Harris 500, goes so far as to include a "harper's song" that denies outright the value of pyramids, temples, and wisdom writings alike:

> The nobles and spirits too,
> being entombed in their pyramids,
> they built chapels, but their cult stations are no more.
> What became of them?
> Now I have heard the sayings
> of Iyemhotep and Hardedef,
> which are quoted in the proverbs so much.
> What are their cult places?
> Their walls are dismantled,
> and their cult places exist no more,
> as if they had never been.

The poet draws a moral from these losses:

> Increase your beauty,
> and let not your mind tire.
> Follow your desire and what is good;
> acquire your possessions on earth.
> Do not control your passion
> Until that day of mourning comes for you.
> The Weary-Hearted does not hear their sobbing,

sobbing cannot save the heart of a man from the tomb.
Chorus: Make holiday,
but tire yourself not with it.
Remember: it is not given to man to take his goods with him.
No one goes away and then comes back.

(Simpson, 306–7)

Uninterested in the afterlife, the love poems' speakers are no atheists. On the contrary, they are eager for the gods to underwrite their earthly passions: "Lover, I am given over to you / by the Golden Goddess of womankind" (317). The poems keep the gods' beneficent influence squarely focused on earthly life, both social life and the elemental natural world that supports it. The entire Egyptian landscape is charged with polymorphous divinity, and the invocation of a city's patron god can expand to an entire pantheon:

> I sail downstream in the ferry by the oarsman's stroke,
> my bundle of reeds in my arms.
> I'll arrive at Memphis,
> and say to Ptah, Lord of Truth:
> Give me my girl tonight!
> The river is wine, Ptah its reeds,
> Sekhmet its foliage,
> the Dew Goddess its buds,
> Nefertum its lotus blossoms.
> The Golden Goddess rejoices
> and the land grows bright at her beauty.
> For Memphis is a flask of mandrake wine
> Placed before the good-looking god.[4]

A general reader is unlikely to know much about Ptah or even to have heard the names of Sekhmet and Nefertum before, yet it is clear enough in context that these are beneficent supernatural beings whose presence supports the lover's passion. Translations of this poem typically have a footnote conveying the information that Ptah is the patron god of Memphis and that "the Golden Goddess" is an epithet of Hathor, goddess of the sky and of love. More specialized knowledge of the other divinities, and of Ptah and Hathor themselves, could further enrich a reading of the poem, yet the essential effect is already achieved as long as the reader can see that the landscape has become surcharged with divine power.

[4] Adapted from Simpson, 299–300, with some readings adopted from Lichtheim, 2:189.

Such culture-specific associations tend to be weakened or erased outright in modernizing translations like Foster's. What Foster is after is both more general and more specific: a comforting universalism that can soothe our troubled souls today. As he says in his introduction, "the speakers in these poems, so long dead yet perennially young, show us that the varieties and moods of love then and in that civilization do not differ from our own" (xv). It is this timelessness that enables them to play a therapeutic role for the weary modern reader. Foster translated the poems between 1969 and 1973 as the Vietnam War wound to its violent and unhappy conclusion, and he alludes to this context in his introduction: "If, at least in our time, history seems to be one intolerable series of wars and rumors of war, songs like these prove that love also endures" (xv). Timeless though they are, to Foster these poems in turn are poised upon the brink of an earlier era of national decline: "the surviving copies of these poems were written down during the later New Kingdom, the time of the Ramesside pharaohs, and perhaps, as seen from a modern perspective, at a time when the long decline had already begun. For by 1000 B.C., the spirit of the place had departed" (xvi).

Fugitive blossoms from "the last great flourishing of Egyptian civilization" (xvi), the poems display an immediacy that is closely linked to their *antiquity*, in a chronology that cordons Egyptian culture off from the birth of European civilization in Greece and Israel early in the first millennium "Before Christ." This is the same strategy we have seen employed by the *Norton Anthology*'s editors for *The Epic of Gilgamesh*, and it makes no more sense here than there. In reality, Egypt remained a significant power in the Mediterranean world for many centuries after the poems were written down, its increasingly syncretistic culture dynamically engaged with Near Eastern and Hellenistic culture well past the time of Christ.

A notable literary expression of this ongoing impact can be found in Apuleius's *Metamorphoses* (also known as *The Golden Ass*), written in the second century C.E. Apuleius begins his narrative by offering "to caress your ears into approval with a pretty whisper, if only you will not begrudge looking at Egyptian papyrus inscribed with the sharpness of a reed from the Nile" (1:3). A speaker of Greek by birth, he apologizes for any awkwardness in his command of Latin, adding that the shifting of languages suits his own theme: "Now in fact this very changing of language corresponds to the type of writing we have undertaken, which is like the skill of a rider jumping from one horse to another. We are about to begin a Greekish story" (1:5). Changed into a donkey, his hero Lucius wanders around the Mediterranean coast, encountering thieves, con artists, and sexual depravity all along the way. Finally he reaches Egypt, where the goddess Isis appears to him and provides the roses that restore him to human form. The story ends with Lucius's initiation into her priesthood, upholders of a pure and ancient wisdom amid the manifold corruptions of the later Roman Empire.

Twelve hundred years after the end of the New Kingdom, then, Egypt was still playing a prominent role in the hybrid culture of the Mediterranean world. Yet from Foster's "modern perspective" this is simply a story of decline: "the spirit of the place had departed." His translations seek to perform a *salto mortale* over the long centuries of decline and warfare that separate us from the lyrical Egyptians of the New Kingdom. Sidelined in this way from the history of European culture, the Egyptian poems can restore the modern reader to a prelapsarian sensual innocence, as we envision ourselves surrounded by "the riot of foods and drinks, the naked servant girls, the singers, musicians, and dancers" (xvi).

We can enter freely into this archaic antiquity thanks to the songs' poetics, which Foster sees as remarkably modern, even American:

> While little is known of the art of poetry in ancient Egypt, my study of these texts has suggested a kind of parallel in the language used by those American poets (Ezra Pound, William Carlos Williams, e. e. cummings, and others) prominent in the earlier decades of the twentieth century writing in the "modernist" style. This prompted me to certain technical decisions: The translations should use the cadenced line, rhythmic, not metered. . . . The diction should be unpretentiously colloquial, simple, except when elevated by the power of strong feeling or slipping over into the sometimes slangy verbal patterns of irony or humor. The language should be conversational, quiet, the usages of personal and private speech. (xviii–xix)

This, of course, is not just American modernism but a certain *reading* of modernism: a surprisingly unpretentious, strangely quiet Ezra Pound is assimilated to the gentler poems of e. e. cummings. Far from being the special province of contemporary world poetry, to recall Steven Owen's argument concerning Bei Dao, a watered-down modernism is a hallmark of bad contemporary translations, whatever the age of the originals, promoting everywhere and at all times what Anthony Appiah has called a "monological universalism" ("Cosmopolitan Reading," 214). Foster's bland, even tone is intended both to save us from modernity and to reinforce a soothing reading of modernity itself. The poems deserve better: they achieve their full force as world literature when we translate them in such a way as to preserve both their immediacy and their distance from us, both their universality and their temporal and cultural specificity.

The work of world literature exists on two planes at once: present in our world, it also brings us into a world very different from ours, and its particular power comes from our doubled experience of both registers together. A work of literature written in our own time and place does this in a way as well, projecting us imaginatively into a situation that can be very different from our own. Yet the real frame of reference remains that of our own world (Norman Mailer's *Ancient Evenings* is hardly about antiquity; still less does it come to us *from* ancient Egypt). The work of world literature adds a further level to our reading experience: we feel ourselves brought into a dynamic engagement with an *actual* other world, in this case New Kingdom Egypt, a world dramatically distant from us in time, space, and culture.

Not that the poems are direct reflections of experience even in that world. Gardiner is surely mistaken in supposing that the necropolis where these poems were set down was the literal setting for the events they describe. ("The disused tombs in the Theban necropolis," he tells us, "will have given ample opportunities for amorous trysts," 36). As the papyrus itself clearly shows, a scribe's daily life had little to do with amorous trysts and everything to do with inventorying goods and composing formulaic panegyrics. In the second year of the brief and inconsequential reign of Ramses V, in the third month of the inundation season, our scribe is engaged in composing yet another encomium on the king: "Thou sittest on the throne of Pre, Great-of-Magic upon thy head, O Ramesse-Amenhikhopshef-beloved-of-Amun, thou Ruler who destroys the Nine Bows. . . ." ("The adulatory epithets here heaped upon Ramses V," Gardiner remarks, "are not calculated to teach us anything new about him . . . and, if the truth be told, this panegyric or Encomium belongs to the very least instructive and dullest types of Egyptian composition," 39–41). The inundation season, when the Nile rises to flood the parched fields, is the time of fertility, joy, new beginnings. The season is slipping by, and our scribe is precisely *not* reclining by the side of the river, under the shade of a fig tree, eating pomegranates and caressing a woman perfumed with scented oils—but such scenes recur again and again in the poems he sings, under his breath, as he dips his brush once again onto his palate. Indulging himself in a daring ligature of the signs 𓑠 and 𓇋, he sees himself, improbably, arranging a feast in the warm mud of the Nile itself, reading the thoughts of the woman who comes, breathless, to meet him:

Figure 9. Scribal statue of Amenhotep, son of Hapu, Eighteenth Dynasty, c. 1400 B.C.E.

> I found my lover at the ford,
> his feet set in the water;
> he builds a table there for feasts
> and sets it out with beer.
> He brings a blush to my skin,
> for he is tall and lean.

(Simpson, 324)

Pharaohs and warriors were typically tall and lean; scribes, as their (usually seated) statues show, were short and overweight, or at least were often so represented (figure 9). It is a mistake to look in these poems for a direct transcription either of the scribe's experience or of our own. Reading this poetry today, we triangulate between our world, the real world of Thebes three thousand years ago, and the erotic world that the poems project outward from the necropolis: a sunlit landscape of endless sensual fulfillment.

While our poem doesn't literally take place in the Theban necropolis, it still remains intimately linked to its culture of origin. If the Egyptian poems really were "Heine pure and simple," we would have little need for them. We already have Heine, not to mention plenty of babes coming at us in the soft-rock lyrics that Foster's assimilative translations echo ("For god's sake, sweet man, it's me coming at you"). Bathetic though they are, however, it is Foster's translations that have been most widely reprinted in recent American anthologies of world literature, presumably because the editors thought they would be "accessible" to contemporary readers.[5] The Egyptian poems can offer us much more than a syrupy version of ourselves, as long as we can keep their difference in play.

It has often been observed that translations age quickly. As a culture's literary values change, a generation's best translations soon turn into period pieces, all too obviously failing to reproduce the source text's tone and values, and no longer working effectively with the evolving culture in which they were produced. But true though it is that few translations outlast their immediate generation, it is a mistake to adopt a position of pure relativism, as though one translation is as good as another, or perhaps as bad as another, since all are contingent, and every translation expresses some person's or group's literary values. Particularly in formalist translation the-

---

[5] Foster's are the translations used, for example, in *The Norton Anthology of World Literature* as well as in a wide-ranging new collection aimed at general readers, *World Poetry: An Anthology of Verse from Antiquity to Our Time,* ed. Katharine Washburn, John S. Major, and Clifton Fadiman (1998).

ory in the seventies and eighties, questions of value were often ruled out of court. Writing in 1982, André Lefevere objected to all critiques of quality in translation:

> The most discouraging feature of the kind of writing on translation under discussion is that it persists in dealing with issues that remain stubbornly undecidable. It is plain impossible to define, once and for all, what a "good" translation is, just as it is impossible to define what good literature is. . . . Standards have changed so often in the history of Western literature that it must be obvious by now that translations are "good" only with respect to a certain place and a certain time, in certain circumstances. ("Literary Theory and Translated Literature," 9)

Lefevere argued, very cogently, that translations never genuinely "reflect" their original, whether faithfully or not; instead, they *refract* their originals. Every translation is a negotiation between "source" and "target" cultures, and as a result all are evidence for shifting literary values. Elsewhere Lefevere criticizes what he sees as a Romantic obsession with fidelity to a quasi-sacred original, "which is not to be tampered with—hence the horror with which 'bad' translations are rejected" ("Mother Courage's Cucumbers," 234).

It is certainly the case that there are translations that are "bad" only because they violate some rival set of literary norms that finally have no better justification than those that underlie the "bad" translation. Yet there are *bad* translations too. Sometimes they result from a wholesale imposition of the translator's cultural norms on the source text, other times from a clever idea, enthusiastically tried, that ultimately didn't pan out. A concern with quality can reflect something other than a Romantic obsession with originality; even if we agree that a translation is a creative work in its own right, it nonetheless has a different status from the original work, since it is a re-creation of that work. As George Steiner emphasized in *After Babel*, a translation is always an interpretation of the source text, and as a result a translation is not a faded replica of the original but an expansive transformation of it. The translator has an ethical responsibility to do justice to the original, though a variety of strategies can certainly be employed to that end. Hence there can be several different effective translations of a single work even at a single time, just as a poem can have a range of critical interpretations. By the same token, though, there can also be bad translations of a work, just as there can be bad interpretations.

What makes a bad translation? Like any interpretation, a translation can fail in two basic ways: either by outright error—simply getting it wrong—or by failing to convey the force and beauty of the original. Lefevere is right that it is impossible to codify any clear set of rules by which to judge such effectiveness, but our situation is no different with translations than with any other form of interpretation: the good ones are the ones that, under close inspection, are seen to do justice to the original. A literalistic reproduction of the original text's syntax and vocabulary produces more of a crib to the original than an effective work in its own right. A heavily assimilative translation, on the other hand, absorbs the text so fully into the host culture that its cultural and historical difference vanishes. Translation theorists from Steiner in the mid-seventies to Lawrence Venuti today have called for "foreignizing" translations, versions that resist assimilation and point up the work's difference, its translated quality. Foster's Egyptian translations fail according to this standard; once Amun has been reduced to "god" and the speaker to a very early Britney Spears, we have lost the very difference that made the Egyptian poem important to translate in the first place.

Of course, one may or may not share this preference for "minoritizing" or "foreignizing" translations. Their popularity today clearly accords with the rise of multiculturalism and our new attention to ethnic difference; just as the melting pot has lost favor as a model for immigrant experience, so too assimilative translation is increasingly disfavored. "Foreignizing" efforts are the translational correlate of the contemporary championing of ethnic identity. A proponent of a more universalist view of world literature could well object that foreignness can be overdone: it can produce potentially unreadable texts, and it can create a separatist mode of translation that undermines the reader's sense of connection to a common human experience. Yet even a reader with universalist principles should object to a translation that simply assimilates the foreign work to contemporary American values, a process that gets us to no common ground beyond our own local cultural position.

The desire to turn the text to our own desires, even to appropriate it outright, is no modern invention; its traces can be seen on Nakht-Sobek's papyrus itself. We are in the unusual situation of knowing, from the papyrus's own headings, not only its Theban provenance but even the month and year when at least part of it was written. We would know even more, the actual name of the compiler of the collection of poems we have been examining, had it not been for Nakht-Sobek's acquisitive enthusiasm. As the manuscript now stands, the songs are titled "The Sweet Sayings Found in a Collection of Writings, Composed by the Scribe of the Necropolis Nakht-Sobek." Nakht-Sobek, however, has replaced the actual composer's name with his own: "An impudent usurpation," as Gardiner sternly comments, "so badly written and over so imperfect an erasure, that it could deceive no one" (1, 6). Yet this overwriting has succeeded all too well: though Nakht-Sobek can never in fact become the composer of these lovely lyrics, he has forever erased his predecessor's identity.

Then again, any such regret is anachronistic. Authorship was rarely noted in ancient Egypt, and then often falsely. The phrase "*ir.n*," which Simpson translates as "composed by," may well have been intended simply to mean "assembled by." Nakht-Sobek and his predecessor alike were probably claiming credit only for compiling the collection, not for composing the poems. The names we have in Egyptian colophons are usually not those of original authors but of the scribes who copy an older text, as in the colophon to "The Story of the Shipwrecked Sailor": "It has come, from its beginning to its end, as it has been found in writing, in the writing of the scribe excellent of fingers, Ameny's son Amen-aa" (Simpson, 56). Far from asserting authorship, such a colophon simply attests to the accuracy of transmission. Despite Gardiner's indignation, Nakht-Sobek's "usurpation" is not after all so different from the modern practice of transmission whereby his collection in turn has become part of "Papyrus Chester Beatty no. 1," which for its own part reaches print under a new title, itself bearing yet another added name—Gardiner's own: *The Library of A. Chester Beatty: Description of a Hieratic Papyrus . . . by Alan H. Gardiner, F.B.A.*

The ancient authors of the poems in the papyrus would hardly have been surprised to have retained the anonymity they probably had from the very outset. They would, however, have been profoundly shocked to imagine that their poems could ever outlast the age-old reign of Amun Re, sustainer of earthly life and of Egypt's immemorial social and political order. The phrase translated "as Amun lives," *wa'h Imn,* could more properly be rendered "as Amun endures": the verb signifies age-long or everlasting continuity. The poet who used this oath would never have envisioned the strange reversal whereby Amun, guarantor of the lovers' passion, has vanished from the world and is brought to an audience today thanks to the poem's lasting erotic power. Amun no longer endures, but the poem comes to us afresh, multiply refracted through the shifting lens of translation.

5

The Afterlife of Mechthild von Magdeburg

Near the beginning of *Virgin Machine*, a 1988 film by the avant-garde German director Monika Treut, the heroine, Dorothee, stages a paper-doll puppet show with her half-brother Bruno, with whom she has been having an affair. Speaking in the voice of one of the puppets, she declares, "Lady Love, you have stolen everything I have achieved on earth." Speaking as Lady Love, Bruno replies, "I have given you eternal freedom in exchange!" Dorothee's puppet goes on to accuse Lady Love of robbing her of her youth, her friends, her very flesh and blood; Bruno's puppet serenely maintains that her reward awaits her in heaven. Dorothee receives Lady Love's assurances with joy, and soon after this scene she flees her home in Hamburg, leaving both her brother and a collapsed marriage, and moves to the earthly paradise—San Francisco—in search of her mother, who had moved there years before to work as a stripper. Though she never finds her mother, Dorothee finds a new sexual identity and a new life in San Francisco's lesbian community, free from the either/or choices available to her back in Germany.

Unidentified in the film, the puppets' dialogue that sets this transformation in motion is taken from one of the most remarkable books of the Middle Ages, a series of visions, reflections, and poems by a long-forgotten thirteenth-century mystic, Mechthild von Magdeburg. In her own age ambiguously situated in relation to the dominant traditions of male theology, Mechthild has been recovered in modern times. She can now be seen as an early feminist and can even serve—in a development that would have astonished Mechthild herself—as an inspiring source for a contemporary filmmaker's radical re-presentation of gender identity.

Translation can carry works across many sorts of borders: not only geographical and temporal but social as well, including the boundaries of gender. Such crossings, however, can be difficult. Mechthild's uncanny prose poetry already posed formidable difficulties for her first audiences and continues to challenge her modern readers today. Her literary activity came as a surprise to Mechthild herself. She was living and working quietly in the northern German town of Magdeburg, where she had become a Beguine, one of a group of women living a religious life and ministering to the poor and the sick but without taking formal vows or assuming full membership in an established convent. Then, in 1250, she began to have intense visions: of departed friends, of purgatory and hell, of the Virgin Mary, and of God himself. She experienced these visions for more than thirty years, many of them focused on her love and longing for Christ.

Her troubles began when, at Christ's command, she started to record these visions, either writing them down herself or dictating them to her nonplussed confessor, a monk named Heinrich von Halle. Collected into several (ultimately seven) books under the overall title *A Flowing Light of the Godhead*, her visions and associated writings found some admirers but aroused violent opposition as well. She was mocked, attacked as unorthodox, even for a time denied access to Holy Communion, as she started to stray into theological matters that women weren't supposed to deal with, and as she—or rather, God himself in her visions—became sharply critical of church affairs. As if her forays into theological debate and church politics weren't bad enough, many of the visions were strikingly erotic in tone and content. Male theologians before Mechthild, writing in Latin, had developed the theme of the Church or the soul as the bride of Christ; Mechthild draws most directly on the Cistercian traditions inaugurated in the previous century by Bernard of Clairvaux, whose *Sermons on the Song of Songs* had lingered on the spiritual meaning of the divine lover's kisses and his praises of the body of the beloved. Bernard, however, had constantly stressed that his listeners must not fall into the error of taking the Song of Songs literally, and Latin had provided an insulating medium in which he could allegorize the poem's erotic imagery for a select, spiritually attuned audience. As he says at the start of his sermons, "To you, brothers, one should speak of different things, or at least in a different *way*, than to those in the world" ("Vobis, fratres, alia quam de aliis de saeculo, aut certe aliter dicenda sunt," *Sermons*, 1:1).

Mechthild was one of the first writers to translate this kind of discussion into the secular languages of the emerging European vernaculars, and she performed this translation in a particularly bold way, combining mystical theology with the courtly-love traditions developed by the German minnesingers. The result of this double translation was "the boldest erotic poem that we possess from the Middle Ages" (Mohr, "Darbietungsformen," 393) and yet also "a milestone in the theological development of medieval German mysticism" (Lüers, *Sprache*, 314). Mechthild presented God and the soul as spiritual lovers with a new intensity and sensual vividness:

> *God Compares the Soul to Four Things*
> You taste like a grape,
> your scent is like balsam,
> you shine like the sun,
> you are an increase of my highest love.
>
> *The Soul Praises God in Five Things*
> O God, overflowing in your gifts!
> O God, outpouring in your love!
> O God, burning in your longing!
> O God, melting in union with your love!
> O God, resting on my breasts!
> I cannot live without you.[1]

Other entries go further, describing Mechthild's encounters with her divine lover:

> So the best-beloved comes to the Most Fair in the hidden chambers of invisible divinity. There she finds the bed of love and its furnishings, divinely prepared by God. Then our Lord says, "Stand still, Lady Soul!" "What do you request, Lord?" "You shall undress yourself!" "Lord, what is to become of me?" "Lady Soul, you are so formed in my nature that nothing may come between you and me. No angel has ever been so honored as to have for one hour what is given to you for eternity. Therefore you must lay aside both fear and shame and all outer virtues; only what you carry within your nature shall you eternally cherish. That is your noble longing and your endless desire; this I will forever fulfill through my infinite mercy." "Lord, now I am a naked soul, and you in yourself a richly adorned God. Our joint companionship is eternal life without death." Then comes a holy silence, as both of them wish. He gives himself to her and she to him. She alone

---

[1] Book 1, chapters 16 and 17. Many of Mechthild's chapters are short poems or epigrammatic utterances like these; others extend for several pages. I will continue to cite by book and chapter, as these are consistent in different editions. When a specific translator is not under discussion, I have translated directly from Hans Neumann's edition of the Middle High German text.

knows what happens to her now, and I content myself with that. Now this cannot continue long; when two lovers come secretly together, they often must part without farewells. (1.44)

As Mechthild's fame spread, she was sought out for spiritual counsel; the later sections of her book include an increasing number of entries giving advice on religious life and on struggles against temptation. Mechthild acutely analyzes the temptations of power, and she condemns the luxury and moral laxity of the established monastic orders, not sparing the pope himself: "Alas, crown of holy priesthood, how you are worn away! Nothing remains but a husk, that is, priestly power, with which you war against God and his chosen friends." This vision ends with God appearing to the pope: "Pope, my son," he warns, "your predecessors' lives were short because they did not fulfill my secret will" (6.21).

Mechthild's contemporaries were both fascinated and unsettled by these visions. One entry indicates that even Mechthild's confessor, Heinrich von Halle, was taken aback by some of her visions, but God assures Mechthild that she must persevere even though she is a mere woman:

> *How God Replied to a Brother Concerning What Is Written in This Book*
>
> Master Heinrich, you wonder at many words that are written in this book. I wonder that you wonder at them. It has ever grieved me to the heart that I, a sinful woman, must write, that I can only describe the true knowledge and the sublime holy revelations in these words, which seem to me far too poor for this eternal truth. I asked the eternal Master what he thought about this. He replied: "Ask him how it happened that the apostles, for all their faint-heartedness, became so fearless as to receive the Holy Spirit. Ask further, where Moses was, when he saw nothing other than God. And ask further, how it was that Daniel could speak so well when still a youth." (5.12)

A chastened Heinrich suppressed his discomfort and determined to spread Mechthild's writings beyond her local circle. This would require translation, as few people spoke (and fewer read) her dialect of Low German. To circulate around Europe, the book would have to be translated into Latin; either Heinrich himself or fellow Dominican monks at Halle translated the first six books (apparently before Mechthild compiled the final book, late in life, when she had moved to a convent at Helfta). At the same time, Heinrich felt that some alterations were in order if the book was to read properly in the language of churchmen's scholarship and theology; the book's very title gained formality and even elegance when *Ein vliessendes Lieht der Gotheit* became *Lux Divinitatis* (no disorderly "flowing" in the Latin title). As Heinrich says in his preface, he "cut, smoothed, and softened" the original (Menzies tr., xxii), and the materials were rearranged by subject matter, producing a far more coherent—and conventional—book, one in which both eroticism and criticism of Church authorities were muted.

Heinrich's approach to the book's eroticism is signaled by how he chose to translate the name of the allegorical figure of Love, "Frau Minne." With this figure, Mechthild is expressing the love of God in the secular imagery developed by Walther von der Vogelweide and his fellow minnesingers; Heinrich weakens this connection by translating *Minne* simply as "Caritas," a term with a safely spiritual significance uncontaminated by the figure of Amor or Eros. Throughout his translation, the language of lovers' passion is regularly toned down: "du bist ein sturm mînes hertzen" ("you are a storm of my heart") becomes "status cordis mei est" ("he is the bulwark of my heart"). Sometimes a more explicit phrase is erased altogether: the Latin text simply drops the vivid line "je das minnebet enger wird, je die umbehalsunge naher gât" ("The narrower the bed of love, the closer is the embrace").[2]

In addition to toning down Mechthild's eroticism, the Latin translation clarifies the lines of authority behind her work. The book opens with a brief prologue in which it is quite unclear in the Middle High German version whether Mechthild is claiming direct authorship or is attributing the book's authorship to God:

This Book is Called "A Flowing Light of the Godhead"

Ah, Lord God, who has made this book? I have made it in my weakness, for I could not hold back my gift. Ah, Lord, what name should be given to this book that serves your honor alone? It shall be called A Light of my Godhead flowing into all hearts who live without falsehood.

As writers of Mechthild's era didn't use quotation marks, this paragraph could either be meant to show Mechthild in dialogue with God or could be her own assertion of authorship. The passage hovers (perhaps deliberately) between both possibilities. Heinrich wanted no ambiguity on this point, and so he inserted dialogue markers into the Latin: "*I said:* Ah, Lord God, who has made this book? *The Lord replied:* I have made it. . . ." Heinrich's clarifi-

---

[2] These and other interesting examples are discussed by Grete Lüers in *Die Sprache der deutschen Mystik des Mittelalters im Werke der Mechthild von Magdeburg*, 45–55.

cation, however, introduced a problem, as whoever is speaking the second sentence is admitting to "weakness" or "powerlessness" (*unmaht*). This is a word that Mechthild never otherwise uses of God or any heavenly figure but only of herself and other weak mortals. Heinrich solved this problem by a simple change of prefix: instead of confessing to powerlessness, *impotentia* in Latin, God instead makes the book through his *omnipotentia*, his omnipotence.

This softened translation is the one that achieved general circulation, and eventually the original text was lost altogether. Fortunately, in the 1340s a Swiss cleric named Heinrich von Nördlingen had made an independent translation from Mechthild's Low German dialect into the more standard Middle High German. Long lost, this translation was rediscovered in 1861 in a Swiss monastery, so that we now have a version that is at least relatively close to the lost original, both in language and evidently also in content. Even this apparently faithful translation, however, is prefaced in such a way as to put Mechthild in her proper place and order the reader's attention accordingly. The translation begins with a Latin introduction in which Heinrich von Nördlingen emphasizes Mechthild's humility and her obedience to the men in authority around her: he describes her as "a virgin holy in body and spirit, through grace inspired by the Lord, who in humble simplicity, in the poverty of an exile, weighed down by contempt, in celestial contemplation, as this writing makes clear, served the Lord for more than forty years with the greatest devotion, following perfectly the footsteps of the order of preaching friars, from one day to the next always becoming more proficient and always better." Heinrich then gives a new and highly selective table of contents. He tells his reader that Mechthild's book

contains many good things, as is set out in the titles:

On the Trinity: Book 2, Chapter 3; Book 3, Chapter 9; Book 4,
Chapters 12 and 14; Book 5, Chapter 26.
On Christ: Book 1, Chapter 2; Book 4, Chapter 24; Book 5,
Chapter 23.
On Our Lady: Book 1, Chapter 4; Book 2, Chapter 3; Book 5,
Chapter 23.
On the Nine Orders of Angels: Book 1, Chapter 6; Book 3,
Chapter 1; Book 5, Chapter 1. . . . (Neumann ed., 3)

And so on. These headings reorient the reading of Mechthild's work away from eroticism and critique alike and toward standard topics of men's theological inquiry. Even the entries on Christ are carefully selected to point the reader to chapters in which Jesus is either an innocent babe in Bethlehem or a sublime prince enthroned in heaven, blessing his saints: none of the chapters listed concerning Christ includes any of Mechthild's private encounters with her divine lover. A single one of Heinrich's headings, *De Caritate maxime*, seems to hint at the book's erotic content, but the sole chapter included under this heading shows Mechthild at her most abstract and impersonal: "The gentle love of holy compassion banishes hollow honor and wicked sickness. . . . The proclaimed love of God's teaching gladly bends down even to a child" (3.13).

The two Heinrichs succeeded only too well in creating acceptable translations of Mechthild's book. It circulated for over a century in these and other, derivative versions, all of which followed their lead in highlighting certain chapters, often dropping the rest of the book entirely. The diffusion of Mechthild's work in Latin was wide enough so that Dante could paraphrase some of her verses in his *Divine Comedy*, having found them in an intermediate source, a Latin life of Saint Dominic by a late-thirteenth-century writer named Dietrich von Apolda. Yet Mechthild's impact became more and more diffuse as her work was diffused. Dietrich is typical in lifting one of her poems out of context, and he credits her simply as "a certain person who loved Saint Dominic," without even identifying her by name. As Gisela Vollman-Profe has noted in her preface to Neumann's edition of the *Flowing Light*, "Mechthild's book was endangered from the start by the unusualness of its form and through its loose overall construction. Since its unity closely depended on the person of its author and her life story, it was almost inevitably lost as soon as interest in Mechthild had faded, and along with it concrete historical knowledge about her. . . . The book became a quarry for the most varied new uses" (1:xiii). Assimilated to the interests and values of mainstream theology, Mechthild's book lost its integrity and gradually fell out of currency; it was forgotten by the end of the fourteenth century.

Half a millennium later, nineteenth-century scholars began seeking out and publishing medieval texts in great numbers. The Middle High German text of the *Flowing Light* was discovered in 1861 and published in 1869, and the Latin translation followed in 1877. At first read only by specialists, the *Flowing Light* began to reach a broader audience in the twentieth century, when more people started to take an interest in medieval mysticism. The great scholar Evelyn Underhill showcased Mechthild in her seminal 1912 book *Mysticism* and in several later works, and in 1953 Underhill's student and friend Lucy Menzies published the first translation of the book into English, under the title *The Revelations of Mechthild of Magdeburg (1210–1297): or, The Flowing Light of the Godhead.* Mechthild had emerged into a new world.

New, but not entirely different, as Mechthild's modern readers were often still uncomfortable with her eroticism. In a 1939 book on *The Flowering of Mysticism,* Rufus Jones praised Mechthild's "lyric genius" and the holiness that allowed her to stand "on the most intimate speaking terms with the highest celestial Beings," and yet just that intimacy disturbed him. "There is a large element of pathology in the story," he remarks, "far too much reproduction of the experiences reported in the Song of Solomon, and unwholesome dialogues of love intimacies which mark this type of amorous, cloistered mysticism" (49). A decade and a half later, when Lucy Menzies translated the book, she downplayed Mechthild's eroticism and also assimilated her to the dominant tradition of male theology. The first chapter of Mechthild's book stages the confrontation between Frau Minne and the Soul that Monika Treut would later pick up, its dialogue based on the secular poetic form of the *minneklage,* or complaint against love. In an introductory footnote, Menzies notes the dialogue's courtly imagery but emphasizes that "its matter is also religious and philosophical. The philosophy is that of early German mysticism, pointing back to the Neo-Platonism of the fourth century" (4). Connecting Mechthild securely to the male philosophical tradition, Menzies systematically softens the stark physicality of Mechthild's language. The soul's first accusation is that Love has behaved highly improperly. In Menzies's translation, these lines read as follows:

> SOUL
> Love, thou didst wrestle long years
> With the Holy Trinity
> Till the overflow fell once for all
> In Mary's humble lap!
> LOVE
> But, O Queen, these things were done
> For thy honour and thy delight.
>
> (1.1)

Frank Tobin, Mechthild's most recent and best translator, renders the Soul's accusation much more directly: "Lady Love, you struggled many a year before you forced the exalted Trinity to pour itself utterly into the humble virginal womb of Mary."[3] This is only one of several passages in which

---

[3] *The Flowing Light of the Godhead,* tr. Frank Tobin, 39. Tobin is following the shrewd guess of Margot Schmidt in her 1955 modern German translation of Mechthild, in which the

Mechthild meditates on the conception and gestation of her beloved Jesus, but the openness with which she presents the event is obscured in Menzies's translation.

In other instances, Menzies censors passages outright. She says in her preface that "Having translated the whole book . . . it is with regret that owing to the high cost of printing, I have been obliged to omit a few unimportant chapters, and here and there, unimportant paragraphs" (xxvi). These omissions, however, were not made on economic grounds alone. Consider the early scene, quoted above, in which the Soul comes to God's chambers and finds the bed of love prepared, receives God's order to undress, and then achieves mystical union with him. When God commands her to undress (*ir soent úch usziehen*), Menzies renders this as "Thy SELF must go!" (1.44). As for the *minnebet*, or bed of love, it disappears altogether, replaced by a chaste ellipsis: "Then the beloved goes in to the Lover, into the secret hiding place of the sinless Godhead. . . . And there, the soul being fashioned in the very nature of God, no hindrance can come between it and God."[4]

New possibilities have emerged in the half-century since Menzies made her pioneering translation, as can be seen in another moment of intimacy, rendered by Menzies as: "The more the fire burns, the more her light increases. The more love consumes her, the brighter she shines" (1.22). Christiane Galvani has done better justice to the Middle High German by rendering this in clearly sexual terms: "The more excited she remains, the sooner she is enkindled. The more feverish she is, the more she glows." Galvani allows Mechthild's body its full role; though Mechthild often speaks of her body as a dog or a beast of burden, she also insists that her spiritual visions must permeate her every member: "*The Writing of This Book Is Seen, Heard, and Felt in All Limbs:* I neither can nor may write, unless I see it with the eyes of my soul, and I hear it with the ears of my eternal spirit and feel the power of the Holy Spirit in every limb of my body" (4.13).

If the sexuality of Mechthild's visions is becoming more visible in

---

Trinity "allzumal ergoß / In Mariens demütig jungfräulichen Schoß" (*Das Fliessende Licht der Gottheit*, 54). In giving the rhymed pairing *ergoß/Schoß* ("discharged"/"womb"), Schmidt has restored the rhyme that was likely present in the original Low German. It seems that Heinrich von Nördlingen was already embarrassed by this scene: his Middle High German translation sacrifices the rhyme in order to suppress the term for "womb," instead having the Trinity spill out more abstractly into Mary's humble "maidenhood" (*magetuom*).

[4] A 1991 translation by Christiane Galvani restores the bed of love, but even Galvani follows Menzies's lead when it comes to stripping: instead of commanding the Soul to undress, Galvani's God says that "You shall take leave of yourself."

contemporary translations, so is her frequent opposition to the male hierarchies of her era. Galvani's introduction gives less weight to neoplatonic
continuities than to Mechthild's manifold challenges to the men around her,
and this is also the emphasis of the most widely circulated recent selection
from Mechthild's writings, included in an ambitious collection by two Bel-
gian medievalists, Emilie Zum Brunn and Georgette Epiney-Burgard. This
collection, published in 1988 under the eloquent title *Femmes Troubadours
de Dieu,* was translated into English the following year under the more prosaic title *Women Mystics in Medieval Europe.* Zum Brunn and Epiney-
Burgard begin their Mechthild selections with one of the starkest passages
in her book:

> I have been warned about this book
> And this is what I have been told:
> That unless I had it buried
> It would become a prey to fire!
> And so, as had been my wont since childhood,
> Being sad, I began to pray.
> I addressed myself to my Beloved
> And said to Him: "Ah, Lord, behold me afflicted
> For the sake of Your honor.
> Will you leave me without consolation?
> For it is You Who have led me here,
> You Who ordered me to write this book."

> (2.26)

God then appears to Mechthild, carrying the book itself in his right hand,
and reassures her:

> He said: "My Beloved, do not despair like that,
> Nobody can burn the Truth.
> He who wishes to take this book from My hand
> Must be stronger than I am."

God goes on to say that Mechthild's feminine humility and lack of learning
have made her a better conduit for his words than a sophisticated scholar
would be.

Powerful as this passage is, this is not how Mechthild begins her collection; this scene is taken from the end of her second book. Mechthild's own
lead-in is far less confrontational. God first addresses the reader not in opposition but with words of invitation:

This book should be gladly received, for God himself speaks its words

I send this book as a messenger to all spiritual people, both good and evil, for if the pillars fall, the structure cannot stand, and it portrays me alone and admirably reveals my secrecy. Whoever wants to understand this book should read it nine times.

The men who circulated the book were clearly impressed by this divine endorsement: the Middle High German version begins with a preface by Heinrich von Nördlingen that echoes God's words even as it emphasizes the work's transmittal through a man's hands: "A brother of the same order collected and wrote this book and there are many good things in it, as is shown in the table of contents. You should read it nine times, prayerfully, humbly, and thoughtfully" (Neumann, 1:2).

Zum Brunn and Epiney-Burgard have given half the story: they portray men's opposition to Mechthild but leave out the passages that show her enlisting God himself as her publicist and successfully setting in motion a male line of transmission to the wider world beyond her community. The bulk of the Belgians' selections have a similar effect, emphasizing passages of loneliness, abandonment, and isolation both from the surrounding community and from God. Thus their longest selection, several pages long, consists of a melancholy chapter entitled *How the Fiancée Who Is United to God Refuses the Consolation of All Creatures, Desiring Only That of God, and How She Sinks into Suffering.* At the heart of this chapter, the abandoned Soul welcomes its own abandonment and even prays for God to increase it:

> Then came the constant estrangement of God and wrapped itself closely around the Soul, so the Soul said: "Welcome, most holy estrangement! How fortunate I am to have been born, to have you as my handmaid; for you bring me unaccustomed joy and inconceivable wonders and unbearable sweetness as well. But, Lord, take the sweetness from me, and leave me with your estrangement alone. Ah, how fortunate I am, dear God, that I have this to bear after my soul has been transformed! I cannot express how pleasing it is to my soul; gall has been turned to honey for me on the palate of my soul. . . . Now God's mastery over me is complete, and God deals wonderfully with me, for now his estrangement is dearer to me than He himself."
>
> The Soul well knew that God wished to comfort her amid the great estrangement, and so she said: "Think, Lord, who I am, and withdraw yourself from me." Then our Lord spoke to her: "Allow

me this, to cool with you the heat of my divinity, the longing of my humanity, and the joy of my holy spirit!" Then she answered: "Yes, Lord, but moderately, so that it pleases you and not me." (4.12)

Zum Brunn and Epiney-Burgard follow this chilling chapter with a final entry on prayer for lost souls, closing with Mechthild's fears for "imperfect religious persons":

> Outwardly they seem wise, but, alas, they are all fools within! This child has the most difficulty to recover, for he sinks first into obstinate quarrels, then into inertia, then into false consolation, followed by despair and finally, alas, he is deprived of all grace. And so it is very difficult to say which direction this strayed soul will take. (5.8)

Their selections end with these gloomy words. Yet this is no more the ending of Mechthild's book than their first selection is her opening. In Mechthild's book, the passage just quoted is immediately followed by a far more positive chapter, *Of the Honor of Seventy Men Who Gave Witness to Christ* (5.9). The fifth book as a whole ends with a chapter titled *How Sister Mechthild Thanks and Praises God and Prays for Three Kinds of People and for Herself*, concluding with a prayer "that Lord, by your sweet pleasure and my long desire I may behold you forever, so the eyes of my soul may play upon your godhead and your sweet love's joy may course through my soul out of your divine breast" (5.35). The mood is now one of joyful and trusting anticipation, rather than anxiety and self-denial.

Zum Brunn and Epiney-Burgard's choice and arrangement of selections produce a very specific sort of Mechthild, constructed as an alienated modern heroine, starkly opposed to her surroundings and enmeshed in an abusive relationship with an arbitrary and inaccessible God. If Lucy Menzies translated and edited Mechthild in such a way that one could almost forget she was a woman, Zum Brunn and Epiney-Burgard have reconstructed a Mechthild who scarcely seems to be connected to the Christian community around her.[5]

The reciprocal difference between the two versions can be found both in overall editorial shaping and also at the level of specific translation

[5] The impact of Zum Brunn and Epiney-Burgard's editorial choices is at variance with the much more balanced presentation given in their introduction to Mechthild's life and work (39–53), which effectively combines feminist perspectives with discussion of patristic roots and the contemporary theological context.

choices. Early in the book, the Soul comes to God's court, where she is described in the Middle High German text as *wise und wol gezogen*. Menzies renders this as "discreet and modest," but in Zum Brunn and Epiney-Burgard the Soul becomes something quite different: "wise and courtly." The Soul then *gert unmesseklich sines lobes*—in Menzies, the Soul "longs above everything to praise Him"; in Zum Brunn and Epiney-Burgard, the Soul longs "that *He* should praise *her*" (1.4; emphasis added). Each of these translations is defensible in itself, but it is noteworthy how each translator's choices silently reinforce the selective overall pattern of their edition: Menzies creates a humble soul who wants to fit in, while Zum Brunn and Epiney-Burgard create a powerful and attractive heroine whose experience of the dark night of the soul, they say in their introduction, was "lived in a way that might be termed modern" (52).

It may be hard to resist fixing Mechthild in one way or another, because she is otherwise so hard to grasp at all. She defers at times to men around her, yet she also plays Heinrich von Halle like a lute; she bemoans her poor command of German and her lack of Latin, yet she also associates herself with such powerful prophetic figures as Moses and Daniel. She often sees herself as abandoned by God as if by an inconstant lover, yet at other times she is caught up into intimate communion with him. Further, she experiences heavenly encounters not only with an inscrutable Christ but with the Virgin Mary as well, whom she elevates to virtually divine status in her own right: "Her son is God," Mechthild says of Mary, "and she is the goddess" (3.1). Empowered by association with Mary, the Soul can become divine as well: "The Heavenly Father shared his divine love with the Soul and said: 'I am the God of all gods, and you are the goddess of all creatures'" (3.9).

If God is characterized by mystery and withdrawal, Mary is a figure of intimacy and nurturing presence. In her fifth book, Mechthild has a vision of Jesus' birth in Bethlehem, focusing on a tender scene in which Mary gives her breast to the baby, conveying to him not only nourishment but her own personality:

> Now hear a wonder! The bright blossoms of her lovely eyes and
> the spiritual beauty of her maidenly countenance and the flowing
> sweetness of her pure heart and the marvelous playfulness of her
> noble soul, these four things came together in her maidenly breast
> by the Father's will and the Son's need and the Holy Spirit's
> desire. Then the sweet milk flowed from her pure heart without
> any pain; the child sucked in a human way and his mother
> rejoiced in a holy way. (5.23)

Interestingly, in this vision Mechthild finds herself at Mary's side in place of Joseph; when Mechthild asks where Joseph is, Mary replies that he has gone to town to buy groceries.

Mary's maternal power even predates her own birth: in another vision, Mary says, "I suckled the prophets and sages, before I was born" (1.22). Mechthild then sees the Soul being nourished by the combined flow of Mary's milk and the crucified Jesus's blood. In contrast to God's constant withdrawal, moreover, Mary has no choice but to be present and to nurture the Soul. As the Soul tells Mary in the conclusion of this vision:

> Lady, now must you suckle us, for your breasts are still so full that you cannot restrain it. If you no longer wished to nurse, the milk would pain you greatly. For indeed I have seen your breasts so full that seven streams poured out all at once from one breast onto my body and onto my soul. . . . So you must suckle us until the Last Day: you must empty yourself until God's children and yours are weaned and fully grown in their eternal body. Ah! Then we shall know and see with limitless joy the milk and even the very same breast which Jesus kissed so often. (1.22)

Taken as a whole, *A Flowing Light of the Godhead* undercuts the most basic dichotomies it plays with: powerlessness and power, humanity and divinity, female and male, body and soul. Mechthild despises her body and longs to leave it behind, and yet at the very end of her book she closes with a dialogue between body and soul, mirroring the opening dialogue between the soul and Lady Love. In place of the anger in the earlier dialogue, the tone is now one of mutual respect and thanks:

> Thus the suffering body speaks to the sorrowing Soul: "When will you fly with the wings of your longing through the marvelous heights up to Jesus, your eternal love? Thank him there, lady, for me, that though I am base and unworthy, even so he wanted to be mine, when he abased himself and took our humanity upon himself. Pray too that he may keep me guiltless in his pure grace until a holy end, when you, most beloved Soul, depart from me."
>
> The Soul: "Alas, my best-beloved prison in which I am confined, I thank you for everything in which you have followed me. Though I have often been troubled by you, yet you have come to my aid. All your suffering will be taken from you on the Last Day. So let us lament no more; what God has done with us will bring us comfort, if you can now stand fast in sweet hope." (7.65)

Gender too is mutable. The Soul, so often presented as the longing woman, is masculine as well. Addressing the Soul in one vision, Faith declares, "Seeing you, O loving Soul, you are so lovably, beautifully made! A glowing light was given so that I could see you, or this could never have happened to me. You are threefold within yourself, so you may well be God's image: You are a virile man in battle, you are a beautifully adorned maiden in the palace before your Lord, you are a joyful bride in your divine bed of love" (2.19). An interesting analogue to Gilgamesh's heritage: where he was one-third human, two-thirds divine, here the Soul is one-third male, two-thirds female.

No translation has yet done justice to Mechthild's many-sided work, in part because no translation has yet come to terms with her extraordinary style, which transcends yet another classic dichotomy: that between prose and verse. All of the translations discussed above, and my own sample passages, alternate between lyrics and paragraphs of prose. Yet most of Mechthild's book is actually written in a flexible rhymed prose, usually rhythmic but rarely employing a set meter, often using true rhymes but also using a wide variety of off-rhymes as well, in a mode that hovers between poetry and prose as we know them and even as most of Mechthild's contemporaries knew them.

Given the spareness of Mechthild's vocabulary and the differing weight of German and English, it is hard to reproduce this style without producing something that sounds like doggerel. Still, a poet attuned to Mechthild's style and highly skilled in the use of off-rhymes and modulated repetitions could do a great deal. The only modern edition to take any account of this distinctive language is Neumann's 1990 edition of the Middle High German, which spaces out Mechthild's rhymes and verbal echoes to emphasize them, while keeping the paragraph format in which the chapters are written. Thus the passage just quoted, in which Faith praises the Soul's threefold beauty begins as follows: "O minnendú sele, ich sach dich a n, du bist harte minnenklich wunderlich g e t a n. Ein lieht wart darzuo g e l ú h e n, das ich dich moehte b e s e h e n, es were mir anders nie b e s c h e h e n" (1:49). True rhymes (*an/getan*) appear along with the off-rhyme *gelúhen/besehen,* and there is a rough but inconsistent meter. The balance of the passage, however, has no rhymes at all and shades back into ordinary prose. In their recent translations, both Tobin and Galvani translate this passage as poetry; but though it is far from prosaic, it is actually something other than verse.

As Gisela Vollman-Profe says in her introduction to Neumann's edition, the first editor of the Middle High German text in 1877, Gall Morel, "knew only prose on the one hand and verse on the other" and arbitrarily set some passages as prose and others as verse. "This procedure, however, obscured the distinctive flow of Mechthild's speech, which employs many intermediate forms to create sliding transitions from prose to verse and from verse to prose" (1:xxii). No modern translation has yet taken up the challenge of Mechthild's flowing style, so appropriate an embodiment of her uncanny visions and her profound reflection on them.

Mechthild was deeply aware that her language always fell short of the radiance of her visions: in heaven, she says, "the light is so exceptionally splendid that I neither can nor may describe it. . . . I can only say a little bit, no more than a honeybee can carry away on its feet from a full hive" (3.1). As little as she could convey, she was also concerned that books could be *over*read, becoming an end in themselves, breeding pride and spiritual isolation. In her third book she records a terrifying vision of a deceased friend who had read not wisely but too much:

> I saw in pain a spiritual man of whom I had a great opinion during his life. . . . He was pale and in a white mist. I asked him: "Alas, why have you not reached heaven?" He answered me with uncertain words, in remorseful shame; he was reading a book, and the words shrieked out, as they rose around him like smoke along with all the books he had ever read. He said: "I had too much worldly love of thoughts, of words, and of deeds." Two dragons lay at his feet, sucking out of him all the comfort he should have received from holy Christianity but for his sickly obedience, since he needlessly preferred to follow his own will and not his prelate's teaching. (3.17)

This vision dramatizes the danger of Mechthild's own work. Fervently orthodox yet fiercely loyal to her private vision, Mechthild could hardly have fit comfortably into any established medieval community of interpretation. Her distinctive poetic prose was the vehicle by which she sought to convey the inexpressible and to alter her readers' perceptions beyond their ordinary boundaries. From the first, the radicalism of her presentation aroused suspicion. In his "softened" Latin translation, Heinrich von Halle sounds a note of caution as early as his preface. He praises Mechthild's holiness and asserts that "all who are troubled and confused will find comfort in this book," but then he adds a word of warning: "All, however, who seek any other comfort, will only be led still further astray by what is said within this book" (Schmidt tr., 53).

Mechthild's book may perhaps have led some readers astray over the centuries, or at least may have inspired some people, like Monika Treut's heroine Dorothee, to strike out on their own countercultural path. The printed record, though, shows more of the opposite problem: Mechthild's editors have consistently worked to bring her *back* into the fold, whether of medieval neoplatonism or of modern feminism, even as her translators have regularized her ambiguous paragraphs of prose poetry, turning them either into lyric poetry or into prosaic exposition. Just as it has no set style, Mechthild's book has no clear narrative or thematic structure; instead, it reflects shifting moods and perceptions, sometimes staking out contradictory positions and at other times transcending dualities of every sort. It has been difficult for translators and editors, from Heinrich von Halle in the 1280s to Zum Brunn and Epiney-Burgard in the 1980s, to avoid an overemphasis on one side or another of the many divides that mark Mechthild's book. The modern translators restore something of the flow that Heinrich left out of his *Lux Divinitatis*, yet a certain fixity remains, beginning as early as the book's title. Neumann, Schmidt, Menzies, Zum Brunn and Epiney-Burgard, and Tobin all use the definite article, *das*, or *la*, or *the*, as the first word: what Mechthild's prologue announces as *a* flowing light of the Godhead has been fixed as *the* flowing light. We still need a translation that will catch the particular spectrum of Mechthild's individual vision, for as she herself stressed, the divine light is seen differently by different people:

> Saint John says: "We shall see God as he is." That is true. But the sun shines according to the weather. There are many sorts of weather under the earthly sun, just as there are many mansions in heaven; as far as I can bear him and see him, thus he is to me. (4.12)

6

Kafka Comes Home

Works that attain a lasting status as classics of world literature are ones that can weather a variety of tectonic shifts in the literary landscape. As they do so, their translations change along with their interpretations. Ours is an age of translation and also an era of retranslation, as translations are revised or replaced outright in order to bring works into conformity with new standards of translation and new interpretations of the works themselves. New translations of Dante appear almost annually; Seamus Heaney's *Beowulf* and Robert Fagles's *Iliad* are released on tape in readings by Hollywood actors. Even modern works are being retranslated with increasing frequency: C. K. Scott Moncrieff's classic translation of Proust's *Recherche* has been revised not once but twice in recent years, even as rival translations have also begun to appear.

A particularly far-reaching transformation has been occurring with the works of Franz Kafka, who is being revised both in translation and even in German. These revisions are noteworthy because they reflect the broad movement in literary studies toward cultural context, a shift that is especially significant for many works of world literature. No longer privileged chiefly for their universal qualities, more and more works of world literature are now favored for displaying specific ethnic identity or cultural difference. New attention is given to figures from "marginal" cultures (the Guatemalan Rigoberta Menchú, for example, or the Saint Lucian Derek Walcott), and major figures already in the canon are being newly positioned. If archetypal modernist masters like Kafka and Joyce were usually seen as metaphoric or literal exiles from a decayed or paralyzed home society, now they are more and more often being invited home again, reconnected to roots they may not have severed so fully as had been thought.

In Kafka's case, portraits of the artist as a culture-transcending figure are giving way to portraits of the artist as a Prague Jew. An earlier generation's publishers and scholars had sought to gain acceptance for difficult modernist writing by creating a kind of instant great tradition of central figures like Proust, Joyce, Mann, and Kafka. Now, though, Kafka's status as a "major" writer is underwritten by accounts of him as an exemplary *minor* figure, to use the term advanced in Gilles Deleuze and Félix Guattari's influential 1975 book *Kafka: Pour une littérature mineure*. Kafka's adaptability to this contemporary concern has fueled a new wave of critical and general attention, as a result of which he now seems to be eclipsing Thomas Mann, who was more prominent than Kafka in the fifties and sixties but is much less visible today, both in scholarly discussion and in popular culture.[1]

It seems unlikely, for example, that any television special is now being made featuring Thomas Mann in a remake of a Frank Capra film. Kafka, however, has had just such a role in Peter Capaldi's *Franz Kafka's "It's a Wonderful Life,"* produced for Scottish television in 1993. Appropriately, Capaldi's film is both hilarious and intense, showing the young Franz Kafka seated at his beloved desk, struggling to write the opening lines of *The Metamorphosis*. The film builds on a host of details known through the work of Kafka's biographers and the publication of his diaries and letters: his fondness for elegant clothing; his obsession with absolute silence while writing; his ambivalence toward women; his tendency to seize on an object at hand as a stand-in for the subject of his story. In the film, Kafka can't decide how to represent Gregor Samsa, who keeps turning into whatever Kafka's eyes light upon (a banana, a housefly) or whatever comes randomly to mind (a kangaroo). He is continually distracted by a noisy party going on beneath him in his rooming house, held by a seductive group of young women, who try to persuade him to dance with them. A ludicrous, but also ominous, episode ensues, involving a threatening knife grinder who accuses Kafka of killing his pet cockroach; the women come to Kafka's rescue by catching the missing insect. Life is wonderful, and *The Metamorphosis* is born; Kafka is saved both from the grinder's knives and from the anguish of his writer's block. "Perhaps things aren't so bad, Mr. K," one of the young women declares. "Perhaps you're right," Kafka replies, adding, in a momentary burst of warmth, "But please—call me F."

---

[1] The *MLA Bibliography* shows that during the sixties, Mann was more often written about in English (142 items) than Kafka (111 items). They were in a dead heat in the seventies (476 entries for Mann, 478 for Kafka), and then Kafka took a decisive lead in the eighties, rising to 530 while Mann dropped dramatically to 289. Kafka dipped somewhat in the nineties, to 411 items, but still retained a substantial margin over Mann, who had 277.

Attention to Kafka's life and times intensified through the eighties and into the nineties, as can be seen in titles like Mark Anderson's 1989 collection *Reading Kafka: Prague, Politics, and the Fin de Siècle* and Krolop and Zimmermann's *Kafka und Prag,* based on a major international conference held in 1992. By 1994 the Scottish scholar Ritchie Robertson could declare the battle won: "Post-structuralist and similar approaches based narrowly on textual study," he wrote, "increasingly seem trite and unrewarding," whereas "the most exciting recent studies of Kafka have tried to contextualize his work" ("In Search of the Historical Kafka," 107). This new wave of Kafka studies has revealed his multiple connections to his mixed cultural surroundings, prominently including his linguistic interests. Like most educated Jews in the Prague of his day, Kafka spoke and wrote in German, but unlike many of his social circle, he learned Czech as well and subsequently studied Yiddish and Hebrew. His own prose turns out to reflect a variety of linguistic influences, and he drafted his manuscripts in a local Prague German that differs significantly from standard German.

This revisionary trend has led to new editions of Kafka's texts, most of which had been left in manuscript upon his death. His literary executor, Max Brod, having refused his friend's deathbed request to burn the manuscripts, set about getting them published, and as he prepared the unpublished novels and stories for publication, he systematically normalized vocabulary, spelling, and punctuation. The result was the publication of Kafka's works in a pure, clear, regionally unmarked style that in turn formed the basis for the influential English versions done in the 1930s by two Scottish translators, Willa and Edwin Muir. These translations began to receive wide attention at a time when Kafka's work was banned in Nazi Germany, and so Kafka became famous in English when he was known to only a few in German. Following Brod's lead, the Muirs and their publisher, Schocken, worked to produce a universalist Kafka, a creator of symbolic quests for spiritual meaning, a writer who could become a central figure for modern self-understanding rather than someone who needed to be read in the context of turn-of-the-century Prague or even of German culture at large.

The shift from a universal Kafka to an ethnic Kafka has meant a move away from the formalism that had generally characterized Kafka criticism, particularly in the United States. As Mark Anderson wrote in 1992:

Whether Freudian, existentialist, New Critical, structuralist, or poststructuralist, these interpretations have offered readings of individual texts in terms of a critical methodology that tended to eclipse the historical dimensions of Kafka's texts. Rooted in no particular culture or period, so ran the implicit assumption, his writings seemed to be meant for all cultures, thus providing an example of the hermetic, anonymous, *sui generis* modern artwork that apparently validated these very formalist, ahistorical methodologies. (*Kafka's Clothes*, 9–10)

Anderson's revisionary perspective is clearly signaled by the temporally and geographically specific subtitle to this book: *Ornament and Aestheticism in the Habsburg Fin de Siècle*. With historicist models now often eclipsing formalist models, it becomes a strength of Kafka's work that his texts can be reconsidered, and retranslated, to validate the assumptions of the *new* methodologies.

Anderson's list of older approaches begins with Freudian and existentialist perspectives, neither of which was actually formalist or disconnected from social concerns. Yet these approaches tended to create an intensely, even exclusively *individualist* Kafka, engaged with society in a purely alienated, antagonistic mode; *Seul, comme Franz Kafka* was the title of a widely cited Freudian study by Marthe Robert (1979). A good example of this treatment of Kafka in America can be found in an early collection, *The Existential Imagination*, edited by Frederick Karl and Leo Hamalian. Published in 1963 by Fawcett Books as a mass-market paperback, this anthology was intended to bring the philosophical insights of Dostoevsky, Sartre, Kafka, and other writers to a broad American public. Kafka is one of four authors highlighted in red on the back cover (along with the Marquis de Sade, interestingly adopted as a very early existentialist). The editors' introduction describes existentialism as the quintessential modern response to the collapse of religious and social certainties: "how was the individual to come to terms with existence in a technological civilization? As a result of man's new role, his doubt and skepticism have turned inward and led to despair; man has lost most of his familiar props, and those that still remain prove insufficient" (11).

Karl and Hamalian see the existentialists as providing an entirely individual, inward response to modernity: "Man here floats in a foreign world in which human existence is feeble, contradictory, and contingent upon an infinity of other forces. . . . He must be alone; for in his very aloneness is his salvation" (11). Even Sartre's wartime involvement in the Resistance was not a form of solidarity but a confrontation with an essential and even exemplary solitude:

A good deal of Sartre's philosophical point of view was established during the Second World War when France suffered the Nazi occupation. Under the occupation, the resistance movement consisted of individuals, like Sartre himself, who daily had to make decisions that directly affected dozens of lives, including his own. Yet each decision had to be made in solitude. If a member of the resistance was caught, he had no redress. . . . Man's capacity for resisting torture and death became, under these conditions, the limits of his liberty. "Total responsibility in total solitude" Sartre gives as the very definition of liberty. (15–16)

This radically disconnected individualism sets the terms for the editors' discussion of Kafka: "In Franz Kafka, man is always judged and always found guilty, in a kind of punishment without crime. He is the innocent victim of an unappeasable power, a horrible and recurrent outrage. . . . Kafka's vision goes beyond that of Dostoevsky in its immutability: it denies man's freedom, it denies him the terror of choice, and finally it denies him the possibility of grace" (26–27). Frederick Karl went on to write a variety of books on modernism and began to look closely at the social and intellectual background of his writers. In 1989 he published a biography of Faulkner, whom he presented in a national context as *William Faulkner: American Writer.* Karl then turned to Kafka, for whom he set a far broader frame, titling his book *Franz Kafka: Representative Man.* Karl's massive biography—eight hundred pages long—reflects the growing critical interest in ethnicity and local roots; as he stresses at the outset, "we cannot separate Kafka from Prague" (9). Such a separation is actually just what the previous generation of critics, including Karl himself, had performed, but now the balance will be righted.

A turn to history, however, does not automatically produce a new Kafka. Even as he details Kafka's multicultural upbringing, Karl carries over into his new biography his former emphasis on the artist's alienation and isolation. Kafka's representativeness, for Karl, is a function of his *disconnection* from his family and from his society as a whole. As a frontispiece, he gives a photograph of a soulful young Kafka with a dog; a note on the copyright page says that "The complete photograph includes a waitress on the other side of the dog," but she is not shown. Karl then opens with a preface built around a meditation on this picture, again emphasizing Kafka's isolation as he had in *The Existential Imagination* almost thirty years earlier:

From Kafka's glare, we would hardly recognize that his photo is part of a larger one, with a waitress to his right and a collie dog between them. From Kafka's gaze, he seems alone, although the collie is leaning against his arm and the waitress is quite attractive. Kafka has taken over the photo because he has no recognition of any other existence. There is the slightest smile on his thin lips, but that does not draw us in. The piercing eyes do it. . . . The upturned collar and black tie, the overwhelming black suit, with one white hand protruding, suggest a funeral. Despite the force of will inherent in the gaze, Kafka here is a death figure. (xvi)

It is Karl himself, however, who has chosen to crop the woman out of the photo. Mark Anderson prints the full photo as evidence of the young Kafka's fondness for fine clothing and free-living companions, and identifies "the waitress" rather differently: "One celebrated image, although often cropped to display him alone, is of Kafka sitting in formal dress next to a jauntily smiling prostitute (Hansi the 'Trocadéro Valkyrie') and her dog" (*Kafka's Clothes*, 2). The companionable grouping in the full photo certainly gives a different effect from the "death figure" evoked by Karl (see figure 10).

Karl's emphasis on Kafka's existential isolation sets the tone for his biography, which programmatically presents Kafka as multiply dislocated from his culture of origin: "We see both victor and victim in the Czech Jew whose face reflects the annihilation of Eastern Europe's Jews; and, further, we see a Czech Jew who was not much of a Jew and a Czech who wrote, not in Czech, but in German, the language of Goethe and Schiller" (xv–xvi). By the end of Karl's preface, Kafka's body has become a microcosm of the collapse of Europe itself: "There is, still further, the Kafka of the piercing eyes that were aware of the internal disaster of his condition as his body deteriorated from tuberculosis; and through those eyes a reflection of Europe burning itself up, as though caught by a gigantic disease" (xviii–xix).

Though Karl wants to reconnect Kafka to Prague, the chapter entitled "Prague and Kafka, Kafka and Prague" is almost unrelievedly negative: "Everything was deceptive and illusive about Franz Josef's empire" (32); "feelings of exile and displacement . . . were set very early" (32); "Kafka spent most of his mature life seeking the mode by which he could discharge what he felt as a small child, when his brothers died, his mother seemed to desert him, [and] he was placed in the charge of Czech outsiders" (35); "it was Prague that helped to generate the very lack of centeredness that gave Kafka so much of his material" (36). In sum: "This was the young Kafka's world in Prague: ringed by enemies, invaded by dead and dying brothers, displaced by inner and outer dictates, he himself made marginal" (37).

Karl ends his biography, more than seven hundred pages later, by returning to the theme of Kafka's total alienation from his world:

Figure 10. Kafka alone and with Hansi Szokoll, "the Trocadéro Valkyrie"

If we view life as somehow overpowering or trapping us . . . then we enter Kafka's world of the Kafkaesque. The adjective really goes back to his own situation in the waning days of the Austro-Hungarian Empire, to the time when the Dual Monarchy was a patchwork of concessions and compromises lacking central power, direction, or even will. From that context, there came the sense of a Kafkaesque world that had little to do with the individual living within it, especially when, as in Kafka's case, that individual was further divided by language and racial/ethnic origin. Caught as he was among the aspects of virtually every defining characteristic—language, race, religion, ethnicity, cultural identification—Kafka was in a prime position to fashion himself as the representative outsider and victim. (758–59)

Against this purely depressive background, Karl reads Kafka's fiction as a series of expressions of alienation and victimization. This leads him to view Kafka's final novel, *The Castle,* for example, in wholly negative terms:

Kafka's idea was not to bring K. enlightenment, but to demonstrate how entombed he becomes even as he delves more deeply into his role as land-surveyor. K.'s profession is particularly ironic, since there is no land to survey, there are no spatial measurements for him to make, there is no clear assignment of what externals are at stake. Thus, while he seeks the land to survey, or those who can so instruct him, he is being buried in his quest. His journey from home and family has not been a journey into achievement or attainment, but into a negation of everything meant by journey. (694)

Kafka's hero is so alienated from reality that the book's setting is hardly a real place at all: "From the first paragraph, we must also suppose that the journey is not outward, to a real place, but inward to a state of mind, that Kafka is hallucinating, as it were, fantasizing an inward journey" (704). This is perhaps a viable reading of the novel, and yet Karl himself seems dissatisfied with the melancholy portrait of extreme alienation that he believes Kafka has painted: "The opening chapters of *The Castle* are murky, often lacking that sharpness of observation that was his characteristic quality, and lacking that edge of irony and wit we have come to expect. . . . It is as though Kafka had to let a novel emerge, since the urge to write was clear, while the material was itself vague to him. Or else at this stage of his life, he was incapable of a long work" (698–99). Either Kafka's novel is the failing last effort of a dying artist, or Karl has missed something.

Karl has indeed missed something. Criticizing *The Castle*'s opening chapters for their murkiness and their lack of irony, Karl takes K. at face value as a land surveyor struggling to make his way in a hostile environment. With the Castle's officials inexplicably refusing to admit that they have commissioned K. to come and work for them, K. becomes the last of those "innocent victims" whom Karl had earlier presented as Kafka's archetypical protagonists. What Karl has missed here is the fact that K. is *lying* when he tells the villagers that he is a land surveyor who has been called in by the Castle's Count Westwest. Like many readers before him, Karl has fallen into a trap that Kafka deliberately set in the ambiguous twilight of his opening chapters. On K.'s first arrival in the unnamed village where the novel takes place, he simply seeks a bed in the inn for the night. Told that he cannot stay without official permission from the Castle, he reacts with surprise: "What village have I wandered into? So there is a castle here?" (2). Informed that he must leave town immediately, he retorts, "Be advised that I am the land surveyor sent for by the Count. My assistants and the equipment are coming tomorrow by carriage" (3).

As the novel proceeds, the Castle officials seem to accept his claim, despite the fact that K.'s supposed assistants and equipment never arrive and there is no surveying for him to do. What happens instead is that the officials, apparently wanting to buy time while they try to discern the interloper's true intentions, send two assistants to him from the Castle. Unable to produce any assistants of his own, K. accepts these substitutes as though they were his own men, in a scene that becomes surreally hilarious when one realizes that he is having to deal with being taken up on his own falsehood, even as the hapless assistants struggle to hold up their end in this war of deceptions:

> "Who are you?" he asked, glancing from one to the other. "Your assistants," they answered. "Those are the assistants," said the landlord softly in confirmation. "What?" asked K., "you are the old assistants whom I told to join me and am expecting?" They said yes. "It's a good thing," said K., after a little while, "it's a good thing that you've come." "By the way," said K. after another little while, "you're very late, you've been most negligent!" "It was such a long way," said one of the assistants. "A long way," repeated K., "but when I met you, you were coming from the Castle." "Yes,"

they said, without further explanation. "Where did you put the instruments?" asked K. "We don't have any," they said. "The instruments I entrusted you with," said K. "We don't have any," they repeated. "Oh, you're a fine sort!" said K., "do you know anything about surveying?" "No," they said. "But if you are my old assistants, then you must know something about it," said K. They remained silent. "Well, come along then," said K., pushing them ahead into the inn. (17)

The first chapter ends with this comic nonresolution—or at least, it does now. Unable to see the point of this exchange, Max Brod apparently felt it was too weak an ending for the first chapter, and so he ended the chapter a scene early and moved the encounter with the "assistants" into the second chapter.

Max Brod and the Muirs missed the deceitful truth about K., perhaps in Edwin Muir's case because he had little patience for the fragmented narratives and unreliable narrators often favored by modernist writers. In a book published in 1928 as he and his wife were beginning their translation of *The Castle,* Muir attacked Joyce's *Ulysses,* saying that "its design is arbitrary, its development feeble, its unity questionable" (*The Structure of the Novel,* 127). Unlike the Muirs, Brod was a novelist and an active member of modernist literary circles, and yet for Brod a recognition of K.'s deceptiveness would have undercut his deeply held belief that Kafka's protagonist is "a man of good will through and through," a frustrated seeker of salvation: "the castle, in the peculiar symbolic language of the novel, stands for divine guidance" (*Franz Kafka,* 186, 189). Further, in Brod's view K. is at once a projection of Kafka himself and a figure of universal significance, a hero with whom the reader should directly, and positively, identify: "Kafka's *Castle,* for all the individuality of the character it describes, is a book in which everyone recognizes his own experiences. Kafka's hero, whom he calls simply K., in autobiographical fashion, passes through life alone. He is the loneliness-component in us, which this novel works out in more-than-life-size, terrifying clarity" (186). Most readers and critics followed the lead of Brod and the Muirs; as Kafka's fame spread in the fifties, K. became an archetypal existentialist hero, the lonely individual battling the absurdities of modern secular, bureaucratic life. Only in the midsixties did two scholars, independently, arrive at a more critical understanding of K.'s self-presentation. In 1965 Erwin Steinberg published an article in *College English* entitled "K. of *The Castle:* Ostensible Land-Surveyor," in which he pointed out that "there is little evidence to support K.'s claim that he is a land-surveyor or that he was hired by the Castle. And there is a good bit of evidence to the contrary" (25). In a book on Kafka that was in press when Steinberg's article appeared, Walter Sokel was more blunt. He chastised Kafka's interpreters for having been "duped by K.'s colossal fraud." Detailing the evidence against K.'s claims, Sokel argued:

> This close reading of the text alters the whole basis of
> interpretation of Kafka's last and greatest novel. It can no longer
> be maintained that the conflict between justice and injustice, no
> matter on what level, is its theme. Its theme is rather K.'s attempt
> to make everyone, including the reader, believe that justice is the
> problem. . . . Kafka has K. conduct his campaign so skillfully and
> emphatically that he persuades most readers to believe him,
> contrary to the textual evidence he himself provides. In his richest
> and most profound work Kafka depicts the victory of fiction over
> reality. The deception perpetrated by his character triumphs not
> over the other characters—for no one in the novel really believes
> K.—but over the reader. (*Franz Kafka,* 32–33)

Interpreting *The Castle* as a text primarily about reading, Sokel rather implausibly denied that the novel had any concern with justice at all, "no matter on what level." Subsequent critics, on the other hand, have been able to use his and Steinberg's discovery to deepen our understanding of the book's ethical concerns, concerns from which K. himself is not exempt. Attending to the social and political dynamics of Habsburg Prague has helped criticism move beyond simple accounts of isolation and victimization and to recognize that without ever mentioning Judaism or the Austro-Hungarian Empire by name in his novel, Kafka was deeply engaged in exploring the complex and contradictory investment of educated, assimilated Jews in a society in which they were simultaneously aliens and an important economic force. In his early biography of Kafka, Max Brod had already interpreted *The Castle* as a coded story of the struggles of a Jew who seeks membership in a hostile society (*Franz Kafka,* 187–92); contemporary criticism has revisited this theme, departing from Brod in seeing the book as finally having less to do with religious transcendence than with immanent social and political concerns.

Critical reassessments have proceeded in tandem with textual revisions. Even as Malcolm Pasley and other textual scholars were producing new editions of Kafka's German texts that would retain his localisms and his idiosyncratic punctuation, critics of the Muirs' English translations have increasingly argued that they had not done justice even to Brod's standardized first editions. Rather, in keeping with their fundamentally religious views, the Muirs produced a kinder, more sympathetic K. in English than appeared in German. As Ronald Gray has written of their presentation of Joseph K. in *The Trial*, "K. is altogether a better-disposed character, as he emerges from the translation, than he is in the original" ("But Kafka Wrote in German," 249). In an extended "Translator's Preface" to his retranslation of *The Castle*, Mark Harman says that "since the Muirs see K. as a pilgrim in search of salvation, they tend to overlook the criticism that Kafka directs at his namesake. I have sought to make K. as calculating and self-serving in English as he is in the original" (xviii).

Harman admirably attends to the shifting ambiguities of Kafka's tone and style, following Pasley's 1982 critical edition of the German text in removing punctuation that Brod had added to normalize Kafka's syntax, and breaking with the Muirs' practice of inserting connective and explanatory phrases to help make sense of things. Where a reader like Frederick Karl was put off by the "murkiness" of many passages in the book and saw them as signs of the author's failing powers, Harman sees such episodes as marvelously and often humorously expressive of the protagonist's differing moods and situations. At times the prose is clear and precise, but elsewhere

> the prose slows down and is almost asphyxiated by clotted passages of opaque verbosity. That wordiness may well parody the prolixity of Austro-Hungarian officials, which, incidentally, occasionally amused Kafka, who once embarrassed himself by erupting in uncontrollable laughter during a speech by the president of the Workers Accident Insurance Company in Prague. In the course of one key chapter in *The Castle* an official called Bürgel drones on in almost impenetrable pseudo-officialese, which I have tried to keep as murky in English as it is in German. (xv)

Harman's version renounces the smooth surfaces and the rhetorical eloquence of the Muirs' prose, even as he conveys a K. who is more antihero than icon.

How successful has this revisionary process been? Are the new editions simply "better" than the old according to the shifting standards of literary taste, or are they in some sense objectively *better* as well? If we now see a Prague Jew where an earlier generation saw an international modernist, are we getting closer to the essence of the writer and his work, or simply projecting our current interests into both? If Harman's calculating and self-serving K.

can now be at home in the America of *Gravity's Rainbow* and *Seinfeld* in a way that the Muirs' innocent K. would not be, is the new K. a more accurate one, or merely closer to our own present predilections? Are the new German editions and English translations justifiably "minoritizing" Kafka or in fact subtly assimilating him to contemporary multicultural values?

At the most basic level of *getting it right,* the new translations are indeed clearly better than the early translations of the modernists. Translators of the thirties had no compunction about rearranging and clarifying things they didn't understand, and they often played up their favorite themes in the process. Like the Muirs, for example, Scott Moncrieff had a fondness for religious imagery, whether it was there in Proust's text or not. Thus, in the book's opening scene, Proust uses an anatomical metaphor to describe how a magic lantern projects a figure across a doorknob in the narrator's bedroom: the figure of Golo is supposed to be "transvertebrated" in the process, but Moncrieff has Golo undergo a Christlike "transubstantiation" instead (*Swann's Way,* 8). In addition, translators of the time often had to work quickly and for poor pay; contemporary literary translators tend to have academic employment or grants that allow them time to do their work at leisure. (Mark Harman is a professor at the University of Pennsylvania and acknowledges further support in the form of a grant from the Austrian Ministry of Education and Art—a delicious irony, to have a government bureaucracy commissioning revisions of Kafka's writing!) The Muirs, moreover, had only begun to learn German in their midthirties, a few years before they undertook their translation of *The Castle,* and they periodically blundered in basic comprehension, often seeing what they really wanted to see rather than what was actually on the page. In an article "On Translation Mistakes, with Special Attention to Kafka in America," Stanley Corngold has discussed several emblematic errors, such as a line that ought to read "he felt rising within him a sorrow" but which was rendered as "he felt rising within him a *song,*" the Muirs having translated the word *Leid* (sorrow, pain), as though it were *Lied.*

More broadly, Mark Harman's colder, more calculating K. reflects the new and genuinely more accurate understanding of the novel's basic situation, which Steinberg and Sokel demonstrated conclusively in the mid-sixties.[2] As a result, the book's tone can at once darken and become funnier

[2] Somewhat surprisingly, the 1982 "definitive edition" of the German text by Malcolm Pasley refers on its dust jacket to K. as "der Landvermesser" pure and simple. In a 1989 article on Kafka's composition process, Pasley similarly speaks of K. as "the land-surveyor" without any indication that this designation is uncertain, much less false ("The Act of Writing and the Text," 211). I would agree with Sokal, however, that people who take K. at his word are misreading (or at

than it was in the Muirs' rather pious version. Like other modernist writers, and indeed like Mechthild von Magdeburg in the 1950s, Kafka was originally introduced into English in stylistically and intellectually softened terms. As Harman says, the early translators' strategies were logical in their time, but we can now do better justice to the modernists' intentions and their real achievements:

> Those of us who set about retranslating the modernists endeavor to render the tone of the original with greater accuracy than that sought, or even desired, by our predecessors, whose priorities lay elsewhere. The efforts of the first English translators of the modernists were, of course, highly effective. Thanks to their elegant renditions, countless English-speaking readers gained access to important modernists. Given the barriers facing all foreign-language authors in a culture so notoriously self-sufficient as the Anglo-American one, that in itself is a remarkable achievement. However, it is clear now that the ease with which these authors were naturalized points to a weakness in the translations themselves. The first translators were often more interested in making their translations conform to traditional aesthetic criteria, e.g. elegance, vividness, smoothness of texture, than in the painstaking effort to echo the prose style of the original. ("Retranslating Franz Kafka's *Castle*," 140–41)

Harman is wonderfully sensitive to the modulations of Kafka's self-deconstructing sentences. The Muirs often failed to convey the subtle ironies embedded in Kafka's play with German possibilities of word order and phrasing. Such ironies are hard to render in English, which has less latitude in the ordering of clauses and the placement of subjects, verbs, and objects. Harman's translation supplies good equivalents in many of these cases. To give one example, when K. first catches sight of the Castle, his reaction, as given by the Muirs, is this: "On the whole this distant prospect of the Castle satisfied K.'s expectations" (Muir tr., 11). This straightforward sentence fails to convey the uncanny insecurity of the original, which interrupts the primary statement, that the view is satisfying, with an extended qualification, much stronger than the Muir's discreet "this distant prospect." The German reads: "Im Ganzen entsprach das Schloß, *wie es sich hier von der Ferne zeigte,* K.'s Erwartungen" (17; emphasis added). Harman renders this much more ef-

---

the least, seriously underreading) the text. Harman's new translation may be helpful in winning further acceptance for a complex understanding of K.'s character and role.

fectively: "On the whole the Castle, as it appeared from this distance, corresponded to K.'s expectations" (8). The German remains slightly stronger, as Kafka has been able to put the verb near the start of the sentence, using his qualifying phrase to divide subject from object and undermine the correspondence the sentence begins by asserting; but Harman captures the essential effect using the options available in English.[3]

Finally, retaining Kafka's nonstandard punctuation gives his prose a heightened and entirely appropriate intensity. As Robert Alter said, reviewing Harman's *Castle* for the *New Republic*, the new translation "gives us a much better sense of Kafka's uncompromising and disturbing originality as a prose master than we have heretofore had in English." Schocken liked this assessment enough to quote it on their back cover, along with a similar response by J. M. Coetzee: "Semantically accurate to an admirable degree, faithful to Kafka's nuances, responsive to the tempo of his sentences and to the larger music of his paragraph construction. . . . For the general reader or for the student, it will be the translation of preference for some time to come."

The only problem with this new, uncompromising accuracy is that it violates Kafka's own practice. Though he wrote a locally inflected German, so lightly punctuated as to create frequent run-on sentences, he meticulously regularized his spelling and punctuation when he prepared manuscripts for publication. This is a point that Deleuze and Guattari fudged when they advanced him as their model of "a minor literature." They quoted various diary entries and letters in which Kafka spoke of the advantages of writing in a small, peripheral country, free from the constraints of a "major literature." Yet in these passages Kafka was referring, like Goethe before him, not to style but to themes and to relations to literary tradition. "A small nation's memory," he wrote in 1911,

> is not smaller than the memory of a large one and so can digest
> the existing material more thoroughly. There are, to be sure,
> fewer experts in literary history employed, but literature is less a
> concern of literary history than of the people. . . . What in great
> literature goes on down below, constituting a not indispensable
> cellar of the structure, here takes place in the full light of day,

[3] Some of Kafka's effects, of course, simply can't be conveyed within the norms of English grammar. Soon after he arrives in the village, K. describes himself to the innkeeper using a string of what look like positive assertions, which are undermined at the very end by a final *not:* "mächtig bin ich nämlich, in Vertrauen gesagt, wirklich nicht" (16)—literally, "powerful am I, indeed, to speak in confidence, truly not."

what is there a matter of passing interest for a few, here absorbs
everyone no less than as a matter of life and death. (*Diaries,*
149–50)

Deleuze and Guattari extend this perspective to language and style, emphasizing Kafka's need to create "his own *patois.* . . . to become a nomad and an
immigrant and a gypsy in relation to one's own language" (*Kafka: Toward a
Minor Literature,* 18–19). As Mark Anderson has said, Deleuze and Guattari's argument builds from "a flagrant but insightful misreading" of the
diary entry just quoted (*Reading Kafka,* 11). Kafka had no interest at all in
"dialect" writing. Indeed, later in the very same entry, he speaks of German
prose style as returning to Goethe "with strengthened yearning . . . in order
to rejoice in the completeness of its unlimited dependence" (152). While
Kafka's loose punctuation reflects the way he would read a text aloud, he
clearly distinguished print from oral delivery, and the several stories he published during his lifetime all appeared in standard High German.

    Kafka has become more "authentic," and his books have become
more "faithful" to him, by a process of denial, a suspension of our knowledge of Kafka's own practice. In normalizing his style as he prepared Kafka's unpublished works for publication, Max Brod was simply doing what
Kafka would have done himself. He sometimes did more than this, unfortunately—for example, when he rearranges material and drops fragmentary
passages in order to create a far more coherent *Castle* than existed in manuscript, arguably a more coherent book than Kafka himself would ever have
produced. Though Pasley has been hailed for undoing all this work ("Not
by Brod Alone" was the elegant title of Ritchie Robertson's glowing review
in the *Times Literary Supplement*), he has been criticized, particularly in
Germany, for having denied Kafka the standard German he always favored
for publication. On this argument, Kafka would no more have published
The Castle in "Prague German" than he would have set the Castle itself in
Prague: his published style is consistently delocalized, just as the stories
themselves are purified of identifiable local content or topical references. In
his preface to his translation of *The Castle,* Mark Harman admits that "one
could reasonably argue that Kafka might have gone through the manuscript
and inserted conventional punctuation had he prepared the text for publication" (xxi). It would be more accurate to observe that this is what Kafka
invariably did when he prepared a manuscript for publication.

    It is not surprising that Harman didn't follow Brod and the Muirs
in adding punctuation, given his commitment to following Pasley's edition
of the manuscript. What is surprising is that he didn't follow Pasley a good

deal farther. He makes no effort to convey the flavor of Kafka's regional German, though this is a major emphasis of Pasley's corrected German edition. In a "Publisher's Note" at the beginning of Harman's translation, Schocken's editorial director, Arthur Samuelson, describes the manuscript's complex publication history and the need for a new translation based on Pasley's critical edition. He adds, however, a caveat: "Although many of the novelties of the German critical text (such as Kafka's unorthodox spelling and his use of an Austrian German or Prague German vocabulary) cannot be conveyed in translation, the fluidity and breathlessness of the sparsely punctuated original manuscript have been retained" (xii). But why *can't* a translation employ unorthodox spelling or find equivalents for a regional dialect? Of course it can. This could be done quite neutrally, by inventing direct equivalents for Kafka's regional spellings, which often shorten infinitives, for example (*gehn* instead of *gehen*), and use an *ie* where standard German would use an *i* (*gieng* instead of *ging*). A translation could reproduce such spellings by using, say, "stoln" in place of "stolen." Alternatively, a translator could find an actual American dialectical equivalent for Kafka's German. After all, any number of American Jewish writers have experimented with prose styles that incorporate elements of Yiddish or Eastern European Slavic syntax and vocabulary. In his Kafka-inspired masterwork *Maus,* for example, Art Spiegelman very effectively gives his father just such a dialect, using more pronounced distortions of standard English than would be needed to convey Kafka's specific locutions.

A translator might go farther still, taking seriously Deleuze and Guattari's idea that a "minor literature" is not so much the literature of a small country as a minority group's dialect carved out of a major language. For an American audience, a logical analogue to the Prague Jew would be the inner-city African American, as witness our reuse of the term "ghetto" in this context. The resources of Black English could very readily be employed to render Kafka's uses of in-group vocabulary and his dialectical spellings and contractions. As Deleuze and Guattari themselves point out, "Prague German is a deterritorialized language, appropriate for strange and minor uses," and they add that "this can be compared in another context to what blacks in America today are able to do with the English language" (*Kafka,* 17).

Unlikely as this option may seem at first sight, it is perfectly possible that such translations will be produced a generation from now, if the present interest in ethnicity continues to gain strength. Such a translation strategy has ample precedent; contemporary translators often seek American equivalents for foreign minority dialects. We can think of visual analogues as well. When he used the imagery of cats and mice for his story of Nazis versus Jews, Art Spiegelman was only partly inspired by Kafka's great story "Josephine the Singer, or the Mouse Folk." Equally, he was adapting cat-and-mouse imagery he had tried to use for comics set in Harlem in the early seventies.[4] Nor need we go so far afield as Spiegelman to find authority for an African-American strategy for rendering Kafka's style, for Kafka himself first made the comparison: "Almost every word I write jars against the next, I hear the consonants rub leadenly against each other and the vowels sing an accompaniment like Negroes in a minstrel show" (*Diaries*, 29).

A perennial problem translators face, when dealing with any work written before their own generation, is whether to render the text in a manner consistent with the time in which it was first written or in something close to contemporary style—"to make Virgil speak such English," as Dryden famously proposed, "as he would himself have spoken, if he had been born in England, and in this present age" ("Dedication of the Aeneis," 72). Each approach has its pitfalls. A purely modern Virgil is a kind of historical falsification, and yet it would be completely impossible to translate Virgil into the English of his own age, as English did not yet exist two thousand years ago. A translation into some early form of West Saxon would serve little purpose today, while some compromise like Middle English would seem ludicrous today, dislocated both from Virgil's time and from ours. Even proponents of "foreignizing" translation, like Lawrence Venuti, are usually quite sparing in their use of archaisms or outmoded turns of phrase; a little goes a very long way. The same problem confronts us with Kafka: we now like his uncorrected manuscript style better than his corrected style because we have passed through postmodernism's love of fragments, internal contradiction, and incompletion, even as we have also acquired a new interest in ethnicity and local dialect. Pasley and Harman give us a *Castle* that Kafka might have published had he been born in 1950 and writing in a postmodern age. The new *Castle* even concludes with a postmodern ending in midsentence: "She held out her trembling hand to K. and had him sit down beside her, she spoke with great difficulty, it was difficult to understand her, but what she said" (316).

[4] In a 1989 article in the *Village Voice,* Spiegelman wrote about his early effort: "I had my theme: Racial Oppression in America. The Blacks would be mice. . . . For about 15 minutes, I had my theme. I didn't know *beans* about being Black in America, even though, under the pseudonym Artie X, I *had* scripted a comic strip called 'Super-Colored Guy' for a weekly Harlem newspaper. . . . Anyway, through the alchemy of intuition I shifted thematic territory to my own 'ethnic background' and found the notion of using cats and mice had as much, or more, relevance" ("On Looney Tunes, Zionism, and the Jewish Question," 21).

In many ways Pasley and Harman's versions do give us a better text than we've ever had before. Even if the text is in some respects only "better" than Brod's and the Muirs' version because it assorts better with prevailing interests, this is an almost inevitable feature of translation, and indeed of interpretation in general. Acknowledging this, however, may help us to keep other options alive. Ideally Kafka's works can be made available in more than one form (multiple translations, in fact, already exist of *The Metamorphosis*), some of which would preserve a more modernist—or a more universalist—Kafka than the newer editions have given us.

Equally, we could have versions that strike some sort of compromise between the modernist and postmodernist Kafkas. Suppose that Kafka had carried out his periodic fantasy of emigrating to Palestine and that the change had done his lungs a world of good; suppose that late in life he had finally decided to publish his still unfinished draft of *The Castle,* prompted perhaps by repeated urgings from his friend Walter Benjamin (whom we can also bring safely to Tel Aviv for the sake of an argument he would have enjoyed). In 1970, say, still vigorous at the age of eighty-seven, Kafka sees that the changed literary climate allows him to publish his text while retaining his private punctuation, and he sees that the book really never needed the perhaps too obvious conclusion he had planned, in which a dying K. was to have been informed that he was finally being hired by the Castle. He might then have published a book that would look rather like Harman's version. Even so, it seems unlikely that Kafka would ever have wanted a book to end in midsentence; the endings of his completed works are usually ambiguous, but they are always definite endings nonetheless. Still unhappy with the paragraph he left unfinished, he might choose to end his manuscript with the last *complete* paragraph, simply dropping the two-and-a-half sentences of the final, incomplete paragraph. In that event, the book would end on a rather different note: instead of a trembling hand, great difficulty speaking, and a blank space following "what she said," the book would now end with a moment of mutual understanding and a perfect image of laughter in the dark:

> "I know why you want to take me with you," K. said finally. What K. knew was of no concern to Gerstäcker. "Because you think I can get something out of Erlanger for you." "Certainly," said Gerstäcker, "why else would I be interested in you?" K. laughed, took Gerstäcker's arm, and let himself be led through the darkness. (316)

PART THREE

Production

7

English in the World

In the summer of 1909, a young and impecunious British writer, known to his many friends as "Plum," arrived in New York. He was hoping to write for the lucrative American magazine market, for the Broadway stage, or preferably for both at once. Money was a constant concern. A decade earlier his father, a magistrate in Hong Kong, had made a bad bet with a friend: that he could walk the entire perimeter of the colony in a day. He won his wager but came down with sunstroke and had to retire to England on a small disability pension. His younger son was forced to abandon his plans to follow his older brother to Oxford; he went to work as a bank clerk. Like T. S. Eliot a few years later, he devoted his evenings to writing, and within a few years he broke free of his bank job, earning a modest living as a humor columnist and as a writer of pulp fiction, particularly boys' school stories. He was still searching, however, for a distinctive style and subject matter and for the real success these might bring. America offered a fresh field of activity, and in New York he began to develop contacts both in publishing and in the theater. Still just making ends meet, he stayed on when war broke out in 1914. Before the war had ended, he had achieved his goals. Not only had he become a best-selling author on both sides of the Atlantic; he had also become a major figure in the developing world of the musical theater. In 1917 he had no fewer than five shows running on Broadway at once—a record never matched before or since.

This young writer was P. G. Wodehouse, and he made his name on Broadway by revolutionizing the writing of song lyrics. Before him, writers would write the book and lyrics for a show, and then the composer would set the lyrics to music. Wodehouse reversed this process: he would set words to the tunes once they were written by his collaborators (Jerome Kern,

George Gershwin, and others). The effect was a jazzier, syncopated, free-flowing style, much less like conventional poetry. His lyrics were also hilarious. Wodehouse had an extraordinary ear for verbal incongruity, perhaps fostered in his early childhood years in Hong Kong, then reinforced once his parents sent him home to school in England, where he received an intensive classical education (his favorite subject in high school was Greek, and his classmates later recalled that he could compose comic verse in Latin as rapidly as in English). His early school stories were already built on the humor of clashes of speech, high and low. In his 1903 *Tales of St. Austin's,* for example, a boy is confronted with the unwelcome news of a pop quiz: "He would have liked to have stalked up to Mr. Mellish's desk, fixed him with a blazing eye, and remarked, 'Sir, withdraw that remark. Cancel that statement instantly, or—!' or words to that effect. What he did say was, 'Oo, si-i-r!'" (9).

Wodehouse found new markets in New York, but he also found something even more valuable to him as a writer: a polyglot exuberance of styles of speech—Midwestern American English, German-American English, Yiddish-American English, Italian-American English, Brooklynese, Upper-East-Side-ese, and other varieties in between. To his British ear, this dialectical riot spelled a golden opportunity, and he gradually began to exploit what he was hearing and the incongruity of his own position as an observer from outside.

Wodehouse's breakthrough came with a pair of novels he published in 1915, and together they established him as a genuinely *transatlantic* author. As early as the eighteenth century there had been an active book trade in both directions across the Atlantic, and in the nineteenth century writers like Mark Twain and Mrs. Trollope had crossed the Atlantic and written of their experiences for their respective home audiences; some writers, like Henry James, had emigrated outright. Wodehouse intensified the process. He began to write stories simultaneously for audiences on both sides of the Atlantic, interpreting British culture for American readers and American culture for British readers. *Psmith Journalist,* one of his 1915 novels, features a languid Oxbridge aesthete (he has added the silent *P* to his name to give it style) who comes to New York on a lark and takes up muckraking journalism amid the social ferment he finds in the unsettled New World. Conversely, *Something New* is set in an imaginary England of haughty butlers and apologetic earls. The first of what would prove to be the great series of Blandings Castle novels, *Something New* is also a portrait of the artist as a young hack writer, or more precisely as a pair of young hack writers: Ashe Marson, who writes detective stories for men's magazines, and Joan Valentine, who writes tales of lords and ladies for women's magazines. Drawing directly on his own experience, Wodehouse portrays the plight of the young writer trapped writing the monthly "Adventures of Gridley Quayle, Detective" for the Mammoth Publishing Company: "The unholy alliance had been in progress now for more than two years, and it seemed to Ashe that Gridley grew less human each month. He was so complacent and so maddeningly blind to the fact that only the most amazing luck enabled him to detect anything. To depend on Gridley Quayle for one's income was like being chained to some horrible monster" (14–15). Happily for Ashe, he meets the lovely and creative Joan Valentine, and they succeed in pooling their genres to solve a mystery at the Earl of Emsworth's country estate, setting themselves on the road to social success as well as marital bliss.

Wodehouse had never had much luck at home with stories of country-house life, but the American market was ready for a satirical account of the aristocracy of the old country, and the *Saturday Evening Post* paid Wodehouse the immense sum of thirty-five hundred dollars for serial rights to the novel. "I was stunned," Wodehouse wrote in a preface to a new edition of the novel half a century later; "I had always known in a vague sort of way that there was money like $3,500 in the world, but I had never expected to touch it" (6). Even as *Something New* was appearing in America, he began work on *Psmith Journalist* for publication in England. He prefaced the book with words of guidance for his British audience:

> The conditions of life in New York are so different from those
> of London that a story of this kind calls for a little explanation.
> There are several million inhabitants of New York. Not all of
> them eke out a precarious livelihood by murdering one another,
> but there is a definite section of the population which murders—
> not casually, on the spur of the moment, but on definitely
> commercial lines at so many dollars per murder. The "gangs" of
> New York exist in fact. I have not invented them. Most of the
> events in this story are based on actual happenings. (7)

Throughout the book Wodehouse assumes that his readers are British: he says in passing, for instance, that Psmith has come to America with a friend who plays cricket for "the M.C.C.," not pausing to inform us that this stands for the Marylebone Cricket Club, as few American readers would know.

The story begins with the narrator serving as guide to a reader who, like Psmith himself, has no previous American experience. In his opening paragraphs Wodehouse celebrates America's cultural and linguistic variety:

The man in the street would not have known it, but a great crisis was imminent in New York journalism.

Everything seemed much as usual in the city. The cars ran blithely on Broadway. Newsboys shouted "Wux-try!" into the ears of nervous pedestrians with their usual Caruso-like vim. . . . Nevertheless, the crisis was at hand. Mr J. Fillken Wilberfloss, editor-in-chief of *Cosy Moments,* was about to leave his post and start on a ten weeks' holiday.

In New York one may find every class of paper which the imagination can conceive. Every grade of society is catered for. If an Esquimau came to New York, the first thing he would find on the book-stalls in all probability would be the *Blubber Magazine,* or some similar publication written by Esquimaux for Esquimaux. Everybody reads in New York, and reads all the time. The New Yorker peruses his favorite paper while he is being jammed into a crowded compartment on the subway or leaping like an antelope into a moving street car. (9)

Like his Esquimau counterpart, Wodehouse found his niche in New York, and his foreigner's ear was attuned to the exotic speech patterns of Caruso-like newsboys, portly German-American waiters, and Irish-American gangsters working the borders of Chinatown and Little Italy. In a very real sense, Wodehouse began writing world literature in 1915. Not only was his work often focused on themes of transatlantic travel and linguistic incongruity; he was actually writing directly *for* an international market, comically exploiting each country's myths about the other and playing with the many varieties of English he encountered. After the war ended, Wodehouse began to commute back and forth between New York and London, criss-crossing the Atlantic to work on productions of his musicals and stage plays, writing his novels in both countries and on board ship en route. Wodehouse's work soon entered world literature in the more strict sense of translation as well: his subtly delocalized portrayals of urban America and rural England proved to be readily readable farther afield, and in his own lifetime Wodehouse was translated into thirty languages.

Intimately linked to translation as it is, world literature can also be found when a work circulates across cultural divides separating speakers of a single widespread language like Arabic, Spanish, or French. A Senegalese novel written in French can enter world literature in an effective sense when it is read in Paris, Quebec, and Martinique; translation is only a further stage in its worldly circulation. Commuting between England and America—famously described by Dylan Thomas as two cultures "separated by the barrier of a common language"—Wodehouse was participating in the growing globalization of English. After World War I the old global influence of the British Empire began to be superseded by the expanding international reach of American economic activity. Writing on the cusp of this major economic and cultural shift, Wodehouse benefited equally from the new wealth of America and from the surviving trade routes of the old Empire. To this day, he and Agatha Christie are the two novelists sold at every railway station in India: Bertie Wooster is alive and well in Bombay.

Wodehouse's spectacular international success was closely connected with his cultural double vision. A work can enter world literature by embodying what are taken to be universal themes and values, so that local cultural detail can be considered secondary or even irrelevant, an approach that worked particularly well with the early response to Kafka, who rarely alluded directly to his contemporary cultural context. Wodehouse's fiction operates differently: it is closely tied to the concrete realities of modern British and American life, but these cultures are written about *as if from outside.* He could write so well for foreign readers in part because he himself was so foreign to each of his environments. Almost the opposite of a cosmopolitan or citizen of the world, Wodehouse was out of place in fundamental ways everywhere he went, even in England, though he should have been entirely at home in Lord Emsworth's environs. He was descended from an ancient English family, which traced its lineage back to one Bertram of Wodehouse Tower in Yorkshire—a clear model, if only in name, for his famous character Bertie Wooster, whose frequent evocations of "noblesse oblige" and "the Code of the Woosters" have a Wodehouse family resonance. As Wodehouse was growing up, three Wodehouses were members of Parliament, and a distant cousin, the Earl of Kimberly, was William Gladstone's foreign minister during the early 1890s. On his mother's side, a great-uncle was the prominent churchman (and great prose stylist) Cardinal Newman.

Yet Wodehouse was a younger child of younger children, and his father's medical disability pushed the family to the very fringes of respectability. It was all Wodehouse's father could do to get his son a job with the Hong Kong and Shanghai Bank; he would be promoted to Hong Kong after three years as a clerk in the London office. Like Austin Henry Layard before him, though, Wodehouse had no wish at all to settle into a colonial life, and Hong Kong in any case was completely foreign to him. Though his parents had stayed there through the 1890s, they had shipped young Plum home when he was a small child; he rarely saw his parents for the remainder of his childhood and adolescence. His father's disastrous circumambulation must have rendered Hong Kong still less attractive to Wodehouse, and he wrote furiously at night precisely in order to save himself from the fate of being sent out to the land of his earliest years. This reality underlies the movements of his early hero Psmith, who comes to New York after resigning from a thinly veiled version of Wodehouse's own bank: "something seemed to whisper to me," Psmith tells a friend, "even in the midst of my triumphs in the New Asiatic Bank, that there were other fields" (*Psmith Journalist*, 34).

It is a mistake to think of Wodehouse purely as a writer of comfortable fantasies of upper-class life, as even his supporters often seem to suppose. In a BBC broadcast in 1961 in honor of Wodehouse's eightieth birthday, Evelyn Waugh tried defusing the charge of literary conservatism by insisting that Wodehouse wasn't writing about the real world at all:

> Mr. Wodehouse's characters are not, as has been fatuously
> suggested, survivals of the Edwardian age. They are creations
> of pure fancy. . . . The language of the Drones was never heard
> on human lips. It is all Mr. Wodehouse's invention, or rather
> inspiration. . . . His characters have never tasted the forbidden
> fruit. They are still in Eden. The Gardens of Blandings Castle are
> that original garden from which we are all exiled. ("An Act of
> Homage and Reparation," 561–62)

Waugh's praise misses the underlying realism of Wodehouse's fantasy world. His dialogues are built out of close attention to the language heard on human lips, and his Edenic world has a notably Darwinian character. Here is Ashe Marson's first view of Blandings Castle's dependent village, Market Blandings:

> The church is Norman, and the intelligence of the majority of the
> natives palaeozoic. To alight at Market Blandings Station in the
> dusk of a rather chilly Spring day, when the south-west wind has
> shifted to due east, and the thrifty inhabitants have not yet lit
> their windows, is to be smitten with the feeling that one is at the
> edge of the world with no friends near.
>
> Ashe, as he stood beside Mr. Peters' luggage and raked the
> unsympathetic darkness with a dreary eye, gave himself up to
> melancholy. Above him an oil lamp shed a meagre light. Along
> the platform a small but sturdy porter was juggling with a milk-
> can. The east wind explored his system with chilly fingers.
> (*Something New*, 83–84)

If this is an Eden, it is one that Kafka's Herr K. would recognize. The Castle itself is ruled, like Kafka's, by a lord who hides from his guests, making his appearance as rarely as possible. In his absence, Ashe and Joan must often deal with minor functionaries like Beach the Butler, and Wodehouse gives a brilliant portrayal of life in the servants' quarters, drawing on long childhood hours spent in pantries while his many aunts and uncles—he had over twenty—were visiting together in drawing rooms. Beach typifies the servants' obsession with their masters' social status and their own reflected glory: "Butlers as a class seem to grow less and less like anything human in proportion to the magnificence of their surroundings. . . . Blandings Castle was one of the more important of England's show-places, and Beach, accordingly, had acquired a dignified inertia which almost qualified him for inclusion in the vegetable kingdom" (90). As always, Wodehouse catches the nuances of the servants' speech, and he explores their attention to its class implications. In *Pigs Have Wings* (1952), when a servant from London makes the mistake of addressing Beach as "Cocky," "ice formed on the butler's upper slopes" (93). Already in *Something New,* Beach's sense of the dignity of his position lends his own speech an oracular quality: "I have a Weak Stomach. The Lining Of My Stomach is not what I could wish the Lining Of My Stomach to be" (92–93). Less self-absorbed servants relax by mocking their masters' English: "And Freddie says, 'Oh, dash it all, guv'nor, you know, what!'" (105). Wodehouse pauses here to have Ashe note "a curious fact that while the actual valet of any person under discussion spoke of him almost affectionately by his Christian name, the rest of the company used the greatest ceremony and gave him his title with all respect" (105–6). Wodehouse views Blandings Castle, like the streets of New York, with an ethnographer's eye.

The innocence that Waugh celebrated in Wodehouse's world is a selective sort of innocence. An atmosphere of genial hilarity reigns, and good-hearted heroes and plucky heroines remain pure before marriage and faithful thereafter; and yet financial realities press in on many characters, and family relations are deeply strained, comically though those strains are manifested. These strains themselves are grounded in economic as well as emotional pressures. The kindly and lovable Lord Emsworth has no visible affection for his son Freddie, one of Wodehouse's many shiftless, fatuous younger sons:

> Like many fathers in his rank of life, the Earl of Emsworth had suffered much through . . . the problem of What To Do With The Younger Sons. It is useless to try to gloss over the fact, the

Younger Son is not required. You might reason with a British peer by the hour—you might point out to him how, on the one hand, he is far better off than the male codfish, who may at any moment find itself in the distressing position of being called on to provide for a family of over a million. . . . but you would not cheer him up in the least. He does not want the Younger Son. (23)

Twenty years later, in *Blandings Castle* (1935), Lord Emsworth still regards his son as "a worse menace to the happy life of rural England than botts, green-fly, or foot-and-mouth disease. The prospect of having him at Blandings indefinitely affected Lord Emsworth like a blow on the base of the skull" (45).

Relations among the older generation are similarly uneasy. The Earl's younger brother Galahad, a free-living character and great raconteur, is a thorn in the side of their censorious sister Constance. In *Pigs Have Wings*, she describes an occasion when Gally came close to drowning: "'just as he was sinking for the last time, one of the gardeners came along and pulled him out,' she added, speaking with a sort of wild regret." Wodehouse underscores Constance's regret, having her fall silent for a moment, "brooding on the thoughtless folly of the chuckle-headed gardener" (155–56).

Blandings is not simply seen through rose-colored glasses; it is, in fact, seen through monocles, pince-nez, and horn-rimmed glasses as well. At the time he was writing *Something New,* Wodehouse published "In Defense of Astigmatism," an essay on the modern novel, in which he used eyeglasses as his example of the realities that his bold contemporaries were too timid to treat: "This is peculiarly an age where novelists pride themselves on the breadth of their outlook and the courage with which they refuse to ignore the realities of life. . . . Why, you can hardly hear yourself think for the uproar of earnest young novelists proclaiming how free and unfettered they are. And yet, no writer has had the pluck to make his hero wear glasses" (19–20). Wodehouse goes on to imagine a scene involving a young lover named Clarence, who polishes his pince-nez tenderly as he woos his sweetheart. Next comes a dramatic scenario ("Clarence adjusted his tortoise-shell-rimmed spectacles with a careless gesture, and faced his assassins without a tremor"), followed by two comic scenes based on eyeglasses fogging up when someone enters a room from outdoors, all illustrating "the latent possibilities for dramatic situations in short sight" (21). In *Something New,* Clarence, Earl of Emsworth, does indeed wear pince-nez; the urbane Galahad sports a monocle, whose mocking glitter alone can drive Constance up to her room to bathe her temples; and Clarence's malevolent personal secretary, the Efficient Baxter, peers at the world through rimless glasses. Grounded in realistic detail, the world of Blandings is more socially and psychologically layered than it first appears to be.

This does not at all mean that Wodehouse's works are faithful transcripts of the daily lives of the British aristocrat and the New York gangster. An oeuvre in which sex and death are absent and every ending is happy can hardly be considered as displaying a rigorous, come-what-may realism. What Wodehouse gives us instead is a stylized world whose realistic details are ludicrously exfoliated into an increasingly conventionalized system of their own. This abstraction from reality is a key element in Wodehouse's success as a writer of world literature: one would never mistake the Blandings novels for regional realism of the sort written by Wodehouse's contemporary R. H. Mottram, a writer taken more seriously than Wodehouse between the wars but whose work never traveled well and is forgotten today. Wodehouse began his career writing about both England and America as an outsider, and for outsiders, but he soon began developing his abstracted world for its own sake, giving his international audience the pure pleasure of watching him play endless variants on his own conventions.

As early as 1928, a reviewer accused Wodehouse of self-plagiarism, a charge that Wodehouse hilariously took up in the preface to his next novel, *Fish Preferred* (1929), a new Blandings story: "A certain critic—for such men, I regret to say, do exist—made a nasty remark about my last novel that it contained 'all the old Wodehouse characters under different names.' . . . With my superior intelligence I have outgeneralled the man this time by putting in all the old Wodehouse characters under the same names. Pretty silly it will make him feel, I rather fancy" (quoted in Phelps, *P. G. Wodehouse*, 158).

In his later fiction Wodehouse exploits to the full the surprises that occur when long-familiar characters appear in unexpected guises. Having intimidated Bertie Wooster in several novels over the years, in 1960 the formidable psychiatrist Sir Roderick Glossop suddenly turns up, disguised as a butler named Swordfish, at the country house of Bertie's Aunt Dahlia. This apparition gives a severe jolt to the heroic sangfroid that Bertie believes himself to possess: "In the eyes of many people, I suppose, I seem one of those men of chilled steel you read about, and I'm not saying I'm not. But it is possible to find a chink in my armor, and this can be done by suddenly springing eminent looney-doctors on me in the guise of butlers" (*How Right You Are, Jeeves*, 29). Bertie really ought to have been prepared for this role change, though, since a quarter of a century earlier he and Sir Roderick had both donned blackface to disguise themselves as traveling minstrels (*Thank*

You, Jeeves, 1934). Conversely, in *Uncle Fred in the Springtime* (1939), Frederick, fifth Earl of Ickinham, stays at Blandings Castle disguised as Sir Roderick himself. Writing his new preface to *Something New* in 1968, Wodehouse noted that "Blandings had impostors the way other houses have mice." Eighty-seven years old at this point, he was looking forward to more of these metamorphoses: "It is about time that another was coming along," he concluded; "without at least one impostor on the premises, Blandings Castle is never itself" (7).

Like Kafka, Wodehouse can be read along two registers, the ethnographic and the universal. His Blandings Castle and his Drones Club cannot be found on any map, as Waugh might say, but neither can Count Westwest's castle or the Penal Colony. All are closed societies whose arcane rules are gradually laid bare for the reader, often through the efforts of an intruder or impostor; all are unique cultures whose rituals nonetheless speak to us of the human condition at large. Like Kafka's symbolist locales, Wodehouse's farcical settings lie somewhere between the realms of pure fantasy and of literary realism, providing an intermediate ground on which the system can develop according to its own internal logic, even as it continually refers obliquely back to the world as we experience it from day to day.

When Wodehouse does incorporate direct contemporary references into his fiction, he plays with the absurdity of juxtaposing real-world characters and events with those of his fictive universe. In a short story from 1926 called "The Clicking of Cuthbert," for instance, a Russian novelist named Vladimir Brusiloff is taking time away from the ongoing political upheavals in Russia by making a lecture tour in America. Invited to address a suburban women's literary club, Brusiloff rebuffs every attempt to draw him out concerning contemporary fiction. A brooding, Dostoevskian novelist, "Vladimir specialized in grey studies of hopeless misery, where nothing happened till page three hundred and eighty, when the moujik decided to commit suicide" (390). In person he is brusque and withdrawn, chiefly because he knows all too well what to expect from his audience:

> What was wrong with him was the fact that this was the eighty-second suburban literary reception he had been compelled to attend since he had landed in the country on his lecturing tour, and he was sick to death of it. . . . realiz[ing] that eight out of ten of those present had manuscripts of some sort concealed on their persons, and were only waiting for an opportunity to whip them out and start reading, he wished that he had stayed at his quiet home in Nijni-Novgorod, where the worst thing that could

happen to a fellow was a brace of bombs coming in through the window and mixing themselves up with his breakfast egg. (391–92)

The hero of this tale, Cuthbert Banks, attends this dismal soiree not because of any interest in literature but because his only passion in life, apart from golf, is the hostess's niece, Adeline, whom he hopes to impress by feigning an interest in high culture. Unable to think of anything to say to Brusiloff, Cuthbert is hopelessly outclassed by his rival, a rising young novelist named Raymond Parsloe Devine, who has deeply impressed Adeline. World literature is all the rage—the club's last lecture had been on "the Neo-Scandinavian Movement in Portuguese Literature" (389)—and Adeline adores Devine's work because she sees him as transcending any merely national context:

> "Mr. Devine," replied Adeline, blushing faintly, "is going to be a great man. Already he has achieved much. The critics say that he is more Russian than any other young American writer."
> "And is that good?"
> "Of course it's good."
> "I should have thought the wheeze would be to be more American than any other young American writer."
> "Nonsense! Who wants an American writer to be American? You've got to be Russian or Spanish or something to be a real success." (388)

Flush with pride at his certified Russianness, Devine tries to impress the visitor with his enthusiasm for the novelists Sovietski and Nastikoff. Devine's ploy fails, however, for like many writers, Brusiloff despises his contemporaries almost without exception. Having humiliated Devine for even mentioning his rivals' names—thereby clearing the way for Cuthbert to win Adeline's hand—Brusiloff continues glowering until he chances to discover that Cuthbert has won the French Open. "Brushing aside one or two intellectuals who were in the way," he drags Cuthbert into a corner to talk golf. "Let me tell you one vairy funny story about putting," he says, and now the political violence of midtwenties Russia comes directly, surreally, into the picture:

> It was one day I play at Nijni-Novgorod with the pro against Lenin and Trotsky, and Trotsky had a two-inch putt for the hole. But, just as he addresses the ball, someone in the crowd he tries to assassinate Lenin with a rewolwer—you know that is our great

national sport, trying to assassinate Lenin with rewolwers—and the bang puts Trotsky off his stroke and he goes five yards past the hole, and then Lenin, who is rather shaken, you understand, he misses again himself, and we win the hole and the match and I clean up three hundred and ninety-six thousand rubles, or five dollars in your money. (396)

In classic Wodehousian fashion, the humor of this anecdote has a double basis, social and linguistic. Wodehouse is never happier than when showing authoritarian figures in an absurd light, and the ridiculousness of Lenin and Trotsky's golfing mishap is underscored by the comic chaos of dialects in which the story is conveyed: Brusiloff's Russian-American dialect ("rewolwer," "it was one day I play") is leavened with technical golfing language ("just as he addresses the ball") and pure Americanisms ("I clean up"). He can mix several dialects in a single outburst: "My dear young man, I saw you win ze French Open. Great! Great! Grand! Superb! Hot stuff, and you can say I said so!" (396). Brusiloff's great compatriot Mikhail Bakhtin could hardly have found a better example of dialogistic heteroglossia even in his beloved Dostoevsky.

Brusiloff himself clearly admires Wodehouse's talents. As he concludes his tirade against his rival novelists, Brusiloff denounces the entire world of letters, allowing only two exceptions apart from himself: "No novelists any good except me," he declares, his words emerging vatically from the dense undergrowth of his beard; "Sovietski—yah! Nastikoff—bah! I spit me of zem all. No novelists anywhere any good except me. P. G. Wodehouse and Tolstoi not bad. Not good, but not bad. No novelists any good except me" (394). Courteously giving his creator pride of place even over Tolstoy, Brusiloff presciently enshrines Wodehouse at the heart of world literature.

Immersed in exploring the laws of his fictional world, Wodehouse took less and less interest in the outside world as such, apart from the hothouse worlds of the New York and London theater. Gradually tiring of shuttling across the Atlantic, he and his wife moved to France in the thirties, settling in the seaside resort of Le Touquet, south of Calais, in a beautiful half-timbered house conveniently close to a major casino. Characteristically, Wodehouse promptly began to make literary use of his new locale, adding yet another layer of worldly transformation and dislocation to his fictional universe. In his 1932 novel *Hot Water*, for example, a wealthy American, J. Wellington Gedge, has reluctantly succumbed to his wife's blandishments and leased Château Blissac, located on the outskirts of a town called

St. Rocque, a fishing village distinguished by its gold-domed casino. J. Wellington Gedge, however, longs to be home in the California of his working-class roots. "The poet speaks of a man whose heart was in the Highlands, a-chasing of the deer. Mr. Gedge's was in Glendale, California, wandering round among the hot dogs and filling-stations" (1–2). The novel is peopled by English and American expatriates, including no fewer than five impostors, two of whom are posing as French aristocrats, their charade somewhat hampered by the fact that neither of them speaks French.

As the Germans marched on Paris in 1940, the Wodehouses resisted friends' appeals to come to England, in part because of quarantine problems involving their Pekinese dogs. The Germans arrested Wodehouse when they occupied Le Touquet, and he was interned at a prisoner-of-war camp in Silesia for a year. Wodehouse bore his internment with good humor, taking his turn at peeling potatoes and writing away, not making any concessions to his uncomfortable environment. He wrote an entire novel, *Money in the Bank,* and half of a second novel while interned; neither shows any overt trace of the setting in which they were composed.

Wodehouse's approach toward his situation made life tolerable but caused enormous problems for him thereafter, once he was released from the camp and allowed to stay at a hotel in Berlin, joined by his wife and the Pekinese dogs. While in internment, he had written a comic sketch of camp life for an American magazine; getting wind of this, the German propaganda ministry inquired whether he might care to broadcast a few humorous talks to America. Pleased to renew contact with his transatlantic audience, Wodehouse never considered the fact that, as England by this time was locked in mortal combat with Germany, many of his countrymen would regard comic sketches of occupation life as traitorous propaganda on behalf of the enemy. Wodehouse made five radio broadcasts from Berlin in the summer of 1941. They received little attention when broadcast to America but caused a storm of protest when they were rebroadcast to England. People being bombed nightly by the Luftwaffe were not prepared to appreciate an ironic, self-mocking account of encounters with well-meaning German soldiers:

> One's reactions on suddenly finding oneself surrounded by the
> armed strength of a hostile power are rather interesting. There is
> a sense of strain. The first time you see a German soldier over
> your garden fence, your impulse is to jump ten feet straight up
> into the air, and you do so. About a week later, you find that you
> are only jumping five feet. And then, after you have been living

with him in a small village for two months, you inevitably begin to fraternize and to wish that you had learned German at school, instead of Latin and Greek. All the German I know is "*Es ist schönes Wetter*" and this handicaps conversation with a Bavarian private who knows no English. After I had said "*Es ist schönes Wetter*," I was a spent force and we used to take up the rest of the interview beaming at one another.[1]

Acutely aware of the social nuances of every variety of English under the sun, Wodehouse had no idea how an embattled British public would react to his use of words like "fraternization." Bitter articles were written in England against his broadcasts; he was called a "a fool and a louse" and even a traitor. Letters to the *Daily Telegraph* proposed that Oxford should rescind the honorary degree they had bestowed on him in 1939. In one letter, the Irish playwright Sean O'Casey implied that the real problem was not Wodehouse's politics but his readers' literary taste:

> The harm done to England's cause and to England's dignity is not the poor man's babble in Berlin, but the acceptance of him by a childish part of the people and the academic government of Oxford, dead from the chin up, as a person of any importance whatsoever in English humorous literature, or any literature at all. It is an ironic twist of retribution on those who banished Joyce and honoured Wodehouse.
>
> If England has any dignity left in the way of literature, she will forget for ever the pitiful antics of English Literature's performing flea. (Sproat, 18–19)

Wodehouse had defenders as well as accusers. Malcolm Muggeridge, then a young intelligence officer, interviewed Wodehouse after his release and concluded that "it wasn't that he was other-worldly or unworldly, as much as that he was a-worldly. Wodehouse's true offense was to have disinterested himself in the war" (Phelps, 223). In 1945 George Orwell wrote an essay "In Defence of P. G. Wodehouse," in which he emphasized the disconnectedness of Wodehouse's world. Instead of seeing his novels as unreal, as Waugh was later to do, Orwell presented them as a conservative portrayal of a long-vanished Edwardian age: "Bertie Wooster, if he ever existed, was killed round about 1915" (324). Arguing that "in the case of Wodehouse,

---

[1] Donaldson, *P. G. Wodehouse*, 224. The full text of Wodehouse's broadcasts can be found in Iain Sproat, *Wodehouse at War* (107–28), though this particular passage is transcribed inaccurately in Sproat, so I quote here from Donaldson.

if we drive him to retire to the United States and renounce his British citizenship, we shall end by being horribly ashamed of ourselves," Orwell offered an acute analysis of politicians' readiness to believe the worst of Wodehouse and denounce him: "He was the kind of rich man who could be attacked with impunity and without risking any damage to the structure of society. To denounce Wodehouse was not like denouncing, say, Beaverbrook" (327–28).

Indifferent to great-power politics, Wodehouse was not as apolitical as Muggeridge thought, or as backward-looking as Orwell implied. In the twenties and the thirties he periodically satirized political figures, particularly those whose motives he saw as the vices of Blandings writ large. A lover of convention, Wodehouse was a mocker of conventionality: he loved to skewer authoritarian personalities, and Lenin and Trotsky have miniature analogs in the Efficient Baxter and the Earl of Emsworth's censorious sister Constance. These self-righteous manipulators are sharply contrasted to figures like Constance's younger brother, the effervescent man-about-town Gally Threepwood. Gally is notably unconcerned with class distinctions or people's financial standing. Free of his sister's snobbery and money-consciousness—perhaps just because, as a Younger Son, he has no secure financial position—Gally befriends butlers, barmaids, and dukes alike.

The true coin of Wodehouse's realm is not money or class position but anecdotes; what his free spirits collect as they move through life is a fund of stories, and these tales bestow upon their owners a toleration for the vagaries of human contact and also an intense sociability: they need an audience with whom they can share their accumulated narrative capital. In *Pigs Have Wings*, forced into company with an earnest young prig named Orlo Vosper, Gally has no need to snub Orlo in favor of more congenial company, for to Gally all company is congenial: "Orlo Vosper belonged to the human race, and all members of the human race were to Gally a potential audience for his stories. It was possible, he felt, that the young man had not heard the one about the duke, the bottle of champagne and the female contortionist, so he welcomed him now with a cordial wave of his cigar" (119).

Unlike some of the British aristocracy who had been covertly or even overtly profascist in the interwar years, Wodehouse was never drawn to authoritarianism in any form. In 1938 he openly parodied Sir Oswald Mosley's British fascist movement in his novel *The Code of the Woosters*, which has a scene in which Bertie sharply reproves Spode, a would-be dictator who has founded the Black Shorts party. Typically, Wodehouse focuses his satire on the fascists' clothing, which resembles soccer players' shorts ("footer bags"). "The trouble with you, Spode," Bertie remarks, is that just because you have succeeded in inducing a handful of half-wits to disfigure the London scene by going about in black shorts, you think you're someone. You hear them shouting "Heil, Spode!" and you imagine it is the Voice of the People. That is where you make your bloomer. What the Voice of the People is saying is: "Look at that frightful ass Spode swanking about in footer bags! Did you ever in your puff see such a perfect perisher?" (118)

Such passages were not remembered in the press of war, and some readers began to look back at Wodehouse's prewar writing through the lens of his Berlin broadcasts: as one letter writer put it, "the embryo of the Fascist mentality was revealed in his whole set of characters, who were essentially undemocratic, unprogressive and reactionary" (quoted in Sproat, 19).

Wodehouse never replied to such criticisms, and he continued after the war to portray all the old Wodehouse characters with undiminished vigor, responding only obliquely to his critics. Picking up O'Casey's disparagement of his work, for instance, he actually gave a postwar collection of letters on theater the title *Performing Flea*. The most direct reflection of his wartime experiences that I have found in his fiction occurs in the opening of his 1946 novel *Joy in the Morning:*

After the thing was all over, when peril had ceased to loom and happy endings had been distributed in heaping handfuls and we were driving home with our hats on the side of our heads, having shaken the dust of Steeple Bumpleigh from our tyres, I confessed to Jeeves that there had been moments during the recent proceedings when Bertram Wooster, though no weakling, had come very near to despair.

"Within a toucher, Jeeves."

"Unquestionably affairs had developed a certain menacing trend, sir."

"I saw no ray of hope. It looked to me as if the blue bird had thrown in the towel and formally ceased to function. And yet here we are, all boomps-a-daisy. Makes one think a bit, that."

"Yes, sir."

These (for Bertie) sober reflections do not, however, refer to the just-ended World War at all, but to "the super-sticky affair of Nobby Hopwood, Stilton Cheesewright, Florence Craye, my Uncle Percy, J. Chichester Clam, Edwin the Boy Scout and old Boko Fittleworth—or, as my biographers will probably call it, the Steeple Bumpleigh Horror" (1–2).

Wodehouse could return to his fictional world with undisguised relief, but returning to England was another matter. When the scandal of his broadcasts broke out, Britain's foreign minister, Anthony Eden, accused him of having "lent his services to the Nazi propaganda machine" (Sproat, 14). He was denounced in Parliament as a traitor, and successive foreign ministers refused to rule out the possibility that he might be tried for treason if he ever returned to England. He never did. He moved to New York City in 1947, and then in 1955 bought a house on several wooded acres on Long Island, where he lived for the remaining twenty years of his life, rarely leaving home even for a night.

In *English as a Global Language* (1997), David Crystal analyzes the ongoing spread of English as the second language of choice in many parts of the world. He argues that English has now become, in fact, the first truly global language in history, spoken in over a hundred countries altogether, as a first or more often second or third language. Writing from a position as someone deeply involved in the preservation and promotion of Welsh language and culture, Crystal doesn't have a simple or triumphalist view of this development. He argues, instead, that the world's citizens need to develop a multilingual competence, learning and using national and minority languages even as they adopt English as the best means of international communication. As he asks in his conclusion, "In 500 years' time, will it be the case that everyone will automatically be introduced to English as soon as they are born (or, by then, very likely, as soon as they are conceived)? If this is part of a rich multilingual experience for our future newborns, this can only be a good thing. If it is by then the only language left to be learned, it will have been the greatest intellectual disaster that the planet has ever known" (140). What Crystal says of languages in general applies to English itself as well. "Global English" may come to mean nothing more than a minimum competence, a bland, watered-down commercial and touristic language whose use could dampen down the linguistic richness of English even in its original home locales. Alternatively, English can be enriched as it finds new uses around the globe, and literature has a critical role to play in this process. Crystal is a linguist, and he focuses on political and commercial uses of English as a means of international communication, but it is notable that he quotes the great Nigerian novelist Chinua Achebe to illustrate the way in which English can grow as it is used by more and more people:

> The price a world language must be prepared to pay is submission to many different kinds of use. The African writer should aim to

use English in a way that brings out his message best without altering the language to the extent that its value as a medium of international exchange will be lost. He should aim at fashioning out an English which is at once universal and able to carry his particular experience. . . . I feel that English will be able to carry the weight of my African experience. But it will have to be a new English, still in full communion with its ancestral home but altered to suit its new African surroundings. (136)

Though Achebe's prose in this essay doesn't yet embody the "new English" he calls for, a wide range of novelists and poets have carried further the sorts of experiment in hybridization that Wodehouse and others were undertaking in the early decades of the century. Two decades before Achebe wrote his essay, a little-known writer in London, G. V. Desani, completed a remarkable picaresque novel, *All About H. Hatterr,* a comic masterpiece of the emerging literature of what we would now call global English. By day Desani was working for the BBC, but in his free time he was inventing a new English. In one scene, H. Hatterr's best friend urges him to come to a concert:

> "If music be the food of love, play on. Give me excess of it! . . .
> The festival will be grand entertainment for you. It will make you
> forget your present predicament. In fact, I can pat my back at this
> choice. Indeed, knowing your real soul, I can say, I have a good
> eye, uncle. I can see a church by daylight."
> "Did Shakespeare write that?"
> "Correctly, honest Iago."
> "Damme, if you think that's great writing, I am a ruddy crab! I
> am a laughing hyena! I am a silver monkey with a mad cockatoo
> at my heels!"
> "Maybe, Mr. H. Hatterr. But you must not underrate the great
> Bard. He observed Life. He held an untarnished mirror to Mother
> Nature. He reported Truth faithfully. Maybe, in his day, the
> ophthalmic optician's art was not as advanced as it is today. Only
> rich and well-to-do people could afford glasses. If a poor man
> could see a church by daylight, without spectacles, it must be
> assumed that he had a good eyesight. There was also a great deal
> of fog in Elizabethan England." (165)

This passage is a kind of haywire version of the discussions Bertie Wooster has with Jeeves, trying to parse the logic of some half-remembered passage from Shakespeare, complete with a discussion of eyeglasses. The difference is that both of Desani's interlocutors have profoundly skewed relations with the Queen's English, and there is no outside narrative voice to mediate between characters and reader. H. Hatterr's friend goes on to say that the star of the concert will be a singer known as Sri Harrow-voo, a Wodehousian impostor with a multicultural pedigree:

> "Who the hell did you say? Banerrji, that *can't* be an Indian name!"
>
> "Not at all, Mr. H. Hatterr. On the contrary, Sri Harrow-voo hides the identity of the well-known Mr. A. Singha. As he studied at Harrow School in England, also because he has invented an Indian form of Tyrolese and Swiss yodelling, *voo-o! vooo-o!* he is famous among the Indian masses as Sri Harrow-voo, rather than as Mr. A. Singha. He has introduced a very great artistic advance because India did not have her own mountain music. He has added the falsetto to the Indian half-notes. . . . He is completely Indian. His early schooling has in no way spoilt him. You will love to meet him. He is a poet." (165–66)

If his older contemporary Wodehouse plied the transatlantic literary trade routes, Desani traveled farther still. Born in Nairobi, he moved to India before emigrating to England in the thirties; after writing his novel during the war, he returned to India for years of yogic practice, living and studying in Japan as well. He then turned to journalism, writing essays for the *Times of India's Illustrated Weekly,* including, in the sixties, an opinion column called "Very High and Very Low." Having made intermittent stays in the United States, he eventually became a professor of philosophy at the University of Texas at Austin.

All About H. Hatterr was praised on publication by T. S. Eliot, albeit in somewhat ambiguous terms: "In all my experience," he wrote, "I have not met with anything quite like it." Quoting these words in an introduction to a reissue of the book in 1969, Anthony Burgess discussed Desani as a *métèque,* a resident alien with a skewed relation to the Queen's English. From this point of view Burgess placed Desani in the company of the great modernist outsiders Conrad and Joyce: "if we are to regard Poles and Irishmen as *métèques,* there are grounds for supposing that the *métèques* have done more for English in the twentieth century . . . than any of the pure-blooded men of letters who stick to the finer rules" (7). Burgess was uncomfortable with his own comparison, however; noting that the term *métèque* is "pejorative, like 'wop' or 'dago,'" he shifted gears, saying that we should see Desani not as "a dweller on a cultural fringe who did remarkably well when one considered his disadvantages but as a man squarely set in the great linguistic mainstream" (7–8).

Perhaps Burgess wouldn't have needed to insist so strongly on Desani's "mainstream" qualifications if he had remembered the readiness with which T. S. Eliot had adopted the term *métèque* for himself. Eliot did this, interestingly, in a speech praising one of Desani's direct literary forebears, Rudyard Kipling. Speaking to the 1958 annual luncheon of the Kipling Society, Eliot anticipated his audience's surprise that a difficult and experimental poet like himself would avow enthusiasm for Kipling's "barrack-room ballads." Eliot emphasized the commonality of their cultural situations, seeing Kipling, like himself, as a lifelong resident alien in British culture:

> Kipling passed his early childhood in India; he was brought back to England for his schooling; he returned to India at the age of seventeen. Two years of his life were spent in America. Later, he settled in Sussex, but came to pass his winters in the more benign climate of South Africa. He had been a citizen of the British Empire, long before he naturalised himself, so to speak, in a particular part of a particular county of England. The topography of my own life history is very different from his, but our feeling about England springs from causes not wholly dissimilar. The word *metic* is perfectly good English, though to many people the French *métèque* may be more familiar. It does not apply perhaps in the strictest sense to either of us, since we come both from wholly British stock; but I think Kipling's attitude to things English, like mine, was in some ways different from that of any native-born Briton. ("The Unfading Genius of Rudyard Kipling," 120)

If resident aliens like Kipling, Eliot, and Wodehouse helped set the stage for the emergence of global English today, they also began the process of reconceiving England itself in a global context. Appropriately, Wodehouse's Blandings Castle is a prime source for the Booker Prize–winning novel of yet another immigrant to England, Kazuo Ishiguro. *The Remains of the Day* (1988) treats the moral decay of the old country-house system, as seen through the eyes of a butler named Stevens, who is clearly descended from Wodehouse's Beach. Ishiguro builds on Wodehouse's sharp analyses of the complex internal hierarchies of the world below stairs at Blandings Castle and the servants' taking of self-definition from the masters they serve.

Upstairs, his Lord Darlington bears a family resemblance as well to Lord Emsworth, though with a dark twist: the lord of Ishiguro's manor bumbles his way into collaboration with the Nazis and their English fascist friends. Reviewing the novel when it appeared, Salman Rushdie was probably the first to draw the connection to Wodehouse, though he saw the relation purely negatively, with Ishiguro overturning the comfortable myths of Wodehouse's world:

> The surface of Kazuo Ishiguro's new novel is almost perfectly still. . . . It is, in fact, July 1956; but other, timeless worlds, the world of Jeeves and Bertie Wooster, the upstairs-downstairs world of Hudson, Mrs Bridges and the Bellamys, are also in the air. . . . Just below the understatement of the novel's surface is a turbulence as immense as it is slow; for *The Remains of the Day* is in fact a brilliant subversion of the fictional modes from which it at first seems to descend. Death, change, pain and evil invade the Wodehouse-world; the time-hallowed bonds between master and servant, and the codes by which both live, are no longer dependable absolutes but rather sources of ruinous self-deceptions; even the gallery of happy yokels turns out to stand for the post-war values of democracy and individual and collective rights which have turned Stevens and his kind into tragi-comic anachronisms. (*Observer*, 21 May 1989, 53)

Rushdie's comments seem to reflect Wodehouse's contemporary reception more than the terms of Wodehouse's novels themselves, particularly the foundational works of the teens and twenties.[2] The fundamental differences between Beach and Stevens, Lord Emsworth and Lord Darlington, are differences of mode rather than of myth: Ishiguro develops as tragedy what his predecessor staged as comedy. In Wodehouse's world as in Ishiguro's, social codes are no longer dependable absolutes but are sources of self-deception, and in both worlds myths struggle against the pressure of intractable realities. Even the unsettling change that sets the scene for Ishiguro's novel—the sale of Lord Darlington's country estate to an American millionaire—is a

---

[2] Rushdie has subsequently introduced Wodehouse into his own fiction as well, though perhaps not on the basis of fresh rereading. In his 2001 novel *Fury*, a puppet named Little Brain reveals that Spinoza's favorite novelist was, anachronistically, P. G. Wodehouse—appropriately, the narrator notes, as Spinoza in turn was the favorite philosopher of "the immortal shimmying butler" Jeeves (17). Rushdie has clearly read Wodehouse closely (the apt use of Spinoza, the fond reuse of the Wodehousian "shimmying"), though he probably hasn't read him recently (hence the slip in labeling Jeeves a "butler").

stock element of Wodehouse's world as early as *Something New,* in which the estate next to Blandings has just been rented by the American industrialist J. Preston Peters. Over the course of Wodehouse's career, Americans buy up much of "heritage Britain" outright.

Kazuo Ishiguro himself has discussed his book as a variation on Wodehouse's mythic world. In a 1990 interview in Texas, Ishiguro said that "I actually think it is one of the important jobs of the novelist to actually tackle and rework myths. I think it's a very valid ground on which a novelist should do his work. I've deliberately created a world which at first resembles that of those writers such as P. G. Wodehouse. I then start to undermine this myth and use it in a slightly twisted and different way" (Vorda and Herzinger, "An Interview," 140). In this interview Ishiguro rejects interpretations of his novel as a commentary on the Suez Crisis or a dissection of British responses to fascism in the thirties. As he rings new changes on Wodehouse's self-revising myths, Ishiguro writes like Wodehouse for an international audience, fashioning ethnographies of a society at once realistic and mythic in nature. English literature is now as much a global as a national phenomenon, and both its language and its thematic resources can be multiply exploited, at once from inside and from outside, as writers triangulate among the local, the international, and the personal landscapes of their worlds. As Ishiguro told his interviewer in Sugar Land, Texas:

> The kind of England that I create in *The Remains of the Day* is
> not an England that I believe ever existed. I've not attempted to
> reproduce, in an historically accurate way, some past period.
> What I'm trying to do there . . . is to actually rework a particular
> myth about a certain kind of mythical England. . . . And usually
> the further I get from Britain the happier I am with the readings,
> because people are less obsessed with the idea of it just being
> about Britain. . . . I feel like I'm *closing in on some strange, weird
> territory* that for some reason obsesses me and I'm not sure what
> the nature of that territory is, but with every book I'm kind of
> closing in on this strange territory. (139–40, 149–50)

Interviewed during his own American lecture tour in the twenties, the great Vladimir Brusiloff could hardly have put it better himself.

8

Rigoberta Menchú in Print

In January 1982, the then-unknown Guatemalan activist Rigoberta Menchú
spent a week in Paris with Elizabeth Burgos, an anthropologist deeply interested in Latin American revolutionary politics. Burgos tape-recorded
Menchú's testimony of her life story and her family's struggles during the
brutal civil war then still under way in Guatemala. Menchú's testimony is a
prime example of a work consciously produced within an international setting, intended from the start to circulate far beyond the author's national
sphere. It is a book that couldn't even have been published in Guatemala,
whose government was suppressing any publications critical of its genoci-
dal policies toward the indigenous population, and whose army would
gladly have murdered Menchú herself, as they had murdered several members of her family, had she set foot in her homeland. Menchú had been living in exile in Mexico for several years, and now she and several associates
had come to Europe to campaign in Geneva at the UN, and more generally
to rally support in their long struggle.

So fully international was the book's production that it was actually first published by Gallimard in French translation in 1983 before it appeared, later that year, in Spain in its original language, and the rights to the
book have continued to be controlled by Gallimard. Within a year, it had
been translated into English and soon thereafter into a dozen more languages. It became an international best-seller, significantly increasing public awareness of the "dirty war" that few had attended to outside Guatemala.
Menchú herself received the Nobel Prize for Peace in 1992, the first indigenous writer ever to be so honored and only the second Guatemalan ever to
receive a Nobel Prize, the first having been the novelist Miguel Angel Asturias in 1967. Asturias's prize had been for literature, but given the close

connection of literature and politics in Latin America, it is appropriate that Asturias was serving as ambassador to France at the time, and he had received the Lenin Peace Prize just the year before.

For its part, *Me Llamo Rigoberta Menchú* is a highly literary work. The genre of *testimonio* to which it belongs gives a personal shape to broader social events, and the most successful *testimonios* (like the best autobiographies in general) are rhetorically charged and artistically shaped narratives that often read like nonfiction novels. Menchú and Burgos's book succeeded as much through its eloquence and its narrative drama as through the information it provided on village life and the army's violence during the 1970s. It rapidly became a standard against which other testimonies were judged, and is now often taught in literature courses along with more fully novelistic reality-based fictions. In 1991 it figured in America's culture wars when it was adopted as a text for Stanford's core great-books course, and in his *Illiberal Education* Dinesh D'Souza made it a prime example of the spread of Marxist propaganda on American campuses under the guise of victim-friendly multiculturalism.

I, Rigoberta Menchú, as the book is called in English, tells the story of the highland village of Chimel, whose Mayan inhabitants struggle to preserve traditional values and customs amid the harsh conditions of life imposed by the dominant mestizo population ("ladinos," in Guatemalan parlance). Forced from better land by encroaching ladino landowners, Menchú's father, Vincente, leads a group of families to unsettled mountainous terrain, where they establish Chimel; they eke out a basic existence there, traveling down periodically to coastal farms (*fincas*) to work in conditions of virtual serfdom, returning to their mountain village when they can. Persecuted anew by rich ladinos who want to steal the land he has cleared, Menchú's father begins to question his situation and joins a new peasant organization, the Committee for Peasant Unity (CUC). In 1978, the government of Fernando Romeo Lucas García having come to power, the simmering civil war widens and intensifies. The conflict now spreads into Chimel's province of El Quiché, and the army begins kidnapping and torturing anyone suspected of collaborating with the insurgents, including union members and priests and laymen associated with Catholic Action, an organization that had begun promoting the social activism of liberation theology. Late in 1979, the army kidnaps Menchú's sixteen-year-old brother Petrocinio; Menchú describes in detail how, after torturing him secretly, they burn him and several others alive in the central square of Chajul, a village not far from Chimel. A year later, Vincente Menchú and thirty fellow CUC members take over the Spanish embassy in Guatemala City, hoping to dramatize the repression under way in El Quiché; the police storm the embassy, trapping them in a room, where they are burned to death. Several months later, the army kidnaps Menchú's mother, raping and torturing her and finally leaving her to die, naked, in the open; as she dies, the soldiers stand over her and urinate in her mouth.

Rigoberta Menchú's riveting descriptions of these horrific events form the dramatic core of her book, which as a whole provides a kind of emblematic compendium of the problems she and her compatriots faced, concretely illustrated in her own life and that of her family: she watches a young brother die of malnutrition while the family is working on a lowland *finca;* ladinos manipulate the legal system to cheat the villagers of Chimel out of their land; as a teenager, Menchú works as a maid in Guatemala City for a woman who treats her as a virtual slave; and finally, as the villagers attempt to organize themselves and protest their lot, the army's vicious repression descends upon them and the family is torn apart. Two of Menchú's sisters flee into the mountains and join the guerillas; Menchú herself goes into exile in Mexico and joins the struggle to organize opposition across the border and to rally support internationally. Illiterate until then, and only speaking a few words of Spanish at all, she says, she determined at age nineteen to learn Spanish and to learn to read, so as to spread her message more broadly. At the time she met Burgos, she had only known Spanish for three years, she says, a fact that the Mexican edition of her book highlights on its back cover, in language adapted from Burgos's introduction:

> Rigoberta was born in San Miguel Uspantán, El Quiché Province, in Guatemala. She is 23 years old, and learned Spanish three years ago, without books, teachers, or school. She learned it through her ferocious will to break the silence in which the Indians of Latin America live. She appropriated the language of the colonizer, not in order to integrate herself into a history that has never included her, but to make valued, through the medium of words, a culture which is part of that history.[1]

Grounded both in her own experience and in centuries-old oral tradition, Menchú's highly personal testimony proved to be far more effective than any statistical report by Amnesty International could have been, and its appeal was underwritten by the personal authority of her eyewitness

[1] Interestingly, this description removes Menchú from history even as it emphasizes her struggle with history: "She is 23 years old," it tells us, the age she was when she first met Burgos in 1982. The book cover still uses the present tense on its fifteenth edition in 1998, by which point Menchú was actually 39.

account of most of the events she describes. Thus she describes walking all night to reach Chajul, where she witnesses her brother's burning, and her description is unsparing:

> I, I don't know, every time I tell this story, I can't hold back my tears, for me it's a reality I can't forget, even though it's not easy to tell of it. My mother was weeping; she was looking at her son. My brother scarcely recognized us. Or perhaps . . . My mother said he did, that he could still smile at her, but I, well, I didn't see that. They were monstrous. They were all fat, fat, fat. They were all swollen up, all wounded. When I drew closer to them, I saw that their clothes were damp. Damp from the moisture oozing out of their bodies. . . . They looked half dead when they were lined up there, but when the bodies began to burn they began to plead for mercy. . . . Many people hurried off for water to put out the fires, but no-one fetched it in time. It needed lots of people to carry the water—the water supply is in one particular place and everyone goes there for it—but it was a long way off and nothing could be done. The bodies were twitching about. Although the fire had gone out, the bodies kept twitching. (179–80)

The only problem with this riveting scene is that it never actually took place. In the late 1980s an anthropologist named David Stoll was working in highland Guatemala on native responses to the years of civil war, finally ended in part thanks to the pressure of Menchú's book. To his surprise, people who had known the Menchús recalled many events very differently. Petrocinio was indeed kidnapped and murdered along with several friends, but he was shot secretly, not burned to death in public; for all the visual drama of Menchú's eyewitness account, the residents of Chajul say that no such event ever occurred.

As Stoll began to look further into the factual basis of her testimony, he found more and more discrepancies; he eventually gathered his findings into an exhaustively researched book, *Rigoberta Menchú and the Story of All Poor Guatemalans* (1999). Stoll has found that Menchú never had a younger brother who died on a *finca;* her mother was murdered in secret, not with the spectacular public brutality Menchú describes; Menchú herself was being schooled by nuns during the period when she says she was employed as a maid by a racist rich woman; far from having been an unschooled illiterate at the time she left Guatemala, she had in fact been fluent in Spanish from childhood and had furthermore received a junior high school education as a scholarship student in Guatemala City and in Huehuetenango. Her father's decades-long land struggles, moreover, were not conducted against wealthy ladinos but against his own in-laws, the Tums: what her book presents as a stark tale of ladino against Indian was in reality a messy family dispute. Further, Stoll found no evidence that Vincente had ever actually joined the CUC or espoused any political views at all. Instead, he concludes that after Rigoberta Menchú's family members had been killed and she found shelter among the revolutionaries along the border with Mexico, she retrospectively enrolled her family and her whole village in the revolutionary movement. In Stoll's view, it was the guerillas who brought the violence to Menchú's area, leaving the local peasants to pay the price when the army responded with massive repression. Whatever people's motives actually were in the late seventies, a decade later most of the peasants Stoll talked to in El Quiché thought of themselves as apolitical people who had gotten caught in the crossfire between the radical left and the radical right. As he soberly comments:

> What I heard about in Uspantán was almost more awful than what so many have read in those pages, where at least campesinos die for a cause that is their own. What I heard about in Uspantán was a preemptive slaughter of peasants who had little or nothing to do with the guerillas, who at most had listened to a few speeches, and who had little conception of the larger cause for which they were dying. Surely they died for something, but what that might be is still being worked out by the families they left behind. (138–39)

Stoll's research has stirred up sharp controversy. People who had never been sympathetic to Menchú's leftist ideology seized on Stoll's findings to attack *I, Rigoberta* as a tissue of lies. If Menchú had formerly seemed to be a kind of Guatemalan Gandhi, now she and Elizabeth Burgos began to look more like Tawana Brawley and the Reverend Al Sharpton, a comparison directly made in a polemical newspaper review by Michael Skube called "As Academia Embraces Lies of 'Larger Truth,' True Scholar Prevails." People who actually work on Guatemala, however, have tended to dispute Stoll's central claims. They argue that the struggle against the government was indeed broad-based, and that the government was using the guerilla insurgency as an excuse to crack down on every sort of dissent, including long-standing Indian efforts to organize themselves and improve their conditions.[2] Concerning the factual truth of Menchú's story, her supporters allow

[2] See for example Peter Canby, "The Truth about Rigoberta Menchú," and Greg Grandin and Francisco Goldman, "Bitter Fruit for Rigoberta." In her preface to the second

that Stoll has uncovered discrepancies between her account and her family's actual experience. They point, however, to the common understanding of *testimonios* as shaped reconstructions. Writing in a special issue of *PMLA* on "Globalizing Literary Studies," Arturo Arias argues:

> *Testimonio* was never meant to be autobiography or a sworn testimony in the juridical sense; rather, it is a collective, communal account of a person's life. . . . for Mayas there is no clear separation between an individual subject and a community, between being and belonging. . . . If her text, which did not make any historical truth claims, achieved the goals of ending massacre and creating respect for Mayan culture, does it matter if it did not conform to how Western science contextualizes documentary facts? ("Authorizing Ethnicized Subjects," 76–87)

Peter Canby closes his *New York Review of Books* essay by quoting a friend and supporter of Menchú, the Guatemalan historian Arturo Taracena:

> You don't see anyone else attacking autobiographies like this: there's a hidden racism. If Stoll is an anthropologist and doesn't know that Indian people speak collectively, that she expressed the voice of the collective conscience, then I don't know what he knows. . . . The magic of the book is the first-person narrative. There are things that she heard from other *militantes,* things that she didn't see, things that she put in her own voice. What she was narrating was the life of the Maya. (33)

In light of Stoll's findings, it becomes clear that *I, Rigoberta Menchú* fits rather better into the ambit of world literature than it had appeared to do; in important respects it is as much a documentary novel as an eyewitness account. Arias and Taracena protest too much in insisting that anyone familiar with the collective nature of Indian memory would never have expected literal truth from Menchú's story. Her book became a reference point for discussions of the genre of *testimonio* during the late eighties and through the nineties, and almost without exception these discussions take the book's key scenes as direct reports of Menchú's own experiences and those of her family. Thus, in their 1990 book *Literature and Politics in the Central American Revolutions,* John Beverley and Marc Zimmerman treat *I, Rigoberta Menchú* as a leading example of the genre of *testimonio,* which

---

edition (1991) of *Time and the Highland Maya,* on the other hand, Barbara Tedlock describes the peasants as Stoll does, as having been caught between the army and the guerillas (xiii–xiv).

they define as a narrative "told in the first-person by a narrator who is also the actual protagonist or witness of the events she or he recounts" (173). They emphasize that "each testimonio evokes an absent polyphony of other voices, of other possible lives and experiences" (175), but this polyphony is invoked because the speaker's own experiences are understood to be exemplary of the struggles of an entire group or class.

A similar perspective is found in an excellent 1996 study of oral testimony by Elena Zayas, *La Historia de Vida: La Oralidad Camino de la Historia,* published in Guatemala City by the University of San Carlos de Guatemala, in a series entitled Documentos para la Historia. Introducing Zayas's monograph, the series editors say that Menchú's story is emblematic of her people's experiences in general, but at the same time they stress the truth of Menchú's eyewitness account: she is someone who "ha visto caer asesinados a sus seres queridos" ("she has seen her loved ones fall, murdered," 2). Zayas gives an intriguing account of a complex scene of *autobiografía indirecta,* in which one person tells a story for a particular purpose to a writer who then publishes it for further purposes thereafter: "This involves a situation of interlocution in which the narrator, as a social actor, elaborates his account at a given moment, not only of his personal history but of a collective history as well" (4). All the same, Zayas takes as literally true Menchú's stories of Petrocinio's death, her father's struggle against the ladino landholders, and her late decision to learn Spanish (41–42, 56). Similarly, Linda Craft uses *I, Rigoberta* as a factual benchmark in her 1997 study of testimony-inspired fiction, *Novels of Testimony and Resistance from Central America.* Detailing a range of novelistic uses of techniques of oral testimony, Craft considers Menchú's book to be "the best example of Guatemalan testimony per se (testimony written without fictionalization or excessive regard for aesthetic value, as opposed to the testimonial novel)" (43).

Rigoberta Menchú herself, in fact, is quite clear within her own book that she distinguishes between what she has seen and what she might reconstruct. When her father and his fellow protestors were burned to death inside the Spanish embassy, many assumed that the police had set the fire, whereas others believed that the trapped protestors themselves had set off Molotov cocktails that they had brought with them, in an attempt either to drive the police away or to create a spectacular martyrdom before they could be subdued, led away, and murdered out of sight. In her discussion of her father's death, Rigoberta Menchú explicitly refuses to speculate on what actually happened: "As I said to someone who asked me for specific details of what happened in the Spanish embassy, I can't invent my own personal version from my imagination. None of our *compañeros* can know exactly" (*I, Rigoberta*, 187).

Menchú knew just what she was doing when she expanded her personal experiences into a collective history. In considering her story within the context of world literature, the real surprise to emerge from Stoll's research is not that her book is so literary but that it is so *worldly*. Though Elizabeth Burgos found her (and perhaps wanted to find her) "childlike" and "astonishingly young" (*I, Rigoberta*, xiv), Rigoberta Menchú had been evolving her story, and her self-presentation, in many public forums over the previous two years. She and her friends were desperately seeking to break through the international indifference that was enabling the Lucas García regime to murder tens of thousands of innocent people with impunity. In a new book, *Rigoberta: La Nieta de los Mayas,* Menchú describes their efforts to rouse apathetic UN bureaucrats to pay attention to what was going on in Guatemala, always being assured that the matter would be looked into soon:

> That's how it went, year after year. . . . Papers and more papers that passed from hand to hand. The photocopying machines were busier than the diplomats. There were always lines of people eagerly waiting to take advantage of the photocopiers. . . . Always the same arguments, the same words we'd hear year after year, in a cold place, cold, as if the cold of the snow had gotten into the bodies of the bureaucrats and the diplomats when it came to hearing about human rights.
>
> It's true, we were bothering them, because we were the only ones who got into the corridors of the UN, defying the police, defying everyone. But who were we? Nobody. (203)

In telling her story to Burgos, Menchú set out to become someone, or more precisely to become many people: as she says in the opening paragraph of *I, Rigoberta,* "The important thing is that what has happened to me has happened to many other people too: My story is the story of all poor Guatemalans" (1). As Greg Grandin and Francisco Goldman have put it, "Her story was a call to conscience, a piece of wartime propaganda designed not to mislead but rather to capture our attention. It relied upon a classic Dickensian technique of pulling together different individual experiences into one character's heart-rending story. Such distortions were probably necessary to break through the wall of media indifference" ("Bitter Fruit for Rigoberta," 25). John Beverley has made a related argument that Menchú's selective idealization of her village's life was "in part realistic, in part heuristic or utopian," consciously elaborated with the strategic goal of fostering "a broad movement of Indian and peasant resistance and an international solidarity network to support it" ("Second Thoughts on Testimonio," 97).[3]

Thus Menchú distilled real-life events into an emblematic, quasi-novelistic account intended to have direct real-world effects, as indeed it did. She could not, however, do this on her own. She was hampered less by any weakness in her Spanish than by her multiply marginal position as a Guatemalan Indian woman. In Europe she met Arturo Taracena, then living in exile in Paris. As Menchú recalls in her second book, he proposed that her story ought to become a book, but only in the right way:

> He was anxious for the book to become known and to reach a large public. He knew Elizabeth Burgos. It was Teracena who proposed to señora Burgos that we should do the book. He maintained that if he and I wrote the book, an exile and an indigenous woman, no one was going to pay attention to it, it would seem like a kind of family pamphlet. We needed someone with a name and an entry into the academic and publishing world. (*La Nieta*, 313)

In this way Burgos became Menchú's collaborator, in an ambiguous relation whose outlines remain unclear. In *La Nieta*, Menchú says that Taracena and a Canadian friend accompanied her to Burgos's apartment and took part in the recording sessions; she says further that once Burgos had transcribed and shaped the narrative, Taracena edited the final manuscript, and they had expected this collective work to be acknowledged (253). In her preface to *I, Rigoberta Menchú*, however, Burgos makes no mention of other collaborators, instead representing Menchú as appearing alone at her door one winter's night and staying alone with her for the week of recording, after which Burgos herself created the manuscript. She then approached Gallimard and signed contracts as the book's sole author, which is how she is listed to this day in the Spanish and Mexican edition. While early editions make no mention at all of Taracena's contribution, he has since been included in a prefatory list of acknowledgments in some, but not all, editions of the book. The English translation, published by Verso in 1984, has no acknowledgments and leaves the question of authorship ambiguous: no author at all is listed on the front cover or spine. On the title page and back cover, the book is described as "edited by Elisabeth Burgos-Debray."[4]

[3] A range of valuable articles on this debate has been collected by Arturo Arias in *The Rigoberta Menchú Controversy* (2001).

[4] In seeking a collaborator "with a name," Taracena in fact found someone with two. Burgos had been married to the prominent French anthropologist and revolutionary theorist

In effect, Menchú's *story* became Burgos's *book,* and Burgos's framing and shaping of the story were crucial to the book's runaway success. As an anthropologist, Burgos was as interested in Menchú's accounts of village life as she was in the story of the civil war; against the advice of associates of Menchú who wanted the book to concentrate heavily on the abuses they sought to publicize, Burgos set Menchú's personal history within a broad, timeless ethnographic frame. Thus, the first three chapters are titled "The Family," "Birth Ceremonies," and "The Nahual," giving an overview of social structure and traditional religious beliefs before we reach the first directly autobiographical chapter, "First Visit to the *Finca.*" The body of the book is punctuated by general chapters on such topics as "Marriage Ceremonies," "Fiestas," and "Death."

Burgos was remarkably successful in creating this mixed presentation. Far from diluting the autobiographical drama, the ethnography has a powerful effect in opening the story out, giving a sense of the tragic disruption of traditional modes of life and also pacing the narrative, offering the reader a chance to recover after each new act of oppression or brutality. The result is something in between a direct *testimonio* and a work like Carlos Castaneda's *The Teachings of Don Juan: A Yaqui Way of Knowledge,* the bestselling 1968 book in which a doctoral candidate in anthropology encounters the timeless wisdom (and the drugs that impart it) of the Yaqui sorcerer known as don Juan.

As the doctoral student Elizabeth Burgos would later do, Castaneda set his encounters with don Juan in an ethnographic frame. He starts with an introduction describing his methods of research and writing and ends the book with a long "structural analysis." Castaneda's work differs markedly from Burgos's, of course, in that "don Juan" later proved to have been Castaneda's outright invention, a means of focusing and dramatizing his research into peyote cults in northern Mexico and the American Southwest. In both books, however, the sober passages of ethnography underwrite and even heighten the vivid immediacy of the personal autobiography. As the anthropologist Walter Goldschmidt wrote in a preface to Castaneda's book, "We are indebted to him for his patience, his courage, and his perspicacity in seeking out and facing the challenge of his dual apprenticeship, and in reporting to us the details of his experiences. In this work he demonstrates the

---

Régis Debray; they were separated at the time Burgos met Menchú and later divorced. While the Spanish edition of *I, Rigoberta* gives her name simply as Burgos, the English edition continues to list her as Burgos-Debray. Apparently Debray's name is an advantage for the English market, a disadvantage for the Latin American and Spanish markets.

essential skill of good ethnography—the capacity to enter into an alien world" (viii). The result, as a quote from the *Los Angeles Times* informs us on the back cover, is "a remarkable experience, a jarring and total immersion into a wholly alien but irresistibly fascinating sensibility . . . the happenings themselves told with such immediacy, honesty and clarity that the reader becomes a part of them."

In much the same way, in her introduction to *I, Rigoberta* Burgos tells us that in her transcript of Menchú's words "we actually seem to hear her speaking and can almost hear her breathing. . . . Quietly, but proudly, she leads us into her own cultural world. . . . As we listen to her voice, we have to look deep into our own souls for it awakens sensations and feelings which we, caught up as we are in an inhuman and artificial world, thought were lost forever" (xii). The early readers and reviewers of the book generally accepted this invitation into what Elzbieta Sklodowska has called "the heartland of phonocentrism." As she says, "most critics did not read testimonial texts—they read the official voices of these texts, confusing the tongues of the editor and his/her surrogates."[5]

Burgos's ethnographic framing made Menchú's stark story attractive to many readers who might otherwise have preferred to avert their eyes from such scenes of violence, and who might (as Taracena had feared) have rejected an Indian activist's account as ideologically motivated propaganda. Burgos short-circuited these reactions by constructing the cultural setting in such a way as to validate Menchú's self-presentation as an innocent eyewitness, a person whose political ideas have grown organically from her village's timeless way of life and from an age-old cultural conflict of pure Indians against mixed-race ladinos who have lost touch with their roots. Menchú's words can then be presented, on the cover of the Spanish edition, as "not simply ones of denunciation and protest. They are above all an energetic affirmation of a manner of being, of a right to be what one is: a specific culture, a comprehension of the universe, an interaction with nature."

And yet, effective though it was, the book's ethnographic framing is regrettable, as it actually magnifies problems in Menchú's account of her society. Burgos says that Menchú was eager to give a full picture of her culture, to talk about her people's customs as well as their recent experiences. It was perhaps inevitable that in the process a twenty-three-year-old, exiled from her shattered village and her lost homeland, would romanticize her

---

[5] "Spanish American Testimonial: Some Afterthoughts," 86, 98. This and other important articles (by Doris Sommer, George Yúdice, and others) are reprinted in Georg Gugelberger, *The Real Thing: Testimonial Discourse and Latin America.*

childhood and village life and politics. Trying to make sense of her radically disorienting experiences, Rigoberta Menchú presented Burgos with a shifting and unstable cultural history, part Rousseauian idyll, part Manichean dystopia, in which unchanging ancestral wisdom is constantly opposed to the oppressive demands of the encroaching ladinos, whose culture is diametrically opposed to Mayan culture in every way.

In presenting this cluster of views, Menchú systematically minimizes conflicts within the Mayan community and passes over the many ways in which Mayans and ladinos have developed in a fraught but dynamic relation to one another over the past five hundred years. As she describes her culture, Menchú paints a remarkably ideal picture of pre-Conquest Mayan life: "Children haven't always died young. Our forefathers told us that our old people used to live until they were a hundred and twenty-five, and now we die at thirty or forty" (68). "Many of our race now know how to kill. The whites are responsible for this" (69). Even in the present, she prefers not to dwell on conflict within her own community. Discussing the village's treatment of boys and girls, for example, she worries round the topic without wanting to draw the conclusions her own examples clearly suggest:

> When a male child is born, there are special celebrations,
> not because he's male but because of all the hard work and
> responsibility he'll have as a man. It's not that machismo doesn't
> exist among our people, but it doesn't present a problem for the
> community because it's so much a part of our way of life. . . .
> Boys are given more, they get more food because their work is
> harder and they have more responsibility. At the same time, he is
> head of the household, not in the bad sense of the word, but
> because he is responsible for so many things. This doesn't mean
> girls aren't valued. Their work is hard too and there are other
> things that are due to them as mothers. . . . The girl and the boy
> are both integrated into the community in equally important
> ways, the two are inter-related and compatible. Nevertheless, the
> community is always happier when a male child is born and the
> men feel much prouder. (14)

While Menchú plays down conflict within her community, she often exaggerates the differences between Mayans and ladinos. She is not alone in doing this. John Hawkins has argued in his book *Inverse Images: The Meaning of Culture, Ethnicity and Family in Postcolonial Guatemala* that contemporary Mayan and ladino Guatemalans tend to see themselves as members of two separate cultures, each defined programmatically as the inversion of the other—with the dominant ladinos typically taking possession of the more desired trait in every opposition. In Hawkins's view, this dynamic has produced not two cultures at all but a single, interdependent cultural system, in which ladinos "are" literate, Spanish-speaking, Westernized city dwellers, and Mayans "are" illiterate, non-Spanish-speaking, non-Westernized country dwellers. Each group clings to these self-images, which continue to seem like the underlying truth even though many ladinos are in fact rural farmers and some Indians are educated city dwellers.

Menchú's account shows many instances of this kind of self-reinforcing cultural differentiation. Though she lived for several years in Guatemala City, she never felt at home there—and never felt she *should* feel at home there: "The city for me was a monster, something alien, different. 'Those houses, those people,' I thought, 'this is the world of the ladinos.' For me it was the world of the ladinos. We were different" (32). Menchú associates ladino culture with all forms of mixture and adulteration, from sexual relations to food:

> In the past, our ancestors grew wheat. Then the Spaniards came and mixed it with egg. It was a mixture, no longer what our ancestors ate. It was the whites' food, and the whites are like their bread, they are not wholesome. The blood of our most noble ancestors was mixed with the blood of the whites. They are a mixture, just like their food. . . . We must not mix our customs with those of the whites. So we don't eat bread. It is not our tortilla. (71)

Menchú's insistence on her late acquisition of Spanish and of literacy may reflect pressure from her family to conform to this dualistic system of values. Indeed, she describes her father as opposing her learning Spanish during his lifetime:

> I told my father this, that I wanted to learn to read. Perhaps things were different if you could read. My father said, "Who will teach you? You have to find out by yourself, because I can't help you. I know of no schools and I have no money for them anyway." I told him that if he talked to the priests, perhaps they'd give me a scholarship. But my father said he didn't agree with my idea because I was trying to leave the community, to go far away, and find what was best for me. He said, "You'll forget about our common heritage. If you leave, it will be for good. If you leave our community, I will not support you." (89)

All in all, it is not surprising that the young Rigoberta Menchú would play out these deep-seated, though partly fictive, paradigms in her talks with Elizabeth Burgos. What is remarkable is that, far from making any effort to tease out the contradictions in Menchú's cultural self-understanding, Burgos herself went well beyond Menchú in elaborating the image of timeless native wisdom unaffected by Western culture. Thus, in dividing the taped material into chapters, Burgos chose epigraphs for each chapter, taken chiefly from three sources: statements by Menchú herself; passages from Asturias's novels depicting native culture; and quotations from the *Popol Vuh*, the classic Mayan story of creation and early history. This is, however, a text that Menchú herself never mentions and seems never to have seen. The sacred text that she does refer to, frequently, is the Bible—naturally enough, as she was raised as a devout Christian, and like her father she became a catechist, instructing children in Catholic doctrine and leading Bible study groups in her village. In her introduction, however, Burgos notes Menchú's use of the Bible only to minimize it: "Rigoberta borrows such things as the Bible, trade union organization and the Spanish language in order to use them against the original owner. For her the Bible is a sort of ersatz which she uses precisely because there is nothing like it in her culture" (xvii).

Burgos is denying the plain fact that the Bible *is* an important part of Menchú's culture, because to recognize this would be to allow for a serious interplay with ladino culture. Instead, the quotations that Burgos imports from the *Popol Vuh* emphasize a timeless, unchanging native truth, as in the epigraph to the first chapter: "We have always lived here: we have a right to go on living where we are happy and where we want to die. Only here can we feel whole; nowhere else would we ever feel complete and our pain would be eternal" (1). Similarly, the chapter on marriage ceremonies begins with this epigraph: "Children, wherever you may be, do not abandon the crafts taught to you by Ixpiyacoc, because they are crafts passed down to you from your forefathers. If you forget them, you will be betraying your lineage" (59). Yet a close reading of Menchú's actual account reveals a very different picture: the very customs she now identifies as embodying the timeless wisdom of her ancestors have been profoundly influenced by centuries of Christian belief and practice, in a further evolution of the hybridization already well under way in the seventeenth century in Ruiz de Alarcón's rural village in Guerrero. Not only have the Maya long acceded to the missionaries' key demands (abandoning human sacrifice, accepting baptism for their children, attending Mass and celebrating the major saints' days); they have actually adopted the Bible's history as a model for their own. As Menchú says: "A lot of it is familiar. For example, we believe we have ancestors, and that these ancestors are important because they're good people who obeyed the laws of our people. The Bible talks about forefathers too. So it is not something unfamiliar to us. We accept these Biblical forefathers as if they were our own ancestors, while still keeping within our own culture and our own customs" (80).

This assimilation to biblical models is no new phenomenon, no ad hoc adoption of an "ersatz" that can be erased in favor of the "real" story of an ongoing separate, chthonic identity. One of the earliest surviving Quiché Mayan texts, the *Title of the Lords of Totonicapán,* was written in 1554 some seventy-five miles southwest of Menchú's village. The authors of this document recount their people's history as a way of legitimating their claims to their land. They begin by describing how the Quiché were led from over the sea by the founder of their culture, Balam-Qitzé: "When they arrived at the edge of the sea, Balam-Qitzé touched it with his staff and at once a path opened, which then closed up again, for thus the great God wished it to be done, because they were sons of Abraham and Jacob" (Recinos, *The Annals of the Cakchiquels,* 170). Clearly aware of the conquistadors' speculation that the remarkably sophisticated native population might be the lost tribes of Israel, the Lords of Totonicapán embrace this history. They assimilate Moses directly to Balam-Qitzé, who goes the Bible one better by leading his entire people—thirteen tribes in all—safely across the sea, and then ratifies a covenant with them by the side of a sacred mountain, giving them permanent possession of their promised land (171–72).

The Mayan uses of biblical models should not be thought of as some passive, unthinking "syncretism," a term increasingly disfavored by people who study modern Mayan culture. Instead, both the Lords of Totonicipán and Rigoberta Menchú engage in an active process of selecting and reforming elements that will be useful to them, in a dynamic that Barbara Tedlock has described as involving a "complementary dualism" in which opposed elements are given interlinked functions and made to coexist (*Time and the Highland Maya,* 44). Interestingly, while Menchú opposes cultural mixing in other aspects of life, she speaks positively of mixtures in the case of religion: "Catholic Action is like another element which can merge with the elements which already exist within Indian culture. . . . This is where you see the mixture of Catholicism and our own culture. We feel very Catholic because we believe in the Catholic religion but, at the same time, we feel very Indian, proud of our ancestors" (80–81).

The mixture created by such a complementary dualism can evolve over time, and can also vary at a given time within a single community.

Many highland Maya think of themselves as Christians and yet also continue practices long associated with the worship of pre-Columbian deities, particularly those involving planting and harvest. Yet villages have divided sharply when pressed to make a firm choice. Tedlock (40–41) describes a priest in the town of Momostenango, who in the midfifties demanded that his parishioners abjure all remnants of polytheistic worship, and one-fifth of the village actually went along with his demands. Then the priest went farther and locked his church to a group who wished to use it, as they had long done, to initiate new diviners, at which point a delegation visited him and informed him that he would be killed if he stayed in the village. He fled.

In Menchú's region, there were presumably some residents who had little use for Christianity, others who were blending "pagan" and Catholic traditions in a variety of ways, and still others (not mentioned by Menchú) who were converting to the newly spreading teachings of evangelical Protestantism, whose missionaries were much more hostile to traditional culture than many Catholic priests were at this period. Menchú herself expresses great loyalty to old Mayan religious beliefs, and yet her own beliefs seem closely assimilated to Catholicism. Thus she describes the divinities of earth and sky in much the same way that she describes the Catholic saints. Just as the saints are "channels through which we communicate with the one God" (72), so too a tree "has its image, its representation, its *nahual*, to channel our feelings to the one God" (80). Menchú regards the old Mayan deities in a highly metaphorical way: praying to the sun, she says, "when we evoke the colour of the sun, it's like evoking all the elements which go to make up our life. The sun, as the channel to the one God, receives the plea from his children" (58). Similarly, when planting corn, "We say the names of the earth, the God of the earth, and the God of water. Then we say the name of the heart of the sky—the sun. . . . So you see it's a different world. This is how we make our pleas and our promises. It doesn't refer so much to the real world, but it includes part of our reality" ("No se refiere tanto a la realidad. Pero sin embargo lleva parte de la realidad que uno vive" [57 in English, 81 in Spanish]). She adds—in sentences interestingly omitted from the English translation—"This praying is the same as the Catholics do when they talk to a saint or an image. . . . But it varies. It depends on the people" (82).

In discussing her people's beliefs, Menchú even denies, or half denies, that they are polytheistic at all:

> From very small children we receive an education which is very different from white children, ladinos. We Indians have more

contact with nature. That's why they call us polytheistic. But we're not polytheistic . . . or if we are, it's good, because it's our culture, our customs. We worship—or rather not worship but respect—a lot of things to do with the natural world, the most important things for us. For instance, to us, water is sacred. Our parents tell us when we're very small not to waste water, even when we have it. Water is pure, clean, and gives life to man. Without water we cannot survive, nor could our ancestors have survived. The idea that water is sacred is in us children, and we never stop thinking of it as something pure. (56)

Loyal though Menchú is to her ancestors' beliefs, they seem to have little remaining theological content, and to have evolved into a general ecological awareness, fully compatible with Christian belief and practice.

The point is not that contemporary Mayan culture as a whole has effectively abandoned pre-Columbian religious beliefs and practices. The point is rather that Mayan culture "as a whole" is made up of many different strands, even within a single group like the Quiché and even in a single village, where different people may hold very different beliefs. As he worked on his luminous translation of the *Popol Vuh* in the midseventies, Dennis Tedlock sought assistance from a diviner named Andrés Xiloj, who helped him unravel the meaning of many obscure terms in the text, as they referred to rituals that Xiloj still carried out.[6] Rigoberta Menchú, an active Catholic and the child of highly committed Catholics, is hardly the representative Burgos would like her to be of a pure and separate Mayan identity.

Such a romanticization can often serve to set the foreign culture off as something safely distant, wholly other, but Burgos seems to have had an opposite motive. She was led to oversimplify Menchú's culture and views because she became entranced with a direct recovery of herself. Having told us that Menchú's words take us back to a time of innocence we thought we had lost, Burgos describes how they became close, during their week together, by preparing refried beans and tortillas, a process that "brought back my childhood in Venezuela" (xv). Burgos closes her introduction by saying that "It remains for me to thank Rigoberta for having granted me the privilege of meeting her and sharing her life with me. She allowed me to discover another self. Thanks to her, my American self is no longer something 'un-

---

[6] See Dennis Tedlock's preface to *Popol Vuh*, 13–21. Xiloj himself had never seen a copy of the *Popol Vuh* before Tedlock showed it to him, and he also was a practicing Christian as well as a traditional *ajk'ij* (diviner or "daykeeper"). Even so, he mixed these elements in a very different proportion than Menchú does.

canny'" (xxi). Burgos has recovered her childhood self, and she has done this by suspending her adult role as analzyer of culture. Indeed, she even experiences the bliss of ignorance: "Initially, I thought that knowing nothing about Rigoberta's culture would be a handicap, but it soon proved to be a positive advantage. I was able to adopt the position of someone who is learning. Rigoberta soon realized this: that is why her descriptions of ceremonies and rituals are so detailed" (xix).

This self-suspension actually allows Burgos a double advantage: she can disappear, and by doing so have an even freer hand in shaping the material. As she reviewed her taped interviews, Burgos says:

> I soon reached the decision to give the manuscript the form of a monologue: that was how it came back to me as I re-read it. I therefore decided to delete all my questions. By doing so I became what I really was: Rigoberta's listener. I allowed her to speak and then became her instrument, her double by allowing her to make the transition from the spoken to the written word. I have to admit that this decision made my task more difficult, as I had to insert linking passages if the manuscript was to read like a monologue, like one continuous narrative. I then divided it into chapters organized around the themes I had already identified. I followed my original chronological outline, even though our conversations had not done so, so as to make the text more accessible to the reader. (xx)

As Anuradha Dingwaney and Carol Maier have put it, Burgos displaces her handicaps as an interlocutor "by appropriating Menchú's identity, her world, her cause, even her voice itself" ("Translation," 305). It is interesting that Burgos becomes Menchú's "double" in the process, as the double or *nahual* is a key concept in Mayan belief. As Rigoberta Menchú says in the third chapter, "The Nahual," "Every child is born with a *nahual*. The *nahual* is like a shadow, his protective spirit who will go through life with him. . . . The *nahual* is our double, something very important to us. We conjure up an image of what our *nahual* is like. It is usually an animal" (18). The identity of a child's *nahual* is hidden even from the child until adolescence, and is always to be concealed from outsiders thereafter. Menchú several times speaks of secrets of her culture that she won't reveal, and the identity of her *nahual* is prominent among them, a metonymy for her identity itself:

> We Indians have always hidden our identity and kept our secrets to ourselves. This is why we are discriminated against. We often

find it hard to talk about ourselves because we know we must
hide so much in order to preserve our Indian culture and prevent
it being taken away from us. So I can only tell you very general
things about the *nahual.* I can't tell you what my *nahual* is
because that is one of our secrets. (20)

As it turns out, Burgos has no need for Menchú to confess the name of her
double, her representative, the protective spirit that enables her to communicate with the world: it has become Burgos herself.

As Gayatri Spivak has said with reference to testimonial writing in
India, "the gendered subaltern woman . . . can yield 'real' information as
agent with the greatest difficulty, not least because methods of describing
her sympathetically are already in place. There is a gulf fixed between the anthropologist's object of investigation and the activists' interlocutor."[7] In his
critique of Burgos and Menchú's book, David Stoll is relatively undisturbed
by Menchú's assimilation of dramatic incidents to her family story; he
agrees that these incidents were all too typical of what actually was happen-
ing during those years. His real criticism of the book is that its romanticized
portrayal of Mayan culture made it appear that the entire population accepted leftist political views that were in fact only held by a minority, and
that the book's readers readily accepted these views as naturally Mayan just
because they so closely mirrored the Western reader's displaced hopes and
wishes: "Certainly Rigoberta was a representative of her people, but hiding
behind that was a more partisan role, as a representative of the revolutionary movement, and hiding behind that was an even more unsettling possibility: that she represented the audiences whose assumptions about in-
dígenas she mirrored so effectively" (246). Stoll overstates his case, here as
elsewhere: Menchú and Burgos's book reached multiple audiences, surely
with a range of assumptions. Burgos herself, however, is just such an audience as Stoll describes, and indeed the process of mirroring, far from hidden, is just what she describes in her introduction to the book.

Like Eckermann reworking his conversations with Goethe, Burgos
finds in herself a doubling or *Spiegelung* of her compelling interlocutor's life
and mind. With one key difference: whereas Eckermann was the provincial
participant in the dialogue, often denied authorial credit for his own book,
Burgos is the one with the name and the entrée into the Parisian publishing

---

[7] "How to Read a 'Culturally Different' Book," 143. For detailed case studies
concerning this and related problems, see Amal Amireh and Lisa Suhair Majaj, *Going Global: The
Transnational Reception of Third World Women Writers.*

world, and it is she who holds the copyright to the joint work. For several years she transferred the book's royalties to Menchú, but when Menchú began to demand authorial rights and the right to establish her own contracts, the two fell out and ceased to be in contact. When questions began to be raised about the book's accuracy, Rigoberta Menchú told a Guatemalan newspaper that the responsibility lay with Burgos:

> That is not my book. It is a book by Elisabeth Burgos. It is not my work; it is a work that does not belong to me morally, politically, or economically. I have respected it greatly because it played an immense role for Guatemala. . . . But I never had the right to say if the text pleased me or not, if it was faithful to the facts of my life. . . . Anyone who has doubts about the work should go to [Burgos] because, even legally, I do not have author's rights, royalties or any of that. (Quoted in Stoll, 178)

The foreshortening of cultural reality that occurred as Menchú's story became Burgos's book only increased as the book circulated into English. The translation tones down the vivid oral style of the Spanish, producing a more orderly, even prosaic, prose. To give one example: Menchú's opening account of her story is a breathless run-on sentence: "Quisiera dar este testimonio vivo que no he aprendido en un libro y que tampoco he aprendido sola ya que todo esto lo he aprendido con mi pueblo y es algo que yo quisiera enfocar" (*Me Llamo Rigoberta Menchú*, 21). This single, unpunctuated sentence becomes a much calmer, more decorous three sentences in Ann Wright's translation: "This is my testimony. I didn't learn it from a book and I didn't learn it alone. I'd like to stress that it's not only my life, it's also the testimony of my people" (*I, Rigoberta*, 1). Even as it further ethnicizes Menchú with a faux-naif cover portrait against a childishly painted multicolored background, the English translation mutes Menchú's style and weakens its actual historicity. This process can be epitomized by the difference in titles. In Spanish, the book's full title is *Me Llamo Rigoberta Menchú y Así Me Nació la Conciencia:* "My name is Rigoberta Menchú and this is how my awareness was born" (*conciencia* here meaning political consciousness or awareness). Both the folktale phrasing and history itself disappear from the English title: *I, Rigoberta Menchú: An Indian Woman in Guatemala.*

Me Llamo Rigoberta Menchú was quickly written and published, in urgent circumstances, by people who couldn't know what a major and lasting impact it would have. Menchú herself came to regret deeply that she had not retained control over her story; as she says in *La Nieta*, "My dream is to recover the rights to *I, Rigoberta Menchú* and to expand it. I want to give it back to Guatemala and the coming generations as part of their history. . . . you can't change history. You can only learn from experience, and not make the same mistakes again" (114–15). When she decided to write a second book, she determined not to repeat her earlier mistake. By now she was the one with the name and the entrée to the international publishing world, and she took care to ensure that the copyright would be held by the Fundación Rigoberta Menchú, which she had established with her Nobel Prize winnings as a nonprofit foundation to promote social justice in Guatemala. Still not thinking of herself as a professional writer, she again enlisted collaborators: she developed an outline with a Mexican friend, Eugenia Huerta, and then she worked with a Guatemalan writer, Mario Matute, to tape record her ongoing story after the time she first came to Europe: her years in obscurity lobbying the UN in Geneva; the campaign to award her the Nobel Prize; her triumphant return to Guatemala after the war's end; and her continuing struggles thereafter.

Having recorded this new set of tapes, she asked an Italian writer, Gianni Minà, to edit and arrange the transcribed material; and finally she enlisted "the talents, the devotion, and the compassion of a great compatriot, Dante Liano" to accommodate her prose to Spanish usage while retaining its strongly oral flavor. Her goal in assembling this multinational team was resolutely international, even global: "We made great efforts with Dante Liano to reconcile the manner of life, thought, understanding and expression, for much of my life in Q'iché, so that it could be perceived, experienced, understood and respected in Spanish, and, we hope, in all the languages of the planet" (*La Nieta*, 26). Reflecting the book's collective creation, its cover and title page describe it as "Por Rigoberta Menchú, con la colaboración de Dante Liano y Gianni Minà."

Menchú was concerned to shape the book's reading as well as its writing. *Rigoberta: La Nieta de los Mayas* begins with no fewer than five prefatory texts: a preface by the writer Eduardo Galeano; a "presentation" by Esteban Beltrán, head of the Spanish branch of Amnesty International; a prologue by Gianni Minà; an introduction by a Quiché poet, Humberto Ak'abal; and, finally, extended acknowledgments by Menchú herself. The book concludes with an appendix summarizing the peace process leading up to the pivotal peace accords in Guatemala at the end of 1996. When the book came out in April of 1998, Menchú introduced it not only in Guatemala but also in Mexico and in Spain, with major press events at which prominent figures commented on it. At last, she had the power to shape her work as she pleased and to introduce it to the world herself.

It is astonishing, then, to see how fully all these efforts were undercut as soon as the book left her immediate control and went into translation. Here I will look in some detail at the English translation, which appeared in the summer of 1998, just three months after the original. Like her earlier book, it was published in England and in America by Verso, once again translated by Ann Wright. In a "Translator's Note" Wright thanks the Rigoberta Menchú Foundation "for their help and advice," but the English version systematically undoes Menchú's framing of her book and makes major changes in organization, content, and style throughout. Menchú is at least still listed as the author, but, remarkably, neither Dante Liano nor Gianni Minà is mentioned on the title page or anywhere else. Instead, the book is presented as Menchú's product alone, now "Translated and Edited by Ann Wright."

Taking over Burgos's role, Wright actually goes far beyond Burgos in asserting editorial control over the material—content as well as style. All five of the Spanish version's introductory texts have been dropped, as has its appendix giving the peace accords, and the book as a whole has been cut by 20 percent. Perhaps some of the prefatory materials would have meant little to the book's English-language readers, but the appendix on the peace process provides information that would be even more useful to a foreign audience than to Guatemalan readers, and it is hard to see why Menchú's acknowledgments deserved to be cut. Not only do they detail the interesting process of the book's composition; they also end with a touching dedication, at once deeply personal and forcefully public:

> With all my heart I dedicate this book to my adorable son, Mash Nawalja', who has changed my life with his smiles and his caresses, despite the fact that I couldn't always be with him during the first days and months of his life. And to my beloved, loving and patient husband, Ángel Francisco Canil, who has always been a light in my life. And to the love of my entire family and to Guatemala, the land that saw my birth. *Our ancestors teach us that no one makes history alone. Freedom for the Indigenous Peoples wherever they want to be.* (26–27)

This dedication is particularly noteworthy, as near the end of *I, Rigoberta Menchú* she had renounced marriage and motherhood, at least for the duration of the struggle, as luxuries she couldn't afford.

Not only has the English version lost the original framing; the body of the book has been rearranged and reoriented in large and small ways. Again, titles are emblematic: in English, the book's Spanish title would be "Rigoberta: Granddaughter of the Maya." Verso's version, however, is titled *Crossing Borders*. Its Rigoberta Menchú is first and foremost the world-traveling celebrity; the awarding of the Nobel Prize, which concludes the book in Spanish, now begins the English version, while the original first chapter, set in Guatemala City, now comes second. This reorganization anticipates the new ways the book would likely be received and read by new audiences in England and North America, and the translation quite directly accommodates this outsider's perspective: where in Spanish Menchú speaks of her decision to return from exile as "coming back here" (*llegar aquí*, 73), the English version has her deciding "to live in Guatemala" (55).

In this respect *Crossing Borders* is interesting for so openly, even preemptively, changing the original so as best to catch the attention of an international market. Having led off with the Nobel Prize account, the translation closes this new first chapter with a passage taken from later in the original book, in which Menchú describes how she is regularly treated with extreme disrespect when she is crossing international borders. Her pointed account makes a fitting contrast to the glamor of the Nobel Prize, and nicely illustrates the ambiguity of the border-crossing theme that the English version highlights:

> I always travel like any other citizen of the world, squat and dark-skinned as I have always been. I will always have the face of a poor woman, my Mayan face, my indigenous face. . . . Customs and immigration officials act impatiently. They take my things out one by one, even my underclothes. . . . After they have finished going through my things, taking out my *huipils*, and making me pack my case again, I always try to teach them a little awareness. You need humanity wherever you are. "The world should be a fairer place," I tell them, "it should be more humane, less aggressive and less racist." I start to give them a talk.
>
> When my case is finally packed again, I take out my identity papers and say, "Look, I'm a humble winner of the Nobel Peace Prize." . . . They are of course very surprised. I know they will never forget me. (21)

She adds—optimistically, or in a concluding irony?—that these customs officials "will probably be among the most avid readers of this book. So everything serves some purpose."

Wright has made several creative choices of this sort in her reconstruction, leading the reader from the international scene into the intractable ambiguities of ethnic and national identity. She closes the English version with a poetic passage on the theme of identity as both a personal and a social reality: "Identity passes through the community, it passes along pavements, it passes down veins, it passes through the being, and it exists in thoughts. . . . It is another shadow, it is like the *nagual,* the copy, the shadow that accompanies you. It is the other, the one beside you. . . . Or it can be a mere shadow carried on the wind or scurrying along paths. . . . You cannot think of your identity as something alone in the world" (227). Though this wasn't Menchú's ending for the book, it makes an effective conclusion for an Anglo-American audience interested in the politics of identity.

Such structural changes represent a heartfelt attempt to bring Menchú's message to the largest possible audience. Unfortunately, having decided to take such an active role in adapting the book to its new readers' presumed interests, Wright couldn't resist systematically trimming and toning down Menchú's vividly oral, colloquial style, opting for a much more orderly, decorous, low-key prose, even—or especially—in moments of emotional intensity. The book begins, in Spanish, with a harrowing chapter called "El enemigo en casa" (the second chapter in the English version, "Trouble in the Family: The Enemy Within"), describing a grim sequence of events in 1995 when a young grandnephew of Menchú's is kidnapped outside her house in Guatemala City, in the midst of an election campaign in which she is active in promoting registration of Indian voters. No ransom demands come; the boy is returned after a long delay, and a chilling call from one of the kidnappers informs Menchú that they had meant to catch her own small son, Mash Nawalja', but had picked up her grandnephew by mistake.

This, however, is not the worst of the story. Persistently trying to sort out what happened when her nephew disappeared, Menchú eventually discovers that he had been taken away and hidden by *his own father,* the ne'er-do-well husband of Menchú's niece. (At the time of the writing of her book, her nephew is in jail for this crime; Menchú believes, but can't be sure, that he had become mixed up with criminals who pressured him into staging this false kidnapping in order to distract and intimidate her.) As she confronts her shiftless nephew, who claims to know nothing but who has been oddly passive in attempting to locate his missing son, her tone becomes urgent. If he won't talk to her, she says, he should at least talk to his parents: "*Decilo* enfrente de ellos, no enfrente mío ¡Pero *decí* qué *ocultás*! Estoy segura de que algo importante *guardás* en tu corazón" (45, her emphasis). In the English version, this impassioned speech becomes, simply, "Tell them in

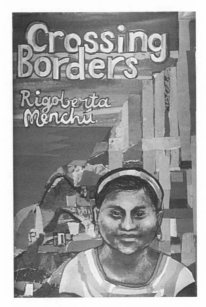

Figure 11. Two versions of Rigoberta Menchú

private. You don't have to tell me. I'm sure you're keeping something important in your heart" (36).

The translation consistently dampens down Menchú's prose, as when she describes the death of her brother Víctor, her niece's father. "Fue asesinado su padre, fue fusilado, fue enterrado en una fosa común en Uspantán" (31). Wright renders this incantatory sentence as: "Her father had been shot and dumped in a communal grave in Uspantán" (26). Yet even as the translation domesticates Menchú for an English audience, it carries on the old pattern of ethnicizing her as a figure of childlike innocence. Already a problematic project when Menchú was an unknown twenty-three-year-old, it is even stranger when applied fifteen years later to the Nobel Prize winner. Yet what is allowed to cross borders remains a highly stylized image. Here too, Menchú went to considerable lengths in the original: in place of the naive-style portrait on the cover of the earlier book, *La Nieta* has a glowing color portrait of the mature Rigoberta Menchú as she appears today. Instead of using this photograph, the cover of the English version once again gives a folkloristic portrait (figure 11), with Menchú looking, if anything, younger than she had on the cover of her earlier book. Though this image vaguely suggests Mayan folk art, it is actually the work of a British illustrator, Sophie Herxheimer, the same person who had done the previous cover.

Inside the book, further emphasizing the reality of the events discussed—and perhaps implicitly responding to the reports already circulating that she had exaggerated and even invented parts of her earlier book—Menchú included sixteen pages of documentary photographs, showing aspects of the struggle during the civil war and Menchú's activities since then. The English version has a studio portrait of Menchú as a frontispiece, but there are no other photographs at all. Instead, at the beginnings and endings of each chapter we are given more folkloristic vignettes, crude little line drawings showing ears of corn, peppers, a woman with a baby, pre-Columbian artifacts, and occasionally an airplane or automobile. Documentary evidence has been replaced by airport art.

Wright has succeeded in tightening up a sometimes rambling book, but in the process she has reduced its real power. Reviewing it for the *New York Times,* Central American correspondent Tim Goldin ended by commenting on a line from the book: "'Many things have changed for me since I won the Nobel Peace Prize,' Menchú writes in her introduction to *Crossing Borders.* What seems not to have changed is the difficulty readers will have in seeing the woman behind the symbol" (29). This difficulty is precisely what the English version has produced, both by magnifying the symbol and by muffling the voice that so vividly expresses Menchú's personality in Spanish.

Reading the translation, the *Washington Post*'s reviewer sees little more in Menchú's new book than a fantasy of return to "an ancient culture based on seasonal rhythms, simple values and a mystical vision of harmony." Trying to be sympathetic, the reviewer concludes that "it is clear that her ultimate quest is to re-create a highland paradise where no one is greedy or corrupt, time is meaningless and patience is inexhaustible. Even if such a pristine world never really existed, who can blame her?" (Constable, 9). This is exactly the cosy mythification that the English translation promotes, but it is not at all Menchú's mature perspective. Even the translation, if read carefully, reveals a far more interesting cultural stance than Menchú had expressed in her early twenties. Far from idealizing a timeless paradise, she now emphasizes the dynamism of cultural development over time, and instead of exalting indigenous purity over against ladino mixtures, as she often did in her first book, she now rejects any such separatism:

> Looking back, I think perhaps it was a mistake to turn the
> Quincentenary celebrations into a kind of battlefield. Many
> people want to return to the old Inca and Mayan ways of five
> hundred years ago. It is impossible to do that! How can we go

back and be the same? Indigenous tradition itself says that time is long and wide, and it has its own signs. Each sign has a different meaning. . . . Culture isn't pure, it is dynamic, it is a kind of dialectic, it is something that progresses and evolves. . . . I think the whole idea of purity is damaging, it leads to sectarianism, intolerance, segregation and racism. (182)

She even criticizes her earlier depictions of non-indigenous Guatemala: "The bad country we have described does indeed exist; a bloodthirsty, repressive, racist, dirty, backward country. Yet it is also true that we have not always been magnanimous enough to balance the good and the bad. We always say that it is bad or it is good. We have not been sufficiently generous to merge the two" (45). Breaking with her earlier indigenist hostility to city life, she has settled permanently in Guatemala City, and she has a new understanding of her own ambiguous position as an educated woman, no longer a part of an organic rural community. This is why she calls herself a granddaughter, rather than a daughter, of the Maya: "I am no philosopher. I am simply a granddaughter of the Mayans—not even a daughter, because a daughter is closer. I'm a grandchild of the Mayans and I believe that some day things will be different. Women now have influence in many spheres. Ordinary women have challenged dictatorships, and perhaps they can go on to challenge injustice all over the world" (87).[8]

Even as she newly identifies with the broader, transnational collectivity "the Maya"—a term she hardly ever used in *I, Rigoberta Menchú*—she gives a newly complex account of her personal background. Underlying her father's long dispute with his in-laws were deep social tensions based on class and ethnicity within the many subgroupings of Mayan society. Her mother's mother came from a well-to-do Mam family and caused a scandal when she married Menchú's grandfather Tum, who was a Chiquimila. "The Chiquimilas are like Gypsies in other parts of the world," Menchú says: landless, dark-skinned, and despised by other Indians. "Other ethnic groups discriminate against them. . . . We sort of wanted to hide our identity when we were little, and even when we were teenagers, because everybody used to laugh at us. When they wanted to insult us, they called us 'Chiquimulas'"

---

[8] Menchú's calling herself a granddaughter of the Maya is particularly apt since, as we first learn in *La Nieta*, she was named after her mother's mother. Her grandmother was not named Rigoberta, however, but M'in. Yet when her father went to register her birth at the town office, the registrar would not accept a Mayan name: "they gave him a list of saints' names, and he chose Rigoberta. I don't know why he chose it. None of my family could ever pronounce it, especially Mama. She always said 'Beta' or 'Tita.' At home, they always called me M'in" (74).

(76–77; *mula,* literally "she-mule," is also slang for "trash" and for "drunkard"). In so insistently disputing his Tum in-laws' land claims, Vincente Menchú was challenging the right of his Chiquimila relatives to own land at all.

A more nuanced book than *I, Rigoberta* was, both more capacious and more accurate in its cultural presentation, *La Nieta* is also charged with a new kind of poetry, especially when Menchú retells dreams she has had and continues to have. Aware that she can never, in fact, return to her childhood community, she revisits Chimel as much to visit the dead as to see the living. As she makes her return trip, she says, "People believe that all those who were murdered there actually inhabit Laj Chimel and Chimel, and are the real owners of the village and the lands. They guard it" (203). Chimel has become more a dreamscape than a landscape for her. Dreams, in fact, frame her book in the Spanish version as much as do the several prefaces and the historical appendix. She begins her acknowledgments by saying that "For years I dreamed [*soñé*] of writing another book" (25), and as the book unfolds this proves to be no casual metaphor. She has shocking premonitory dreams shortly before the murders of her mother and of her father (112–13; 72–73 in English); while in exile she constantly dreams of returning home; and the very last paragraph of her book is a kind of elegy to her village, preserved only in dreams. Not because Chimel no longer exists—she has just been back to see it—but because *her* Chimel no longer exists, and she herself is no longer the person who once lived there. So she concludes her book by evoking the reality of dreams:

> The only thing I've been able to salvage from Chimel was dreams. There are wonderful nights in my life when I dream of Chimel. I feel as if I'd made a long journey and I'd managed to come back. I look at my mother, I speak with her, I look at our house—if I was a painter I could paint this house. I see the rabbits that peek out through the bars. I see the peach grove. I see the short path that goes to the river. I see the long path that goes out of the village to Uspantán. I see the slope alongside Chimel, I see the whole village, and I see a little house at the bottom of the town. I remember the scent of the earth when the rain falls: a lovely scent that the soil gives off. I feel nostalgia. It's dreams that keep me company. Dreams make me travel in the mountains. They hold my imagination at work. They make me go there. Dreams make me go back, they make the past seem present. Dreams take me to a strange new day, they show me a mysterious future. I don't

know how many dreams I've left strewn along all those roads, but I always come back to them, like a pilgrim who returns to his birthplace, feet covered with dust. I keep on living, dwelling in dreams, for the only place we really exist is in dreams. (338)

Rigoberta Menchú is one of the most international of contemporary authors, her work produced for a global audience and often written on her laptop while traveling the globe. Yet she also remains deeply tied to a small country where she still lives but where she can never return home, except perhaps in her poems and in dreams. In the interplay between these dreams and the complex realities of waking life, *Rigoberta: La Nieta de los Mayas* becomes a compelling work of world literature. Though the English translation illustrates all too well the vicissitudes that can attend a work's life in the world, something of Menchú's very worldly literariness survives in *Crossing Borders* as well, if we read it attentively. We can't actually read the original concluding paragraph just quoted—it has fallen victim to Wright's editorial clean-up—but Wright has at least preserved another version of this dream, which appears in the middle of the book. In this retelling of the dream, Menchú returns to her childhood home and there meets her lost mother. Now they converse, in a few charged words that Menchú gives in Quiché and then herself translates for us, carrying us across several borders at once:

> The strange thing is that every time I dream, I dream of the same place. I see a log, fairly large. I see an area that was like the kitchen. I see ears of corn, I see corn hanging from the porch. I even see the noses of the rabbits looking out between their bars. . . . This house is there for me, just as I knew it and just as I dream of it. Every time I dream, I come back to the scent of the damp earth, when the Sun comes out after a good rain. I come back to the scent of tortillas just taken off the *comal.* I always find my mother there, seated on the log. I come up and she says: *Xat peetik wal"* ("So you've come, child!"). "*Xin peetik nan*" ("Yes, Mamá, I've come"). (135/91)

9

The Poisoned Book

According to the preliminary notes to Milorad Pavić's *Dictionary of the Khazars,* his book is a reconstruction of a long-lost encyclopedia concerning a people who lived around the Black Sea until the tenth century, when they disappeared from history. Published in Prussia in 1691 by a Polish printer named Johannes Daubmannus, the *Lexicon Cosri* was destroyed a year later by the Inquisition. Only two privately held copies survived. One, fastened with a golden lock, was printed in poisoned ink; it had a companion copy, not poisoned, fitted with a silver lock:

> Insubordinates and infidels who ventured to read the proscribed dictionary risked the threat of death. Whoever opened the book soon grew numb, stuck on his own heart as on a pin. Indeed, the reader would die on the ninth page at the words *Verbum caro factum est* ("The Word became flesh"). If read simultaneously with the poisoned copy, the auxiliary copy enabled one to know exactly when death would strike. Found in the auxiliary copy was the note: "When you wake and suffer no pain, know that you are no longer among the living." (6)

Pavić's book is one of a growing number of recent novels that take the writing and circulation of world literature as an explicit theme. A novel in dictionary form, or rather in the form of three different encyclopedias concerning the Khazars (who, unlike the poisoned encyclopedia, did genuinely exist), *Dictionary of the Khazars* has been widely celebrated as a tour de force of metafictional play. Its cross-referenced entries invite the reader to abandon the narrative progressions of ordinary novels and consider whole new ways of reading, signaled from the start by the fact that the book is published in two different editions, "Male" and "Female." As the front cover of the Female Edition dramatically announces (with corresponding language on the cover of the Male Edition):

> This is the FEMALE EDITION of the Dictionary.
> The MALE edition is almost identical. But NOT quite.
> Be warned that ONE PARAGRAPH is crucially different.
> The choice is yours.

Clearly, readers of this novel have new opportunities, and new responsibilities.

Pavić had been a respected poet and scholar of Serbian literature but was almost unknown outside Yugoslavia until he published his novel, which rapidly became a runaway success around the globe. As with *I, Rigoberta Menchú* not long before, the French rights to the novel were acquired while the book was still in press, and it was published in Paris as well as in Belgrade in 1984, by which time another dozen translations were already under way. By the late nineties, it had been translated into no fewer than twenty-six languages, including Japanese and Catalan, and had sold several million copies in all. Yet the book's international success involved the neglect or outright misreading of its political content. As his country began to disintegrate after Tito's death, Pavić spoke out bitterly on behalf of the cause of Serbian nationalism, his international reputation giving weight to his words at home. The metaphysical magician turned out to have an angry joker up his sleeve. *Dictionary of the Khazars* contains a political polemic, hidden in plain sight, that eluded international audiences, who had welcomed the book as "an Arabian Nights romance," "a wickedly teasing intellectual game," and an opportunity "to lose themselves in a novel of love and death," as the flyleaf of the American edition describes it. How should we read this novel now, and what can its double life tell us about the worldliness of world literature?

The nationalist undercurrent of Pavić's book could remain invisible abroad not only through outsiders' relative ignorance of local concerns but also because in many ways the book appears to be a satire of any one-sided viewpoint. The three encyclopedias represent three limited, warring points of view, Christian, Muslim, and Jewish: each encyclopedia tells the story of the Khazars' conversion to its compiler's religion. Pavić based this multiple tale on a dialogue by the medieval poet and philosopher Judah ha-Levi, the *Kitab al-Khazari* or *Book of the Khazars,* written in Arabic in Spain in around 1140. Judah ha-Levi in turn was meditating on historical sources that told of the conversion of the Khazars to Judaism in around 740 C.E. No other case is known of a non-Jewish country ever having converted to Judaism in this way, and apparently the kingdom remained at least nominally Jewish until it was defeated and dismantled by Russian invaders late in the tenth century. In Judah ha-Levi's account, the Khazars' heathen ruler, the Kaghan, has a dream in which an angel tells him that his intentions are pleasing to God but his deeds are not. The Kaghan decides that he must determine which of the world systems surrounding him makes the most sense, and so he summons to his court a Greek philosopher, a Christian scholastic, and a Muslim theologian, and probes the basis of their beliefs. Dissatisfied by each of their answers, he reluctantly invites a rabbi as well; "I had not intended to ask any Jew," the Kaghan remarks, "because I am aware of their reduced condition and narrow-minded views, as their misery left them nothing commendable" (Judah ha-Levi, *The Kuzari*, 40). The rabbi, however, gives the most persuasive arguments in favor of Judaism, stressing the events of Hebrew salvation history accepted by Muslims and Christians alike, whereupon the Kaghan and his people convert.

Pavić used this remarkable dialogue as the basis for his set of three one-sided encyclopedias. He added further entries to trace later research on the Khazars, centering on the efforts of a seventeenth-century Walachian nobleman, Avram Brankovich, to reconstruct these early events in the form of the original lexicon, destroyed a year after he published it in 1691; still further entries describe several modern scholars' efforts to reconstruct Brankovich's destroyed book. They are frustrated in their efforts by the Devil—or rather, three devils, one for each of the three faiths—who exert themselves to keep the scholars from reassembling the three parts of the encyclopedia. Having long divided and conquered the world, the devils wish human beings to continue to see only one side of reality, each group trapped in its own partial viewpoint. Thus the struggle to create (and then to recreate) the multilingual dictionary becomes a cosmic battle to piece reality together into a whole, or to hold it apart in fragments.

Dictionary of the Khazars has a multinational pedigree. It is directly descended from the imaginary encyclopedia of Tlön in Borges's story "Tlön, Uqbar, Orbis Tertius," with the ambitious twist that where Borges only described his encyclopedia, Pavić actually writes one, or at least three hundred pages' worth of the supposed fragments of its three versions. Other Borges stories, like "The Library of Babylon" and "Death and the Compass," are certainly in the background as well. Like Borges's stories, the novel plays on Mallarmé's dream of a book as "a spiritual instrument" that would encompass the entire world within its covers. *Dictionary of the Khazars* is also, as its cover says, "an Arabian Nights romance," complete with tales embedded within tales, references to Haroun al-Rashid, and a Shahrazad-like poet-princess, Ateh; if the lost language of the Khazars survives at all, it is among a group of Black Sea parrots, descendants of parrots whom Ateh taught to sing her poems. Finally, in its use of a medieval Jewish source text, the *Dictionary* was surely inspired by Danilo Kiš's 1976 story sequence *A Tomb for Boris Davidovich*, published just two years before Pavić began his novel. Kiš's title character, Boris Davidovich Novsky, is a modern reincarnation of a skeptical fourteenth-century rabbi, Baruch David Neumann, an actual person who was interrogated by the Inquisition. This interrogation was recorded at the time and is retold in modified form by Kiš, who footnotes the sources he is transforming, just as Pavić does in turn.

Building on his wide network of literary and historical sources, Pavić gives his characters a global perspective as well. His modern scholars form a multinational trinity: a Polish-born, Yale-trained professor, Dorothea Schultz; an Egyptian Hebraist, Abu Kabir Muawia; and a Serbian archaeologist, Isailo Suk, professor at Novi Sad, a center of Serbian culture where Pavić himself long taught literature. These characters and their earlier counterparts are all flamboyantly multilingual, sometimes using different languages for specific purposes. Already in the seventeenth century, Avram Brankovich's family "count in Tzintzar, lie in Walachian, are silent in Greek, sing hymns in Russian, are cleverest in Turkish, and speak their mother tongue—Serbian—only when they intend to kill" (25). Brankovich himself "cannot stay with one language for long: he changes them like mistresses and speaks Walachian one minute and Hungarian or Turkish the next, and he has begun to learn Khazar from a parrot. They say he also speaks Spanish in his sleep, but this language melts by the time he is awake" (28). In a dream he is told a poem in Hebrew, a language which he doesn't know; when he manages to get it interpreted, it proves to be a famous poem by Judah ha-Levi concerning the poet's divided self, living in Spain far from his distant homeland: "My heart is in the East, but I am at the end of the West. / . . . Zion is in Edom's bondage, and I am in Arabian fetters" (29). Only a reader of Hebrew can know this, as Pavić places the reader into Brankovich's position by giving the poem only in Hebrew, without translation, though for centuries this has been the most widely translated medieval Hebrew poem. It is this poem that leads Brankovich to Judah ha-Levi's *Book of the Khazars*, setting him off on his increasingly obsessive quest for information about the Khazars.

In a confidential report to the Viennese court, which is always on the watch for challenges to its imperial authority, an incarnation of the Devil named Nikon Sevast describes Brankovich's efforts to assemble materials and to create a complete account of Khazar history and culture:

> Brankovich had eight camel-loads of books brought to Constantinople from the Zarand district and from Vienna, and more are still arriving. He has sealed himself off from the world with walls of dictionaries and old manuscripts. . . . Brankovich's card file, created along with the library, encompassed a thousand pages, covering a variety of subjects: from catalogues of sighs and exclamations in Old Church Slavonic to a register of salts and teas, and enormous collections of hair, beards, and moustaches of the most diverse colors and styles from living and dead persons of all races, which our master glues onto glass bottles and keeps as a sort of museum of old hairstyles. His own hair is not represented in this collection, but he has ordered that strands of it be used to weave his coat of arms with a one-eyed eagle and the motto "Every master embraces his own death." (45)

The dictionary may well be the death of the reader if not of Brankovich himself, as the only surviving copies are the gold- and silver-locked volumes; a reader who finds a copy thus has an equal chance of being enlightened or murdered by the book on reaching the words *Verbum caro factum est* on the ninth page.

Isailo Suk and Abu Kabir Muawia are murdered in Istanbul in 1982, just before they and Dorothea Schultz succeed in reassembling the dictionary, and so Pavić's 1984 novel can only be a partial reconstruction, incomplete and full of conflicting information. Late in the book, for example, Pavić actually reprints the ninth page of a Latin and Hebrew translation of Judah ha-Levi's Arabic dialogue, published in 1660 as *Liber Cosri* and obviously prefiguring Brankovich's lost *Lexicon Cosri*. The ninth page of Judah ha-Levi's treatise does indeed discuss Christ's incarnation, yet the fatal words from John's gospel cannot be found there. Instead, in ha-Levi's text the Christian sage paraphrases the Bible, interestingly translating within Latin itself between physical and metaphysical terms: "incorporata (*incarnata*) est Deitas, transiens in uterum virginis" ("God was incorporated [*incarnated*], passing through a virgin's womb," 298). Source and reconstruction together might even complete the true dictionary's destruction: Judah ha-Levi's *Liber Cosri* and Pavić's *Dictionary* may resemble certain Khazar mirrors, made of polished salt, which come in two varieties, slow and fast, reflecting past or future events rather than the present. Princess Ateh is said to have died when her servants foolishly brought her a pair of these mirrors at daybreak. She was wont to sleep with sacred letters drawn on her eyelids by blind scribes, letters that would kill whoever saw them, so that enemies could not surprise her in her sleep. But she unthinkingly looked into the fast and slow mirrors before the fatal letters had been washed off her eyelids: "She saw herself in the mirrors with closed lids and died instantly. She vanished between two blinks of the eye, or better said, for the first time she read the lethal letters on her eyelids, because she had blinked the moment before and the moment after, and the mirrors had reflected it. She died, killed simultaneously by letters from both the past and the future" (24).

To an unusual degree, Pavić's book openly anticipates its international circulation after publication. Pavić actually arranges matters so that his book *needs* to be translated in order to achieve a full expression of his themes. Intent upon breaking up linear ways of reading, Pavić stresses a consequence of the multilingualism of the "lost" original: its entries would have been alphabetized differently in Greek, Arabic, and Hebrew, so that readers in each language would inevitably have been reading different books, arranged in a different order in each translation. Pavić's original novel can only describe this difference without embodying it, since he doesn't really want to limit his readership to the few people who could read those three languages, even assuming that he could write them all himself, which doesn't appear to be the case. His book is written in Serbo-Croatian throughout, though he asserts that Daubmannus's 1691 *Lexicon Cosri* was "printed in Arabic, Hebrew, and Greek," as well as—improbably—Serbian (239). In his Preliminary Notes, Pavić describes his book's monolingualism as "the main shortcoming of the current version in relation to the Daubmannus edition," adding that at least the reader can choose to read the book's entries out of order: "it can be read in an infinite number of ways. It is an open book, and when it is shut it can be added to: just as it has its own former and present lexicographer, so it can acquire new writers, compilers, and continuers" (11).

Only a fiction in the original novel, the multilingual mobility of the entries became a reality once the *Dictionary* was translated. Pavić noted this fact with great satisfaction in a 1998 article:

> I have always wished to make literature, which is a nonreversible art, a reversible one. Therefore my novels have no end in the classical meaning of the word. . . . The original version of *Dictionary of the Khazars,* printed in the Cyrillic alphabet, ends with a Latin quotation: "sed venit ut illa impleam et confirmem,

Mattheus." My novel in Greek translation ends with a sentence: "I have immediately noticed that there are three fears in me, and not one." The English, Hebrew, Spanish, and Danish versions of *Dictionary of the Khazars* end in this way: "Then when the reader returned, the entire process would be reversed, and Tibbon would correct the translation based on the impressions he had derived from this reading walk." ("The Beginning and the End of Reading," 143)

Pavić goes on to quote the closing sentences of the versions in Swedish, Dutch, Czech, German, Hungarian, Italian, Catalan, and Japanese. Foreign translations collectively create a multiple book, extending the original novel's monolingual reconstruction of Daubmannus's supposedly quad-rilingual original.

Pavić's international framework and his experimental emphases re-inforced each other for his international audience, leading foreign readers to overlook any local implications of his book and instead to emphasize its metafictional concerns. Even after Yugoslavia had fallen into civil war, dis-cussions by non-Slavic scholars continued to focus almost exclusively on apolitical readings of the book. This approach can be typified by the theo-rist of science and postmodernism N. Katherine Hayles, in a 1997 article flamboyantly entitled "Corporeal Anxiety in *Dictionary of the Khazars:* What Books Talk about in the Late Age of Print When They Talk about Losing Their Bodies." Giving a detailed and interesting reading of the theme of tex-tual production and destruction, Hayles emphasizes the novel's "radical in-determinacy" (804) and the operations of "a closed, self-referential loop" within it (811). She says nothing at all about the book's political themes or the cultural context of its composition and publication, apart from a pass-ing reference in a footnote to an article by Petar Ramadanović, "Language and Crime in Yugoslavia," which she describes as taking "a sociological ap-proach" (819 n).

In the first extended critical presentation of Pavić in English, the *Review of Contemporary Fiction* devoted over a hundred pages in the sum-mer of 1998 to a cluster of a dozen pieces on Pavić's novels, centering on the *Dictionary* and including a long interview with Pavić as well as his article "The Beginning and End of Reading." Nowhere in these dozen pieces is there anything more than vague, passing mention of the tragic events that un-folded in the former Yugoslavia beginning in 1987, when resurgent mi-cronationalisms tore the nation apart. The articles have titles like "*Dictio-nary of the Khazars* as an Epistemological Metaphor" and "Milorad Pavić and Hyperfiction." Even an article entitled "Culture as Memory" concerns intertextuality and makes no reference to battles over cultural identity and memory in the former Yugoslavia of the eighties and nineties.

For his own part, Pavić says nothing at all about politics in his article on reading; he focuses entirely on formal issues and the future of the novel. In the interview, conducted by a Greek journalist named Thanassis Lallas, Pavić speaks mostly of his ancestors and of his metafictional concerns, mentioning only in very general terms that "For a while I was not able to publish my writing in my own country. There were political reasons for it. . . . I had to wait until 1967, when the appropriate conditions were established that allowed me to publish my first book in my country" ("As a Writer, I Was Born Two Hundred Years Ago," 133). Asked directly about events in Serbia, Pavić replies with a kind of gentle, distanced irony that gives little indication of his personal views, even speaking of the Serbs as "they" rather than "we": "It is a nation deprived of memory. They never forgive, but forget immediately. They are good warriors, but the worst diplomats. They win wars, and lose battles. . . . They always have their enemies in mind and they do not care a lot for their friends" (133–34). He then quickly turns the conversation to a discussion of Serbia's prominent writers and filmmakers and to his own fiction. As the interview draws to a close, Pavić sidesteps a question as to whether he has ever been a Communist and replies, "I am the last Byzantine" (140).

Nowhere in this interview, conducted in Belgrade by a foreign journalist for international consumption, does Pavić make anything resembling a direct political statement. He describes his life's goal as "to rescue as many pieces of beauty as possible. Tons of beauty sink every day in the Danube. Nobody notices. The one who notices it must do something to rescue it" (135). Asked specifically about the current situation in Serbia, he expresses a hope that the international success of novels like his may be "an assurance that love will overcome savagery in this world where there is always more beauty than love. . . . Let us for an instant count readers, not voters" (141). This is just what Pavić's personal website actually does: the home page displays a tally of how many people have visited the site to date. Reflecting an awareness of the foundation of his global appeal, Pavić's site is registered not in his own name but as www.khazars.com. Appropriately, like the *Dictionary* itself the site comes in two parallel versions, not male and female but Serbian and English (in a good illustration of David Crystal's theme of the emergence of English as the international language of choice in much of the world). A capsule biography on the home page says pointedly that Pavić "is not a member of any political party." Instead of party affiliation, the biography lists Pavić's membership in the Serbian Academy of Sciences and Arts and in several European cultural organizations, with no hint of the fact that the Serbian Academy was extensively involved in Serbian cultural politics in the eighties and nineties.[1]

Pavić's stance had been very different in the late eighties, when Slobodan Milošević came to power vowing to restore the greatness that had once been Serbia's, with himself as the dominant unifying force. According to an account by Rajko Djurić, Milošević's party modified the traditional nationalist "four-S" slogan, *Samo sloga Srbina sparava* (only *unity* can save Serbia) to read *Samo Slobodan Srbina sparava.* Speaking for domestic consumption, Pavić expressed his forceful support for the new government's goals in a range of articles and interviews for Belgrade newspapers, reinforcing nationalist messages of Serbian ancestral greatness, a favorite theme of Milošević's. As Pavić declared in 1989, "In Serbia people were eating with golden forks in the thirteenth century, while the Western Europeans were still tearing raw flesh apart with their fingers" (quoted in Djurić, "Kultur und Destruktivität," 163–64).

Language was a crucial arena for the nationalist program of Serbian resurgence, spearheaded by activities of the Serbian Academy of Sciences and Arts, to which Pavić was elected in 1991. "Croats, Serbs, and Muslims used to speak a common language before the war," Petar Ramadanović has written; "now they speak 'Croat,' 'Serbian,' and 'Bosnian.' Serbo-Croat, the vanquished language, has no people, no folk anymore. But Serbo-Croat, the language of a ghost, the language of people who have lost their country, remains as a trace, as a witness of the un-speakable crime that is committed in the Balkans" (185). Pavić, on the other hand, saw Serbo-Croatian as a political fiction created to suppress local identity, most specifically the historical greatness of Serbia and of the Serbian language. As he said in 1989, using the rhetoric of victimhood that would undergird Milošević's declarations of war against Slovenia and Croatia in 1991, "The Serbs come from the midpoint of the world, from the navel of the Indo-European peoples, and the Serbian language is an ancient language, the ancestor of all the Indo-European languages. And so everyone hates us out of envy; they sense that we are the most ancient of all the peoples between the Himalayas and the Pyrenees" (quoted in Djurić, 164).

[1] I am describing the site as of February 2002. It has been set up and maintained by Pavić's wife, Jasmina Mihajlović, herself a critic and writer, who has written extensively on Pavić and is keenly concerned with his reception and reputation both at home and abroad. Appropriately, the site includes a hypertext story by Pavić, "Damascene: A Tale for Computer and Compasses," with "forks" at which the reader chooses the order of episodes and the ending.

These statements give a chilling cast to one aspect of the Brankovich family's multilingualism: they use Serbian "only when they wish to kill" (25). Written words function as weapons throughout *Dictionary of the Khazars*, from Princess Ateh's death-dealing letters to the invention of the Cyrillic alphabet by Saint Cyril. Summarizing the move from the rounded early Slavonic alphabet (Glagolitic) to the angular Cyrillic, Pavić describes the process of alphabetization in violent terms: "While the Slavs besieged Constantinople in 860 A.D., [Cyril] was setting a trap for them in the quiet of his monastic cell in Asia Minor's Olympus—he was creating the first letters of the Slavic alphabet. He started with rounded letters, but the Slavonic language was so wild that the ink could not hold it, and so he made a second alphabet of barred letters and caged the unruly language in them like a bird" (63–64). In order to fit the Slavonic language within the cage of their script, Cyril and his brother Methodius "broke it in pieces, drew it into their mouths through the bars of Cyril's letters, and bonded the fragments with their saliva and the Greek clay beneath the soles of their feet" (64).

The monastic theocracy on Mount Athos in northern Greece, where this scene takes place, has long been a focus of Slavic Orthodox identification; Pavić gives a further literary and heroic twist to the locale by identifying it with Olympus, a site he associates with Homer. In his interview with Thanassis Lallas, he cites Homer and the later Serbian bards as his predecessors in epic creation from oral material (138). Pavić went on to make Athos a key locale in his 1988 novel *Landscape Painted with Tea*, and well before he began the *Dictionary* he gave Athos pride of place in a poem called "Monument to an Unknown Poet," in which several of his characteristic themes are already fully evident. "My eyes are full of blood and wine like plaster on Athos' walls," the poem begins; in the second stanza, the speaker develops the link between literature and liturgy:

> My tongue three times peeled off its shirt of years
>   and three languages forgot within me
> But my tongue still recognizes the language of lost liturgies.
> My feet are tired from choosing the staff that will not break
> But my heart still makes a pilgrimage to your words set on fire.

In the poem's conclusion, these Khazar-like lost languages are redeemed in an internalized homeland:

> My tongue three times peeled off its shirt of time
>   and three languages forgot within me
> But my heart has tasted the rock of your homeland
>   and found in it the flavor of hearth,

Although I was the apprentice of a poet who doesn't exist,
    a poet without a poem.

(28)

From the eyes full of blood in the opening line to the "flavor of hearth" at the end, this poem resonates with the pre-Nazi tradition of celebrations of *Blut und Boden*—blood and soil, symbols of ethnic rootedness typically mobilized against Jews and other newcomers who are thought to be supplanting the original inhabitants in their own land. There are, of course, no real monuments to unknown poets, just as no poet can exist without a poem: Pavić is playing on the imagery of monuments to the Unknown Soldier, here a man without a country fighting for his rightful home and hearth.

For all the ironic detachment of his interview with Thanassis Lallas, Pavić speaks rather differently on his website. To be sure, he belongs to no political party, and a brief "Autobiography" on his site insists that "I have no biography. I have only a bibliography." Yet this autobiography closes with a direct self-identification with an unjustly persecuted Serbia:

> I have not killed anyone. But they have killed me. Long before my death. It would have been better for my books had their author been a Turk or a German. I was the best known writer of the most hated nation in the world—the Serbian nation.
> XXI century started for me avant la date 1999, when NATO airforces bombed Belgrade and Serbia. Since that moment the river Danube on whose banks I was born is not navigable.
> I think God graced me with infinite favor by granting me the joy of writing, and punished me in equal measure, precisely because of that joy perhaps.
>
> Milorad Pavić.

Www.khazars.com is thus still developing the themes of writing, victimization, and divine inscrutability that pervade *Dictionary of the Khazars*.

The novel complicates these themes by its use of a Jewish source text. Pavić treats Jewish mysticism, in fact, with insight and sympathy as the utopian vision of an eternally displaced people. Having printed Judah ha-Levi's "Song of Zion" in Hebrew early in the book, he gives a partial prose translation two hundred pages later, describing the poet composing the poem as he finally makes his longed-for journey from Spain to the Holy Land at the end of his life:

> It was on this trip that he wrote his most mature poems, among them the famous *Song of Zion*, which is read in synagogues on the

Day of the Holy Abba. He landed on the holy shores of his original homeland and died within reach of his destination. According to one account, just as he laid eyes on Jerusalem he was trampled to death by Saracen horses. Writing about the clash between Christianity and Islam, he said: "There is no port in either East or West where we might find peace. . . . Whether Ismael wins or the Edomites"—Christians—"prevail, my fate remains the same—to suffer." (246)

The Jewish section of the *Dictionary* is the longest of the three; placed at the end, it is the section where the book's many threads are drawn together. If the true Lexicon could ever be assembled, it would represent the hidden body of Adam Ruhani or Adam Cadmon, a figure from kabbalistic mysticism, whose instantiation would redeem the fallen universe: "The Khazars saw letters in people's dreams, and in them they looked for primordial man, for Adam Cadmon, who was both man and woman and born before eternity. They believed that to every person belongs one letter of the alphabet, that each of these letters constitutes part of Adam Cadmon's body on earth, and that these letters converge in people's dreams and come to life in Adam's body" (224–25). Samuel Cohen, a contemporary of Avram Brankovich's and compiler of the Hebrew version of the Dictionary, struggles to assemble a text that will fully embody Adam Cadmon: "I know, my Khazar dictionary includes all ten numbers and twenty-two letters of the Hebrew alphabet; the world can be created out of them but, lo, I cannot do it. I am missing certain names, and as a result some of the letters will not be filled" (229).

Far from treating Judaism slightingly or with hostility, Pavić does just the opposite: throughout his book, he implicitly identifies the Serbs *with* the Jews. Judah ha-Levi, trapped between Christianity and Islam, becomes the model for Pavić himself, philosophical poet who records his country's fate, caught between the Austro-Hungarian Empire on one side and imperial Russia on the other. At the very beginning of the *Dictionary,* the Khazars stand in for the Balkans when their independence is brutally crushed by the Russians:

A Russian military commander of the 10th century, Prince Svyatoslav, gobbled up the Khazar Empire like an apple, without even dismounting from his horse. In 943 A.D. the Russians went without sleep for eight nights to smash the Khazar capital at the mouth of the Volga into the Caspian Sea, and between 965 and 970 A.D. they destroyed the Khazar state. Eyewitnesses noted that

the shadows of the houses in the capital held their outlines for
years, although the buildings themselves had already been
destroyed long before. They held fast in the wind and in the
waters of the Volga. (2–3)

Before Yugoslavia plunged into civil war, it was natural enough to read such
passages as expressing the heroic resistance of an indomitable nation to the
oppression of imperial invaders. With Pavić identified as "Yugoslavian" and
his book as "translated from the Serbo-Croatian," the *Dictionary* could be
read in a way pleasing to Western liberals and conservatives alike, as a general plea for Yugoslavian self-determination in the face of Soviet repression.

This turns out not to be what Pavić had in mind. Far from defend-
ing Yugoslavia, he wanted to see it taken apart. Once in power, Slobodan
Milošević and his ultranationalist allies began to disassemble Yugoslavia and
even Serbo-Croatia into separate ethnic identities and languages. Formerly
virtually indistinguishable from Croatian except in script (Cyrillic versus
Roman), Serbian now became a distinct language, and Pavić took the opportunity to have his book "translated" *into* Serbian. Though for most books
this would have meant little more than transliteration, in the case of the *Dictionary* the new version acquired a new order of entries, and the "Serbian
version printed in the Latin alphabet" is one of the translations Pavić points
to as differing from the original ("The Beginning and the End of Reading,"
143). Christina Pribićević-Zorić's widely praised English translation is described in the British and American editions as "translated from the Serbo-
Croatian," and yet when this same translation was locally reissued in Belgrade in 1996, it was labeled as "translated from Serbian." We are used to
seeing alternate translations differ from one another as they reinterpret a
common source language. Here just the opposite has occurred: the identical English version is presented as a translation of two *different* original languages, as Serbo-Croatian is torn asunder.

Within the book itself, Pavić focuses the rhetoric of suppression
and victimhood on the Khazars. Modifying Judah ha-Levi's dialogue, Pavić
adapts the theme of the Jews as archetypal oppressed minority to describe
the Khazars as an oppressed *majority* in their own multicultural land: a
translation of Serbian nationalist hostility toward Tito's efforts to create a
unified Yugoslavia. Tito's program is sharply satirized in an extended discussion of the organization of the Khazar state, in which the causes of Serbian resentment can be seen in heightened form. Whereas the Serbs, with
some 40 percent of the population, were a plurality but not at all a majority
in Yugoslavia, "the Khazars are the most numerous in the empire, the others all constituting very small groups. But the empire's administrative orga-

nization is designed not to show this" (146). The state is divided into districts, with more districts for the minorities than for the Khazar majority. Legal and political representation, however, are proportional to the number of districts rather than to population. Moreover, the major Khazar region has been split up: "In the north, for instance, an entirely new nation was invented, which gave up the Khazar name, even the Khazar language, and it has a different name for its district" (146). Names are a crucial battleground: "Given this situation and this balance of forces, promotions hinge on blind obedience to the non-Khazar representatives. Just avoiding the Khazar name is already a recommendation in itself, enabling one to take the first steps at court. The next step requires fiercely attacking the Khazars and subordinating their interests to those of the Greeks, Jews, Turkmen, Arabs, or Goths, as the Slavs are called in these parts" (147). It will be noted that this listing makes the Khazars the oppressed majority among a total of six ethnic groups, a number corresponding to Yugoslavia's six constituent republics.

The Khazars' struggle is economic as well as cultural. In a grim parody of Tito's policy of giving preferential economic treatment to the smaller, less developed republics, the Khazar government sells specially dyed bread to non-Khazar regions:

> Dyed bread is the sign of the Khazars' position in the Khazar
> state. The Khazars produce it, because they inhabit the grain-
> growing regions of the state. The starving populace at the foot
> of the Caucasus massif eats dyed bread, which is sold for next
> to nothing. Undyed bread, which is also made by the Khazars,
> is paid for in gold. The Khazars are allowed to buy only the
> expensive, undyed bread. Should any Khazar violate this rule and
> buy the cheap, dyed bread, which is strictly forbidden them, it will
> show in their excrement. Special customs services periodically
> check Khazar latrines and punish violators of this law. (149–50)

The Khazar state, in Pavić's presentation, becomes the ultimate dystopia of a totalitarian multiculturalism.

The Khazars are exemplary victims geographically as well as socially, for the three hells of Christianity, Islam, and Judaism meet under their lands (52). The devils' influence continually percolates upward, though naturally the devils themselves hate what they have wrought. As one of the three devils says to Dr. Muawia at the end of the book:

> Look at the results of this democracy of yours. Before, big nations
> used to oppress small nations. Now it's the reverse. Now, in the
> name of democracy, small nations terrorize the big. Just look at

the world around us. White America is afraid of blacks, the blacks are afraid of the Puerto Ricans, Jews of the Palestinians, the Arabs of the Jews, the Serbs of the Albanians, the Chinese of the Vietnamese, the English of the Irish. Small fish are nibbling the ears of the big fish. . . . Your democracy sucks. . . . (330)

Having expressed his views on democracy, the devil orders Muawia to open his mouth so that his teeth won't be spoiled, and shoots him in the mouth.

A novel that achieved rapid worldwide success as "an Arabian Nights romance" and "a novel of love and death" actually contains more death than love, and it even helped to usher in the death it most longed for, the destruction of a multiethnic Yugoslavia. In "Pavić's Literary Demolition of Yugoslavia," Andrew Wachtel points out that Pavić's use of postmodernist techniques could be read in Western Europe as pure play or as a healthy corrective to Enlightenment certainties, whereas Pavić could deploy these techniques to very different effect in a Yugoslavia whose very creation expressed an Enlightenment ideal of unity in diversity based on a common, reasoned public discourse:

> The philosophical demolition job Pavić performed on the synthetic concept of Yugoslavia grew out of his own importation of a particular postmodernist mode of thought into Yugoslav discourse. But on Yugoslav soil, the Lyotardian vision of separate and incommensurable language games did not remain a metaphor. It was embodied, instead, in a series of nationalist micronarratives whose primary mode of communication turned out to be shooting. (640)

Perhaps we were reading the poisoned copy of the book all along?

If *I, Rigoberta Menchú* aroused controversy when it proved to be partly fictional, *Dictionary of the Khazars* becomes unsettling when it proves to be far more historical than it seemed, far less fantastic in character. Closely connected to contemporary reality, the *Dictionary* was a pointed and polemical intervention in cultural debate in the uncertain years leading up to Yugoslavia's vicious civil war. How should we read the book in light of this new understanding, or should we continue to read it at all? Certainly a book marketed as a romantic escape into hyperfiction would have attracted fewer readers if it had been presented as "A Playful Apologia for Ethnic Cleansing." One might regard the novel as a sort of con job, much as Rigoberta Menchú's conservative critics are seeing her book today. Foreign readers haven't realized that they were sold a bill of goods: nationalist propaganda falsely marketed as international postmodernism.

To take such a view, though, risks a kind of textual essentialism, as though a book really is one thing and has one meaning wherever and whenever it is read. Few of us still believe this in theory, thanks to a generation's worth of poststructuralist discourse, and yet in practice it is all too easy to fall into essentialist language in describing a book's themes and effects, even though what we are really describing may largely be our own reading of it at a given time. But we needn't go to the opposite extreme, and maintain that a book has an infinite multiplicity of meanings and perhaps no real ethical impact at all. Despite Pavić's enthusiasm for his text's reversibility, there are finally always going to be forty-five entries that collectively present the same elements for the reader to absorb. Further, readers don't read in a private cultural vacuum. Though a range of readings is always possible at a given time and place, this range is limited, not infinite, and the readings produced in a particular cultural context will tend to have a definite family resemblance.

What the double life of *Dictionary of the Khazars* demonstrates is the major difference between a work's life in a national context as opposed to a global context. As a work of Yugoslavian literature, written in Serbo-Croatian and printed in Cyrillic script, the Хазарски Речник had one kind of impact, or a range of impacts, that began to change as Yugoslavia broke apart and the book became *Hazarski Rečnik,* written in Serbian and printed in Roman script. In both forms, it would naturally be read in a direct relation to the local literary, social, and political history that Pavić shares—and disputes—with his readers. Individual Serbian, or Bosnian, or Montenegrin readers might approve or reject Pavić's satiric implication that the Khazars are the forerunners of modern Serbs as a majority oppressed in their own country, but most of these readers would recognize the theme at once, however they assessed it. Probably many readers around Eastern Europe would be attuned to this level of the text, as it would resonate so strongly with issues close to home.

Farther afield, however, *Hazarski rečnik* changed as it became a work of world literature, whether as *Diccionario Jázaro* or as מילון הכוזרים. The novel's nationalism remained subordinate to its internationalism for most foreign readers even after Milošević came to power and ethnic tensions mounted throughout the Balkans, and it didn't take the expanse of the Atlantic to effect such a shift. In a 1995 survey of the French reception of the *Dictionary,* Milivoj Srebro finds French-speaking reviewers and critics consistently reading Pavić as the playful heir to Calvino, Cortázar, and Perec. She quotes a Swiss reviewer in 1988 describing the novel as "une machine infer-nale," but this is not at all a political assessment; instead, the reviewer con-cludes, "the demoniacal Pavić teaches us that reality, like truth, is a sweet il-lusion" ("Le Coup médiatique de Milorad Pavić," 277). The reviewer makes no reference to any Balkan realities, even though at their closest point the borders of Switzerland and the former Yugoslavia are less than a hundred and fifty miles apart.

The pressures of local context are certainly reduced when a work travels abroad. Yet acknowledging this shift doesn't mean that it is good to remain as clueless as the Swiss reviewer allowed himself to be, at a time when it would have behooved Western readers to pay much closer attention to the issues Pavić was raising. Having found one French critic (an Eastern Euro-pean émigré) who "has even been tempted to see in this work a parable of the destiny of the Serbs," Milivoj Srebro dismisses such an interpretation as denying the book's universality. "It is precisely this universality," she adds, "that makes the difference between a masterpiece and an ordinary work" (284). Even Srebro, though, ends by admitting that French responses to the novel have been one-sided: "To be sure, if we take up the formulation of Jean Starobinski, according to which 'the critical trajectory develops, so far as possible, between *accepting everything* (through sympathy) and *situating everything* (by comprehension),' one could say that the reviews of *Dictionary of the Khazars* have stayed fairly close to the first pole of this trajectory" (284–85). It should not be necessary to treat a foreign work with an un-comprehending sympathy in order to appreciate its excellence. It does no service to works of world literature to set them loose in some deracinated space, whether the "great conversation" of a fifties-style academic human-ism or the "closed self-referential loop" of poststructuralist metafiction. Aes-thetically as well as ethically, a pure universalism of either variety is finally reductive, missing the real complexity of a work, just as much as would an opposite insistence that a work can only be read effectively in the original language, untranslatably linked at all points to its local context. An informed reading of a work of world literature should keep both aspects in play to-gether, recognizing that it brings us elements of a time and place different from our own, and at the same time that these elements change in force as the book gets farther from home.

Understanding the cultural subtext of Pavić's Khazars is important for foreign readers, as otherwise we simply miss the point of much of the book. As Petar Ramadanović says, Pavić was composing an "appeal for com-passion with the Serbian problem . . . addressed to the international com-munity" (190). However we choose to react to that appeal, a full reading should be aware of it and should confront the ethical choices that the novel is pressing us to make. At the same time, when we read a work of world literature we have a great deal of freedom in deciding what use we will make of such contextual understanding. This freedom can most readily be seen when we are reading a work from a distant time as well as place: we need to know who Amun is, if we are to understand the Egyptian love poet's invocation of his power, but the poem is unlikely to move us to start offering sacrifices to him. The same may be said of a Christian composition. It seems to me a trivialization to treat *The Divine Comedy* as an essentially secular work, though various modern commentators have chosen to focus on Dante as "poet of the secular world," in Erich Auerbach's phrase. Auerbach went so far as to claim that Dante's realism overwhelmed his theology "and destroyed it in the very process of realizing it" (*Mimesis,* 202). We can dispute such a claim on both historical and aesthetic grounds, taking seriously the possibility that *The Divine Comedy* was a successful Christian poem. Even so, appreciating Dante's profound religious vision does not require us to convert to Catholicism, or to take a stand on issues of Florentine politics, though both of these responses are ones that Dante might well have desired. A work of world literature has its fullest life, and its greatest power, when we can read it with a kind of *detached engagement,* informed but not confined by a knowledge of what the work would likely mean in its original time and place, even as we adapt it to our present context and purposes.

Pavić himself raises this theme repeatedly. The son of a house builder, he often uses architectural metaphors in talking about his books. He has tried, he says, to construct books with many exits rather than a single ending, so that the reader "can come out not only through one exit but also through other exits that are far from each other. . . . Slowly I lose from my sight the difference between the house and the book, and this is, perhaps, the most important thing I have to say in this text" ("The Beginning and the End of Reading," 144). We can extend Pavić's metaphor: a book offers us many ways in as well as many ways out, some of which are most readily accessible from a local standpoint, while others are more visible from a distance. For Pavić, indeed, it is the reader who has the true freedom of the text; caught within a web of circumstance and fatality, the writer has far less. It is the Devil in Istanbul who declares that "your democracy sucks," but by giving this speech to the Devil Pavić doesn't mean to distance himself from this viewpoint, as he regularly identifies himself with the Devil. Poet of a radically fallen world, Pavić creates a book from his own passions and prejudices, expecting that different readers may find ways out of his book that he himself cannot take or perhaps even find.

A clear stand-in for Pavić within the book is the devil Nikon Sevast, a master calligrapher who spends his time painting frescoes in Moravian churches before he goes on to encounter Avram Brankovich and serve as a copyist of the *Lexikon*. Describing his fresco technique to a fellow monk, Sevast says, "I work with something like a dictionary of colors, and from it the observer composes sentences and books, in other words, images. You could do the same with writing. Why shouldn't someone create a dictionary of words that make up one book and let the reader himself assemble the words into a whole?" (96). In so doing, the reader will not merely share in the creative process but will actually experience a freedom denied to the devil/artist himself: "It is not I who mix the colors but your own vision," Sevast tells his fellow monk. "I only place them next to one another on the wall in their natural state; it is the observer who mixes the colors in his own eye, like porridge. . . . Therefore, faith in seeing, listening, and reading is more important than faith in painting, singing, or writing" (95).

Reading gives access to a realm of freedom that provides strength to the dreamer, who is otherwise caught in the trials of the waking world. For Pavić it is world literature that typifies the possibility of escape from the tragedies of individual circumstance. Just as reciting Dante gave Primo Levi strength in Auschwitz, so too Pavić has Saint Methodius think of Homer while undergoing torture at the order of hostile German bishops:

> He was brought to trial before a synod in Regensburg, then tortured and exposed naked to the frost. While they whipped him, his body bent over so low that his beard touched the snow, Methodius thought of how Homer and the holy prophet Elijah had been contemporaries, how Homer's poetic state had been larger than the state of Alexander of Macedonia, because it had stretched from Pontus to beyond Gibraltar. . . . He thought of how Homer had seas and towns in his vast poetic state, not knowing that in one of them, in Sidon, sat the prophet Elijah, who was to become an inhabitant of another poetic state, one as vast, eternal, and powerful as Homer's own—an inhabitant of the Holy Scriptures. (88–89)

Recalling his reading of Homer and Elijah, a poet and a prophet who themselves could not perceive the overlapping of their verbal realms, Methodius can ignore the whips that seek to break his spirit.

Isaac Sangari, Hebrew representative before the Kaghan in the great religious debate, is intensely loyal to his language and tradition, but not exclusively so:

He made a point of stressing the values of the Hebrew language, but he knew many other languages as well. He believed that the differences between languages lay in the following: all languages except God's are the languages of suffering, the dictionaries of pain. "I have noticed," he said, "that my sufferings are drained through a rupture in time or in myself, for otherwise they would be more numerous by now. The same holds true for languages." (274)

The only truly free characters in Pavić's book are a select sect of "dream hunters," devotees of a cult headed by Princess Ateh, an alternative to all existing religions. The dream hunters travel from one person's dream to another, seeking pairs of people who unknowingly dream of one another; the rifts in the universe can be healed if the dream hunters can unite these pairs, who are the potential lexicographers of the full Dictionary. As a devil named Ibn Akshany remarks to one of these dream hunters, his hunt is the most privileged form of reading, and it is better than writing itself: "Anybody can play music or write a dictionary. Leave that to others, because people like you, who can peer into the crack between one view and the other, that crack where death rules supreme, are few and far between" (183).

Pavić's book enters world literature both by its international circulation and also by opening out directly, so far as possible, into the reader's world. Though the Dictionary proper ends differently in different languages, in every edition Pavić follows it with a "Closing Note on the Usefulness of this Dictionary," in which he evokes the reader, or more specifically a pair of readers, male and female. These readers will each have read one of the book's two editions and will now meet in the square of their town: "I see how they lay their dinner out on top of the mailbox in the street," he says, "and how they eat, embraced, sitting on their bicycles" (335). In *Dictionary of the Khazars*, the nightmare of history becomes the dream of world literature, a space of freedom from the limited viewpoints that enmesh nations and individuals alike, not excluding the book's own author. The readers' meal on the mailbox, and its hinted romantic aftermath, can form an antidote to the poison with which the book itself was written.

Figure 12. The Great Sphinx at Giza, 1798

World Enough and Time

And so, what *is* world literature? I have conceived this book as a demonstration as much as an essay in definition, seeking to show the kinds of work now in our view and some of the ways they can be approached. I have dwelt on some of the texts that have obsessed me over the years and that seemed particularly suggestive on issues of circulation, translation, and production. In the process, much as Eckermann gives us *his* Goethe, I have given you my world literature, or at least a representative cross-section of it, while recognizing that the world now presents us with material so varied as to call into question any logic of representation, any single framework that everyone should adopt and in which these particular works would all have a central role. A leading characteristic of world literature today is its variability: different readers will be obsessed by very different constellations of texts. While figures like Dante and Kafka retain a powerful canonical status, these authors function today less as a common patrimony than as rich nodes of overlap among many different and highly individual groupings.

Amid all this variety, family resemblances can be found among the different forms of world literature circulating today, emergent patterns that lead me to propose a threefold definition focused on the world, the text, and the reader:

1. *World literature is an elliptical refraction of national literatures.*
2. *World literature is writing that gains in translation.*
3. *World literature is not a set canon of texts but a mode of reading: a form of detached engagement with worlds beyond our own place and time.*

Each of these points merits discussion.

Elliptical refraction of national literatures. For the past half-century, world literature in its North American guises has usually been opposed to national literature. A genial disregard, if not outright hostility, often obtained between the devotees of the two. With most literature faculty based in departments organized along national lines, in many schools "world literature" was treated as an introductory course, suitable for beginning students but fundamentally vague in conception and unrigorous in application, a preliminary stage prior to serious work in a literature major based on close study of a culture and its language. Even the most elaborate comparative to scholarship often raised serious reservations among committed specialists. No less a book than Erich Auerbach's *Mimesis* (1946), probably the most ambitious and impressive synoptic study of its generation, was roundly criticized by reviewers based in one or another of the specific areas his book traversed. The classicist Ludwig Edelstein, for example, noted that Auerbach had dramatically foreshortened Greco-Roman literary history, ignoring the findings of classical scholarship to produce his stark contrast of Hebrew and Greek cultures, whereas "in the historical view, even the fifth century is not a unity" (431). Similarly, the medievalist Helmut Hatzfeld criticized Auerbach for reading the *Chanson de Roland* "with the eyes of an enlightened pacifist" rather than with an understanding of what the medieval author would have believed (335). Even René Wellek, in a review filled with faint praise, felt that Auerbach's results were "peculiarly shifting and disconcertingly vague" (305). *Mimesis* won this battle, but it lost the war. Widely admired and discussed to this day, it has had few, if any, successors: Auerbach's own students became specialists in a much more limited range of languages and eras.

Comparatists in the postwar era often returned the specialists' disregard, holding out messianic hopes for world literature as the cure for the ills of nationalistic separatism, jingoism, and internecine violence—and, by implication, advancing the comparatist as the transcendent heir to the narrowness of monolingual specialization. Comparative literature was to be the grand corrective for "the nationalistic heresy," as Albert Guérard put it in a lead article in the *Yearbook of Comparative and General Literature* in 1958. Looking ahead to European unification, Guérard anticipated that "Comparative Literature will disappear in its very victory; just as 'foreign trade' between France and Germany will disappear in the Common Market; just as the 'foreign relations' between these two countries will be absorbed by a common parliament" ("Comparative Literature?" 4). For Guérard, the overriding question in 1958 was "How and When Shall We Commit Suicide?" His answer: "Not just yet: we are needed so long as the nationalistic heresy has not been extirpated" (5).

We can no longer proceed as though this heresy is about to disappear. The European Parliament in Brussels is unlikely to supplant Europe's national governments during our lifetimes, and in an academic context the very great majority of teachers and scholars of literature continue to be located in nationally based departments. What does the ongoing vitality of national literary traditions mean for the study of world literature? An understanding of world literature as an elliptical refraction of national literatures can help to clarify the vital, yet also indirect, relation between the two. With the possible exception of a few irreducibly multinational works like *The Thousand and One Nights,* virtually all literary works are born within what we would now call a national literature. The modern nation is, of course, a relatively recent development, but even older works were produced in local or ethnic configurations that have been subsumed into the national traditions within which they are now preserved and transmitted. A "nation" itself, in early modern English, could designate an ethnic group or culture: in the King James Bible, "the nations" translates the Hebrew *ha-goyim,* the Septuagint's *hoi ethnoi.* Understanding the term "national" broadly, we can say that works continue to bear the marks of their national origin even after they circulate into world literature, and yet these traces are increasingly diffused and become ever more sharply refracted as a work travels farther from home.

This refraction, moreover, is double in nature: works become world literature by being received *into* the space of a foreign culture, a space defined in many ways by the host culture's national tradition and the present needs of its own writers. Even a single work of world literature is the locus of a negotiation between two different cultures. The receiving culture can use the foreign material in all sorts of ways: as a positive model for the future development of its own tradition; as a negative case of a primitive, or decadent, strand that must be avoided or rooted out at home; or, more neutrally, as an image of radical otherness against which the home tradition can more clearly be defined. World literature is thus always as much about the host culture's values and needs as it is about a work's source culture; hence it is a double refraction, one that can be described through the figure of the ellipse, with the source and host cultures providing the two foci that generate the elliptical space within which a work lives as world literature, connected to both cultures, circumscribed by neither alone.

I advance the image of an elliptical refraction as a convenient metaphor, but I don't mean to imply a scientific precision that the extremely varied phenomena of world literature would not support. For those who would prefer a more literary image, I might suggest the two-headed "pushmi-pullyu" from the Doctor Dolittle books. The pushmi-pullyu is an appropriately multicultural animal, related "to the Abyssinian gazelles and the Asiatic chamois, on my mother's side," as he tells the doctor, adding that "my father's great-grandfather was the last of the unicorns" (*The Story of Doctor Dolittle,* 76). He seems well suited for a multitemporal comparatism as well, as he has two ancient precursors: Janus, the Roman guardian of portals, whose two-headed image Hugh Lofting would certainly have known, and also an older, more exact analog that Lofting probably did not know: the Egyptian hieroglyph , determinative for the verb *khns,* , "to go in two directions at once."

Still, the pushmi-pullyu suggests a divided or splitting self that is at odds with the coming together from separate worlds that I take to be the essence of the circulation of texts into the ambient of world literature. A better image for this elliptical process might be what takes place around nine o'clock in the evening at Disneyland, when a crowd gathers along the shoreline of Rivers of America, seeking something more magical than the androidal simulacrum of Main Street, U.S.A. Street lights dim; music swells; then a sheet of water jets up from a phalanx of nozzles hidden in the sand out on Tom Sawyer's Island. From the opposite shore powerful beams of light shoot across the river and converge on the screen of mist, where they project a moving image: Mickey, the Sorcerer's Apprentice, introducing the evening's son-et-lumière extravaganza, formed in the shimmering conjunction of projected light and refracting water.

In literature proper, the complex process of elliptical refraction means that the circulation of world literature is much more than what René Wellek disparaged as merely "the foreign trade of literature" ("The Crisis of Comparative Literature," 283), and it doesn't lead to a transcendent universalism in which cultural difference is a mere "heresy" that should wither away as Marx and Engels expected the state to do. At the same time, recognizing the ongoing, vital presence of the national within the life of world literature poses enormous problems for the study of world literature. It is far from clear how to proceed if we want to broaden our focus beyond one or two periods or national traditions: who can really know enough to do it well? Bad enough that there are many more works of literature than anyone can read—must we really learn all about their home cultures too? The ellipse of world literature may seem comprehensible enough when we are thinking of only a single text or group of texts, but as we begin to look more widely we soon find ourselves amid a multitude of partially overlapping ellipses, all sharing one focus in the host culture but with their second foci distributed ever more widely across space and time.

The specter of amateurism haunts comparative literature today.

Lacking a deep knowledge of more than a very few cultures, are comparatists doomed either to stay within a limited range of material or else to succumb to the scholarly tourism I began by criticizing? Students of world literature increasingly experience what Djelal Kadir has described as "the simultaneously productive and melancholy precariousness of the comparatist's existence" ("Comparative Literature Hinternational," 245). The situation was very different when Auerbach and Wellek came to the United States: then it was supposed to be the *national* traditions that were in a precarious state, but this no longer seems to be the case. Much recent literary study has taken a dim view of nationalist ideologies and their imperial projections, and yet in an odd way the critique of nationalism has turned out to coexist quite comfortably with a continuing nationalism in academic practice. The more one needs to know, say, about the courts of Queen Elizabeth and King James I in order to understand Shakespeare, the less time one has available to learn much about the cultural underpinnings of French drama or Greek tragedy, and one tends to downplay the importance of what one doesn't know.

Moving beyond a regionally linked set of traditions becomes harder still. The more committed today's Shakespeareans become to understanding literature within cultural context, the less likely they are to feel comfortable in comparing Shakespeare and Kalidasa. Indeed, even within a single region a range of disparate literatures can seem too daunting to tackle. Several years ago I was on a search committee looking to hire a junior medievalist; one of the hottest topics we found among our applications was the dissection of the origins of nationalism in the medieval kingdoms that were struggling for mastery in the British Isles. The several writing samples on aspects of this theme all took a critical attitude toward the efforts of Anglo-Saxons and Anglo-Normans to promote themselves culturally and extend their sway politically, and yet none of the scholars who furnished these samples was doing any work in Irish or Welsh literature. Not on principle, surely, as the richness of both traditions in the medieval period is widely recognized: the medievalists simply hadn't had *time* to learn those languages along with everything else they were studying. Rather than include material they could read only in translation and without a close cultural knowledge, they left it out of account altogether. Yet works like the Irish *Táin* and the Welsh *Mabinogi* would be full of interest for explorations of cultural identity, while poets like Dafydd ap Gwilym have fascinating satirical things to say about Anglo-Saxons and Anglo-Normans alike. Deconstructing nationalism in theory, these medievalists had succumbed to it in practice.

How to do better? A logical but too rarely chosen way to study an extensive range of material is to work collaboratively, as Henry H. H. Remak already argued forty years ago in a pointed article called "Comparative Literature at the Crossroads: Diagnosis, Therapy and Prognosis." Even so great a scholar as Erich Auerbach lacked world enough and time for his European-based study of the representation of reality, but two or three people working together can collectively encompass more of the world than any one person can do. Collaborative work can help bridge the divide between amateurism and specialization, mitigating both the global generalist's besetting hubris and the national specialist's deeply ingrained caution.

There are encouraging signs of a growth in such work. For thirty years now the International Comparative Literature Association has been sponsoring an ambitious multivolume comparative literary history project, latterly headed by Mario Valdés of Toronto, each of whose volumes has been produced by national and regional specialists working in collaboration. World literature anthologies today are often the product of extended collegial interaction among a dozen or so broad-minded specialists, and all of us who have been working on such projects can testify to the intellectual excitement they entail. Team teaching is also more and more common both in world literature survey courses and in courses covering more focused cross-cultural topics. Yet it also has to be said that our graduate programs really have yet to begin to adapt to this shift. We essentially do nothing to encourage doctoral students to work together, still less to train them to work together well. While individual scholarship and teaching will always remain important, those who work on world literature are increasingly going to find that a significant share of their work is best done in collaboration with other people. Our graduate programs have some serious rethinking to do.

Equally, whether it is pursued individually or collaboratively, work on world literature should be acknowledged as *different in kind* from work within a national tradition, just as the works themselves manifest differently abroad than at home. This does not mean that we should simply ignore the local knowledge that specialists possess, as literary theorists of the past generation often did when developing their comprehensive theories (neither Northrop Frye in *Anatomy of Criticism* nor Roland Barthes in books like *S/Z* and *Sade, Fourier, Loyola* made any serious use at all of scholarship on the authors they chose as illustrations of their elegant conceptual schemes). A student of world literature has much to gain from an active engagement with specialized knowledge.

At the same time, though, this knowledge is best deployed selectively, with a kind of scholarly tact. When our purpose is not to delve into a culture in detail, the reader and even the work itself may benefit by being spared the full force of our local knowledge. The need for selectivity can be seen especially clearly in the case of works that come from a different era and from outside the usual norms of literary discourse, such as Mechthild's *Flowing Light of the Godhead.* Her book has acquired an extensive secondary literature, most of it written by specialists in medieval theology and church history. Much of what they have to say is only tangentially relevant to a literary analysis, particularly one focused not on Mechthild's relations to her precursors and contemporaries but on more general issues of gender or of poetics. Of course, Mechthild develops her poetics and expresses her gender position in part through her engagement with theologians like Bernard of Clairvaux and poets like Walther von der Vogelweide and Neidhard von Reuenthal, but for most purposes it's sufficient to demonstrate such relations at a few key points; not all of her known intertexts need to be elucidated.

While writing on Mechthild for this book, I several times had to resist digressing into discussions of Walther, Bernard, or Hildegard of Bingen. I finally felt that these digressions really weren't furthering the discussion so much as reflecting my own insecurity (the need to show specialists that I really had read these writers) or, worse yet, my vanity (the wish to impress my nonspecialist readers, who would probably not have been entranced in any event by displays of irrelevant erudition). While I did have good reasons to take direct account of Mechthild's treatment of the Virgin Mary, I said nothing about her Christology. A full contextual reading of her book would require extended treatment of all these aspects and more, but a comparative study is a much more selective enterprise.

Selective, but not merely reduced from the plenitude of full local knowledge. Intimately aware of a work's life at home, the specialist is not always in the best position to assess the dramatically different terms on which it may engage with a distant culture. Looking at such new contexts, the generalist will find that much of the specialist's information about the work's origins is no longer relevant and not only can but should be set aside. At the same time, any work that has not been wholly assimilated to its new context will still carry with it many elements that can best be understood by exploring why they came to be there in the first place. The specialist's knowledge is the major safeguard against the generalist's own will to power over texts that otherwise all too easily become grist for the mill of a preformed historical argument or theoretical system.

When I distinguish "specialists" from "generalists," I mean to characterize approaches as much as individuals. Just as a work can function either at home or abroad, so too any given person can be both a specialist in some areas and a generalist in others. When we are employing a generalist approach, we should not simply cast off our specialist selves—or our specialist colleagues. Generalists have much to learn from specialists, and should always try to build honestly, though selectively, on the specialists' understandings, ideally even inspiring the specialists to revise their understandings in turn. Too often, a generalist who alludes dismissively to the narrow-minded concerns of specialists merely ends up retailing a warmed-over version of what specialists had been saying a generation earlier. Instead, the generalist should feel the same ethical responsibility toward specialized scholarship that a translator has toward a text's original language: to understand the work effectively in its new cultural or theoretical context while at the same time *getting it right* in a fundamental way with reference to the source culture.

This brings us to my second point: *World literature is writing that gains in translation.* There is a significant difference between literary language and the various forms of ordinary, denotative language, whose meaning we take to be largely expressed as information. A text is read as literature if we dwell on the beauties of its language, its form, and its themes, and don't take it as primarily factual in intent; but the same text can cease to work as literature if a reader turns to it primarily to extract information from it, as when George Smith read *The Epic of Gilgamesh* to confirm the biblical history of the Flood, regretting that the account had been "disfigured by poetical adornments." Informational texts neither gain nor lose in a good translation: their meaning is simply carried over with little or no effective change. Treaties and contracts can be complex documents, but if well drafted and well translated, they are understandable to all parties concerned. They may be breached from the pressure of changing circumstances or through misinterpretations that apply to all the document's versions, but treaties rarely fail because of problems arising from translation per se.

At the other extreme, some works are so inextricably connected to their original language and moment that they really cannot be effectively translated at all. Purist views of literary language often take all poetry as "what is lost in translation," in Robert Frost's famous phrase, since whatever meaning a new language can convey is irretrievably sundered from the verbal music of the original. "A poem should not mean / But be," as Archibald Macleish wrote in 1926 in his "Ars Poetica," in lines that convey their own declarative meaning with surprising success.[1] Much poetry, including Frost's

[1] *Collected Poems,* 107. Frost and Macleish alike are rejecting elaborate interpretations,

and Macleish's, has been translated with great effect into many languages. It is more accurate to say that *some* works are not translatable without substantial loss, and so they remain largely within their local or national context, never achieving an effective life as world literature.

It is important to recognize that the question of translatability is distinct from questions of value. A work can hold a prominent place within its own culture but read poorly elsewhere, either because its language doesn't translate well or because its cultural assumptions don't travel. Snorri Sturluson's dynastic saga *Heimskringla* is a major document in medieval Nordic culture, but it only makes compelling reading if you are fairly knowledgeable about the political history of Norway and Iceland, and it remains unknown abroad outside specialist circles. By contrast, Norse mythological texts like the Elder Edda and Snorri's own *Prose Edda* have been widely translated and much appreciated. They are actually harder to understand than the *Heimskringla*, but they treat themes of broad interest in striking, if often mysterious, language. Equally, a work's viability as world literature has little to do with its author's perspective on the world. There can be no more global work, conceptually speaking, than *Finnegans Wake,* yet its prose is so intricate and irreproducible that it becomes a sort of curiosity in translation. *Dubliners,* a far more localized work, has been much more widely translated and has had a far greater impact in other languages.

Literary language is thus language that either gains *or* loses in translation, in contrast to nonliterary language, which typically does neither. The balance of credit and loss remains a distinguishing mark of national versus world literature: literature stays within its national or regional tradition when it usually loses in translation, whereas works become world literature when they gain on balance in translation, stylistic losses offset by an expansion in depth as they increase their range, as is the case with such widely disparate works as *The Epic of Gilgamesh* and *Dictionary of the Khazars.* It follows from this that the study of world literature should embrace translation far more actively than it has usually done to date. This is not to argue, though, for a return to the kind of ungrounded cosmopolitanism seen a century ago in world literature collections. Too many world literature courses have tended to assume that undergraduate courses should be the last refuge

---

as well as translations, of their immutable, self-identical poems. When Frost told Louis Untermeyer that poetry is what is lost in translation, he was dismissing critical efforts to unfold the implicit meanings of his poem "Stopping by Woods on a Snowy Evening." As he told Untermeyer, "You've heard me say—perhaps too often—that poetry is what is lost in translation. It is also what is lost in interpretation. That little poem means just what it says it means, nothing less but nothing more" (Untermeyer, *Robert Frost: A Backward Look,* 18).

for a high-minded amateurism, a busman's holiday from any real engagement with the works' cultures of origin. Committed teachers of world literature are increasingly finding ways to give students access to cultural context, via corollary readings and through collaborative student explorations of websites and print resources. At the opposite end of the university spectrum, scholars have often feared to touch a work in translation at all as they develop critical analyses for publication. In her article on *Dictionary of the Khazars,* N. Katherine Hayles notes with regret that few people outside Slavic studies have ever written about Pavić, and she urges more to do so, even if they don't know Serbo-Croatian. Admirable as this plea is, it is regrettable that Hayles took her own ignorance of the original language as a license to ignore the book's cultural context outright, even though much information about that context is available in English.

The fullest response to this problem would, of course, include learning more languages. Only a very few foreign languages are presently studied in North America for general academic purposes: French, German, Spanish, and Latin about exhaust the list. Most of the world's other languages are only learned by native speakers or by specialists in a given area: even world languages like Chinese and Arabic are mastered mostly by Sinologists and Arabists, while less commonly spoken languages like Irish or Serbo-Croatian are taught only in a handful of small programs and are studied almost exclusively by people who want to connect to their ethnic roots or who plan to specialize in the area. This situation needs to change. Just as the literary canon has opened up and become less unified, there is no longer a set canon of languages that any educated comparatist ought to know. Twenty-five years ago, it is safe to say that the true mark of a serious comparatist, prior to any substantive knowledge, was a really good *accent* in three major Continental languages. There is little logic now in requiring a common set of languages for all students, and very good reasons to encourage all students to develop a serious knowledge of at least one culture beyond their own. The learning of languages provides a crucial mode of access to other cultures, the best way to ensure that the student will become more than a cultural ecotourist. Indeed, there is much to be said for everyone involved with world literature, students and faculty alike, to see language study as an ongoing activity. Language study should not be a preliminary to literary study but a partner for life: a powerful stimulus to learning a language can be to fall in love with its literature in translation, and such encounters can happen at any time.

Even with a major improvement in the breadth of language study, and even with a substantial increase in collaborative projects, it will be necessary to make active scholarly use of translation if we are not to continue cutting our topics down to the size of whatever linguistic bed is available to us at a given moment. Understanding world literature as writing that gains in translation can help us to embrace this fact of contemporary intellectual life and to use translations well, with a productively critical engagement.

It is only possible to engage critically with works in translation if we can allow that literary meaning exists on many levels of a work. Translation can never really succeed if a work's meaning is taken to reside essentially in the local verbal texture of its original phrasing. José Ortega y Gasset gave a classic expression to this view in his 1937 dialogue "The Misery and the Splendor of Translation"—an essay that, in its reference to Balzac's novel *Splendeurs et misères des courtisanes,* links translation with prostitution. Ortega y Gasset began from the assumption that style is everything in a literary work, and he had a modernist's view that a writer's style is achieved precisely by its difference from all other styles, just as languages are defined by their difference from all other languages:

> An author's personal style, for example, is produced by his slight deviation from the habitual meaning of the word. The author forces it to an extraordinary usage so that the circle of objects it designates will not coincide exactly with the circle of objects which that same word customarily means in its habitual use. The general trend of these deviations in a writer is what we call his style. But, in fact, each language compared to any other also has its own linguistic style. . . . Since languages are formed in different landscapes, through different experiences, their incongruity is natural. It is false, for example, to suppose that the thing the Spaniard calls a *bosque* the German calls a *Wald,* yet the dictionary tells us that *Wald* means *bosque.* . . . an enormous difference exists between the two realities. It is so great that not only are they exceedingly incongruous, but almost all their resonances, both emotive and intellectual, are equally so. (51)

A silence ensues after the dialogue's lead figure makes this claim, and one of his interlocutors comments that "this silence that has risen among us has a funereal character. You have murdered translation, and we are sullenly following along for the burial" (52). Ortega y Gasset's narrator replies that he really means to present translation as the emblem of the noble futility of all human endeavors, but this is a resolution that takes away as much as it gives.

Ortega y Gasset's stark view of language reflects a modernist emphasis on radically isolated individuals. "What have I in common with

Jews?" Kafka famously asked himself in a mood of dark irony. "I have hardly anything in common with myself" (*Diaries,* 252). At the extreme, from this point of view even a single language may disintegrate within the fragmented consciousness of a single user, and different speakers of the same language are doomed to mean different things with every word they say. For someone who grew up in Maine, as I did, the term "forest" includes many more evergreens than it would for people raised in Maryland, and many fewer eucalyptus trees than for a southern Californian. Yet such idiosyncratic differences are not eternally given and insurmountable: two friends from different countries could take a walk together in what one of them would call a *Wald* and the other a *bosque,* but they would both be referring to precisely the same surroundings. The modernists surely exaggerated the extent of stylistic novelty in literature: even a distinctive voice will usually ring a marked but finite series of changes on a common literary language.

It is often said that quite apart from individual innovation, literary language is particularly hard to translate since so much of the meaning depends on culture-specific patterns of connotation and nuance. Yet one could equally make a very different argument: after all, literature is often distinguished from film and television by the fact that the reader is *required* to fill in the scene, which is not given outright as it is on the screen. As Wolfgang Iser argued in *The Act of Reading,* literary narratives work less by communicating fixed information than by creating suggestive gaps that the reader must fill in. Iser further emphasized (against Roman Ingarden) that different readers will necessarily, and productively, fill in these gaps in different ways.

What is true of any literary work is doubly true of world literature. A book read in one language and within one cultural context presents a situation in which, as Iser says, readers will differ but "the text itself cannot change" and exerts a powerful limiting force on the variability of readerly response (167). Traveling abroad, though, a text does indeed change, both in its frame of reference and usually in language as well. In an excellent translation, the result is not the loss of an unmediated original vision but instead a *heightening* of the naturally creative interaction of reader and text. In this respect a poem or novel can be seen to achieve its lasting effect precisely by virtue of its adaptability to our private experience. Readers in Seville and in Berlin may well cover Thomas Mann's magic mountain with rather different flora, but so may two different readers in Berlin itself, just as different readers will likely visualize our Egyptian poem's tunic differently and would continue to do so even if all translators made a common pact to call it an overcoat or a *ghalabiyah.* Far from being short-circuited in translations from *Wald* to *bosque* or from New England to New Mexico, literary meaning gains its full resonance when it is completed according to the reader's individual imagination and circumstances.

Of course, some elements of a literary work are more freely variable than others, and a large part of a translator's interpretive responsibility lies in determining which particular patterns of sound, imagery, or implication are important to carry over as directly as possible. Yet even elements that cannot be directly reproduced in the new language can often be conveyed at a different level of the text. Some of Kafka's self-deconstructing sentences really can't be rendered in English without a substantial loss of ironic play, and yet the irony we label "Kafkaesque" is fully conveyed at the levels of the paragraph and of the scene, even if not always at the level of the individual sentence.

Acutely aware of the difficulties entailed in translation at the level of the word and the phrase, translation theorists have sometimes gone so far as to see the essence of language itself as entailing a basic incommunicability. Thus George Steiner argued in *After Babel* that human societies have multiplied languages not so much to communicate as to *conceal* their secrets and maintain their individual identities against the surrounding world:

> I am suggesting that the outwardly communicative, extrovert
> thrust of language is secondary. . . . The primary drive is inward
> and domestic. Each tongue hoards the resources of consciousness,
> the world-pictures of the clan. . . . a language builds a wall
> around the "middle kingdom" of the group's identity. It is secret
> towards the outsider and inventive of its own world. There have
> been so many thousands of human tongues, there still are,
> because there have been, particularly in the archaic stages of
> social history, so many distinct groups intent on keeping from
> one another the inherited, singular springs of their identity, and
> engaged in creating their own semantic worlds, their "alternities."
> (231–32)

Such a view might seem to make translation impossible, but Steiner offers us a qualified hope: the abyss between languages can indeed be overcome, but it takes a heroic interpretive leap to do so. It takes, in fact, Steiner himself. He proposes an intense focus on style, on the historical and cultural resonances of individual words, producing readings that are often exhilarating but that also begin to edge over into bibliomania:

> No semantic form is timeless. When using a word we wake into
> resonance, as it were, its entire previous history. . . . To read fully

is to restore all that one can of the immediacies of value and intent in which speech actually occurs. There are tools for the job. A true reader is a dictionary addict. . . . Without such quarries as Champion's *L'Argot ancien* and Eric Partridge's lexica of underworld usage, much of Western literature, from Villon to Genet, is only partly legible. . . . A demanding reader of mid-eighteenth-century verse will often find himself referring to the Royal Horticultural Society's *Dictionary of Gardening*. (24)

You will note the silent shift by which "a true reader" becomes "a *demanding* reader."[2] Steiner's book crystallizes the moment of the apotheosis of close reading in the midseventies, reinforced by hermeneutic theory, when the greatness of a work could be measured by its ability to retain its power even after a barrage of critical assaults: "only great art both solicits and withstands exhaustive or willful interpretation" (27).

Steiner's approach involves a politics as well as a hermeneutics. In his theory the work of art becomes a stand-in for the individual who stubbornly resists the seductions of sociability:

There can hardly be an awakened human being who has not, at some moment, been exasperated by the "publicity" of language, who has not experienced an almost bodily discomfort at the disparity between the uniqueness, the novelty of his own emotions and the worn coinage of words. It is almost intolerable that needs, affections, hatreds, introspections which we feel to be overwhelmingly our own, which shape our awareness of identity and the world, should have to be voiced—even and most absurdly when we speak to ourselves—in the vulgate. Intimate, unprecedented as is our thirst, the cup has long been on other lips. (175)

Steiner goes so far as to see this realization as a psychic trauma we encounter early in life: "One can only conjecture," he soberly concludes, "as to the blow which this discovery must be to the child's psyche" (175). Steiner here echoes Jacques Lacan in seeing language as a form of crystallized alienation, and

---

[2] Steiner's scholarly demands may even surpass those of actual specialists in the period. Intrigued by his somewhat implausible evocation of the Royal Horticultural Society's dictionary, I surveyed four eighteenth-century specialists whose work I particularly admire: April Alliston, Jenny Davidson, Stuart Sherman, and my brother Leo Damrosch. I asked them how often they found themselves consulting the *Dictionary of Gardening*, offering the options of "often," "occasionally," "rarely," and "never." All four opted for "never."

Steiner's world-weary child is closely related to the antiheroes of Lacan's "mirror stage," toddlers distraught at the revelation that the entire world is not simply a projection of their own ego.

Too bad, toddlers: you *do* belong to a wider society, and if you grow up to become professors you can never master even a local field so fully as to be free from reliance on a range of other specialists who know things you don't, including other languages. To use translations means to accept the reality that texts come to us mediated by existing frameworks of reception and interpretation. We necessarily work in collaboration with others who have shaped what we read and how we read it. Indeed, any works written in an earlier period in our own country reach us in much the same way that Walter Benjamin describes translation itself: "a translation issues from the original—not so much from its life as from its afterlife. For a translation comes later than the original, and since the important works of world literature never find their chosen translators at the time of their origin, their translation marks their stage of continued life" ("The Task of the Translator," 71). A specialist equipped with ample research materials can do much to approximate a return to the world in which an old or foreign poem was composed. The generalist, concerned with the poem's worldly afterlife, doesn't have that luxury, or even that necessity.

Its relative freedom from context does not require the work of world literature to be subjected to anything like an absolute disconnect from its culture of origin. Anyone involved in translating or teaching works from other cultures must always weigh how much cultural information is needed and how it should be presented. One healthy consequence of the increasing acknowledgment that a translation *is* a translation has been a greater openness in providing contextual information. Often in the past, translators gave no such information at all, or folded it silently into the translation itself so as to preserve the seeming purity of the text—though in reality they had to distort the text in order to avoid disrupting a supposedly direct encounter of reader and work. Especially when the text in question was both old and foreign, translations were forced either to become very loose paraphrases (Burton's *Arabian Nights*) or to assimilate closely to host-country norms (Edward Fitzgerald's *Rubáiyat of Omar Kháyyâm*).[3] Scholarly readers, by contrast, would be given heavily annotated bilingual editions, full of cultural information but with the translation often only marginally readable.

[3] Fitzgerald was quite open about his assimilative program. As he wrote to a friend in 1857, "it is an amusement to me to take what liberties I like with these Persians, who, (as I think) are not Poets enough to frighten one from such excursions and who really do want a little Art to shape them" (quoted in Bassnett, *Comparative Literature,* 18).

This either/or choice is increasingly breaking down. Arthur Waley's classic translation of *The Tale of Genji* bathed the story in the warm glow of an Edwardian prose; in the process, he also suppressed what he apparently regarded as the disruptive effect of the hundreds of poems scattered through the text, deleting most and translating the remainder as prose. Waley also freely paraphrased and expanded passages in order to insert clarifying information for the Western reader. Even his assimilative translation, though, employed footnotes to explain literary and cultural references that couldn't readily be folded into the text itself. Fifty years later, Edward Seidensticker's 1976 translation gave a far more literal (and far less Edwardian) translation, openly setting the text's poems as poetry. Seidensticker also went further than Waley in framing his translation, with an extensive introduction (more than twice the length of Waley's) and with fuller literary references in his footnotes. In his introduction, Seidensticker notes that he had written many more notes than appear in the published translation; his editor at Knopf pressed him to prune them back substantially, evidently fearing that full annotations would put off the general readers for whom the translation was intended, and so the net result is only a small increase over Waley's level of annotation.

The *Genji* has recently been translated once again, by Royall Tyler (2001). Though this translation too is clearly intended for a general audience, Viking has allowed Tyler about three times as many footnotes as Seidensticker was permitted twenty-five years before; many pages have six or more footnotes, offering a stream of cultural information that at once emphasizes the text's foreignness and supplies information to bridge the distances between Japanese and English, medieval and modern worlds. Tyler's translation also concludes with more than fifty pages of explanatory back matter, including maps, house diagrams, and extensive glossaries, not only of names but also of colors, clothing, titles, and offices, all elements that have intricate vocabularies in Japanese which can only be partially suggested in English. The new translation has been widely reviewed in the general press, and the reviewers have specifically praised the wealth of annotation along with the eloquence of the prose.

As André Lefevere has written, a direct presentation of cultural context is often essential if we are to avoid an assimilation to our own norms, and this requires us as readers to accept the translation's mediating role:

> When we no longer translate Chinese T'ang poetry "as if" it were Imagist blank verse, which it manifestly is not, we shall be able to begin to understand T'ang poetry on its own terms. This means,

however, that we shall have to tell the readers of our translations what T'ang poetry is really like, by means of introductions, the detailed analysis of selected texts, and such. We shall, therefore, have to learn to skip the leap we often call "of the imagination" but which could be much more aptly called "of imperialism." The question is whether Western cultures are ready for this. ("Composing the Other," 78)

The sequence of *Genji* translations indicates that more and more readers are indeed becoming ready for just this sort of contextual framing.

At the same time, when we read in the elliptical space of world literature, we don't exactly understand the foreign work "on its own terms," and a leap of the imagination is still needed. Intended for readers of world literature, Royall Tyler's new *Genji* translation still presents much less contextual information than specialists possess. To read scholarly studies, such as Ivan Morris's *The World of the Shining Prince* or Haruo Shirane's *The Bridge of Dreams: A Poetics of "The Tale of Genji,"* is to be introduced to a wealth of historical and intertextual information that far surpasses anything dreamed of even in Lefevere's philosophy of translation. Yet to read Shirane, or to go further and read the older romances and poetry collections that Murasaki Shikibu was raised on, is to take a significant step in following the *Genji* back into its home culture. An endlessly rewarding and fascinating pursuit—but it is an approach that shifts one's understanding into the realm of Japanese literature. By contrast, when we read the *Genji* as world literature, we are fundamentally translating it out of its home culture and into a new and broader context. We can make this translation far more effectively if we attend to the insights that specialists possess, but we will use this information selectively and for different purposes. Whereas the specialist attempts to enter as fully as possible into the source culture, the student of world literature stands outside, very much as Benjamin describes translation itself standing outside a work's original language, facing a wooded ridge that each of us will forest with our own favorite trees: "Unlike a work of literature, translation does not find itself in the center of the language forest but on the outside facing the wooded ridge; it calls into it without entering, aiming at that single spot where the echo is able to give, in its own language, the reverberation of the work in the alien one" (76).

And so to the final part of my definition of world literature: *not a set canon of texts but a mode of reading, a detached engagement with a world beyond our own.* At any given time, a fluctuating number of foreign works will circulate actively within a culture, and a subset of these will be widely shared and enjoy a canonical status, but different groups within a society, and different individuals within any group, will create distinctive congeries of works, blending canonical and noncanonical works into effective microcanons. As Bruce Robbins says of a locally inflected cosmopolitanism, it involves not an ideal detachment but "a reality of (re)attachment, multiple attachment, or attachment at a distance" (*Cosmopolitics,* 3). World literature's attachments are multiplied by the fact that it is at once a collective and an individual phenomenon. A large and multilayered group of foreign works that circulate in a given culture, it is also experienced as a private pleasure by individual readers, in ways that may diverge dramatically from the social goals that usually underlie the defining and formal transmission of a literary heritage. The texts themselves exist both together and alone: when we read Dante, we are aware that we are encountering a major work of world literature, one that draws on a wealth of previous writing and that casts its shadow ahead onto much that will follow it. Yet even as we register such connections, we are also immersed within Dante's singular world, an imagined universe very unlike any envisioned by Virgil or by Saint Paul, and one that Milton, Gogol, and Walcott will radically revise in turn for very different purposes of their own.

The individual text's appeal is beautifully expressed by James Joyce in the lines that form the second epigraph to this book: "(Stoop) if you are abcedminded, to this claybook, what curios of signs (please stoop), in this allaphbed! Can you rede (since We and Thou had it out already) its world?" (*Finnegans Wake,* 184). We forget ourselves in reading (the double sense of "abcedminded"); like Hormuzd Rassam and George Smith striving to decipher the signs on a clay tablet they've gotten out of the ground, we enter into a multiple relation with the work, as Joyce suggests by having us "rede" its world. We read but also enter actively into dialogue with the work (German, *reden:* "to converse"), almost as though we ourselves were writing it with a reed pen.

The great conversation of world literature takes place on two very different levels: among authors who know and react to one another's work, and in the mind of the reader, where works meet and interact in ways that may have little to do with cultural and historical proximity. Someone who reads *Swann's Way* and *The Tale of Genji* together is likely to find them resonating in multiple and profound ways, engaging one another at least as closely as a reader who is attentive to national traditions will find Proust engaging with Balzac, or the *Genji* with *The Tale of the Heike.* World literature is fully in play once several foreign works begin to resonate together in our mind. This provides a further solution to the comparatist's lurking panic:

world literature is not an immense body of material that must somehow, impossibly, be mastered; it is a mode of reading that can be experienced *intensively* with a few works just as effectively as it can be explored *extensively* with a large number.

Auerbach's great book would not have been much improved if he had added further chapters of the sort he wished he'd had world enough and time to write: a chapter on Apollonius Rhodius, to show Hellenistic fiction in greater depth; a full chapter on Proust, now rather awkwardly shoehorned in as an aside to his chapter on Woolf, to give a more rounded account of modernism. Such additions would of course have added something to his argument, but the book is already long enough at 557 pages. He might have gained more if he had *cut* some chapters: if he had discussed a dozen works, rather than twenty, and made active use of the scholarship of those who were spending their lives on the individual periods and cultures he was passing through.

As in scholarship, so in teaching. Anthologies have been growing larger and larger, as teachers and publishers have sought to encompass our ever-expanding canon. When we are presenting a single national tradition, there is still a logic to giving some sense of most of the currently acknowledged major authors, particularly as time and space generally allow the inclusion of a range of less-known figures as well. The task becomes impossible with any truly global vision of world literature, and other approaches are plainly needed. At a minimum, it takes three points to define a plane surface, and perhaps three works, interestingly juxtaposed and studied with care, can define a literary field. *Antigone, Shakuntala,* and *Twelfth Night* can together open up a world of dramatic possibility. *The Tale of Genji* can profitably be read, as I have suggested, along with Proust's *Swann's Way.* There is no evidence that Proust had read Murasaki, though his book does reflect the French *japonaiserie* of his day, but if we want a direct link between the books we could add in Yukio Mishima's *Spring Snow,* which rewrites and subverts both Murasaki and Proust together.

Murasaki could also be seen, to very different effect, in a story-telling context, in combination, say, with *The Thousand and One Nights* and Boccaccio's *Decameron.* Or her book could be used to discuss gender issues in connection with Christine de Pizan's *Book of the City of Ladies* and Gottfried's *Tristan.* Or again, a culturally based comparison could discuss the evolution of women's writing in court cultures, centering on the *Genji* and on Madame de Lafayette's *La Princesse de Clèves.* A comparison of this sort would provide a logical frame for a cluster of several related works around each of the major texts. Along with the *Genji* we could read classic poems from the early collections the *Man'yōshū* and the *Kokinshū*, and we could also include Sei Shōnagon's *Pillow Book*, together with the *Sarashina Diary*, written several decades later by a woman who believed she was a virtual reincarnation of Murasaki herself. *La Princesse de Clèves* could similarly be framed with selections from the memoirs of La Rochefoucauld and from the letters of Madame de Sévigné.

The effect of any of these combinations is very different from what we gain from a semester devoted to medieval Japan or to seventeenth-century France, and it is even different from the net effect of a semester on Japan followed by a semester on France. Immersion in a single culture represents a mode of relatively direct engagement with it, aptly symbolized by efforts to acquire "near-native fluency" in the culture's language. Reading and studying world literature, by contrast, is inherently a more detached mode of engagement; it enters into a different kind of dialogue with the work, not one involving identification or mastery but the discipline of distance and of difference. We encounter the work not at the heart of its source culture but in the field of force generated among works that may come from very different cultures and eras.

This elliptical relation already characterizes our experience of a foreign national tradition, but there is likely to be a significant difference of degree, both because the ellipses multiply and because the angle of refraction increases. Works of world literature interact in a charged field defined by a fluid and multiple set of possibilities of juxtaposition and combination: "intercourse in every direction," in Marx and Engels's apt phrase. As we triangulate between our own present situation and the enormous variety of other cultures around and before us, we won't see works of world literature so fully enshrined within their cultural context as we do when reading those works within their own traditions, but a degree of distance from the home tradition can help us to appreciate the ways in which a literary work reaches out and away from its point of origin. If we then observe ourselves seeing the work's abstraction from its origins, we gain a new vantage point on our own moment. The result may be almost the opposite of the "fusion of horizons" that Friedrich Schleiermacher envisioned when we encounter a distant text; we may actually experience our customary horizon being set askew, under the influence of works whose foreignness remains fully in view.

My concluding image is meant to illustrate this point (p. 280, figure 12). Like a work of world literature, this image can be seen emblematically or with attention to its historical context, a history located neither in the present nor in ancient Egypt. As an emblem, it serves here to suggest the opening up of the world of world literature: what was once largely a European and male preserve, bounded historically as well as geographically, has become a far broader and less familiar terrain. So we have the European men trying to take the measure of a figure that is African, and feminine in appearance, and far more ancient than the antiquity of Greece. The Great Sphinx at Giza, at the time of this etching still buried to the shoulders in sand, puzzles her European interlocutors much as her literary counterpart, brought to life two and a half millennia ago by Sophocles, challenged Oedipus to solve the riddle of human identity.[4]

So far, so good; but we can historicize our image as well. The gentlemen with their plumb line and sketchbook are four of the scientists whom Napoleon brought with him in 1798 when he made his ill-fated attempt to conquer Egypt; this picture was sketched on the spot by one of the expedition's artists, Baron Dominique Vivant Denon, a diplomat, playwright, and painter. In the long history of European conquest, there can have been few invasions so futile in military and political terms. Napoleon's chief purpose in invading Egypt was to strike a blow against England's growing imperial reach: his hope was to begin dismantling the Ottoman Empire before the British could accomplish the task, and ultimately to subdue England itself. "The road to London passes through Egypt," as he declared (Siliotti, *Egypt Lost and Found*, 83). He set out from Toulon in May 1798 with over three hundred ships, manned by ten thousand sailors and carrying thirty-five thousand troops. He and his forces quickly took Alexandria and headed to Cairo, where they drove out the Ottoman general Murad Bey.

But things soon started to go badly for the French. In August 1798 the British navy, commanded by Horatio Nelson, destroyed the French fleet at Alexandria, leaving Napoleon's army virtual prisoners in their newly conquered country. Napoleon sent his brilliant young general Desaix up the Nile to pursue Murad Bey; in a series of bloody battles, Desaix gained control of most of Upper Egypt. Meanwhile a series of violent uprisings in Cairo were launched by Egyptians who were finding the French to be worse oppressors than their Ottoman predecessors. Other battles ensued against an allied army of the Ottomans and the British. By the time he had been in Egypt a year, Napoleon had lost half his army to warfare and plague. He managed to hold on by winning a major battle at Aboukir in July 1799, al-

---

[4] Perhaps under the influence of Greek tradition, in which sphinxes were female, Denon portrayed the Great Sphinx as looking like a Nubian princess, rather than with the markedly masculine features that other artists more accurately conveyed. In his narrative, Denon describes the Sphinx's expression as "douce, gracieuse, et tranquille" and praises the softness of the lips (*Voyage*, 109); all in all, it seems most appropriate to refer to Denon's version of the Sphinx as female.

beit at the cost of thousands of lives, but French defeats in Europe forced him to return to France, sailing secretly out of Egypt so as to avoid the British blockade. Several months later Desaix also returned to Europe, where he was killed in the Battle of Marengo in June 1800. By an odd coincidence, General Jean-Baptiste Kléber, Napoleon's commander in Egypt, was assassinated on the very day that Desaix died, two thousand miles away in Italy.

Napoleon's remaining Egyptian forces eked out several more bloody victories against local and foreign opposition, but then in March 1801 the French were soundly defeated by the British. Shortly before being killed in this climactic battle, Major General Lanusse declared to his commander, Jacques-François de Bussay de Menou, "A man like you should never have commanded the French army. You are not capable of running the kitchens of the Republic" (Siliotti, 87). Three months later the remaining French surrendered to the English, who gave them passage out of the country and assumed control. Napoleon's invasion had cost some twenty thousand lives of his own troops, and took an even greater toll on the Egyptians he was nominally liberating. Far from reducing British power, moreover, the whole sad sequence of events only increased it.

The only thing of any real value to emerge from this misguided adventure was the work of Napoleon's committee of 167 scientists, and the voyage was fatal even for many of them: thirty-two of them died during the course of the expedition, from wounds or from disease. The survivors set about surveying and studying Egypt and its ancient monuments, and their work was crowned by the completely unexpected discovery of the Rosetta stone. Two decades later, Champollion's decipherment of its hieroglyphs laid the groundwork for the recovery of the language, the history, and the literature of ancient Egypt. The excitement surrounding these discoveries in turn inspired Henry Rawlinson to seek out and decipher the cuneiform inscriptions at Bihistun and led to the subsequent recovery of *Gilgamesh* and the literatures of the several major ancient Near Eastern cultures now known to us.

Vivant Denon was the first to stimulate wide public interest in the scientific study of the ancient Near East; his lavishly illustrated account of his journey up the Nile with Desaix became a European best-seller when it was published in 1802 as *Voyage dans la Basse et la Haute Égypte pendant les campagnes du Général Bonaparte*. Denon dedicated his great work to Napoleon, praising him as a worthy heir to the greatest of the pharaohs of old:

> To combine the lustre of your name with the splendor of the
> monuments of Egypt, is to associate the glorious annals of our

own age with the fabulous epochs of antiquity; and to reanimate the dust of Sesostris and Mendes, who like you were conquerors, and like you benefactors. All Europe, on learning that I accompanied you in one of your most memorable expeditions, will receive my work with eagerness and interest. I have neglected nothing in my power to render it worthy of the Hero to whom it is inscribed. (*Voyage*, 31)

The story of Napoleon's ill-fated expedition involves far more loss of life than reanimation. Yet Denon and his colleagues inaugurated the recovery of long-lost artworks and writings that do, in a fashion, reanimate monarchs like the great Twelfth-Dynasty kings Senwosret I–III, known to Denon only from Herodotus's account, a millennium and a half after the fact, of a single figure vaguely remembered as "Sesostris."

The French failed to dominate the Egyptian culture that Napoleon tried to reorganize along French lines, and they didn't even retain possession of the portable antiquities they unearthed, which the victorious English commandeered: the British Museum got the Rosetta stone. Conquest failed, and there now seems something grimly fatuous about Denon's identification of Napoleon with Sesostris—or Napoleon's own self-identification with Alexander the Great, whose footsteps he felt he was following to the Alexandria founded by his conquering predecessor. Master of his destiny during this period in Europe, Napoleon was out of his depth in the sands of Egypt. Yet his fascination with Egyptian antiquity was sincere: "Men," he told his army before the pyramids of Giza, "from the top of these monuments forty centuries are gazing down on you!" (Siliotti, 83). A more detached engagement, though, would have been better all round, a genuinely revivifying encounter such as we can now have when we seek pleasure and enlightenment rather than a possessive mastery of the world's cultural productions. The gentlemen of Napoleon's "Commission des Arts et des Sciences" failed to take the Sphinx's true measure, though we can see them trying literally to get into her head. The Sphinx turns out not to have the direct conversational interests that Sophocles gave her. In Denon's engraving she raises her eyes, parting her lips as if to speak, but not to question the ephemeral mortals, whose presence she ignores; she greets Amun Re, Lord of the Two Lands, who rises at dawn without fail, perfect each day, to shine in power on his eternal kingdom.

BIBLIOGRAPHY

Abu-Lughod, Janet. "Going Beyond Global Babble." In King, *Culture, Globalization and the World-System,* 131–37.

Aldridge, A. Owen. *The Reemergence of World Literature: A Study of Asia and the West.* London and Toronto: Associated University Presses, 1986.

Ali, Tariq. "Literature and Market Realism." *New Left Review* 199 (1993): 140–45.

Amireh, Amal, and Lisa Suhair Majaj, eds. *Going Global: The Transnational Reception of Third World Women Writers.* New York: Garland, 2002.

Anderson, Mark. *Kafka's Clothes: Ornament and Aestheticism in the Habsburg Fin de Siècle.* Oxford: Clarendon, 1992.

———, ed. *Reading Kafka: Prague, Politics, and the Fin de Siècle.* New York: Schocken, 1989.

Appiah, K. Anthony. "Cosmopolitan Reading." In Dharwadker, *Cosmopolitan Geographies,* 197–227.

Apter, Emily. *Continental Drift: From National Characters to Virtual Subjects.* Chicago: University of Chicago Press, 1999.

Apuleius. *Metamorphoses.* Tr. J. Arthur Hanson. 2 vols. Loeb Classical Library, 1989.

Arias, Arturo. "Authorizing Ethnicized Subjects: Rigoberta Menchú and the Performative Production of the Subaltern Self." *PMLA* 116.1 (2001): 75–88.

———, ed. *The Rigoberta Menchú Controversy.* Minneapolis: University of Minnesota Press, 2001.

Asad, Talal. "A Comment on Translation, Critique, and Subversion." In Dingwaney and Maier, *Between Languages and Cultures,* 325–32.

Auerbach, Erich. *Mimesis: The Representation of Reality in Western Literature.* Tr. Willard R. Trask. Princeton: Princeton University Press, 1953.

Barnstone, Willis, and Tony Barnstone, eds. *Literatures of Asia, Africa, and Latin America.* Upper Saddle River, N.J.: Prentice-Hall, 1999.

Barthes, Roland. *Roland Barthes by Roland Barthes.* Tr. Richard Howard. New York: Hill and Wang, 1977.

Bassnett, Susan. *Comparative Literature: A Critical Introduction.* Oxford: Blackwell, 1993.

———. *Translation Studies.* Rev. ed. London: Routledge, 1991.

Bassnett, Susan, and Harish Trivedi, eds. *Post-Colonial Translation: Theory and Practice.* London: Routledge, 1999.

Bei Dao. *At the Sky's Edge: Poems 1991–1996*. Tr. David Hinton. New York: New Directions, 1996.

_____. *The August Sleepwalker: Poetry*. Tr. Bonnie S. McDougall. New York: New Directions, 1988.

Benjamin, Walter. "The Task of the Translator." In *Illuminations*, ed. Hannah Arendt, tr. Harry Zohn, 69–82. New York: Schocken, 1969. Repr. in Venuti, *The Translation Studies Reader*, 15–23.

Bernheimer, Charles, ed. *Comparative Literature in the Age of Multiculturalism*. Baltimore: Johns Hopkins University Press, 1995.

Bernard of Clairvaux. *Sermons on the Song of Songs*. Vols. 2–5 of *The Works of Bernard of Clairvaux*. Tr. Kilian Walsh and Irene Edmonds. Spencer, Mass.: Cistercian Publications, 1971–80.

Beverley, John. "Second Thoughts on Testimonio." In *Against Literature*, 87–99. Minneapolis: University of Minnesota Press, 1993.

Beverley, John, and Marc Zimmerman. *Literature and Politics in the Central American Revolutions*. Austin: University of Texas Press, 1990.

Bierhorst, John, ed. and tr. *Cantares Mexicanos: Songs of the Aztecs*. Stanford: Stanford University Press, 1985.

Block, Haskell, ed. *The Teaching of World Literature: Proceedings of the Conference at the University of Wisconsin, April 24–25, 1959*. Chapel Hill: University of North Carolina Press, 1960.

Bloom, Harold. *The Western Canon: The Books and School of the Ages*. New York: Riverhead, 1994.

Borges, Jorge Luis. *Collected Fictions*. Tr. Andrew Hurley. New York: Viking, 1998.

Brennan, Timothy. *At Home in the World: Cosmopolitanism Now*. Cambridge: Harvard University Press, 1997.

Brod, Max. *Franz Kafka*. Tr. G. Humphries Roberts and Richard Winston. New York: Schocken, 1960.

Budge, E. A. Wallis. *The Rise and Progress of Assyriology*. London: Hopkinson, 1925.

Bueno, Eva Paulino. "Race, Gender, and the Politics of Reception of Latin American Testimonios." In Amireh and Majaj, *Going Global*, 115–47.

Burgos, Elizabeth. *Me Llamo Rigoberta Menchú y Así Me Nació la Conciencia*. Mexico City and Madrid: Siglo Veintiuno, 1985. 15th printing, 1998.

Burns, Robert. *The Merry Muses of Caledonia*. Eds. James Barke and Sydney Goodsir Smith. New York: G. P. Putnam's Sons, 1964.

Canby, Peter. "The Truth about Rigoberta Menchú." *New York Review of Books,* 8 April 1999, 28–33.

Carrasco, Davíd. *Quetzalcoatl and the Irony of Empire: Myths and Prophecies in the Aztec Tradition*. Chicago: University of Chicago Press, 1982.

Carroll, Lewis. *Аня вь странѣ чудесъ: The Nabokov Russian Translation of Lewis Carroll's "Alice in Wonderland."* Tr. "V. Sirin" (Vladimir Nabokov). 1923. Repr. New York: Dover, 1976.

Carvalhal, Tania. "Cultura e Contextos." In Coutinho, *Fronteiras Imaginadas,* 147–54.

Casanova, Pascale. *La République mondiale des lettres.* Paris: Seuil, 1999.

Castaneda, Carlos. *The Teachings of Don Juan: A Yaqui Way of Knowledge.* Berkeley: University of California Press, 1968.

Caws, Mary Ann, et al., eds. *The HarperCollins World Reader.* 2 vols. New York: HarperCollins, 1994.

Chasles, Philarète Euphémon. "Foreign Literature Compared." In Schultz and Rhein, *Comparative Literature: The Early Years,* 21–22.

Cheah, Pheng, and Bruce Robbins, eds. *Cosmopolitics: Thinking and Feeling beyond the Nation.* Minneapolis: University of Minnesota Press, 1998.

Chow, Rey. *Writing Diaspora: Tactics of Intervention in Contemporary Cultural Studies.* Bloomington: Indiana University Press, 1993.

Clendinnen, Inga. *Aztecs: An Interpretation.* New York: Knopf, 1991.

Clerk, Jayana, and Ruth Siegel, eds. *Modern Literature of the Non-Western World: Where the Waters Are Born.* New York: HarperCollins, 1995.

Coe, Michael D., and William T. Sanders. "History of Meso-American Civilization." In *Encyclopaedia Britannica: Macropaedia,* 11:934–54. Chicago: Encyclopaedia Britannica, 1976.

Cole, John Y. *On These Walls: Inscriptions and Quotations in the Buildings of the Library of Congress.* Washington, D.C.: Library of Congress, 1995.

Colenso, John William. *The Pentateuch and Book of Joshua Critically Examined.* London: Longman, Green, 1863.

Constable, Pamela. Review of Rigoberta Menchú, *Crossing Borders. Washington Post,* 26 July 1998, sec. 10, 9.

Coutinho, Eduardo F., ed. *Fronteiras Imaginadas: Cultura Nacional/Teoria Internacional.* Rio de Janeiro: Aeroplano, 2001.

Cooppan, Vilashini. "World Literature and Global Theory: Comparative Literature for the New Millennium." *Symplokē* 9.1–2 (2001): 15–43.

Corngold, Stanley. "On Translation Mistakes, with Special Attention to Kafka in America." In Ulrich Stadler, ed., *Zwiesprache: Beiträge zur Theorie und Geschichte des Übersetzens,* 143–57. Stuttgart: J. B. Metzler, 1996.

Craft, Linda J. *Novels of Testimony and Resistance from Central America.* Gainesville: University Press of Florida, 1997.

Crawford, Robert. *Devolving English Literature.* 2d ed. Edinburgh: Edinburgh University Press, 2000.

Crystal, David. *English as a Global Language.* Cambridge: Cambridge University Press, 1997.

Culler, Jonathan. "Comparability." *World Literature Today* 69.2 (1995): 268–70.

Damrosch, David. "The Aesthetics of Conquest: Aztec Poetry before and after Cortés." *Representations* 33 (1991): 101–20.

———. "Allegories of Love in Egyptian Poetry and the Song of Songs." *Stanford Literature Review* 5 (1988): 25–42.

———. "Gilgamesh and Genesis." In *The Narrative Covenant: Transformations of Genre in the Growth of Biblical Literature,* 88–143. Ithaca: Cornell University Press, 1991.

Deleuze, Gilles, and Félix Guattari. *Kafka: Toward a Minor Literature.* Tr. Dana Polan. Minneapolis: University of Minnesota Press, 1986.

Denon, Dominique Vivant. *Voyage dans la Basse et la Haute Égypte pendant les campagnes du Général Bonaparte.* Cairo: Institut Français d'Archéologie Orientale du Caire, 1989–90.

Desani, G. V. *All About H. Hatterr.* Introduction by Anthony Burgess. Rev. ed. New York: McPherson, 1986.

Dev, Amiya. *The Idea of Comparative Literature in India.* Calcutta: Papyrus, 1984.

———. "Towards Comparative Indian Literature." In Mohan, *Aspects of Comparative Literature,* 35–45.

Dharwadker, Vinay, ed. *Cosmopolitan Geographies: New Locations in Literature and Culture.* New York: Routledge, 2001.

Dhawan, R. K., ed. *Comparative Literature.* New Delhi: Bahri, 1987.

Díaz del Castillo, Bernal. *The Discovery and Conquest of Mexico.* Tr. A. P. Maudslay. New York: Farrar, Strauss and Cudahy, 1956.

———. *Historia Verdadera de la Conquista de la Nueva España.* Ed. Joaquín Ramírez Cabañas. Mexico City: Porrúa, 1983.

Dimock, Wai Chee. "Literature for the Planet." *PMLA* 116.1 (2001): 173–88.

Dingwaney, Anuradha, and Carol Maier. "Translation as a Method for Cross-Cultural Teaching." In Dingwaney and Maier, eds., *Between Languages and Cultures: Translation and Cross-Cultural Texts,* 303–19. Pittsburgh: University of Pittsburgh Press, 1995.

Djurić, Rajko. "Kultur und Destruktivität am Beispiel Jugoslawien." In Jürgen Wertheimer, ed., *Suchbild Europa: Künstleriche Konzepte der Moderne,* 162–67. Amsterdam: Rodopi, 1995.

Donaldson, Frances. *P. G. Wodehouse: The Authorized Biography.* London: Weidenfeld and Nicolson, 1982.

Dryden, John. "Dedication of the Aeneis." In *The Poems of John Dryden,* ed. J. Kinsley, 4 vols., 4:1003–64. Oxford: Clarendon, 1958.

D'Souza, Dinesh. "Travels with Rigoberta." In *Illiberal Education: The Politics of Race and Sex on Campus,* 59–93. New York: Random House, 1991.

Durán, Diego. *The Aztecs: The History of the Indies of New Spain (1581).* Tr. Doris Heyden and Fernando Horcasitas. London: Cassell, 1964.

Eckermann, Johann Peter. *Beiträge zur Poesie, mit besonderer Hinweisung auf Goethe.* Berlin: Morawe and Scheffelt, 1911.

———. *Gespräche mit Goethe in den letzten Jahren seines Lebens.* Ed. Regine Otto. Berlin: Aufbau-Verlag, 1982. For translations, see entries under Goethe.

Edelstein, Ludwig. Review of Erich Auerbach, *Mimesis. Modern Language Notes* 65 (1950): 426–31.

Eliot, Charles W., ed. *The Harvard Classics.* 50 vols. New York: P. F. Collier and Son, 1910; 2d edition, 1917.

Eliot, T. S. "The Unfading Genius of Rudyard Kipling." *Kipling Journal* 26.129 (1959): 9–12. Repr. in Elliot L. Gilbert, ed., *Kipling and the Critics,* 118–23. New York: New York University Press, 1965.

Elzey, Wayne. "The Nahua Myth of the Suns." *Numen,* August 1976, 114–35.

Eoyang, Eugene. "The Many 'Worlds' of World Literature: Pound and Waley as Translators of Chinese." In Lawall, *Reading World Literature,* 241–66.

Étiemble. *Ouverture(s) sur une comparatisme planétaire.* Paris: Christian Bourgois, 1988.

Even-Zohar, Itamar. "The Position of Translated Literature within the Literary Polysystem." *Poetics Today* 11 (1990): 45–51. Repr. in Venuti, *The Translation Studies Reader,* 19–97.

Finkel, Donald, ed. and tr. *A Splintered Mirror: Chinese Poetry from the Democracy Movement.* San Francisco: North Point, 1991.

Foster, John L. *Love Songs of the New Kingdom.* New York: Charles Scribner's Sons, 1974.

Fowler, Barbara Hughes. *Love Lyrics of Ancient Egypt.* Chapel Hill: University of North Carolina Press, 1994.

Fraser, J. Baillie, Esq. *Mesopotamia and Assyria from the Earliest Ages to the Present Time.* New York: Harper and Brothers, 1842.

Friederich, Werner P. "On the Integrity of Our Planning." In Block, *The Teaching of World Literature,* 9–22.

Frye, Northrop. *Anatomy of Criticism.* Princeton: Princeton University Press, 1957.

———. *The Great Code: The Bible and Literature.* New York: Harcourt, Brace, Jovanovich, 1982.

Gardiner, Alan H. *The Library of A. Chester Beatty: Description of a Hieratic Papyrus with a Mythological Story, Love-Songs, and other Miscellaneous Texts, by Alan H. Gardiner, F. B. A.* Oxford: Oxford University Press, 1931.

Garibay K., Ángel María. *Poesía Náhuatl.* Mexico City: UNAM, 1964.

George, Andrew. *The Epic of Gilgamesh: A New Translation.* Harmondsworth, U.K.: Penguin, 1999.

Gilbert, William Schwenck. *The Mikado; or, The Town of Titipu.* In *The Complete Plays of Gilbert and Sullivan,* 345–400. New York: Modern Library, n.d.

Godzich, Wlad. "Emergent Literatures and the Field of Comparative Literature." In Koelb and Noakes, *The Comparative Perspective on Literature,* 18–36.

Goethe, Johann Wolfgang von. *Conversations with Eckermann.* Ed. J. K. Morehead. Tr. John Oxenford. Introduction by Havelock Ellis. London: Everyman, 1930.

———. *Conversations with Eckermann (1823–1832).* Tr. John Oxenford. San Francisco: North Point, 1984.

———. "Duvals Tasso." In *Schriften zur Literatur,* ed. Edith Nahler, 5 vols., 2:171–74, 5:237–43. Berlin: Akademie der Wissenschaft, 1970.

———. "Some Passages Pertaining to the Concept of World Literature." In Schultz and Rhein, *Comparative Literature: The Early Years*, 1–11.

Goldin, Tim. Review of Rigoberta Menchú, *Crossing Borders. New York Times*, 18 April 1999, 7:29.

Grandin, Greg, and Francisco Goldman. "Bitter Fruit for Rigoberta." *Nation*, 8 February 1999, 25–28.

Gray, Ronald. "But Kafka Wrote in German." In Angel Flores, ed., *The Kafka Debate: New Perspectives for Our Time*, 242–52. New York: Gordian, 1977.

Griffin, William. *Clive Staples Lewis: A Dramatic Life*. San Francisco: Harper and Row, 1986.

Guérard, Albert. "Comparative Literature?" *Yearbook of Comparative and General Literature* 7 (1958): 1–6.

Gugelberger, Georg, ed. *The Real Thing: Testimonial Discourse and Latin America*. Durham: Duke University Press, 1996.

Guillory, John. *Cultural Capital: The Problem of Literary Canon Formation*. Chicago: University of Chicago Press, 1993.

Guillén, Claudio. *The Challenge of Comparative Literature*. Tr. Cola Franzen. Cambridge: Harvard University Press, 1993.

Harman, Mark. "Retranslating Franz Kafka's *Castle*." In Lenore A. Grenoble and John M. Kopper, eds., *Essays in the Art and Theory of Translation*, 139–64. Lampeter, Wales: Mellen, 1997.

Hawkins, John. *Inverse Images: The Meaning of Culture, Ethnicity and Family in Postcolonial Guatemala*. Albuquerque: University of New Mexico Press, 1984.

Hatzfeld, Helmut. Review of Erich Auerbach, *Mimesis. Romance Philology* 2 (1948–49): 333–38.

Hayles, N. Katherine. "Corporeal Anxiety in *Dictionary of the Khazars:* What Books Talk about in the Late Age of Print When They Talk about Losing Their Bodies." *Modern Fiction Studies* 43.3 (1997): 800–20.

Higonnet, Margaret, ed. *Borderwork: Feminist Engagements with Comparative Literature*. Ithaca: Cornell University Press, 1994.

Iser, Wolfgang. *The Act of Reading: A Theory of Aesthetic Response*. Tr. David Henry Wilson. Baltimore: Johns Hopkins University Press, 1978.

Ishiguro, Kazuo. *Remains of the Day*. New York: Vintage, 1988.

Jacobsen, Thorkild. "The Gilgamesh Epic: Romantic and Tragic Vision." In Tzvi Abuseh, John Huehnergard, and Piotr Steinkeller, eds., *Lingering over Words: Studies in Ancient Near Eastern Literature in Honor of William L. Moran*, 231–49. Atlanta: Scholars Press, 1990.

Jameson, Fredric, and Masao Miyoshi, eds. *The Cultures of Globalization*. Durham: Duke University Press, 1998.

Janssen, J. J. *Commodity Prices from the Ramessid Period: An Economic Study of the Village of Necropolis Workmen at Thebes*. Leiden: Brill, 1975.

Jones, Rufus. *The Flowering of Mysticism: The Friends of God in the Fourteenth Century*. New York: Macmillan, 1939.

Joyce, James. *Finnegans Wake*. New York: Viking, 1958.

Judah ha-Levi. *The Kuzari*. Tr. N. Daniel Korobkin. Northvale, N.J.: Jason Aronson, 1998.

Kadir, Djelal. "Comparative Literature Hinternational." *World Literature Today* 69.2 (1995): 245–47.

Kafka, Franz. *The Castle*. Tr. Willa and Edwin Muir. London: Secker and Warburg; New York: Knopf, 1930.

———. *The Castle: The Definitive Edition*. Tr. Willa and Edwin Muir, with additional material tr. Eithne Wilkins and Ernst Kaiser. New York: Schocken, 1954.

———. *The Castle: A New Translation, Based on the Restored Text*. Tr. Mark Harman. New York: Schocken, 1998.

———. *Diaries 1910–1923*. Ed. Max Brod. Tr. Joseph Krech, Martin Greenberg, and Hannah Arendt. New York: Schocken, 1976.

———. *Das Schloß: Roman*. Ed. Max Brod. Munich: Kurt Wolff, 1926.

———. *Das Schloß: Kritische Ausgabe*. Ed. Malcolm Pasley. 2 vols. Frankfurt: Fischer, 1982.

Karl, Frederick. *Franz Kafka: Representative Man*. New York: Ticknor and Fields, 1991.

Karl, Frederick, and Leo Hamalian, eds. *The Existential Imagination*. New York: Fawcett World Library, 1963.

Kermode, Frank. *The Classic*. London: Faber and Faber, 1975.

King, Anthony, ed. *Culture, Globalization and the World-System: Contemporary Conditions for the Representation of Identity*. Minneapolis: University of Minnesota Press, 1997.

Kiš, Danilo. *A Tomb for Boris Davidovich*. Tr. Duška Mikić-Mitchell. Normal, Ill.: Dalkey Archive Press, 2001.

Koelb, Clayton, and Susan Noakes, eds. *The Comparative Perspective on Literature*. Ithaca: Cornell University Press, 1988.

Krolop, Kurt, and Hans Dieter Zimmerman, eds. *Kafka und Prag: Colloquium im Goethe-Institut Prag 24.–27. November 1992*. Berlin: de Gruyter, 1994.

Lallas, Thanassis. "'As a Writer I Was Born Two Hundred Years Ago. . . .': An Interview with Milorad Pavić." *Review of Contemporary Fiction* 18.2 (1998): 128–41.

Lanser, Susan Sniader. "Compared to What? Global Feminism, Comparatism, and the Master's Tools." In Higonnet, *Borderwork*, 280–300.

Larsen, Mogens Trolle. *The Conquest of Assyria: Excavations in an Antique Land, 1840–1860*. New York: Routledge, 1996.

Lauter, Paul. "Canon Theory and Emergent Practice." In *Canons and Contexts*, 154–71. New York: Oxford University Press, 1991.

Lawall, Sarah, ed. *Reading World Literature: Theory, History, Practice*. Austin: University of Texas Press, 1994.

Lawall, Sarah, and Maynard Mack, et al., eds. *The Norton Anthology of World Literature*. 2d ed. 6 vols. New York: Norton, 2002.

Layard, Austen Henry. *Autobiography and Letters: From His Childhood until His Appointment as H. M. Ambassador at Madrid*. Ed. W. N. Bruce. 2 vols. New York: Charles Scribner's Sons, 1903.

_____. *Early Adventures in Persia, Susiana, and Babylonia: Including a Residence among the Bakhtiari and Other Wild Tribes before the Discovery of Nineveh.* London: John Murray, 1894.

_____. *Nineveh and Its Remains: With an Account of a Visit to the Chaldaean Christians of Kurdistan, and the Yezidis, or Devil-Worshippers; and an Inquiry into the Manners and Arts of the Ancient Assyrians.* 2 vols. New York: Putnam, 1849.

Lefevere, André. "Composing the Other." In Bassnett and Trivedi, *Post-Colonial Translation,* 75–94.

_____. "Literary Theory and Translated Literature." *Dispositio* 7.19–20 (1982): 3–22.

_____. "Mother Courage's Cucumbers: Text, System and Refraction in a Theory of Literature." *Modern Language Studies* 12.4 (1982): 3–20. Repr. in Venuti, *The Translation Studies Reader,* 233–49.

_____. *Translation, Rewriting, and the Manipulation of Literary Fame.* London: Routledge, 1992.

León-Portilla, Miguel. *Aztec Thought and Culture: A Study of the Ancient Nahuatl Mind.* Tr. Jack Emory Davis. Norman: University of Oklahoma Press, 1963.

_____. *Pre-Columbian Literatures of Mexico.* Tr. Grace Lobanov and Miguel León-Portilla. Norman: University of Oklahoma Press, 1969.

Lewis, Wyndham, et al. *Blast* (1914). Repr. Santa Rosa: Black Sparrow Press, 1981.

Lichtheim, Miriam. *Ancient Egyptian Literature: A Book of Readings.* 3 vols. Berkeley: University of California Press, 1973–1980.

Lodge, Henry Cabot, ed. *The Best of the World's Classics: Restricted to Prose.* 10 vols. New York: Funk and Wagnalls, 1909.

Lofting, Hugh. *The Story of Doctor Dolittle.* London: Jonathan Cape, 1922.

Lüers, Grete. *Die Sprache der deutschen Mystik des Mittelalters im Werke der Mechthild von Magdeburg.* Darmstadt: Wissenschaftliche Buchgesellschaft, 1966.

Mack, Maynard, et al., eds. *The Norton Anthology of World Masterpieces: Expanded Edition.* 2 vols. New York: Norton, 1995.

_____. *World Masterpieces.* 2 vols. New York: Norton, 1956. 2d ed., 1965. 3d ed., 1976.

Macleish, Archibald. *Collected Poems, 1917–1982.* Boston: Houghton Mifflin, 1985.

Magill, Frank, ed. *Masterpieces of World Literature in Digest Form.* 4 vols. Pasadena: Salem, 1949–1969.

Marx, Karl, and Friedrich Engels. *Manifesto of the Communist Party.* Tr. Samuel Moore. In *Marx,* vol. 50 of *Great Books of the Western World,* 415–34. Chicago: Encyclopaedia Britannica, 1952.

Matos Moctezuma, Eduardo. *The Aztecs.* Tr. Andrew Ellis. New York: Rizzoli, 1989.

Mechthild von Magdeburg. *Das fließende Licht der Gottheit.* Middle High German text, ed. Hans Neumann, with introduction and additions by Gisela Vollmann-Profe. 2 vols. Munich: Artemis, 1990.

_____. *Das fließende Licht der Gottheit.* Modern German tr. by Margot Schmidt. Einsiedeln: Benziger, 1955. Rev. ed., Stuttgart: Frommann-Holzboog, 1995.

_____. *Flowing Light of the Divinity.* Ed. Susan Clark. Tr. Christiane Mesch Galvani. New York: Garland, 1991.

_____. *The Flowing Light of the Godhead.* Tr. Frank Tobin. New York: Paulist Press, 1998.

_____. *The Revelations of Mechthild von Magdeburg (1210–1297), or The Flowing Light of the Godhead.* Tr. Lucy Menzies. London: Longmans, Green, 1953.

Melas, Natalie. *All the Difference in the World: Post-Coloniality and the Ends of Comparison.* Stanford: Stanford University Press, forthcoming.

Meltzl de Lomnitz, Hugo. "Present Tasks of Comparative Literature." In Schultz and Rhein, *Comparative Literature: The Early Years,* 53–62.

Menchú, Rigoberta. *Crossing Borders.* Ed. and tr. Ann Wright. London and New York: Verso, 1998.

_____. *I, Rigoberta Menchú: An Indian Woman in Guatemala.* Ed. Elisabeth Burgos-Debray. Tr. Ann Wright. London and New York: Verso, 1984. See also Burgos, Elizabeth.

_____. *Rigoberta: La Nieta de los Mayas.* In collaboration with Dante Liano and Gianni Minà. Madrid: Aguilar, 1998.

Miller, Mary, and Karl Taube. *The Gods and Symbols of Ancient Mexico and the Maya.* London: Thames and Hudson, 1993.

Mitford, Edward Ledwich. *A Land March from England to Ceylon Forty Years Ago: Through Dalmatia, Montenegro, Turkey, Asia Minor, Syria, Palestine, Assyria, Persia, Afghanistan, Scinde, and India.* 2 vols. London: W. H. Allen, 1884.

Miyoshi, Masao. *Off Center: Power and Culture Relations between Japan and the United States.* Cambridge: Harvard University Press, 1991.

Mohan, Chandra. "Comparative Indian Literature: Some Recent Trends." In Mohan, *Aspects of Comparative Literature,* 95–105.

_____, ed. *Aspects of Comparative Literature: Current Approaches.* New Delhi: India Publishers, 1989.

Mohr, Wolfgang. "Darbietungsformen der Mystik bei Mechthild von Magdeburg." In Hugo Kuhn and Kurt Schier, eds., *Märchen, Mythos, Dichtung,* 375–99. Munich: Beck, 1963.

Moran, William L. "The Epic of Gilgamesh: A Document of Ancient Humanism." *Bulletin, Canadian Society for Mesopotamian Studies* 22 (1991): 15–22.

Moretti, Franco. *Atlas of the European Novel, 1800–1900.* London: Verso, 1998.

_____. "Conjectures on World Literature." *New Left Review* 1 (2000): 55–67.

Morris, Ivan. *The World of the Shining Prince: Court Life in Ancient Japan.* New York: Knopf, 1975.

Muir, Edwin. *The Structures of the Novel.* London: Hogarth, 1928.

Murasaki Shikibu. *The Tale of Genji.* Tr. Arthur Waley. 1925. Repr. New York: Modern Library, 1960.

_____. *The Tale of Genji.* Tr. Edward G. Seidensticker. 2 vols. New York: Knopf, 1976.

_____. *The Tale of Genji.* Tr. Royall Tyler. 2 vols. New York: Viking, 2001.

Nabokov, Vladimir. "Problems of Translation: 'Onegin' in English." *Partisian Review* 22 (1955): 496–512. Repr. in Venuti, *The Translation Studies Reader,* 71–83.

Neumeyer, Peter F., ed. *Twentieth-Century Interpretations of "The Castle."* Englewood Cliffs, N.J.: Prentice-Hall, 1969.

Ngal, Mbwil a Mpang. *L'Errance.* Yaoundé, Cameroun: Éditions CLE, 1979.

_____. *Giambatista Viko: ou, Le Viol du discours africain.* Lubumbashi, Zaire: Alpha-Oméga, 1975. Repr. Paris: Hatier, 1984.

Ortega y Gasset, José. "The Misery and the Splendor of Translation." Tr. Elizabeth Gamble Miller. In Rainer Schulte and John Biguenet, eds., *Theories of Translation: An Anthology of Essays from Dryden to Derrida,* 93–112. Chicago: University of Chicago Press, 1992. Repr. in Venuti, *The Translation Studies Reader,* 49–63.

Orwell, George. "In Defence of P. G. Wodehouse." In *Dickens, Dali and Others,* 222–43. London: Reynal and Hitchcock, 1946. Repr. in *The Orwell Reader,* 315–28. New York: Harcourt, Brace, 1956.

Owen, Steven. "What Is World Poetry?" *New Republic,* 19 November 1990, 28–32.

Pavić, Milorad. "The Beginning and the End of Reading—The Beginning and the End of the Novel." *Review of Contemporary Fiction* 18.2 (1998): 142–46.

_____. *Dictionary of the Khazars: A Lexicon Novel in 100,000 Words.* Tr. from the Serbo-Croatian by Christina Pribićević-Zorić. In Female and Male Editions. New York: Knopf, 1988.

_____. *Landscape Painted with Tea: A Crossword-Novel.* Tr. Christina Pribićević-Zorić. New York: Knopf, 1990.

_____. "Monument to an Unknown Poet." In *Four Yugoslav Poets.* Ed. and tr. Charles Simic. Northwood Narrows, N.H.: Lillabulero, 1970. Unpaginated.

Pavić, Milorad, and Jasmina Mihajlović. www.khazars.com.

Pasley, Malcolm. "The Act of Writing and the Text: The Genesis of Kafka's Manuscripts." In Mark Anderson, *Reading Kafka,* 201–14.

Pérez-Firmat, Gustavo. *The Cuban Condition: Translation and Identity in Modern Cuban Literature.* Cambridge: Cambridge University Press, 1989.

Phelps, Barry. *P. G. Wodehouse: Man and Myth.* London: Constable, 1992.

Ponce, Pedro. "Brief Relation of the Gods and Rites of Heathenism." Tr. J. Richard Andrews and Ross Hassig as appendix A to Ruiz de Alarcón, *Treatise on the Heathen Superstitions and Customs,* 211–18.

Posnett, Hutcheson Macaulay. *Comparative Literature.* London: K. Paul, Trench,1886. Repr. New York: Johnson Reprint Co., 1970.

_____. "The Science of Comparative Literature." In Schultz and Rhein, *Comparative Literature: The Early Years,* 183–206.

Pound, Ezra, and Noel Stock. *Love Poems of Ancient Egypt.* New York: New Directions, 1962.

Prempati, D. "Why Comparative Literature in India?" In Dhawan, *Comparative Literature,* 53–65.

Proust, Marcel. *Remembrance of Things Past.* Tr. C. K. Scott Moncrieff. 1928. Repr. New York: Vintage, 1970. Rev. tr. by Terence Kilmartin, 1981. Further rev. by D. J.

Enright, under the title *In Search of Lost Time*. New York: Modern Library, 1992.

Pushkin, Aleksandr. *Eugene Onegin: A Novel in Verse*. Tr. and commentary by Vladimir Nabokov. 2 vols. Bollingen Series, no. 72. Princeton: Princeton University Press, 1964. Rev. ed., 1975.

Ramadanović, Petar. "Language and Crime in Yugoslavia." In David Jordan, ed., *Regionalism Reconsidered: New Approaches to the Field*, 185–96. New York: Garland, 1994.

Rassam, Hormuzd. *Asshur and the Land of Nimrod: Being an Account of the Discoveries Made in the Ancient Ruins of Nineveh, Asshur, Sepharvaim, Calah, Babylon, Borsippa, Cuthah, and Van, Including a Narrative of Different Journeys in Mesopotamia, Assyria, Asia Minor, and Koordistan*. New York: Eaton and Mains, 1897.

———. *Babylonian Cities: Being a Paper Read before the Victorian Institute, or Philosophical Society of Great Britain*. London: E. Stanford, 1883.

Recinos, Adrián, ed. *The Annals of the Cakchiquels; Title of the Lords of Totonicapán*. Tr. Adrián Recinos, Dioniso José Choney, and Delia Goetz. Norman: University of Oklahoma Press, 1953.

Remak, Henry H. H. "Comparative Literature at the Crossroads: Diagnosis, Therapy and Prognosis." *Yearbook of Comparative and General Literature* 9 (1960): 1–28.

Resende, Beatriz. "A Formação de Identidades Plurais no Brasil Moderno." In Coutinho, *Fronteiras Imaginadas*, 83–96.

Robbins, Bruce. "Comparative Cosmopolitanisms." In Cheah and Robbins, *Cosmopolitics*, 246–64.

———. *Feeling Global: Internationalism in Distress*. New York: New York University Press, 1999.

Robert, Marthe. *Seul, comme Franz Kafka*. Paris: Calmann-Lévy, 1979.

Robertson, Ritchie. "In Search of the Historical Kafka: A Selective Review of Research, 1980–92." *Modern Language Review* 89.1 (1994): 107–37.

———. "Not by Brod Alone." *Times Literary Supplement*, 14 October 1983, 1129.

Rodríguez, Ileana. *Women, Guerillas, and Love: Understanding War in Central America*. Minneapolis: University of Minnesota Press, 1996.

Rüdiger, Horst. *Zur Theorie der vergleichenden Literaturwissenschaft*. Berlin: de Gruyter, 1971.

Ruiz de Alarcón, Hernando. *Aztec Sorcerers in Seventeenth-Century Mexico: The Treatise on Superstitions of Hernando Ruiz de Alarcón*. Tr. Michael Coe and Gordon Whittaker. Albany: Institute for Mesoamerican Studies, 1982.

———. *Tratado de las Supersticiones y Costumbres Gentílicas que Hoy Viven entre los Indios Naturales desta Nueva España*. Mexico City: Secretaria de Educación Pública, 1988.

———. *Treatise on the Heathen Superstitions and Customs that Today Live among the*

Indians Native to This New Spain, 1629. Tr. J. Richard Andrews and Ross
    Hassig. Norman: University of Oklahoma Press, 1984.
Ruiz de Alarcón, Juan. *The Truth Suspected.* Tr. Julio del Toro and Robert V. Finney.
    Poet Lore 38.4 (1927): 475–530.
Rushdie, Salman. *Fury.* New York: Random House, 2001.
_____. Review of Kazuo Ishiguro, *Remains of the Day. Observer,* 21 May 1989, 53.
Sahagún, Bernardino de. *Florentine Codex: General History of the Things of New Spain.*
    Ed. and tr. Arthur J. O. Anderson and Charles E. Dibble. 13 vols. Sante Fe,
    N.M.: School of American Research and University of Utah Press, 1950–82.
_____. *Psalmodia Christiana.* Tr. Arthur J. O. Anderson. Salt Lake City: University of
    Utah Press, 1993.
Said, Edward W. *Culture and Imperialism.* New York: Vintage, 1993.
_____. *Orientalism.* New York: Pantheon, 1978.
_____. *The World, the Text, and the Critic.* Cambridge: Harvard University Press,
    1983.
Sandars, N. K., ed. and tr. *The Epic of Gilgamesh.* Harmondsworth, U.K.: Penguin,
    1960.
Schott, Siegfried, ed. and tr. *Altägyptische Liebeslieder: Mit Märchen und
    Liebesgeschichten.* Zurich: Artemis, 1950.
Schultz, Hans-Joachim, and Phillip H. Rhein, eds. *Comparative Literature: The Early
    Years.* University of North Carolina Studies in Comparative Literature, no.
    55. Chapel Hill: University of North Carolina Press, 1973.
Shirane, Haruo. *The Bridge of Dreams: A Poetics of "The Tale of Genji."* Stanford:
    Stanford University Press, 1987.
Siliotti, Alberto. *Egypt Lost and Found: Explorers and Travelers on the Nile.* New York:
    Stewart, Tabori and Chang, 1999.
Simpson, William Kelly, ed. *The Literature of Ancient Egypt: An Anthology of Stories,
    Instructions, and Poetry.* Tr. W. K. Simpson, R. O. Faulkner, and Edward F.
    Wente, Jr. New Haven: Yale University Press, 1972.
Skube, Michael. "As Academia Embraces Lies of 'Larger Truth,' True Scholar Prevails."
    Atlanta Constitution, 7 March 1999, sec. L, 10.
Smith, Barbara Herrnstein. *Contingencies of Value.* Cambridge: Harvard University
    Press, 1988.
Smith, George. *Assyrian Discoveries: An Account of Discoveries on the Site of Nineveh,
    during 1873 and 1874.* New York: Scribner, 1875.
_____. *The Chaldean Account of Genesis: Containing the Description of the Creation,
    the Fall of Man, the Deluge, the Tower of Babel, the Times of the Patriarchs,
    and Nimrod; Babylonian Fables, and Legends of the Gods; from the Cuneiform
    Inscriptions.* London: Sampson Low; New York: Scribner, Armstrong, 1876.
_____. *The Chaldean Account of the Deluge from Terra Cotta Tablets Found at Nineveh.*
    London: Sampson Low, 1874.
Sokel, Walter. *Franz Kafka.* New York: Columbia University Press, 1966. Excerpted in
    Neumeyer, *Twentieth-Century Interpretations of "The Castle,"* 32–35.

Spiegelman, Art. "On Loony Tunes, Zionism, and the Jewish Question." *Village Voice* 6 June 1989, 21–22.

Spivak, Gayatri Chakravorty. "How to Read a 'Culturally Different' Book." In Francis Barker, Peter Hulme, and Margaret Iversen, eds., *Colonial Discourse/ Postcolonial Theory,* 126–50. Manchester: Manchester University Press, 1994.

Sproat, Iain. *Wodehouse at War: The Extraordinary Truth about P. G. Wodehouse's Broadcasts on Nazi Radio.* London: Milner, 1981.

Srebo, Milivoj. "Le Coup médiatique de Milorad Pavić: *Le Dictionnaire Khazar* vu par la critique littéraire française." *Revue de Littérature Comparée* 69.3 (1995): 273–85.

Steinberg, Erwin. "K. of *The Castle:* Ostensible Land-Surveyor." *College English* 32.3 (1965): 185–89. Repr. in Neumeyer, *Twentieth-Century Interpretations of "The Castle,"* 25–35.

Steiner, George. *After Babel: Aspects of Language and Translation.* Oxford: Oxford University Press, 1975.

Stoll, David. *Rigoberta Menchú and the Story of All Poor Guatemalans.* Boulder, Colo.: Westview Press, 1999.

Strich, Fritz. *Goethe and World Literature.* London: Routledge and Kegan Paul, 1949.

Tedlock, Barbara. *Time and the Highland Maya.* Rev. ed. Albuquerque: University of New Mexico Press, 1992.

Tedlock, Dennis, ed. and tr. *Popol Vuh: The Mayan Book of the Dawn of Life.* New York: Simon and Schuster, 1985.

Texte, Joseph. "The Comparative History of Literature." In Schultz and Rhein, *Comparative Literature: The Early Years,* 105–12.

Tigay, Jeffrey. *The Evolution of the Gilgamesh Epic.* Philadelphia: University of Pennsylvania Press, 1982.

Tobin, Frank. *Mechthild von Magdeburg: A Medieval Mystic in Modern Eyes.* Columbia, S.C.: Camden House, 1995.

Untermeyer, Louis. *Robert Frost: A Backward Look.* Washington, D.C.: Library of Congress, 1964.

Venuti, Lawrence. *The Scandals of Translation: Towards an Ethics of Difference.* London and New York: Routledge, 1998.

_____, ed. *Translation and Minority. Translator* 4.2 (1998); special issue.

_____, ed. *The Translation Studies Reader.* Mona Baker, advisory ed. London and New York: Routledge, 2000.

Vorda, Allen, and Kim Herzinger. "An Interview with Kazuo Ishiguro." *Mississippi Review* 20.1–2 (1991): 131–54.

Wachtel, Andrew. "Pavić's Literary Demolition of Yugoslavia." *Slavic and East European Journal* 41.4 (1997): 627–44.

Wallerstein, Immanuel. "The National and the Universal: Can There Be Such a Thing as World Culture?" In King, *Culture, Globalization, and the World System,* 97–105.

Washburn, Katherine, John S. Major, and Clifton Fadiman, eds. *World Poetry: An Anthology of Verse from Antiquity to Our Time.* New York: Norton, 1998.

Waterfield, Gordon. *Layard of Nineveh.* London: John Murray, 1963.

Waugh, Evelyn. "An Act of Homage and Reparation to P. G. Wodehouse." In *The Essays, Articles and Reviews of Evelyn Waugh,* ed. Donat Gallagher, 561–68. London: Methuen, 1983.

Wellek, René. "The Crisis of Comparative Literature." In *Concepts of Criticism,* ed. Stephen G. Nichols, 282–95. New Haven: Yale University Press, 1963.

———. Review of Erich Auerbach, *Mimesis. Kenyon Review* 16 (1954): 299–307.

Wiget, Andrew. "Aztec Lyrics: Poetry in a World of Continually Perishing Flowers." *Latin American Indian Literatures* 4 (1980): 1–11.

Wilkie, Brian, and James Hurt, eds. *The Literature of the Western World.* 5th ed. 2 vols. Upper Saddle River, N.J.: Prentice-Hall, 1997.

Wodehouse, P. G. *Blandings Castle.* Garden City, N.Y.: Doubleday, Doran, 1935.

———. "The Clicking of Cuthbert." In *The Most of P. G. Wodehouse,* 385–97. New York: Simon and Schuster, 1960.

———. *The Code of the Woosters.* London: Jenkins, 1938.

———. *Fish Preferred.* New York: Simon and Schuster, 1929.

———. *Hot Water.* New York: A. L. Burt, 1932.

———. *How Right You Are, Jeeves.* New York: Simon and Schuster, 1960.

———. "In Defense of Astigmatism." In *The Uncollected Wodehouse.* New York: Seabury, 1976. 19–22.

———. *Joy in the Morning.* New York: Doubleday, 1946. London: Jenkins, 1947. Also published under the title *Jeeves in the Morning.*

———. *Performing Flea.* London: Jenkins, 1953.

———. *Pigs Have Wings.* Garden City, N.Y.: Doubleday, 1952.

———. *Psmith Journalist.* London: A. and C. Black, 1915.

———. *Something New.* New York: D. Appleton, 1915.

———. *Tales of St. Austin's.* London: A. and C. Black, 1903.

———. *Uncle Fred in the Springtime.* New York: Doubleday, 1939.

Wordsworth, William. Preface to the Second Edition of *Lyrical Ballads.* In *Selected Poems and Prefaces,* ed. Jack Stillinger, 445–64. Boston: Houghton Mifflin, 1965.

Yu, Pauline. "Alienation Effects: Comparative Literature and the Chinese Tradition." In Koelb and Noakes, *The Comparative Perspective on Literature,* 162–75.

Zayas, Elena. *La Historia de Vida: La Oralidad Camino de la Historia.* Guatemala City: University of San Carlos de Guatemala, 1996.

Zum Brunn, Emilie, and Georgette Epiney-Burgard. *Women Mystics in Medieval Europe.* Tr. Sheila Hughes. New York: Paragon House, 1989.

Calvino, Italo, 140
Canby, Peter, 235–36
Canil, Angel Francisco, 252
Canning, Sir Stratford, 42–43, 46
canonicity, 14–15, 118–44, 281
Capaldi, Peter, 188
Capra, Frank, 188
Carrasco, Davíd, 99
Carroll, Lewis, 157
Carvalhal, Tania, 27
Casanova, Pascale, 27
Castaneda, Carlos, 240–41
Cervantes Saavedra, Miguel de, 97, 130
Champollion, Jean-François, 40, 302
Chasles, Philarète Euphémon, 9
Chow, Rey, 20–21
Christine de Pizan, 299
classics, 15–16, 126
Clendinnen, Inga, 83
Clerk, Jayana, 21
Coe, Michael, 82–83, 101–3
Coetzee, J. M., 201
Colenso, John William, 14, 52
Conrad, Joseph, 51, 227
Cooppan, Vilashini, 22
Corngold, Stanley, 199
Cortés, Hernán, 99, 108
cosmopolitanism, 9, 121–23, 289, 298
Craft, Linda, 237
Crystal, David, 225, 267
Culler, Jonathan, 113
cultural context, 139–41, 148–49, 150–52,
     158–66, 275–79, 286–88, 295–99; for
     Kafka, 187–206 passim
cummings, e. e., 163

Dafydd ap Gwilym, 285
Dante, 22, 278; figure of, 119, 133–35, 281,
     298; translations of, 187; as writer, 18,
     111, 118, 140, 176, 277
Das, Sisir Kumar, 27
Dawa, Zhaxi, 111
Debray, Régis, 240
Deleuze, Gilles, 188, 201–3
Demosthenes, 118
Denon, Dominique Vivant, 301–3
Desani, G. V., 226–28
Dev, Amiya, 27
Dharwadker, Vinay, 24
Díaz del Castillo, Bernal, 108–9
Dimock, Wai Chee, 135, 140

Dingwaney, Anuradha, 248
Djebar, Assia, 138
Djurić, Rajko, 268
Dryden, John, 204
D'Souza, Dinesh, 15–17, 232
Durán, Diego, 100
Duval, Alexander, 7

Eckermann, Johann Peter, 1–3, 6–14, 28–36,
     249, 281
Edelstein, Ludwig, 282
Eliot, Charles W., 120–25, 133
Eliot, T. S., 23, 131, 209, 227–28
Ellis, Havelock, 32–34
Elzey, Wayne, 99
Emerson, Ralph Waldo, 133
Engels, Friedrich, 3, 284, 300
Enkidu, 64, 132, 138–39; as friend of Gil-
     gamesh/Bilgames, 57, 66, 68–71, 76, 133
Eoyang, Eugene, 21
Epiney-Burgard, Georgette, 179–82, 186
Erasmus, Desiderius, 112
Étiemble, 5
eurocentrism, 13, 118–33
Even-Zohar, Itamar, 24

Fadiman, Clifton, 125–26, 134, 166
Fagles, Robert, 187
Faulkner, William, 126–27, 191
Finkel, Donald, 23
Fitzgerald, Edward, 295
Foster, John, 159, 162–63, 166, 168
Fowler, Barbara, 156
Franklin, Benjamin, 118
Fraser, J. Baillie, 40
Freud, Sigmund, 127, 129
Friederich, Werner, 110–11
Frost, Robert, 288–89
Frye, Northrop, 5, 14, 25, 286
Fuller, Margaret, 33

Galeano, Eduardo, 251
Galvani, Christiane Mesch, 178–79, 184
Gardiner, Alan H., 148–155, 158, 164, 169
Garibay K., Angel María, 97
gender politics, 29–30, 170–86, 242, 249
Genet, Jean, 294
George, Andrew, 53, 58, 66–67, 69, 138–39
Ghalib, 130

world systems theory, 25
Wright, Ann, 159, 252–54, 256

Xochiquetzal, 103–4

Yu, Pauline, 5

Yúdice, George, 241

Zayas, Elena, 237
Zimmermann, Marc, 189, 236
Zum Brunn, Emilie, 179–82, 186